Sharing Expertise

Sharing Expertise

Beyond Knowledge Management

Edited by Mark S. Ackerman, Volkmar Pipek, and Volker Wulf

The MIT Press
Cambridge, Massachusetts
London, England

This book was set in Sabon on 3B2 by Asco Typesetters, Hong Kong.
Printed and bound in the United States of America.

Library of Congress Cataloging-in-Publication Data

Sharing expertise : beyond knowledge management / edited by Mark S. Ackerman, Volkmar Pipek, and Volker Wulf.
    p.   cm.
 Includes bibliographical references and index.
 ISBN 0-262-01195-6 (hc. : alk. paper)
  1. Knowledge management. 2. Organizational learning—Management.
3. Information technology—Management. 4. Human-computer interaction.
I. Ackerman, Mark S. II. Pipek, Volkmar. III. Wulf, Volker.
HD30.2 .S53   2003
658.4′038—dc21   2002024418

Contents

Preface

Many companies and organizations find themselves in dynamic and even turbulent environments. Differentiation and customers' specific needs drive their markets, technologies change quickly and often disruptively, and professionals look for sense and personal growth in their work environment. Thus, organizations are required to learn continuously and to reinvent their processes and products. In these processes, employees' individual skills and their ability to share and generate knowledge within their communities and social networks increasingly play a crucial role.

Efficiently sharing expertise is critically important in many areas:

· Enabling organizational learning (e.g., Argyris and Schön 1996), where organizations and subunits can modify their structure and culture according to their experiences

· Augmenting new forms of organizations made possible by information technology (e.g., virtual organizations—Davidow and Malone 1992; Mowshowitz 1997), which often depend on knowing and judging people's competencies

· Creating ad hoc teams to solve time-critical problems

· Providing better technical assistance and presales marketing, and maintaining customer relationships over time

· Developing social capital (Putnam 2000; Cohen and Prusak 2001), including factors such as trust, reciprocity, and shared norms and values in knowledge-sharing processes

Knowledge management examines how organizations can effectively manage, store, retrieve, and augment their intellectual properties. The term *knowledge management* points to an important issue in organizations today—corporations and nonprofit organizations are increasingly dependent on deploying nontangible assets, such as know-how and tactical problem solving, in shorter time frames.

In our opinion, most approaches offering computer support for knowledge management show a rather narrow understanding. In general, there are two views of supporting knowledge management through software. The first exploits the idea of externalizing knowledge and recommends placing more and more information into shared repositories. These information databases or organizational memories have the advantage of using standard computational techniques and offer the hope of easily reusable information. These traditional approaches tend to focus on gathering, providing, and filtering available explicit knowledge.

However, the repository view of knowledge management has some important limitations and cannot be used in all situations. The information in a repository is easily transferable and reusable, but decontextualized information is often not easy to use. Users often need to find either knowledgeable people or people who can help them apply the information to the current situation or problem. Similarly, when the knowledge is tacit, access to people is often indispensable. If there is a complex or innovative problem to be solved, access to experts is often preferred over static documents.

Recently, research and practice has moved to the second type of knowledge management, which we call expertise sharing. Many researchers (e.g., Argyris and Schön 1996; Nonaka 1991) have pointed the way toward this type of knowledge management. The human resources and organizational behavior fields have for years hinted at the importance of personnel in organizational life. Ackerman (1993) argued for the importance of augmenting what he called expertise networks. Bannon and Kuutti (1996) proposed considering the active, constructive aspect of remembering in work activities as an invaluable resource in organizations.

Expertise sharing, then, focuses on the human components—the cognitive, social, cultural, and organizational aspects of knowledge work—in addition to information storage and retrieval. Compared to traditional approaches, which emphasize the role of management in organizing knowledge exchange, our perspective focuses on self-organized activities of the organizations' members. In enabling sharing, organizations try to connect people to one another so as to bolster communication, learning, and organizational knowledge. A variety of technical and social experiments are under way in organizations, and this book examines those efforts. As well, expertise management includes communities of practice and knowledge communities, which attempt to augment and increase communities', professions', and groups' overall expertise.

We believe it is important to further establish and cultivate this second type of knowledge management (expertise sharing). This viewpoint is reflected throughout this book.

Personal Views

Our views of the importance of expertise in knowledge management spring largely from our own research experiences.

Ackerman's work began with a system, Answer Garden, to foster organizational memories, storehouses of commonly required information and activities within organizations (Ackerman 1993; 1998; Ackerman and Malone 1990). This conception of organizational memory included information repositories as well as access to people through the system: if you could not find an answer, the system would route a question to an appropriate human expert. (The expert could then place the question and answer in an information repository, growing it. Thus the system's name.) Research on Answer Garden's use showed the utility of, and the issues in, finding people who knew the answers to organizational problems. Further work (Ackerman and McDonald 1996; Ackerman and Palen 1996) explored these ideas, adding "graceful escalation" through various computer-mediated communication facilities like chat and bulletin boards, to the basic system. In fact, many strands of work (Ackerman and Starr 1996; McDonald and Ackerman 2000) explored how to better tie together what was called the expertise network (Ackerman 1993) of an organization or larger collectivity—how to find people who know things, how to bring people together in ad hoc teams, and how to find the results of those activities. Throughout all this work, the importance of connecting and transforming the social network was key. Managing knowledge could not be about static repositories; information in social settings lives and breathes, and is intimately tied to the social fabric. Sharing and managing expertise has always been a necessary part of knowledge management.

Pipek started working at the research group Human-Computer Interaction and CSCW at the University of Bonn, Germany, after obtaining his master's degree in computer science. He first focused on the organizational dynamics of groupware introduction processes (Pipek and Wulf 1999; Mambrey and Pipek 1999). Sensitized through these experiences to the importance of good knowledge logistics as well as to the power of self-organization, he then focused on systems to support collaboration (discourse-based design) in communities (Pipek et al. 2000; Märker and Pipek 2000). He now leads a project on organizational learning in virtual organizations, which focuses on developing expertise sharing in networks of distributed autonomous actors. The basic motivation for his activities (including his interest in electronic democracy) is the combination of the communication and computing powers of information technology to support self-organization in knowledge-intensive environments.

Wulf worked with groupware design for and with users. POLITeam was a major research project to develop collaborative technologies that supported work in the German political administration. In this effort two facts became clear. First, the design and introduction of groupware is strongly interrelated with processes of organizational development. Second, most of the knowledge relevant to enable these development processes could not be found in the official documentation (organizational charts or task descriptions) but resided in the heads and practice of the workers (Wulf 1997; Wulf 1999; Pipek and Wulf 1999). Based on this experience, Wulf developed the concept of integrated organization and technology develoment (OTD). It became the base for several research projects carried out at the University of Bonn's ProSEC Research Group and the International Institute for Socio-Informatics (Wulf and Rohde 1995; Wulf et al. 1999; Rohde, Rittenbruch, and Wulf 2001). While encouraging organizational learning through process innovations, support for knowledge and expertise sharing became an important research issue.

The Book's Perspective

This book addresses both researchers and practitioners in the knowledge management area. Researchers will find a state-of-the-art book on expertise sharing, detailing the literature and current research frontier. Practitioners will find the critical issues and important perspectives they need to implement viable systems. We have made every effort to make the book readable for all audiences. We believe the review articles will be of lasting value and the technical and empirical chapters helpful for understanding expertise sharing.

We have consciously exposed the complexity and difficulty of sharing expertise. There already are many management books that prescribe how to manage what people know. The six-step process for better utilizing the intellectual capital of a business is close at hand, and the twelve-step process for repairing the damage is not far away. However, while straightforward prescriptive processes are easy to understand and sell, they tell a limited story. Tying together people in new ways is hard work—it is at the frontier of our understanding of management practices, social networks, and technical augmentations. One should not expect simple solutions.

We cannot hope to definitively define the term *expertise* here. A vigorous academic debate is raging around the term. For our purposes, however, *expertise* connotes relative levels of knowledge in people. Relatively few people will claim themselves to be experts, but many people agree they have some measure of expertise in some area. The chapters in this book consider how to inculcate, share, and find expertise so that the resources of an organization (and the people within it) increase.

The book's title uses the term *sharing* instead of *managing* to distinguish our way of thinking from some other approaches in knowledge management, particularly from those researchers strictly examining knowledge sharing from a traditional management perspective. Instead, this book examines a range of possibilities—from traditional management structures to how expertise might be self-organized by knowledge workers. In many views, management may be better able to facilitate than to prescribe or control information activities.

Accordingly, this book views expertise management from alternative and critical stances. By critical, we mean a critical realism stance, viewing current theories and efforts through an empirical lens based in field studies of real organizations. We find this new area of research and its possibilities exciting, but we also wish to avoid both management science and Tayloristic reductions. Instead, the book focuses on the possibilities without losing the complexity and difficulty of the enterprise. The book has been heavily influenced by the computer-supported cooperative work (CSCW) and the alternative information technology (IT) communities.

Structure of the Book

The book has three parts:

• *Part I: Literature review and background chapters.* This part introduces the general topic through surveys of the state of the discussion in the literature and the practice of knowledge sharing in large organizations.

• *Part II: Field/use studies.* This part looks empirically into the actual practice of expertise sharing in different types of organizational settings. It should provide the reader with an understanding of the inherent complexity of expertise sharing. Because expertise is socially arranged and organized, it must be understood through studies of real organizations. We include a number of field studies examining expertise management both as it is currently practiced and how it may be practiced with computational augmentation.

• *Part III: System studies.* This part looks at tools that have the potential to facilitate expertise sharing. A variety of computational systems can be used to route queries, assemble people and work, and augment the naturally occurring social networks inside an organization. We examine technical mechanisms and architectures designed specifically for expertise management, primarily focusing on interesting prototype applications. Some of them have already been evaluated in practice, others still wait for such a proof of concept. The contributions that form this part are based in two distinct research communities: artificial intelligence (AI) and computer-supported cooperative work (CSCW), which we believe contribute to the pool of technological innovations in this emerging field.

References

Ackerman, M. S. 1993. Answer Garden: A Tool for Growing Organizational Memory. Ph.D. diss., Massachusetts Institute of Technology, Cambridge, MA 02139.

———. 1998. Augmenting Organizational Memory: A Field Study of Answer Garden. *ACM Transactions on Information Systems* 16 (3): 203–224.

Ackerman, M. S., and T. W. Malone. 1990. Answer Garden: A Tool for Growing Organizational Memory. In *Proceedings of the ACM Conference on Office Information Systems*, 31–39.

Ackerman, M. S., and D. W. McDonald. 1996. Answer Garden 2: Merging Organizational Memory with Collaborative Help. In *Proceedings of the ACM Conference on Computer-Supported Cooperative Work (CSCW '96)*, 97–105.

Ackerman, M. S., and L. Palen. 1996. The Zephyr Help Instance: Promoting Ongoing Activity in a CSCW System. In *Proceedings of the ACM Conference on Human Factors in Computing Systems (CHI '96)*, 268–275.

Ackerman, M. S., and B. Starr. 1996. Social Activity Indicators for Groupware. *IEEE Computer* 29 (6): 37–44.

Argyris, C., and D. A. Schön. 1996. *Organizational Learning II*. Reading, Mass.: Addison-Wesley.

Bannon, L. J., and K. Kuutti. 1996. Shifting Perspectives on Organizational Memory: From Storage to Active Remembering. In *Proceedings of the Twenty-ninth Hawaii Conference on System Sciences*, vol. 4, 156–167.

Cohen, D., and L. Prusak. 2001. *In Good Company: How Social Capital Makes Organizations Work*. Boston: Harvard Business School Press.

Davidow, H. W., and M. S. Malone. 1992. *The Virtual Corporation: Structuring and Revitalizing the Corporation for the 21st Century*. New York: HarperCollins.

Mambrey, P., and V. Pipek. 1999. Enhancing Participatory Design by Multiple Communication Channels. In *Human-Computer Interaction: Communication, Cooperation, and Application Design*. Vol. 2 of *Proceedings of the Eighth International Conference on Human-Computer Interaction (HCI '99)*, ed. H. J. Bullinger and J. Ziegler, 387–391. London: Erlbaum.

Märker, O., and V. Pipek. 2000. Computer-Supported Participation in Urban Planning from the Viewpoint of Communicative Planning Theory. In *Proceedings of the IFIP 8.5 Working Conference on Advances in Electronic Government*, 43–58.

McDonald, D. W., and M. S. Ackerman. 2000. Expertise Recommender: A Flexible Recommendation System Architecture. In *Proceedings of the ACM Conference on Computer-Supported Cooperative Work (CSCW '2000)*: 231–240.

Mowshowitz, A. 1997. Virtual Organization. *Communications of the ACM* 40 (9): 30–37.

Nonaka, I. 1991. The Knowledge-Creating Company. *Harvard Business Review* (November–December): 96–104.

Pipek, V., O. Märker, C. Rinner, and B. Schmidt-Belz. 2000. Discussions and Decisions: Enabling Participation in Design in Geographical Communities. In *Community Informatics: Enabling Communities with Information and Communications Technologies*, ed. M. Gurstein, 358–375. Hershey, Pa.: Idea Group.

Pipek, V., and V. Wulf. 1999. A Groupware's Life. In *Proceedings of the Sixth European Conference on Computer Supported Cooperative Work (ECSCW '99)*, ed. S. Bødker, M. Kyng, and K. Schmidt, 199–219. Dordrecht, the Netherlands: Kluwer.

Putnam, R. 2000. *Bowling Alone: The Collapse and Revival of American Community*. New York: Simon and Schuster.

Rohde, M., M. Rittenbruch, and V. Wulf, eds. 2001. *Auf dem Weg zur Virtuellen Organization: Fallstudien, Problembeschreibungen, Lösungsansätze*. Heidelberg: Physica.

Wulf, V. 1997. Storing and Retrieving Documents in a Shared Workspace: Experiences from Political Administration. In *Human-Computer Interaction (INTERACT '97)*, ed. S. Howard, J. Hammond, and G. Lindgaard, 469–476. Sydney, Australia: Chapman and Hall.

———. 1999. Evolving Cooperation When Introducing Groupware: A Self-Organization Perspective. In *Cybernetics and Human Knowing* 6 (2): 55–75.

Wulf, V., M. Krings, O. Stiemerling, G. Iacucci, M. Maidhof, R. Peters, P. Fuchs-Fronhofen, B. Nett, and J. Hinrichs. 1999. Improving Interorganizational Processes with Integrated Organization and Technology Development. *Journal of Universal Computer Science* 5 (6): 339–365.

Wulf, V., and M. Rohde. 1995. Towards an Integrated Organization and Technology Development. In *Proceedings of the Symposium on Designing Interactive Systems (DIS '95)*, 55–64.

Acknowledgments

We are deeply indebted to Andrew Cohen, who was very influential in the intellectual formulation of this book. He co-organized the ECSCW '99 workshop on knowledge sharing, which spurred the efforts for this book; participated in the discussions formulating the book; and provided valuable help in outlining the book concept and prospective contributors. We want to acknowledge his valuable assistance; unfortunately, he dropped out as a co-editor because of work commitments after joining an expertise management startup, but we are fortunate in having a chapter of his in the book.

This book was made possible by a number of funding organizations. Mark Ackerman was funded in part by a grant from the National Science Foundation (IRI-9702904, "Augmenting Expertise Networks") as well as institutional support from the Department of Information and Computer Science at the University of California, Irvine, and the Laboratory for Computer Science at the Massachusetts Institute of Technology.

Volkmar Pipek is currently funded by a grant of the German Federal Ministry for Research and Education (No. 01HG9984, "Organizational Learning in Virtual Organizations").

Volker Wulf wishes to thank the German State of North Rhine Westphalia, whose generous support allowed him to pursue this project while staying at the Massachusetts Institute of Technology. Reinhard Oppermann (FhG-FIT) and Markus Rohde (International Institute for Socio-Informatics) took over tasks that made his stay at MIT possible.

At MIT Press Bob Prior has been a great help in creating and producing this book. In addition, the editors would like to gratefully acknowledge the help that Deborah Cantor-Adams, Alice Cheyer, Sharon Deacon Warne, and Yasuyo Iguchi provided in editing and preparing the manuscript. Peter Carstensen helped us with this effort at ECSCW '99. The book and its vision improved through conversations with Jürgen Friedrich, Jonathan Grudin, Christine Halverson, Matthias Jarke, Helge Kahler, John King, Wayne Lutters, David McDonald, Jack Muramatsu, Tim Reichling, and Markus Won. We would like to thank our reviewers as well.

Most of all, we want to thank the contributing authors for their contributions and their patience on this adventure.

I
Overview and Background

This part of the book presents three overview chapters. These contain reviews of the research areas that have had a significant impact on our view of expertise sharing.

First, Hinds and Pfeffer provide a research review of the cognitive and motivational issues that affect expertise sharing. Only with a deep understanding and appreciation for these factors can an expertise-sharing effort succeed. Indeed, these are the background issues for many knowledge management successes and failures. Hinds and Pfeffer provide a rich survey of these critical factors rooted in the social psychology and organizational behavior literatures.

Next, Huysman and de Wit present a general overview of knowledge management. In their analysis, which is empirically grounded, they identify three areas in knowledge management, what they call knowledge retrieval, knowledge exchange, and knowledge creation. Their analysis and literature review show why expertise sharing and management is a critical component of knowledge management as a whole.

Third, Penuel and Cohen survey some of the workplace learning efforts. They examine expertise sharing from the intersection of knowledge management and organizational learning.

In addition to these three overview chapters, Yimam-Seid and Kobsa provide an excellent overview of expertise recommenders, a type of system that suggests other people who might know about a subject. Their chapter has been placed in the systems section, but their review of previous work and their analytical analysis could have fit in this section as well.

1

Why Organizations Don't "Know What They Know": Cognitive and Motivational Factors Affecting the Transfer of Expertise

Pamela J. Hinds and Jeffrey Pfeffer

In today's economy, competitive success is increasingly based on possessing knowledge and intellectual capital rather than financial or other "hard" assets. For instance, Grant (1996) argues that knowledge is the most critical asset for a company, and Spender (1996) maintains that a firm's knowledge and its ability to produce knowledge is at the core of a theory of the firm. Nevertheless, the sharing of expertise within organizations remains a challenge for managers. As the former chief executive of Hewlett-Packard, Lew Platt, is quoted as saying, "If HP knew what HP knows, we would be three times as profitable" (Davenport and Prusak 1998, xii; see also O'Dell and Grayson 1998).

In a recent surge of articles and books discussing the benefits of knowledge sharing and knowledge management, scholars and practitioners have argued that organizations can do more to capitalize on the expertise embedded within them. But many organizations expend incredible efforts in an attempt to promote the sharing of expertise and nevertheless meet with little success. As an example, a survey of 431 U.S. and European organizations by Ernst and Young found that only 13 percent of the respondents thought they were doing a good job at transferring knowledge held by one part of the organization to others in the same firm (Ruggles 1998). Why is it so difficult to harness and disseminate knowledge and expertise?

In her recent book Argote (1999) argues that there are conditions under which it is more difficult to learn and share knowledge within organizations. We agree with Argote and take her premise one step further. In this chapter we argue that there are deep-rooted *cognitive* and *motivational* limitations that interfere with people's ability to share their expertise. Our purposes are to highlight these limitations, to identify realistic expectations for what expertise will be shared and when that will occur, and to identify practices that may help managers improve the sharing of expertise in their organizations.

It is important to note that there is substantial evidence that sharing knowledge and expertise within organizations is problematic. For instance, a case study showed that General Motors learned surprisingly little from its joint venture in California with Toyota, even though it went into that venture with learning as one of the primary objectives (Brown and Reich 1989; Pascale 1990). General Motors also has difficulty transferring lessons from its experience in the Saturn division into the rest of the company (Pfeffer and Sutton 2000). Quantitative data provide a similar picture of the difficulties of transferring knowledge and expertise. Szulanski (1996, 27), studying 122 best-practice transfers in eight companies, notes that "experience shows that transferring capabilities within a firm is far from easy." Data from a number of studies show that there is substantial variation in performance across sites in multisite organizations, indicating that transferring knowledge and expertise is problematic. For instance, one analysis demonstrated that there was no organization-level effect on oil refinery performance (Ricketts 1994)—in other words, there was as much variation in maintenance expenditures and refinery uptime across different refineries *within* a company as there was across refineries owned by different companies. Other studies of the performance of units in multisite organizations have reported similar results concerning the lack of an organization-level effect on performance (O'Dell and Grayson 1998). To have as much variation in performance across sites inside a single organization as there is across sites operating in different organizations clearly suggests that there is inadequate transfer of expertise occurring within organizational boundaries.

1.1   Cognitive Limitations

One set of limitations on sharing expertise is cognitive, that is, the way experts store and process information may make it difficult for them to share that expertise with others regardless of whether or not they are motivated to do so. The cognitive limitations faced by experts come partly from the way that they mentally represent the task. As expertise increases, mental representations become more abstract and simplified (see Sternberg 1997 for a review). For example, in a study of electronic repairmen, Gitomer (1988) found that those with more skill viewed the electronic device as a system of components and conducted trouble-shooting by following a conceptual model of the way the device worked. In contrast, those with less skill described the same device as a group of unrelated parts and spent more time switching parts using a trial-and-error procedure. Similarly, Chi and her colleagues (Chi, Glaser, and Rees 1982) found that experts in physics used a deeper, more conceptual structure to sort physics problems, whereas novices sorted problems using a superficial structure. Adelson (1984) also found that expert programmers used conceptually based (abstract) representations when attempting to describe a programming task, whereas novices used syntactically based (concrete) representations. These studies, along with others (Ceci and Liker 1986; Gobet and Simon 1998; Johnson 1988; Lamberti and Newsome 1989; Chase and Simon 1973; McKeithen et al. 1981), suggest that expertise is characterized by conceptual, abstract representations.

One characteristic of experts' more conceptual, abstract representations is that they appear to be simplified representations of the task. As experts begin to automate aspects of the task, details of the task become less salient and experts begin to view the task in an oversimplified way. In an experiment, Langer and Imber (1979) found that experts' lists of task components contained significantly fewer and less specific steps than did the lists of those with less expertise. Developing abstract, simplified representations of the task allows experts to process information more rapidly, view the task holistically, and avoid getting bogged down in details. As such, abstract and simplified representations generally serve experts well. However, there are situations in which these representations can interfere with experts' ability to share their expertise, particularly with others who have significantly less expertise.

Bridging the Expertise Gap

When experts share their expertise with others, they are frequently in the position of communicating with people less expert than themselves. This requires that they somehow bridge the gap between themselves and those with less expertise. Experts can bridge the gap by providing background and concrete information, and using language that is understandable to those with less expertise. In other words, experts need to establish a common ground with the intended recipients of their knowledge. However, it can be difficult at times to determine what is common ground and to convey information appropriate to the recipient.

One might expect that experts, in conveying expertise to others, would have the flexibility to revert to their concrete understanding of the task or to their own novice experience as a means of bridging the gap between themselves and novices. However, several cognitive limitations interfere with both experts' ability to access their expertise at the concrete level and their ability to articulate that expertise in such as way that those with less expertise can understand it.

In her study of experts' estimations of novice task performance using a cellular telephone (study 1) or building a toy airplane (study 2), Hinds (1999) found that experts severely underestimated novice performance times. In part, experts' inaccuracy was attributable to an availability bias—a bias whereby people recall information that has been more recently triggered or is, for other reasons, more salient in memory (see Tversky and Kahneman 1973). To the extent that experts acquired their expertise at an earlier time than those with less expertise, they may have incomplete and inaccurate recall of their own learning experience because it is less available in memory. Experts, for example, have difficulty recalling how little they knew and how slowly they performed as novices (Hinds 1999). Because experts begin to abstract and simplify their understanding of tasks as they become more expert, they may not be able to recall the complexity and details they and others require as novices to understand the task.

Although little work has focused specifically on how experts share their knowledge, there is some evidence that experts' instructions to novices will be at a level too difficult for novices to grasp. For example, in an experiment in which electronics experts instructed novices on how to complete an electronic circuit, experts gave more advanced, abstract, and less concrete instructions to novices than did those with less expertise (Hinds, Patterson, and Pfeffer 2001). A second experiment then demonstrated that novices performed better on the target task when instructed by those with less expertise. Similarly, in a recent experiment by Finkel, Heath, and Dent (2001) in which they asked participants to provide instructions on how to order a series of abstract shapes, participants with more experience providing instructions to a partner oversimplified their explanations and relied more on idiosyncratic language than did those with less experience explaining the task to others. These studies suggest that experts have difficulty reverting to concrete, detailed explanations of the task even when they know their explanations are intended for novices.

Camerer and his colleagues (Camerer, Loewenstein, and Weber 1989) termed a related bias the "curse of knowledge"—a curse whereby those with knowledge are unable to forget their knowledge even when it would improve their own performance on a task. In their study of student project teams, they found that performers were unable to ignore their current knowledge when making estimates of company earnings. Further, when guessing the mean prediction of uninformed subjects, informed subjects' estimates were biased toward their own knowledge. The curse of knowledge may make it difficult for experts to bridge the gap between themselves and novices because they have difficulty imagining ever having been so ill-informed on the topic and accurately imagining the information that novices might not know.

When attempting to take the perspective of those with less expertise, experts may rely on an anchoring and adjustment heuristic, a method that involves establishing a baseline from which to adjust their estimates of others' behaviors. Often this baseline is derived from the estimators' own experience (Davis, Hoch, and Ragsdale 1986; Nickerson, Baddeley, and Freeman 1987). For instance, Hinds (1999) found that experts anchor on their own current experience and attempt to adjust downward to the level of those with less experience. When decision makers use an anchoring and adjustment heuristic, the adjustment is often inadequate, with the estimate too closely associated with the original anchor. Consistent with this, Hinds (1999) found that experts attempted to adjust their original anchor (on their current performance) by adjusting downward to their own novice performance, but that these adjustments were sorely lacking because experts had inaccurate memories of their own novice performance. Experts may think that they are bridging the gap between themselves and novices because they have made a downward adjustment, but they fall terribly short. The result can be frustration on the part of the novice or, even worse, novices may have an incomplete understanding of the task without realizing it is incomplete. In these cases, novices may believe that they have the knowledge required yet find themselves unable to successfully complete the task.

The availability bias, the curse of knowledge, and an anchoring and adjustment heuristic all are cognitive heuristics or biases that are characteristic of how experts retain, process, and retrieve information related to their expertise. Each makes it challenging to bridge the gap between experts and novices. Moreover, these biases may be difficult to overcome. In their study of students estimating company earnings, Camerer, Loewenstein, and Weber (1989) found that feedback did not improve informed subjects' estimates of uninformed subjects' predictions. Similarly, in her work examining experts' estimates of the performance time of novices using cellular telephones, Hinds (1999) found that experts did not improve when prompted with traditional debiasing methods. Even when prompted to think about their previous experience and consider the types of problems faced by novices, experts had a difficult time including and weighting these factors appropriately. For example, when confronted with the problems faced by new users of cellular phones, one expert stated that these problems were easy to solve and should take mere seconds, although the novices struggled with the problem for several minutes (Hinds 1999). These cognitive limitations suggest that even when experts are willing to share their knowledge with others, they may face the challenge of not being able to revert to a level of concreteness and detail that is needed by novices to understand and build their own expertise at the task.

Articulating Tacit Knowledge

Another cognitive problem in transferring knowledge is the challenge of articulating knowledge that is tacit rather than explicit. As experts learn tasks, they develop both explicit and tacit knowledge. Tacit knowledge is learned through experience and held at the unconscious or semiconscious level (see Polanyi 1966; Leonard and Sensiper 1998). Because tacit knowledge does not reside at the conscious level, it is difficult to articulate and therefore difficult to share with others. Even when experts are able to mentally bridge the gap between themselves and those with less expertise, they may have trouble articulating the specific information novices need to learn and perform effectively. In their study of pizza parlors, Epple, Argote, and Murphy (1996) found that workers acquired both explicit, codifiable knowledge and tacit knowledge. For example, one employee was able to share with others a system for optimizing pizza preparation based on the cooking times of different pizzas. However, employees had difficulty telling others how to hand-toss a pizza because the expertise was tacit and not easily described. In such cases where expertise is tacit, people may inadvertently tell only part of the story—the explicit version—but neglect to share the tacit foundation that makes the knowledge complete.

Another problem in asking experts to articulate knowledge is that knowledge is embedded and difficult to extract from the particular situation or environment (Brown and Duguid 1998; Hansen 1999; Lave and Wenger 1991). Experts may be able to articulate the steps they perform in their own situation, in their own environment. However, these may or may not be the steps that are needed or the approach that is appropriate in a different environment. This phenomenon is so pervasive in organizations that the phrase "not invented here" has been coined to refer to ideas that were developed in a different context and are therefore less valued. While part of the resistance to adopting innovations that were invented elsewhere may be based on competition for status or the derogation of out-groups (e.g., Brewer and Brown 1998), some of the problem may also be based on the genuine challenge of adopting innovations developed in a different context.

In their study of two truck assembly plants whose technologies diverged over time, Argote and Epple (1990) found that managers were reluctant to seek knowledge, arguing that knowledge from the other plant was not relevant to their operations. Similarly, in their study of knowledge seeking and sharing within a consumer products organization, Hinds and her colleagues (2001) found that employees were more resistant to transferring knowledge that required adaptation to a new context. This is consistent with Singley and Anderson's (1989) model of transfer, which argues that transfer of knowledge will be greater if there is more similarity between tasks. Singley and Anderson go on to argue that negative transfer can occur when people attempt to transfer knowledge between tasks when the conditions do not match. This is not to say that expertise cannot be applied across situations, rather to point out the added challenge faced by experts when attempting to codify or articulate knowledge in such a way that it can be applied across multiple situations and in multiple environments.

Finally, there is some evidence that when experts are exhorted to explicate their knowledge, it can detract from their own performance. In the process of explicating knowledge, experts may get unduly committed to the partial knowledge that they have articulated and neglect more subtle, tacit aspects of their tasks. Work by Wilson and Schooler (1991) suggests that being asked to explain what one is doing makes people less effective at performing tasks because it requires that they explicate a plan of action that does not reflect what they would have done if they had relied on their tacit knowledge. In asking experts to convey their knowledge, it may be wise to be cognizant of the potential drop in experts' level of performance if asked to explicate their expertise at a detailed level. The risk is that experts may become more distant from their own expertise as they focus on the details important to novices.

1.2   Motivational Limitations

Although cognitive factors are important in understanding why knowledge and expertise are sometimes difficult to communicate and transfer, cognitive limitations are not the whole story. Differences in perspective between experts and novices, and even the effort required, cannot completely account for the profound problems observed in the transfer of knowledge and skill across units. In thinking about the challenges faced by organizations such as General Motors that have benefited little from efforts designed to increase learning across organizational units, it is clear that there must be some motivational, intentional component to the explanation. It is difficult to believe that individual cognitive biases such as an availability bias would differ substantially across companies, even though some organizations have much more success in transferring knowledge across units than others (Davenport and Prusak 1998). This is not to deny the importance of cognitive issues but to note that there are motivational problems as well.

Competition as a Disincentive

Much, although not all, of the motivational problem comes from the very structure and operating premises of most organizations, which are designed to set people and units against each other and thereby discourage the sharing of information and expertise. In ways too numerous to completely detail and so automatic as to be unexceptional, companies set up internal competitions that pit people and units against each other. People compete for promotions, and indeed promotion has been studied as a "tournament" in which people who win at one round survive to compete in the next round while those who lose are essentially finished in their efforts to win subsequent promotions (Rosenbaum 1979). Economists have even argued that this tournament structure is desirable in ensuring effort and diligence (e.g., Lazear and Rosen 1981). People also compete for raises. The customary way of administering salary is to distribute a fixed proportion of a unit's salary budget to be divided across the members of the unit based on relative performance. By definition this means that what one person receives another cannot, a zero-sum game. Companies offer individual incentives, such as awards (like employee of the month or the year), or incentives to teams, such as bonuses or profit sharing. Although perhaps unintentionally, such individual and team rewards can induce competition because outstanding performance is most often determined *relative* to the performance of others.

Even without such explicit management practices, competition between units may be an inevitable aspect of organizational life. A natural (and often beneficial) result of being organized into units or teams is the tendency for individuals to identify with the team. People see themselves as part of their unit or work team and begin to differentiate themselves from other work teams. According to social identity theory, individuals' desire for positive self-evaluation leads them to have an in-group bias in which they attribute positive characteristics to their own group and negative characteristics to the out-group (Abrams and Hogg 1990). This categorization process results in higher levels of intergroup conflict and reduced cooperation within organizations (Kramer 1991). As Argote (1999) states,

Giving groups distinct names, providing opportunities for members to interact, publicizing the performance of different groups, providing rewards based on the performance of different groups, and other techniques designed to increase group identity are also likely to increase intergroup competition. Intergroup competition, in turn, impairs sharing of information and transfer of knowledge across groups. (177)

Consistent with this, Fisher and his colleagues (Fisher, Maltz, and Jaworski 1997) report less information sharing between the marketing and engineering functions when respondents from the marketing side were more strongly identified with their group than with the organization as a whole. In other words, the very practices that promote high levels of *esprit de corps* within teams create competition between teams and can inhibit the sharing of expertise within organizations.

Competition between individuals and teams is presumed to motivate greater individual or subunit performance. Holding aside whether inducing competition actually has such a desirable effect on individual performance (see Kohn 1992 for evidence that competition does not invariably promote enhanced individual performance), competitive dynamics must inevitably produce less cooperation across people and units in a company. In the case of knowledge sharing or transferring expertise, there exist knowledge markets (Davenport and Prusak 1998) inside organizations, and as in any other markets, exchange dynamics are important. For experts, the cost of sharing expertise in a competitive environment generally outweighs the benefit of sharing. Why would I voluntarily help a competitor—for raises, for promotions, for status—in a system that induces more competitive dynamics? The answer is, I would not. Another way of seeing the same result is to note that knowledge is power, and control over information provides those who have the information, if it is necessary and useful, with more power (e.g., Pettigrew 1972). Sharing expertise, therefore, means sharing power, and one is much less likely to share power in a competitive environment in which those who are receiving the information and expertise may use it against the interests of the person providing it. This logic is why Deming and other writers about total quality management, a process that relies heavily on learning from others to improve operations, were so critical of relative performance evaluations and any other management practices that set people against each other (e.g., Deming 1982).

Consider also the person on the other side of the exchange—the person in need of the knowledge or expertise. As Blau (1955; 1964) showed decades ago, status is accorded to those who provide assistance to others. The providing of status to the helper balances the exchange. If the helper did not receive higher status, then the exchange would be unbalanced—the requester of help would get the help, and the person providing the information would get nothing. In a competitive world individuals in need of expertise may be reluctant to voluntarily engage in an exchange—knowledge for status—that places them in a disadvantageous position and acknowledges their inferior position. However, status is not the only exchange that can be offered. Within organizations there exists a *norm of reciprocity* such that asking for knowledge from others implies the expectation of reciprocation in the future. In an organization in which knowledge is considered to be the property of an individual and where obligations are incurred when knowledge is sought, people should be more reluctant to seek knowledge and expertise from others (see Hollingshead, Fulk, and Monge 2002). Consistent with this, Hinds et al. (2001) found that within a consumer products organization, respondents who reported that norms of reciprocity were operating also were significantly less likely to spend time seeking knowledge from others in the organization.

If inducing competitive dynamics impedes the transfer of expertise within organizations, then it must follow that eliminating the emphasis on internal competition is an important step in enhancing knowledge transfer. Anecdotal case evidence suggests that it is. Davenport and Prusak (1998) note that companies that were most successful in knowledge transfer had both formal and informal reward systems that provided recognition, status, and even material rewards to those who shared expertise and helped others, not to those who developed and maintained knowledge monopolies. They maintain that creating situations where people would feel motivated to share their wisdom with others requires that "organizations ... hire nice people and treat them nicely" (34).

Other Disincentives

In addition to competition, other organizational processes also can act as disincentives for sharing expertise. For example, some organizations insist on "knowledge sharing" by establishing explicit, formalized processes that require the sharing of expertise. These processes are designed to ensure compliance and conformity. However, because knowledge sharing requires the transfer of knowledge across boundaries along with the development of a shared understanding of the material (Brown and Duguid 1998), ideal information-sharing processes allow relationships and shared interpretations to develop with less rigid organizational control. In systems constrained by rules, experts may be less motivated to share their expertise because the process is less satisfying. In fact, reactance theory (Brehm 1966) suggests that forcing people to do something may produce exactly the opposite result, as people rebel against the constraints imposed on them.

A related organizational characteristic that acts as a disincentive to sharing expertise is the status hierarchies that are pervasive in organizational life. Formal hierarchies have traditionally served the purpose of coordinating and making more efficient the flow of information in organizations (Cyert and March 1963; Simon 1962). This is accomplished through a division of labor in which functionally specialized units and unity of command constrain communication flows to those defined by the chain of command (Galbraith 1973). By constraining communication so that instructions flow downward and information flows upward, organizations are made more efficient and predictable. However, people who are accustomed to such a model may be reluctant to share information in ways that violate this model. For example, Leonard and Sensiper (1998) describe the situation of nurses who are reluctant to suggest patient treatments because physicians are of higher status. Similarly, in a study of operating room teams, Edmonson (2000) reported that nurses and others of low status often were reluctant to share their expertise and advice with surgeons because surgeons responded negatively to advice from these lower-status team members. In some cases, this resulted in errors in the operating room because the lower-status team members frequently better understood some aspects of new technologies and procedures. Sanctions against sharing and norms for not sharing across hierarchical boundaries conspire to limit the amount of expertise that flows upward and even laterally inside organizations.

A somewhat related yet distinct motivational issue is the individual's relationship to the organization, not just to others inside the organization. Being motivated to share what you know with others requires trust—not only trusting those others (something that is diminished with competition) but also trusting the larger institution within which the sharing of expertise is occurring. "Workers are more likely to ... expend the additional effort to gather and share information ... when their claims to be stakeholders are recognized by the firm and they have a reasonable expectation of employment security" (Appelbaum et al. 2000, 43–44). In this regard, there is evidence that organizational actions that destroy trust, such as downsizing, induce fear and make the transfer of expertise and experience less likely (Davenport and Prusak 1998; Pan and Scarbrough 1998; Pfeffer and Sutton 2000). For example, in her study of a groupware system, Orlikowski (1993) observed that people were reluctant to share information when they were afraid that the information would be used against them. Pan and Scarbrough (1998) also observed that an environment of trust contributed to active knowledge sharing within a multinational chemical company. Why would a person tell what he knows unless he feels reasonably secure that by sharing knowledge he is not putting at risk his own or his colleagues' organizational position and career?

Leonard and Sensiper (1998) go on to argue that sharing one's expertise can be risky because of the difficulty involved in articulating preferences based largely on tacit knowledge. For example, in designing computer interfaces, some experienced user interface specialists simply "know" but cannot explain why the buttons should be placed in a certain configuration or the colors should be changed on a computer screen. In organizations that insist on hard data, sharing one's tacit expertise via opinions and intuitions can convey a lack of certainty or clarity and undermine one's expert standing in the organization. Sharing expertise requires building a culture of trust, and any organizational practice or action that destroys trust adversely affects the motivation to share information with others.

Lack of Incentives

Competition, rigid business processes, and status differences within organizations can act as disincentives to sharing one's expertise. In addition to organizational practices that create penalties for sharing expertise, organizations can (and often do) inhibit the sharing of expertise by not providing adequate incentives to balance the costs experts invariably incur in the process of sharing their knowledge. Sharing complex knowledge requires time devoted to either personal interaction or thoughtful documentation of one's expertise, or both. Few organizations provide the time required for knowledge transfer, believing that "conversations" are not real work. As Davenport and Prusak (1998, 47) have noted, "Implicit in building a marketplace ... is the need to give members of the organization enough time to shop for knowledge, or to sell it. A Catch-22 of the corporate world is that employees are too busy working to take time to learn things that will help them work more efficiently."

Consistent with theories of motivation, people can be expected to share their expertise more when they are provided incentives for doing so (see Huber 1991; Pan and Scarbrough 1998). The importance of receiving credit for knowledge sharing was evident in an interview reported by Hinds and her colleagues (2001) in which a director from a consumer products organization said, "We are so focused on results and we are measured on results ... and nowhere, anywhere, does it say you should share knowledge, help other people with the knowledge you have and you will be rewarded for it.... I won't make more money by sharing more, and I won't get promoted by sharing more." However, when there was a reward for knowledge sharing, it occurred. Within one division of the same consumer products organization, an award was offered for "information sharing." One director singled out the people in this division as "doing a great job" because they were actively talking to others in the company and sharing knowledge across divisional boundaries.

In his study of the search for knowledge and transfer of expertise within an electronics company, Hansen (1999) found that personal contact that allowed for questions and feedback resulted in more successful transfer of knowledge, particularly tacit knowledge. However, such interactions frequently require patience and effort as the expert attempts to understand the novice perspective, answer questions, provide feedback, and convey knowledge successfully. An alternative to personal contact is the documentation of experts' knowledge. However, this process also can be onerous and time-consuming for the expert. On software development projects, developers are often reluctant to spend hours documenting their code so that others can benefit from their expertise. One reason for developers' reluctance is undoubtedly the lack of incentives for such time-consuming tasks. Knowledge transfer, in other words, requires resources of time and energy. Too many companies want to see a return on their investment in transferring skill and knowledge without making the investment and adequately compensating employees for their time.

1.3 Overcoming Barriers to Transferring Expertise

Our discussion of the cognitive and motivational limitations to sharing expertise paints a pretty dismal picture with regard to sharing expertise within organizations. However, many organizations have successfully shared and transferred expertise between units (see Argote 1999, ch. 5). Although some of the cognitive and motivational limitations that we discussed earlier are extremely difficult to overcome, we believe that there are some management practices that can be implemented to diminish the problem of transferring skill and knowledge.

Overcoming Cognitive Limitations

Cognitive limitations may be more difficult to overcome than motivational ones because the limitations are a result of the way that information is stored in and retrieved from memory. Still, there are some things that organizations can do that may reduce the effects of these cognitive factors. For example, many of the cognitive limitations apply to experts but less so to those with less expertise. Organizations might therefore find more success in disseminating expertise by using people with an *intermediate* level of knowledge as a conduit to transfer information between experts and novices. Some research suggests that those with intermediate levels of expertise may be better suited to sharing expertise with novices because they are closer to the novices' own experience. For example, Hinds (1999) found that those with intermediate levels of expertise were better predictors of how long it would take novices to perform tasks using a cellular telephone than were either experts or novices. Those with intermediate levels of expertise may be able to explicate more of the concrete knowledge required for the task than experts while still providing the abstract information required for task understanding. Organizations might also consider creating teams composed of both intermediates and experts to help provide information to novices at the appropriate level of complexity.

Another way to overcome some of the cognitive limitations is to encourage two-way interaction between novices and experts. This allows novices to ask questions and get feedback from experts. It also allows experts to adjust their presentation style based on novices' questions and performance. One form that such an approach can take is an apprenticeship program in which novices are able to shadow experts and ask questions without relying solely on experts to explicate their knowledge. Such a process puts the burden on the novice to understand the experts' context and to ask the questions that make it possible for novices to transfer this knowledge to their own situation. This process has characteristics similar to that described by Hansen (1999). In his study, strong interpersonal relationships that allowed discussion, questions, and feedback were an essential aspect of the transfer of complex knowledge.

Carlile and his colleagues (Carlile, Carlile, and Rebentisch 2001) have argued that the key to overcoming contextual differences is by representing knowledge through the use of boundary objects. Boundary objects embody and represent essential knowledge and can be shared across domains and levels of expertise. For example, experts can produce prototypes or sketches of products as a way of conveying their thoughts about how a product might work and how it should be designed. The prototype has extensive tacit knowledge embedded within it and can serve as a basis for communication, discussion, and elaboration without requiring that the expert articulate a priori all of her thinking about the product design. Through such boundary objects, people can see for themselves the way that knowledge is represented and negotiate shared meanings.

Overcoming Motivational Limitations

Fortunately for organizations, motivational barriers to sharing expertise are more easily addressed through changes in organizational practices. The motivational issues discussed earlier can be addressed by reducing competition between groups, allowing communities of practice to evolve, deemphasizing status hierarchies, and increasing incentives to share expertise with others.

Organizations can do several things to reduce competition between groups. First, encouraging individuals to focus on organization-level goals rather than individual or team-level goals can reduce intergroup competition by causing employees to identify with the organization as a whole (e.g., Sherif 1966). In Sherif's classic studies of interaction in a boys' summer camp, when groups competed with each other, the boys exhibited hostile behavior. However, when they were given a super-ordinate goal, competing with another camp across the lake, they were amicable toward each other and exhibited cordial, friendly relations. These results, replicated numerous times experimentally, demonstrate that "there is usually more in-group bias, less intergroup liking, and greater intergroup discrimination when groups are objectively in competition than when they are interdependent or must cooperate to achieve a common goal" (Brewer and Brown 1998, 565). Once individuals identify with the organization and see those outside as the competition, the sharing of expertise should increase.

Second, organizations can reduce their reliance on individual and unit-level reward systems that are zero-sum. For example, organizations can allocate raises based upon absolute levels of performance (e.g., vis-à-vis goals) without ranking employees and teams against one another. They can also avoid zero-sum situations where an increase in one person's raise precludes an increase in another person's raise by setting aside enough resources so that all employees can receive the highest possible raises if the company does well as a whole. Further, to promote high levels of cooperation, a significant portion of an individual's compensation can be based on the performance of the organization rather than on the performance of the individual or team. Such organization-level reward systems can be used for salary increases, bonuses, stock options, and so forth. Reducing competition between groups and focusing individuals on collective goals should increase people's willingness to share their expertise with others because all parties benefit from the exchange.

Another method for increasing the sharing of expertise within organizations is to encourage and support communities of practice. Communities of practice are "groups of people who are informally bound together by shared expertise and passion for a joint enterprise" (Wenger and Snyder 2000, 139). These groups tend to interact regularly by meeting face-to-face or relying on technology to facilitate discussion. Members belong to communities of practice because of a desire to exchange knowledge. Organizations can promote communities of practice by creating an organizational environment in which these informal groups can thrive. Wenger and Snyder (2000) describe communities of practice as gardens that need to be tended and nurtured. To the extent that organizations nurture those communities of practice that are keepers of knowledge critical to the mission of the organization, essential expertise is likely to be shared more readily across organizational units.

Another motivational limitation discussed earlier is the status hierarchy that exists within most organizations. To the extent that organizations deemphasize status distinctions, there is likely to be more sharing of expertise. For example, if nurses felt that they were valued as much, or almost as much, as physicians, they would be more willing and able to share their expertise about a patient's history or a new technology. Managers can deemphasize status by reducing the power differential between members of the organization. In the case of nurses and physicians, if physicians had no influence over the schedules, assignments, and careers of nurses, the power differential would be reduced (though unlikely eliminated because of other contributors to status such as level of education). Another way to reduce the negative effects of status is to elicit and encourage minority opinions. If people feel they are appreciated for their new perspectives rather than sanctioned for unpopular opinions, they are more likely to risk sharing their expertise even if they are of lower status or have opinions different from those of others.

Finally, increasing the incentives for sharing expertise should help to offset the costs that experts incur when they take the time and put forth the effort to share their expertise. Although some organizations provide incentives for sharing expertise, rarely are these incentives comparable to incentives for completing other tasks within the organization. People often work to product or project deadlines and are rewarded based on their performance against these goals. To the extent that sharing one's expertise is at least as valued and rewarded as other goals, sharing expertise is likely to be increased.

1.4   The Role of Technology

So far, this chapter has avoided the question of how technology can help to facilitate the sharing of expertise within organizations. The reason for this is twofold. First, the focus of the chapter was intended to be on limitations to the sharing of expertise as a backdrop for understanding organizational processes around the sharing of expertise. Second, the authors are somewhat skeptical about the role of technology in facilitating the sharing of expertise.

We believe that expertise is largely tacit and embedded in the context in which it is being used. Systems that purport to capture expertise for later perusal by those in need often fall short of the goal. This is in part because it is difficult to capture the knowledge of experts in such a form and in part because users find it difficult to absorb expertise from such a system. As we discussed, experts' ability to explicate their tacit knowledge is limited by the way they represent their knowledge in memory. This not only interferes with their ability to articulate this knowledge to novices but makes it difficult to articulate it in such a way that it can be loaded into an information system for later retrieval. Further, experts are unlikely to be motivated to document their knowledge for others to use. For these reasons, our assessment is that these systems generally capture *information or data* rather than *knowledge or expertise*. Information and information systems are extremely useful but do not replace expertise or the learning that takes place through interpersonal contact.

One promising technological development is in the area of expert-finding systems—systems that are available to organization members who want to find experts on particular topics. These systems have the advantage that they are not attempting to disseminate disembodied, decontextualized knowledge but rather are trying to facilitate the development of interpersonal connections around topics of interest. Although a new set of organizational issues arises with the introduction and use of such systems, we believe that being able to locate those with expertise is an important step in building interpersonal ties and communities of practice through which expertise can be shared.

1.5   Conclusion

It is generally recognized that in today's economy it is increasingly the case that all work is knowledge work. Therefore, what the barriers are to developing and transferring expertise within organizations, and the ways of overcoming those barriers, are of interest to both organization theorists and to practicing managers. We have argued in this chapter that (1) sharing knowledge even within an organization is often difficult and not always successfully accomplished; (2) this difficulty arises from both cognitive and motivational issues; (3) organizations that successfully transfer knowledge and share expertise are better at building structures and sets of management practices that overcome these barriers; and (4) in all of this, technology may play an enabling role but is not a critical factor either in the origination of the cognitive and motivational problems or in their solution.

Throughout, we have tried to tie the issue of sharing expertise to some fundamental features and literatures in both cognitive psychology and organization theory. By so doing, we hope to encourage more research that crosses disciplinary boundaries and that investigates the causes of the problems in sharing expertise and their remedies from multiple perspectives.

References

Abrams, D., and M. Hogg, eds. 1990. *Social Identity Theory: Constructive and Critical Advances.* New York: Springer-Verlag.

Adelson, B. 1984. When Novices Surpass Experts: The Difficulty of a Task May Increase with Expertise. *Journal of Experimental Psychology: Learning, Memory, & Cognition* 10: 483–495.

Appelbaum, E., T. Bailey, P. Berg, and A. Kalleberg. 2000. *Manufacturing Advantage: Why High-Performance Work Systems Pay Off.* Ithaca, N.Y.: Cornell University Press.

Argote, L. 1999. *Organizational Learning: Creating, Retaining, and Transferring Knowledge.* Norwell, Mass.: Kluwer.

Argote, L., and D. Epple. 1990. Learning Curves in Manufacturing. *Science* 247: 920–924.

Blau, P. M. 1955. *The Dynamics of Bureaucracy.* Chicago: University of Chicago Press.

———. 1964. *Exchange and Power in Social Life.* New York: Wiley.

Brehm, J. W. 1966. *A Theory of Psychological Reactance.* New York: Academic Press.

Brewer, M., and R. Brown. 1998. Intergroup Relations. In *The Handbook of Social Psychology.* Vol. 2. 4th ed. Ed. Daniel T. Gilbert, Susan T. Fiske, and Gardner Lindzey, 554–594. New York: McGraw-Hill.

Brown, C., and M. Reich. 1989. When Does Union-Management Cooperation Work? A Look at NUMMI and GM-Van Nuys. *California Management Review* 31: 26–44.

Brown, J., and P. Duguid. 1998. Organizing Knowledge. *California Management Review* 40 (3): 90–111.

Carlile, P. 2000. A Pragmatic View of Knowledge and Boundaries: Boundary Objects in New Product Development. Working paper, Sloan School of Management, MIT, Cambridge, MA 02139.

Carlile, P., and E. Rebentisch. 2001. Into the Black Box: The Knowledge Transformation Cycle. Working paper, Sloan School of Management, MIT, Cambridge, MA 02139.

Camerer, C., G. Loewenstein, and M. Weber. 1989. The Curse of Knowledge in Economic Settings: An Experimental Analysis. *Journal of Political Economy* 97: 1232–1254.

Ceci, S. J., and J. Liker. 1986. A Day at the Races: A Study of IQ, Expertise, and Cognitive Complexity. *Journal of Experimental Psychology: General* 115 (3).

Chase, W. G., and H. A. Simon. 1973. Perception in Chess. *Cognitive Psychology*, 4 (1): 55–81.

Chi, M., R. Glaser, and E. Rees. 1982. Expertise in Problem Solving. In *Advances in the Psychology of Human Intelligence*, ed. R. J. Sternberg, 7–75. Hillsdale, N.J.: Erlbaum.

Cyert, R. M., and J. G. March. 1963. *A Behavioral Theory of the Firm.* Englewood Cliffs, N.J.: Prentice-Hall.

Davenport, T. H., and L. Prusak. 1998. *Working Knowledge: How Organizations Manage What They Know.* Boston: Harvard Business School Press.

Davis, H. L., S. J. Hoch, and E. K. Ragsdale. 1986. An Anchoring and Adjustment Model of Spousal Predictions. *Journal of Consumer Research* 13: 25–37.

Deming, W. E. 1982. *Out of the Crisis*. Cambridge, Mass.: Center for Advanced Engineering Study, Massachusetts Institute of Technology.

Edmondson, A. C., R. Bohmer, and G. Pisano. 2000. Learning New Technical and Interpersonal Routines in Operating Room Teams: The Case of Minimally Invasive Cardiac Surgery. In *Research on Managing Groups and Teams: Technology*, vol. 3, ed. E. Mannix, M. Neale and T. Griffith, 29–51. Stamford, Conn.: JAI Press.

Epple, D., L. Argote, and K. Murphy. 1996. An Empirical Investigation of the Micro Structure of Knowledge Acquisition and Transfer Through Learning by Doing. *Operations Research* 44: 77–86.

Finkel, E., C. Heath, and J. Dent. 2001. Expertise and the Curse of Knowledge: The Communication Problems of Specialists. Working paper, University of North Carolina, Chapel Hill, NC 27514.

Fisher, R., E. Maltz, and B. Jaworski. 1997. Enhancing Communication Between Marketing and Engineering: The Moderating Role of Relative Functional Identification. *Journal of Marketing* 61: 54–70.

Galbraith, J. 1973. *Designing Complex Organizations*. Reading, Mass.: Addison-Wesley.

Gitomer, D. H. 1988. Individual Differences in Technical Troubleshooting. *Human Performance* 1 (2): 111–131.

Gobet, F., and H. A. Simon. 1998. Expert Chess Memory: Revisiting the Chunking Hypothesis. *Memory* 6: 225–255.

Grant, R. M. 1996. Toward a Knowledge-Based Theory of the Firm. *Strategic Management Journal* 17: 109–122.

Hansen, M. T. 1999. The Search-Transfer Problem: The Role of Weak Ties in Sharing Knowledge Across Organization Subunits. *Administrative Science Quarterly* 44 (1): 82–111.

Hinds, P. 1999. The Curse of Expertise: The Effects of Expertise and Debiasing Methods on Predictions of Novice Performance. *Journal of Experimental Psychology: Applied* 5: 205–221.

Hinds, P., D. Burgess, J. Pfeffer, and P. Moore. 2001. Laying the Groundwork: The Role of Organizational Context in Knowledge Sharing and Seeking. Working paper, Stanford University, Palo Alto, CA 94305.

Hinds, P., M. Patterson, and J. Pfeffer. 2001. Bothered by Abstraction: The Effect of Expertise on Knowledge Transfer and Subsequent Novice Performance. *Journal of Applied Psychology* 86 (6): 1232–1243.

Hollingshead, A., J. Fulk, and P. Monge. 2002. Fostering Intranet Knowledge-Sharing: An Integration of Transactive Memory and Public Goods Approaches. In *Distributed Work*, ed. P. Hinds and S. Kiesler. Cambridge, Mass.: MIT Press.

Huber, G. 1991. Organizational Learning: The Contributing Processes and the Literatures. *Organization Science* 2: 88–115.

Johnson, E. J. 1988. Expertise and Decision under Uncertainty: Performance and Process. In *The Nature of Expertise*, ed. M. T. H. Chi, R. Glaser, and M. J. Farr, 209–228. Hillsdale, N.J.: Erlbaum.

Kohn, A. 1992. *The Case Against Competition*. Rev. ed. Boston: Houghton Mifflin.

Kramer, R. 1991. Intergroup Relations and Organizational Dilemmas: The Role of Categorization Processes. *Research in Organizational Behavior* 13: 191–228.

Lamberti, D. M., and S. L. Newsome. 1989. Presenting Abstract versus Concrete Information in Expert Systems: What Is the Impact on User Performance? *International Journal of Man-Machine Studies* 31 (1): 27–45.

Langer, E. J., and L. G. Imber. 1979. When Practice Makes Imperfect: Debilitating Effects of Overlearning. *Journal of Personality and Social Psychology* 37: 2014–2024.

Lave, J., and E. Wenger. 1991. *Situated Learning: Legitimate Peripheral Participation*. New York: Cambridge University Press.

Lazear, E., and S. Rosen. 1981. Rank-Order Tournaments as Optimum Labor Contracts. *Journal of Political Economy* 89: 841–864.

Leonard, D., and S. Sensiper. 1998. The Role of Tacit Knowledge in Group Innovation. *California Management Review* 40 (3): 112–132.

Luft, J. 1984. *Group Process*. Palo Alto, Calif.: Mayfield Publishing.

McKeithen, K., J. Reitman, H. Reuter, and S. Hirtle. 1981. Knowledge Organization and Skill Differences in Computer Programmers. *Cognitive Psychology* 13: 307–325.

Nickerson, R. S., A. Baddeley, and B. Freeman. 1987. Are People's Estimates of What Other People Know Influenced by What They Themselves Know? *Acta Psychologica* 64: 245–259.

O'Dell, C., and C. J. Grayson. 1998. *If Only We Knew What We Know*. New York: Free Press.

Orlikowski, W. 1993. Learning from NOTES: Organizational Issues in Groupware Implementation. *The Information Society* 9: 237–250.

Pan, S., and H. Scarbrough. 1998. A Sociotechnical View of Knowledge Sharing at Buckman Laboratories. *Journal of Knowledge Management* 2: 55–56.

Pascale, R. 1990. *Managing on the Edge*. New York: Simon and Schuster.

Pettigrew, A. 1972. Information Control as a Power Resource. *Sociology* 6: 187–204.

Pfeffer, J., and R. Sutton. 2000. *The Knowing-Doing Gap: How Smart Companies Turn Knowledge into Action*. Boston: Harvard Business School Press.

Polanyi, M. 1966. *The Tacit Dimension*. New York: Doubleday.

Ricketts, R. 1994. Survey Points to Practices That Reduce Refinery Maintenance Spending. *Oil and Gas Journal* (July): 37–41.

Rosenbaum, J. 1979. Tournament Mobility: Career Patterns in a Corporation. *Administrative Science Quarterly* 24: 220–241.

Ruggles, R. 1998. The State of the Notion: Knowledge Management in Practice. *California Management Review* 40 (3): 80–89.

Sherif, M. 1966. *Group Conflict and Cooperation: Their Social Psychology.* London: Routledge and Kegan Paul.

Simon, H. A. 1962. The Architecture of Complexity. *Proceedings of the American Philosophical Society* 106: 467–482.

Singley, M., and J. Anderson. 1989. *The Transfer of Cognitive Skill.* Cambridge, Mass.: Harvard University Press.

Spender, J. C. 1996. Making Knowledge the Basis of a Dynamic Theory of the Firm. *Strategic Management Journal* 17: 45–62.

Sternberg, R. J. 1997. Cognitive Conceptions of Expertise. In *Expertise in Context: Human and Machine,* ed. P. J. Feltovich, K. M. Ford, and R. R. Hoffman, 149–162. Cambridge, Mass.: MIT Press/AAAI Press.

Szulanski, G. 1996. Exploring Internal Stickiness: Impediments to the Transfer of Best Practice Within Firms. *Strategic Management Journal* 17: 27–43.

Tversky, A., and D. Kahneman. 1973. Availability: A Heuristic for Judging Frequency and Probability. *Cognitive Psychology* 5: 207–232.

Wenger, E., and W. Snyder. 2000. Communities of Practice: The Organizational Frontier. *Harvard Business Review* (January–February): 139–145.

Wilson, T., and J. Schooler. 1991. Thinking Too Much: Introspection Can Reduce the Quality of Preferences and Decisions. *Journal of Personality and Social Psychology* 60: 181–192.

2

A Critical Evaluation of Knowledge Management Practices

Marleen Huysman and Dirk de Wit

Although knowledge management is popular among academics as well as among organizational practitioners, the concept is still surrounded by ambiguity. We believe that this ambiguity has at least two causes, which we address in this chapter: a limited focus on knowledge-sharing practices and a lack of long-term practical experience.

The academic literature on knowledge management continues to grow (see, for example, recent special issues of academic journals such as *Journal of Strategic Management, Management Science, IS Frontiers*, and *Journal of Strategic Information Systems*). Nevertheless, most of the contributions tend to focus on only one specific aspect of knowledge sharing and to ignore other relevant and interesting knowledge processes. This limited focus arises in part from a tendency to consider only knowledge management practices that explicitly use this concept while failing to consider practices that do not use the popular term. Furthermore, a review of the literature on knowledge management (Huysman and de Wit 2002) shows that most contributions tend to single out one type of knowledge sharing while ignoring potentially valuable others. The literature on knowledge management views knowledge sharing either from a stock approach, in which knowledge can be codified, or from a flow approach, in which knowledge cannot be codified. In addition, a third stream of literature looking at knowledge management from an innovation perspective seems to operate independent of the other two perspectives. In other words, the literature on knowledge management concentrates on managing knowledge retrieval or on managing knowledge exchange or on managing knowledge creation, and seldom on a combination of the three processes. All three perspectives are valuable and increase our understanding of managing knowledge processes. Thus, the research discussed in this chapter complements existing research by using a conceptual framework that covers a broad range of knowledge-sharing activities.

Another reason why knowledge management is surrounded by ambiguity is the mismatch between conceptual orientations and normative guidelines on the one hand and long-term practical experience on the other. Accounts of experience with knowledge management in practice are often based on "best practice" or on short-term projects (Davenport, Long, and Beers 1998; Fahey and Prusak 1998). A problem with best-practice research is that it tends to inform us about positive (managerial) experiences and omit negative ones. And research based on short-term projects does not provide insight on the long-term viability of the knowledge management initiative. To learn effectively from the experience of other organizations, we need information about possible downsides and ways to circumvent them as well as information about long-term, real practice in organizations.

In this chapter we provide insight into a variety of knowledge-sharing practices. We first introduce a conceptual framework that is used to categorize the research into three knowledge management foci: knowledge retrieval, knowledge exchange, and knowledge creation. Then the research insights are used for critical analyses of the practice of knowledge management.

We selected ten large companies that with varying degrees of success engaged in management of knowledge sharing. Using our theoretical framework, we tried to avoid the bias in the literature on knowledge management that results from focusing on one aspect of knowledge sharing while ignoring others. The companies in the studies are active in a wide range of businesses. Thus, we hope to avoid another bias in the literature, namely, the bias toward knowledge-intensive companies such as consultants and law firms (e.g., Hansen, Nohria, and Tierney 1999; Gottschalk 1999). In order to ensure a well-distributed variety of industries and types of knowledge sharing, we focus on three different types of knowledge-sharing initiatives: knowledge retrieval, knowledge exchange, and knowledge creation.

2.1 Knowledge Sharing and Organizational Learning

We connect the concept of knowledge management with a related field: organizational learning. As such, knowledge management is perceived as structural management initiatives to support learning within and by the organization, whereas organizational learning is seen as the process through which an organization (re)constructs knowledge. The focus on collective knowledge construction is in line with more recent contributions to the organizational learning research stream (e.g., Brown and Duguid 1991; Cook and Yanow 1993; Elkjaer 1999; Huysman 2000; Nicolini and Meznar 1995; Pentland 1995; Sims 1999; Weick and Roberts 1993). Perceiving organizational learning and knowledge management as a process of (re)constructing organizational knowledge implies a social constructivist approach to knowledge (Berger and Luckmann 1966; Gergen 1994; Schutz 1971). According to the social constructivist approach, organizational learning is seen as an institutionalizing process through which individual knowledge becomes organizational knowledge. Institutionalization is the process whereby practice becomes sufficiently regular and continuous to be described as institutional. The attention is on the process through which individual or local knowledge is transformed into collective knowledge as well as on the process through which this socially constructed knowledge influences, and is part of, local knowledge (see Nonaka 1994). With organizational or collective knowledge, reference is made to knowledge as in rules, procedures, strategies, activities, technologies, conditions, paradigms, or frames of references around which organizations are constructed and through which they operate (Levitt and March 1988). Important is that organizational knowledge is capable of surviving considerable turnover in individual actors (Pentland 1995).

Berger and Luckmann (1966) describe three phases or "moments" that can be discerned during the institutionalization of knowledge: *externalizing*, *objectifying*, and *internalizing*. Externalizing knowledge refers to the process through which personal knowledge is exchanged with others. Objectifying knowledge refers to the process through which knowledge becomes an objective reality. During internalizing knowledge, this objectified knowledge is used by individuals in the course of their socialization. In relation to organizational learning processes, knowledge sharing can be analyzed as consisting of these three knowledge-sharing activities: externalizing individual knowledge such that knowledge becomes communicated; objectifying this knowledge into organizational knowledge such that knowledge becomes taken for granted; and internalizing this organizational knowledge by members of the organization.

In addition to these three processes, which in combination ensure the institutionalization of organizational knowledge, knowledge management focuses on the creation of new knowledge, or knowledge development. The various processes that make up innovation and institutionalization, or knowledge creation and recreation, can be made visual by the use of a knowledge-sharing cycle (figure 2.1). The cycle

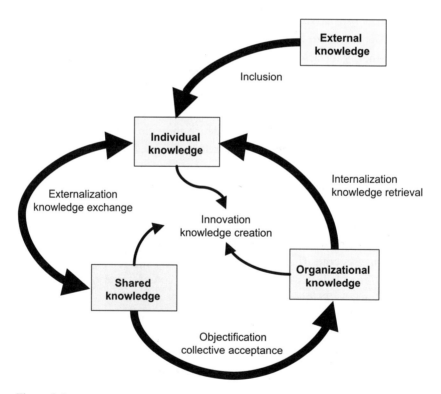

Figure 2.1
Internal organizational learning and knowledge sharing.

provides a simplified picture of knowledge sharing in organizations and is meant to help analyze the management of knowledge sharing.

The knowledge-sharing cycle is based on the social constructivist notion of organizational learning. In order to broaden the scope of knowledge sharing with creative processes, the cycle includes the process of knowledge creation.

It should be noted that the cycle has some similarities with the well-known classification of Nonaka and Takeuchi (1995): socialization, externalization, combination, and internalization. These authors use the concepts to point to other phenomena, namely, the transfer between tacit and explicit knowledge. In order to avoid confusion, we do not make use of the concepts "internalization" and "externalization" but instead refer to their relation with knowledge-sharing processes. More specifically, knowledge internalization is from now on referred to as knowledge retrieval, and knowledge externalization is referred to as knowledge exchange.

These forms of knowledge sharing relate to the learning processes of individuals and groups. Learning at the level of the organization only takes place when the collective treats knowledge as being organizational knowledge, that is, when knowledge has become collectively accepted and used. Collectively accepting knowledge is of strategic importance. Organizations that want to use internal knowledge sharing should pay explicit attention to the collective acceptance of shared knowledge.

Types of Knowledge Sharing
Three basic types of knowledge sharing can be derived from the knowledge-sharing cycle.

• *Knowledge retrieval.* Knowledge sharing from the organization to the individual has the purpose of retrieving existing organizational knowledge. During knowledge retrieval the individual learns from the organization. This type of knowledge sharing is depicted in figure 2.1 with an arrow pointing from organizational knowledge to individual knowledge.

• *Knowledge exchange.* Knowledge sharing from an individual to other individuals has the purpose of exchanging existing individual knowledge. During this process, individuals learn from other individuals. Knowledge exchange is portrayed in figure 2.1 with a mutual arrow between individual and shared knowledge.

• *Knowledge creation.* Knowledge sharing among individuals has the purpose of generating new knowledge. Knowledge creation in the case of internal learning results from new combinations of existing individual, shared, or organizational knowledge. This process of internal innovation is depicted in figure 2.1 within a circle with arrows flowing from the three sources of knowledge.

Collective Acceptance
This is the process during which shared knowledge becomes organizational knowledge. Collectively accepting local knowledge is the process in which the collective—often gradually—starts to accept existing shared knowledge as being part of the organization. This process is not so much one of sharing knowledge as one of sedimentation. For example, a group of technicians might have learned a new way of fixing a machine. This new operational knowledge remains local knowledge until it is accepted by the organization, for example, as expressed in organizational stories, in manuals, and in the training of newcomers. This process of objectification usually takes much longer than do the three knowledge-sharing processes (Dixon 2000; Berger and Luckmann 1966; Douglas 1987).

Because of its time-consuming and highly implicit character, we did not initially include collective acceptance in the empirical research. Nevertheless, our research revealed that ignoring the importance of collective acceptance can be a serious obstacle to organizational learning. In fact, most organizations in the research tended to ignore the outcomes of local knowledge-sharing processes or had problems collectively accepting these outcomes. That knowledge sharing often does not contribute to learning at the level of organizations has important implications that we discuss later.

Information Communication Technology
Knowledge-sharing processes can be distinguished not only by which learning processes they support but also by how they can be supported by information communication technology (ICT) (Hansen, Nohria, and Tierney 1999; Zack 1999).

Supporting knowledge retrieval is mainly needed to enable the knowledge transfer between the organization and the individual. For this purpose, stored knowledge, for example, in reports, databases, and knowledge bases, is most appropriate (Zack 1999). Knowledge management started out from the perspective of creating knowledge management database systems or creating expert systems. It is the organization that shares knowledge with the individual.

The role of ICT in supporting knowledge exchange between individuals is often said to be the domain of electronic networks. Intranets and Lotus Notes tools are the best known and often referred to in this context (Ciborra 1996).

Facilitating knowledge creation also requires the support of networks, although they are far less structured than is the case with knowledge sharing for reuse. Often it is difficult to decide a priori what knowledge should flow between which members, what the outcome or even the purpose of networking would be. In that case, networks resemble more the communities of practices described by researchers like Brown and Duguid (1991). In some instances, groupware technology and electronic communities can facilitate the process of knowledge creation.

Table 2.1 presents the primary purposes of managing knowledge sharing, the types of learning, the types of ICT application used to support the knowledge-sharing activities, and the various companies where we studied knowledge-sharing initiatives.

In the next section we briefly discuss the three types of knowledge sharing and illustrate the findings with examples taken from cases. Because of space limitations, we refer the interested reader who would like to learn more about the individual cases to Huysman and De Wit (2002).

2.2   Introduction to the Research

The research includes ten structured knowledge-sharing practices within ten large companies with more than one thousand workers each. In all these companies, top management supported the initiatives. All initiatives were supported by information communication technology. Along with the types of knowledge sharing that we studied, these ICT applications ranged from knowledge bases to electronic communities.

Table 2.1
Three Types of Knowledge Sharing

	Knowledge Retrieval	Knowledge Exchange	Knowledge Creation
Learning From	Organizational knowledge	Individual knowledge	Community knowledge
Main Purpose	Store dispersed collective knowledge to enhance individual learning	Prevent occurrence of knowledge gaps and redundancy	Combining knowledge to create new ideas and insights
ICT Support	Knowledge base	Networks	Communities
Companies Studied	Railways National Netherlands (NN) Postbank's call center	Cap Gemini IBM ING Barings Schiphol airport	Unilever R&D Stork Ministry of Housing

As the research concentrated on actual experiences and possible problems, we needed to use a different selection of cases than selecting knowledge management initiatives only. Because we only included initiatives that had already been running for a substantial period, we excluded knowledge management practices from which we could not extract empirical lessons. This meant cutting potentially interesting case studies. In fact, most knowledge management initiatives that we at first considered as interesting enough to include in the study appeared to be still in a conceptual stage. As a result, we decided to broaden the range of potential cases by also including practices of managing knowledge sharing that had not (yet) received the label "knowledge management." Consequently, we obtained a rather pragmatic orientation to knowledge management. In short, knowledge management is perceived here as comprising organizational practices that facilitate and structure knowledge sharing among knowledge workers. With successful knowledge management we refer to practices of knowledge sharing that have become embedded in the ongoing work processes of an organization. In other words, we perceive the success of knowledge management as related to the degree in which sharing knowledge has become a taken-for-granted part of the routine practices within the organization.

The multiple case study research we used was mainly exploratory. Because of the ambiguity within the literature in general, we opted for an exploratory research study. We asked the following research questions: Whose knowledge is managed? What knowledge is managed? When is knowledge managed? Why is knowledge managed? How is knowledge managed? Where is knowledge managed? We believe these questions are the most reasonable ones that can be asked when trying to explore a concept in practice.

Exploring the concept also requires an explorative research method. Although we had some prior knowledge about what has been written on knowledge management, interviewees led the way. The research is based on more than fifty open interviews with managers, knowledge workers, and initiators. The interviews were structured so as to avoid "conceptual humbug." Interviews lasted for two hours on average. We also had access to documents reporting about the initiatives and to the ICT tools that were used to support knowledge sharing.

2.3   Knowledge Sharing in Practice

Knowledge Retrieval

The insurance company National Netherlands (NN), the Postbank, and the Netherlands Railways offered insights about their experiences with providing organizational members access to organizational knowledge. Table 2.2 summarizes the findings related to knowledge retrieval at the three companies.

In the case of the Postbank, sales personnel at the front office used organizational knowledge stored in a knowledge base. This knowledge base was used not only to support client interaction but also to support the socialization and training of the call center operators. In the case of the NN, insurance employees made use of organizational knowledge stored in a knowledge base. In addition, employees referred to a structured personal network of insurance experts to learn about the operational processes of the organization. At the railways, train conductors used a mobile knowledge base, the rail pocket, to gain knowledge about the operational process.

Table 2.2
Knowledge-Retrieving Initiatives

	Postbank	NN	Railways
Type of Learning Process	Organization as knowledge owner; domain knowledge for training on the job; match practice with learning	Storing knowledge; integration domain knowledge; individual learning plus personal networks	Support of mobile personnel on the train
Support of Learning Process	Knowledge bases and interactive learning environments	Knowledge bases; structured physical networks	Knowledge bases
Purpose	Knowledge storing, mind mapping, and actualizing to increase client satisfaction, to support and socialize operators	Retain knowledge because of change from product to market-oriented organizational forms	Facilitate job performance
ICT	Infobase	Knowledge base	NS rail pocket (mobile knowledge base)
Role of ICT	Essential, regular use	Essential, regular use	Essential, regular use
Some Experiences	No feedback, speeding up task execution	Friction between hierarchy and knowledge-sharing responsibilities	Dependence on knowledge bases; no feedback; no monitoring
Type of Worker	Sales personnel at call center	Insurance and knowledge worker	Conductor

In all three cases, the purpose of the knowledge-sharing initiative was to retrieve organizational knowledge in order to use it for operational processes. Typical to these knowledge-sharing initiatives was that the organization provided access to explicit formal organizational knowledge in order for individual members to learn from it and transfer it into implicit knowledge. This learning process can be described as internalization: knowledge transfer from organization to individuals.

All three companies made intensive use of knowledge databases. The insurance company (NN) and the Postbank used a knowledge database in their sales and service operation. The bank had created this database through mind-mapping techniques and transferring existing documents. Both organizations felt a need to create a knowledge database when they transformed from a product-driven organization to a market-driven organization. The transformation implied that people had to operate as generalists instead of specialists. In order to maintain an appropriate level of service, employees needed to be supported. In both cases the database was linked to a learning system. New employees could use the database as a tool to quickly become generalists. The insurance company also created a network of people. Knowledge coordinators and knowledge specialists were needed to secure the development of new knowledge and to provide a fallback resource for questions of employees.

The Netherlands Railways provided an interesting example. In this case an employee developed a mobile application to overcome the weight of carrying around travel schedules and handbooks. Senior management quickly took up the idea. The mobile application, called the rail pocket, contains organizational knowledge and gives employees room to input their administrative and day-to-day experiences.

In all three cases it was possible to discern some problems of managing and supporting knowledge retrieval. We discuss these in the next section.

Knowledge Exchange

Our research provided four illustrations of structuring knowledge-sharing initiatives with the purpose of exchanging and reusing knowledge. These companies were IBM, Cap Gemini, Schiphol airport, and ING Barings (table 2.3).

Table 2.3
Knowledge-Exchanging Initiatives

	Schiphol	ING	Cap Gemini	IBM
Typical for Learning Process	Storage of knowledge, such as about personal networks	Making knowledge within various countries accessible	Reuse	Reuse
Support of Learning Process	Knowledge center	Network of countries	Informal networks and electronic networks	Electronic networks
Purpose	Capture personal knowledge and identify networks	Make country information accessible	Make knowledge accessible and increase efficiency	Make knowledge accessible; standardization; ready-made solutions
ICT	Network	Intranet	Intranet	Intranet
Role of ICT	Limited	Important	Important	Essential
Some Experiences	Reassure cooperation	Problems in mobilizing geographically dispersed people	Differences in bottom-up and top-down initiatives; time limitations	Part of transformation; problems in time and recognition
Type of Worker	Policy	Corporate finance, policy	Consultants	Routine consultants

The purpose of these initiatives was to let people learn from each other through reusing individual knowledge. Both social and technical networks were used to facilitate this learning process.

In the case of Schiphol, a knowledge center was initiated that captured personal knowledge and identified existing networks in order to support the knowledge work of policymakers at the airport. At ING Barings, an intranet was introduced to support knowledge exchange between different countries. At Cap Gemini, consultants used both informal personal networks and electronic networks (Cap Com and the Galaxy) to enable reuse of knowledge. Reuse of knowledge was also the main purpose at IBM for installing an intranet. Consultants at IBM used this codified knowledge, especially in case of standardization and ready-made solutions.

Reuse of knowledge created by knowledge workers is a common reason for starting a knowledge management system or an intranet. Consultant firms, especially, see reuse of knowledge as an important strategy. Organizational practice (providing inexperienced people with fit-to-the-situation solutions) and customer pressure create this need for reuse.

An important driver for these organizations to introduce knowledge management is the high turnover of personnel. Management needs to look after the knowledge base, typically with best practice as an application. Another motivator is customer-driven. Customers, especially clients of knowledge-intensive organizations such as the ones discussed here, ask for knowledge that has proven valuable elsewhere. They do not seek for new solutions but rather want a cost-effective solution that has been used already. The different needs and interests also lead to one of the fundamental problems: the difficulty for knowledge workers or professionals of engaging in knowledge sharing. Most knowledge workers find it hard to express what is meaningful in their work. Also, professionals are more often focused on developing their own solutions instead of using other people's ideas (Weggeman 1997). Characteristic of these organizations is that professionals develop their own networks to obtain the knowledge and information they need. Work load and time pressures often prevent knowledge workers from externalizing their knowledge as best-practice recommendations unless a social aspect is part of the process.

In section 2.4 we discuss the problems these four companies experienced in managing knowledge reuse.

Knowledge Creation

Although many organizations start with knowledge capturing, often an ultimate goal is creating new knowledge. In an organization with fixed routines and procedures, this need for generative learning may be less than in an R&D environment. But still, creating new ideas and insights through sharing knowledge is on many business objectives lists. We studied knowledge creation in three different organizations: Unilever, Stork (a high-tech multinational company), and the Ministry of Housing

Table 2.4
Knowledge-Developing Initiatives

	Stork	Unilever	Ministry of Housing
Type of Learning Process	Sharing to get new ideas	Sharing to reuse and develop new knowledge	Sharing to get new input for future policy
Support of Learning Process	Study groups	Knowledge workshops	Virtual communities
Purpose	New insights	Exchange and development of knowledge	Interactive policy development
ICT	Electronic rapport	Knowledge mapping; Lotus Notes	Digital discussion platforms
Role of ICT	Marginal	Present but not essential	Essential
Some Experiences	Structure depends on seniority; ambiguity about outcomes	Combination of respect, status, and physical encounters stimulates community building	Problems of virtual communities without having clear collective purposes
Type of Worker	Experts and managers in high tech	Experts in R&D settings	Policy-making officials, external stakeholders

(table 2.4). In various ways these organizations made use of communities or groups of individuals with shared knowledge interests.

Unilever, for example, gained experience in supporting communities of practice. The company started over five years ago to systematically collect, exchange, create, and leverage knowledge because it saw its innovative ideas being copied by competitors. Using existing knowledge within the company and exchanging this knowledge became one of the strategies to stay abreast. The research department developed this structure as an outcome of so-called knowledge workshops. Unilever now organizes workshops in order to bring members together who share their expertise, for example, about tomato products, but who are geographically distributed. Initially, these workshops were intended to map this distributed knowledge, to identify knowledge gaps, and to store shared knowledge in knowledge databases. Over time the workshops gained another, more fruitful purpose: the facilitation of communities of interest. Because of the physical encounters between otherwise dispersed people with similar interests, people not only share their knowledge at the moment of the actual meeting but tend to get into contact with each other after the workshop. In some cases, these groups become social networks of people who like to explore and develop new ideas. These communities, consisting of geographically dispersed individuals, created fruitful bodies of knowledge that facilitate organizational learning.

The international technology company Stork introduced integrated process innovation (IPI), a structured form of knowledge development through communities. This structure supports different communities in sharing knowledge and allowing new knowledge to come into existence. Although IPI has existed for almost thirty years, only recently has the company stuck the label knowledge management on it. Interestingly, both at Unilever and at Stork, little use is made of ICT. The focus is on connecting people and creating organizational networks rather than technical ones. The Ministry of Housing has electronic communities. It uses the Internet so that communities focusing on a specific theme can exchange thoughts. It also incorporates the results of this type of electronic discussion platform in its future policy development.

In the next section we discuss the experiences with managing knowledge sharing that the ten companies gained over the years.

2.4   Analysis: Identifying Traps and Ways to Avoid Them

We addressed our research material with six exploratory research questions in mind (table 2.5). While addressing these questions, we observed that all initiatives are or have been biased toward various aspects of managing knowledge sharing. The practices of knowledge management also illustrated that these biases might result in potential traps. Organizations might fall into these traps if they are too much focused on certain aspects while overlooking others.

How Knowledge Is Shared and What Knowledge Is Shared: The ICT Trap
The focus on *what* knowledge is shared and *how* it is shared helped us to identify a potential risk for falling into a so-called ICT trap. The ICT

Table 2.5
Six Research Questions and Their Dominant Biases and Related Traps

Research Question	Knowledge-Sharing Bias	Knowledge-Sharing Traps
Why is knowledge sharing managed?	Control bias	Management trap
When is knowledge sharing managed?	Opportunity-driven bias	Management trap
Whose knowledge sharing is managed?	Individual knowledge bias	Local learning trap
Where is knowledge sharing managed?	Operational-level bias	Local learning trap
What knowledge sharing is managed?	Codified knowledge bias	ICT trap
How is knowledge sharing managed?	Technology-driven bias	ICT trap

trap consists of two different yet related biases. We encountered this trap when we asked two questions: What knowledge is shared in practice? and How is knowledge shared in practice? Addressing the first question revealed that many of the initiatives we studied were biased toward a stock approach to knowledge. Addressing the second question showed that these companies were biased toward a technological-driven orientation to knowledge management. In that case, the underlying assumption is that ICT can support and improve knowledge sharing within an organization.

Many articles and books on the concept of knowledge management start their discussion with a definition of knowledge. Almost always, the relation is made between two concepts: data and information. Whereas data are signals, and information comprises signals that make a difference, knowledge is created out of information but is individual-specific. In its most extreme definition, knowledge that belongs to individuals cannot be explicated. At the moment we exchange knowledge, the knowledge becomes signals to the potential receiver. There is a danger that organizations might treat this externalized knowledge as a valuable substitute for knowledge exchanges between individuals. If so, much valuable knowledge will be overlooked. Because technology supports codifying knowledge, this codified knowledge bias is closely connected to the technology-driven bias. Organizations often espouse a technology-driven bias because they rely on ICT to make knowledge retrieval possible. There are several problems with focusing too much on codifying knowledge. First, there is the problem of dependence. Organizations may become dependent on their digitized archives with the risk of relying too much on this aspect of knowledge and overlooking the value of more fluid and personal knowledge. Second, there is the problem of deterioration. Knowledge embedded in documents or in expert systems may quickly become outdated. When sharing embedded knowledge is not part of an explicit culture, knowledge databases fall prone to rapid deterioration. This is not a new phenomenon, yet it requires discipline of the knowledge worker, which in itself forms another problem of knowledge externalization. Discipline may be hampered by the pressing agenda. We observed at various organizations the problem that knowledge workers have in filling in the knowledge system with past experiences while simultaneously gaining new experiences in a new project or work environment. Especially in project-oriented organizations, the pressure to make hours accountable is high.

The obvious solution for management is to allow time in order to enable workers to make their experiences explicit. However, even with adequate time, people will find it hard to make explicit what is truly valuable to the company. We encountered this problem at IBM, where engineers were unable to express their valuable learning experiences. On the other hand, people are reluctant to use the knowledge documented because they prefer using their own solutions rather than those offered by others. Many authors on knowledge management believe that one of the serious problems with externalizing knowledge resides in the unwillingness of knowledge workers to give away their power (e.g., Weggeman 1997; Wiigg 1999; Davenport 1997). The argument goes that because knowledge is power, people are selective in externalizing their knowledge. We did not come across this argument for rejecting knowledge management. Alternatively, we observed that people seem to be resistant to sharing their personal knowledge in case going public with it would increase their vulnerability, in other words, when codifying knowledge would imply opening up individually kept secrets. A final problem is that organizations tend to be focused more on codified than on situated knowledge. Situated knowledge is knowledge that is not embedded somewhere, neither in manuals nor in the heads of individuals. Instead, individuals interacting with each other create situated knowledge in practice. Situated knowledge is therefore situation- rather than individual-dependent (Lave and Wenger 1991).

The technology-driven bias is embedded in the conviction that the introduction of technological facilities will improve knowledge sharing among people and harness the organization against loss of knowledge. Knowledge management is often seen as inherently connected to ICT. For example, the introduction of an intranet is seen as creating the facility for knowledge exchange, often in combination with a reward structure meant to encourage people to share their knowledge. Yet, when the technology itself is not fancy enough, or when the use is not adapted to the people working with the technology, people will be driven away despite rewards or punishments. This will curtail the knowledge management initiative.

We came across several knowledge management initiatives that focused on creating a technological environment but that where unable to reach the people actually using the system. Most of the intranets in our study were widely praised but little used by those who praised them. One of the awkward effects of the technology trap is that a firm belief exists in improving technology in such a way that earlier barriers are overcome.

Unilever learned a lesson over the past years from falling into the ICT trap. The company started out by putting its faith in technology and the opportunities to map expert knowledge in databases. Soon it discovered that creating a network of experts, and facilitating physical encounters, opens a large potential for knowledge sharing. The ICT is introduced after the network has become established.

Why Knowledge Is Managed and When Knowledge Is Managed: The Management Trap

Addressing the question of *why* knowledge is managed reveals a bias among managers toward the need to control knowledge. Addressing the question of *when* knowledge is managed shows that knowledge sharing is taken up by managers and given explicit attention only when they perceive organizational opportunities to do so. This opportunity-driven bias, together with the control bias, was implicitly embedded in many knowledge management initiatives we analyzed. Together, these biases increase the chance for organizations to fall into the so called management trap.

One of the most general risks of knowledge management initiatives is that the concept is perceived from a managerial perspective only. Clearly, for managers there are several advantages to managing knowledge within the organization. One is that knowledge is often scattered within the organization. With the emergence of the knowledge economy in which workers gain more and more knowledge specific to their own work processes, organizations must make these scattered knowledge domains more transparent. Next and related is the argument that transparency is needed to reduce the reinvention of the wheel. The ideal is that when everyone knows what everyone knows, people will contact each other to exchange knowledge or to effectively refer customers and clients. Learning from each other has the additional advantage of filling up knowledge gaps that would otherwise exist when people leave the organization or change positions. The ongoing trend toward globalization, too, calls for the exchange of knowledge among globally dispersed knowledge workers. Another reason why organizations are interested in knowledge management is the growth of awareness that organizational knowledge might be the key to organizational success. Management books and articles demonstrate a growing awareness that the intellectual capital of the corporation is usually worth much more than its tangible book value (Stewart 1997; Edvinsson and Malone 1997). Shareholders have developed a need to gain more insight in the core competence of the organization, which in most cases resides in the (tacit) knowledge shared among the workers within the organization. Facilitating organizational change is yet another managerial reason to engage in knowledge management. Because managers cannot force people to share their knowledge, knowledge management calls for support of knowledge workers.

Knowledge management heavily depends on the willingness of knowledge workers to take part in it. We encountered various reasons for knowledge workers to actually engage in knowledge management initiatives, such as an increase of job efficiency, status, and fun. If the condition of a win-win situation is not established, managers will be confronted with major rejections from the side of the knowledge workers.

These win-win situations do not have to match and might occur when the various actors engage in knowledge sharing for different reasons. For example, knowledge exchanges between various actors at an electronic discussion platform introduced by the Ministry of Housing proliferated, although users had different and sometimes even conflicting reasons to engage in these discussions.

Next to the bias toward managerial control, the management trap also relates to the bias to introduce knowledge management based on opportunity-driven arguments only rather than on (present or future) problem-driven arguments. We saw that knowledge management will be more successful when it addresses existing situations and problems than when it is seen as an opportunity for organizational change.

There are basically three reasons why organizations engage in explicit knowledge management activities, of which the first two are expressions of opportunity-driven motives for introducing knowledge management.

One reason is ICT-driven: knowledge management is often linked to supporting knowledge exchange through ICT. With the rise of the technological possibilities that ICT offers, and especially with the rise of intranets, Lotus Notes, and knowledge and expert systems, new avenues are open for organizations that want to structure their knowledge processes.

Some organizations introduce knowledge management because they have heard of other organizations that engage in forms of knowledge management. As mentioned earlier, a possible fallacy is that most of these stories are based on conceptual orientations only or are told by highly enthusiastic (knowledge) managers. In both cases, the positive stories tend to hide negative experiences or pitfalls to knowledge management. In other words, organizations are seduced to imitate others, while the models they imitate are mostly incomplete. Companies that were only in a conceptual stage of introducing knowledge management often referred to well-known textbooks, well-known best practice, and well-known conference speakers.

A third reason to introduce knowledge management is problem-driven. In such a case, organizations use knowledge management techniques to address existing or future problems. Knowledge workers themselves often initiate problem-driven knowledge management. Interestingly, all initiatives in the research that were introduced to cope with existing problems did not use the term *knowledge management* or only attached it in a later stage when the concept gain popularity. Organizations that introduced knowledge management based on opportunity-driven arguments all explicitly used the label but either had problems in institutionalizing it or were still in a conceptual stage of introduction.

Where Knowledge Is Managed and Whose Knowledge Is Managed: The Local Learning Trap

Another potential problem we encountered has to do with the limited scope of attention to both the process and outcomes of knowledge sharing. This so-called local learning trap is a combination of two related biases: the individual knowledge bias and the operational-level bias. In short, the local learning trap is about the risk of concentrating attention on local knowledge sharing without addressing the issue of how the organization as a whole can benefit from it.

When we look at the actual practices of knowledge management and ask *where* knowledge is managed, we observed that many of the organizations we studied focused their attention on the operational level only. There are various reasons why this focus on the operational level might become a burden to the knowledge management initiative. For many knowledge workers it is important that management act as an example instead of a facilitator only. As a consultant argued, "If they do not share their knowledge, why would I do it?" Knowledge-sharing processes cannot be limited to the operational level only. Much of the knowledge is also shared among managers. Of course, another important condition for successful introduction of knowledge management is for management not only to contribute to knowledge sharing and construction but also to support the initiatives. We did not come across this latter condition during our research because management support was one of the criteria we used to select cases. Nevertheless, lack of management support seems to be one of the serious problems organizations face when introducing knowledge management (e.g., Davenport 1997).

Knowledge management is generally seen as the management of learning processes within organizations. There is however a potential pitfall when this is interpreted as the management of individual learning instead of collective learning. During our research, we saw many initiatives approaching knowledge management as supporting knowledge sharing by individuals more than by collectives within organizations. That the focus tends to be more on individual learning rather than on collective learning is understandable, as managing individual learning is less complicated than managing collective learning. Tools to improve the individual knowledge base are part of every organization, such as training, education, or more explicit tools such as libraries or databases. In contrast, tools to improve the collective knowledge base are much more difficult to imagine. Also, individual learning is easier to control than collective learning. Managers, for example, might ask employees to read an article, to take a course, or to inspect a database. From this information-processing activity, we can predict what the outcome of this learning process will be. Much of the collective knowledge is, however, gained during day-to-day interactions and is less easy to manage (Brown and Duguid 1991). Schiphol, for example, had created a knowledge center that actually functions as knowledge libraries. Individuals can acquire the necessary knowledge from these centers to gain more insights on a particular subject. The other organizations that focused knowledge sharing on knowledge exchange, Cap Gemini, IBM, and ING Barings, used an intranet to store past experiences of knowledge workers so that others could learn from them. These networks merely function as tools to support individual knowledge development rather than collaborative knowledge development. As one consultant remarked, "The system is supposed to store experiences in a database, but that doesn't work; you cannot learn experiences from others as such; knowledge sharing happens through face-to-face communication."

Some organizations have tried to avoid this individual knowledge bias. At Unilever and Stork, for example, the sharing of knowledge among collectives was supported by enabling the existence of communities. During frequent meetings, these communities exchanged valuable experiences and developed new ideas on how to improve their day-to-day activities. Managing communities calls for a different approach than managing individuals. In fact, management has little influence on these communities of practice besides acknowledging their existence. Learning within communities is also often unnoticed by the learners themselves (Ciborra and Lanzara 1994) and is seldom planned. Many communities are continuously in flux, changing place, time, membership, and content. Mapping the knowledge within the organization by mapping the various communities is therefore impossible; even if management were able to map all the existing communities, this would only be a random indication (Brown and Duguid 1991). Consequently, managing collective learning processes such as those that take place in communities of practice is much harder than managing individual learning processes (Orr 1990; Ciborra and Lanzara 1994; Cook and Yanow 1993; Weick and Roberts 1993; Jordan 1989). Because of its flowing, tacit, loose, and emergent character, managing knowledge sharing by managing communities requires a different approach to than what we are used to (De Wit and Huysman 2001). This implies that the role of managers will be pushed to the periphery, where their main contribution lies in the acknowledgment and facilitation of emergent grass-roots community behavior (Wenger and Snyder 2000; Brown and Duguid 2000).

The most crucial consequence of the lack of management involvement is that shared knowledge will most likely remain local knowledge and will not be collectively accepted. This is not always problematic, certainly not when the knowledge is only relevant to this local group of people. In all other cases, where local knowledge might be relevant in a wider context including future workers, active involvement of management to support collective acceptance will stimulate organizational learning processes. Our research showed that most initiatives focus on the learning of individuals and sometimes also of groups. Seldom is there a relation between this learning and learning at the level of organizations. We see this as a potential pitfall because most initiatives have the potential to contribute to organizational improvement.

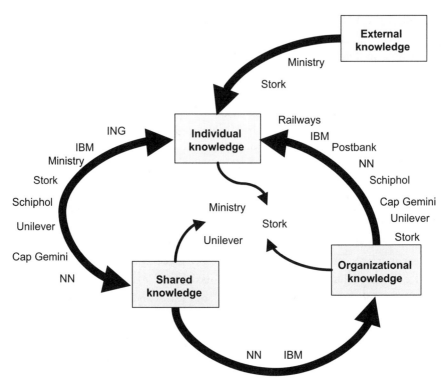

Figure 2.2
Companies and their learning processes.

Collective acceptance is key to bridging the gap between individual learning and organizational learning. Many of the practices analyzed here lack this crucial process of collectively accepting shared knowledge. One of the most important reasons is the lack of collective involvement in local knowledge sharing or learning processes.

Figure 2.2 locates the knowledge-sharing initiatives that we encountered in the frame of different learning processes. As the figure illustrates, we saw that almost all companies were paying attention to supporting individual members in retrieving organizational knowledge. For some companies, such as the Postbank and the railways, this aspect of knowledge sharing was indeed their prime focus.

Many of the initiatives also involved connecting people such that individual knowledge could be exchanged. As mentioned, most companies did so by introducing electronic networks such as intranets, and some relied more on physical networks such as communities and special interest groups. These initiatives supported either individual learning or group learning. There were, however, only two initiatives (IBM and NN) that support all three learning processes:

• Individual learning by giving individuals access to collective knowledge (the arrow pointing from organizational knowledge to individual knowledge)

• Individual and group learning by giving individuals and groups of individuals access to individual knowledge (the mutual arrow between individual and shared knowledge)

• Organizational learning by providing the collective access to shared knowledge (the arrow pointing from shared knowledge to organizational knowledge)

Collective acceptance at IBM mainly occurs through the intervention of a jury of specialists. This jury decides whether individually introduced knowledge in the shared knowledge database is usable, relevant, and interesting enough to the collective to be accepted for publication in the collective knowledge base. The insurance company National Netherlands facilitates collective acceptance through experts, knowledge coordinators, specialists, and contact persons. Because of their expertise and seniority, these people have been given the role of knowledge brokers. In a way, their role is comparable to that of the jury members at IBM. Knowledge gained from contacting these people is considered valuable and as such gets more easily accepted by the collective. The knowledge brokers are not only active in the physical networks but also play an important role in storing shared and distributed knowledge in the organizational electronic networks.

2.5 Concluding Remarks

Knowledge management has received much controversial attention. Although the group of proponents is still growing, the same can be said for a large group of people who perceive the concept as a fad. Although we used a critical perspective, we do belong to the group of proponents who perceive knowledge management as one of the basic organizational processes in present and future organizations. While many different conceptions of knowledge management exist in parallel, almost everyone agrees that knowledge management is about supporting the development and surfacing of knowledge that is shared in organizations. However, based on our research, we observed that there exist many different ways of using these ideas in practice. We classified the concept into three conceptually distinct types of knowledge sharing: knowledge retrieval, knowledge exchange, and knowledge creation. By covering such a broad range of knowledge-sharing practices, we tried to avoid being biased toward one particular aspect of knowledge sharing while ignoring valuable others. This was especially important because the main purpose of the research was to find out what biases and traps exist within the practice of knowledge management.

We observed three general traps into which organizations might fall when introducing knowledge management initiatives. These traps are a result of various biases within the practices of managing knowledge sharing. In sum, a knowledge management initiative seems to last longer and become accepted within the organization as part of daily practice when organizations acknowledge the needs of knowledge workers to exchange their knowledge. When knowledge management involves the support of individual learning processes, knowledge sharing among knowledge workers cannot be guaranteed. Also, knowledge management is more effective in organizations where knowledge exchange is seen from a flow perspective rather than a stock perspective only. When knowledge management is focused on increasing the knowledge stock, problems might arise as a result of differences in interpretation, lack of discipline, and lack of flexibility. The success of knowledge management also depends on the underlying reason for introduction. Initiatives based on a problem-driven introduction seem to have a much longer life span than initiatives based on ICT and an opportunity-driven argument. Futhermore, knowledge management initiatives will only contribute to the organization as a whole when they are centered both on collective and individual learning processes rather than on individual learning processes only. Finally, organizations will only harvest the fruits of knowledge management when the practice is approached as an organizationwide issue rather than an issue relevant to the operational level only.

We would like to close the discussion with our general observation that there is a need to *implicitly manage the implicit.* The general managerial task of supporting knowledge-sharing processes and of introducing and implementing them can range from highly explicit to highly implicit. By implicit management we mean nondirective ways of using power; explicit management is about more directive. By explicit management of knowledge we mean situations in which the manager forces knowledge workers to become involved in knowledge exchange processes. The manager's power can be forced by the use of various incentives, ranging from financial to status-related. Unlike many other conceptions on the topic and supported by observations from practice, our conclusion is that the success of knowledge management lies in the way organizations are able to manage implicit knowledge by processes that are less directive or implicit. Clearly, our research was explorative and needs further work to determine its scientific value. This applies both to the identification of traps and biases and to its implication for management.

References

Berger, P., and T. Luckmann. 1966. *The Social Construction of Knowledge.* London: Penguin.

Brown, J. S., and P. Duguid. 1991. Organizational Learning and Communities of Practice: Towards a Unified View of Working, Learning, and Innovation. *Organization Science* 2 (1): 40–57.

———. 2000. *The Social Life of Information.* Boston: Harvard Business School Press.

Ciborra, C. U., ed. 1996. *Groupware and Teamwork.* New York: Wiley.

Ciborra, C. U., and G. F. Lanzara. 1994. Formative Contexts and Information Technology: Understanding the Dynamics of Innovation in Organizations. *Accounting, Management, and Information Technology* 4 (2).

Cook, S. D., and D. Yanow. 1993. Culture and Organizational Learning. *Journal of Management Inquiry* 2 (4).

Davenport, T. H. 1997. Ten Principles of Knowledge Management and Four Case Studies. *Knowledge and Process Management* 4 (3).

Davenport, T. H., D. W. Long, and M. C. Beers. 1998. Successful Knowledge Management Projects. *Sloan Management Review* (Winter): 43–57.

De Wit, D., and M. H. Huysman. 2001. Implicitly Managing the Implicit. Available at http://www.iamot.org/paperarchive/151A.pdf.

Dixon, N. M. 2000. *Common Knowledge.* Boston: Harvard Business School Press.

Douglas, M. 1987. *How Institutions Think.* London: Routledge and Kegan Paul.

Edvinsson, L., and M. S. Malone. 1997. *Intellectual Capital.* New York: Harper.

Elkjaer, B. 1999. Organizational Learning: A Management Tool or Part of Human Interaction? In *Organizational Learning and the Learning Organization: Developments in Theory and Practice,* ed. M. Easterby-Smith, L. Araujo, and J. Burgoyne. Thousand Oaks, Calif.: Sage.

Fahey, L., and L. Prusak. 1998. The Eleven Deadliest Sins of Knowledge Management. *California Management Review* 40 (3): 265–276.

Gergen, K. J. 1994. *Realities and Relationships: Soundings in Social Construction.* Cambridge, Mass.: Harvard University Press.

Gottschalk, P. 1999. Use of IT for Knowledge Management in Law Firms. *Journal of Information, Law, and Technology* 3.

Hansen, M. T., N. Nohria, and T. Tierney. 1999. What's Your Strategy for Managing Knowledge? *Harvard Business Review* (March–April): 108–116.

Huysman, M. H. 2000. Rethinking Organizational Learning: Analyzing Learning Processes of Information System Designers. *Accountancy, Management, and Information Technology* 10.

Huysman, M. H., and D. de Wit. 2002. *Knowledge Sharing in Practice.* Dordrecht: Kluwer.

Jordan, B. 1989. Cosmo-Political Obstetrics: Some Insights from the Training of Traditional Midwives. *Social Science and Medicine* 28 (9).

Lave, J., and E. Wenger. 1991. *Situated Learning: Legitimate Peripheral Participation.* New York: Cambridge University Press.

Levitt, B., and J. G. March. 1988. Organizational Learning. *Annual Review of Sociology* 14: 319–340.

Nicolini, D., and M. B. Meznar. 1995. The Social Construction of Organizational Learning: Conceptual and Practical Issues in the Field. *Human Relations* 48 (7): 727–746.

Nonaka, I. 1994. A Dynamic Theory of Organizational Knowledge. *Organization Science* 5: 14–37.

Nonaka, I., and H. Takeuchi. 1995. *The Knowledge-Creating Company.* New York: Oxford University Press.

Orr, J. E. 1990. Sharing Knowledge, Celebrating Identity: Community Memory in a Service Culture. In *Collective Remembering: Memory in Society,* ed. P. Middleton and D. Edwards. London: Sage.

Pentland, B. T. 1995. Information Systems and Organizational Learning: The Social Epistemology of Organizational Knowledge Systems. *Accounting, Management, and Information Technology* 5: 1–21.

Schutz, A. 1971. *Collected Papers.* 2 vols. The Hague: Nijhoff.

Sims, D. 1999. Organizational Learning as the Development of Stories. In *Organizational Learning and the Learning Organization: Developments in Theory and Practice*, ed. M. Easterby-Smith, L. Araujo, and J. Burgoyne. Thousand Oaks, Calif.: Sage.

Stewart, T. A. 1997. *Intellectual Capital: The New Wealth of Organizations.* New York: Doubleday.

Weggeman, M. 1997. *Kennismanagement.* Schiedam, Netherlands: Scriptum.

Weick, K. E. 1979. *The Social Psychology of Organizing.* Reading, Mass.: Addison-Wesley.

Weick, K. E., and K. H. Roberts. 1993. Collective Mind in Organizations: Heedful Interrelating on Flight Decks. *Administrative Science Quarterly* 38 (3): 357–381.

Wenger, E., and W. Snyder. 2000. Communities of Practice: The Organizational Frontier. *Harvard Business Review* (January–February): 139–145.

Wiigg, K. M. 1999. What Future Knowledge Management Users May Expect. *Journal of Knowledge Management* 3 (2): 155–165.

Zack, M. H. 1999. Managing Codified Knowledge. *Sloan Management Review* 40 (4): 45–58.

3

Coming to the Crossroads of Knowledge, Learning, and Technology: Integrating Knowledge Management and Workplace Learning

Bill Penuel and Andrew Cohen

As the global economy continues to transform itself at a rapid pace, companies have come to focus more and more on the importance of creating and managing knowledge (Prusak 1997). The rise of knowledge management in companies across industries not typically associated with the production of information comes at a time when businesses are recognizing the role knowledge plays in keeping companies competitive. Companies need both to manage effectively the knowledge they do have, distributed across people, technologies, and organizational practices, and to acquire new knowledge that will enable them to stay competitive in the marketplace.

While companies have made great strides in recent years toward managing knowledge more effectively, few companies have been able to draw connections between knowledge management and workplace learning, another emerging central interest of business today. Companies have begun to examine how concepts like the learning organization are related to knowledge management strategies (Senge 1990), but they are rarely guided by clear definitions of what learning is and how best to support it in the workplace. Here, we aim to draw attention to examples of companies that have integrated an understanding of how people learn into their knowledge management strategies. We pay particular attention to the ways that collaborative technologies have supported companies in developing integrated learning and knowledge management solutions. We recognize that technology has played a critical role in both knowledge management (Prusak 1997) and workplace learning (Cohen et al. 1999).

3.1   Different Learning Processes for Different Situations

Effective companies recognize that there are different kinds of learning for different situations. Similarly, there are different strategies that a company can adopt to manage knowledge in order to meet different learning needs and accomplish the central goal of managing the company's expertise. We consider two different kinds of learning in detail: the learning of newcomers or novices on the job, and the learning of experts. For each group, we identify key learning needs and corresponding knowledge management strategies that address those needs. We also present examples of companies that have used technology successfully to meet learning needs and accomplish knowledge management goals at the same time.

In another publication (Penuel and Roschelle 1999) we outlined several learning principles that can be observed across different learning situations. A central assumption embedded in all the principles is that learning takes place within communities of practice. In other words, we are always learning in context, on the go, as we participate in activities with other people, institutions, texts, and technologies. Those contexts are often defined by a professional community of people who do things together or who share a common professional identity—computer programmers, lawyers, doctors, and so forth. By arguing that learning takes place in a community of practice, we are saying that those professional and institutional contexts are always with us as we learn, and they shape what we learn, why we learn, and how we learn at work.

For a newcomer, learning to become a part of the community of practice at a new job requires first and foremost an understanding of that broader community's resources (table 3.1). Newcomers need to know where expertise is distributed across a company, and how they can access it. They need to know to whom to turn with questions about personnel, marketing, sales, and the like. The company's knowledge management strategy, therefore, needs to provide newcomers with access to experts, opportunities in training and informal settings to rub elbows with more experienced staff. Newcomers also need to learn how to do their jobs, which may involve interaction with experts and require practice in solving the kinds of problems they will face on the job. As they

Table 3.1
Newcomer Learning Needs

Newcomer Learning Need	Learning Principle	Knowledge Management Process	Example
To learn how expertise is distributed across the company	Learning takes place in communities of practice	Distributing representations of expert knowledge	Microsoft SPUD Project
To learn the kinds of tasks they will be expected to perform on the job	Novices learn to become experts through practice in solving a variety of problems in a domain	Simulating work practices. Distributing expert stories	Yellow Pages Sales (ILS)
To take advantage of learning opportunities within ongoing practice	Learning is enhanced through collaborative reflection	Designing forms of strategic assistance that makes problems and solutions visible to learners	Answer Garden

begin to work, there are always "teachable moments" on the job, opportunities within ongoing practice to help newcomers reflect on their practice and gain a deeper understanding of their work and how it contributes to their company's success.

However, supporting learning among experts in a company requires different strategies than supporting novices or newcomers becoming expert in their company's specific practices. Learning among experts, even in companies that are heavily dependent on the knowledge they produce, can be extremely difficult (Starbuck 1992). Experts' learning needs are focused about the requirement to interact with other experts to update continually their expertise (table 3.2).

Opportunities to share stories of successful practice (and dramatic failures) provide experts with ways to expand individual skill to form broader communities of practice. Similarly, knowledge networks can help leverage innovation and provide environments for experts to solve new and emerging problems faced by companies. And where experts

Table 3.2
Expert Learning Needs

Expert Learning Need	Learning Principle	Knowledge Management Process	Example
To expand expertise beyond individual skill	Learning takes place in communities of practice	Collection and sharing of stories among experts	Collection and sharing of stories among experts
To draw from domain expertise to solve new and emerging problems faced by the company	Becoming an expert means applying learning to new contexts	Creating knowledge networks to leverage innovation	Creating knowledge networks to leverage innovation
To escape blinders imposed by professional specialization	Prior knowledge mediates (can enhance and inhibit) learning. Learning is enhanced through reflection	Creating problem-solving environments where diverse experts can interact	Creating problem-solving environments where diverse experts can interact

come from different disciplines, domains, or companies, there are opportunities for experts to begin to escape the blinders imposed by their own specialization (Armstrong 1985).

We believe that these two different kinds of learning constitute the core of the kind of learning most companies need to consider in order to design knowledge management solutions that also support effective workplace learning. Creating effective workplace learning involves much more than devising a knowledge management strategy; it involves a careful implementation of tools and processes that allow for the transfer of knowledge from expert to novice and for the creation of new knowledge as experts interact with one another. Knowledge transfer and knowledge creation are thoroughly social processes, involving much more than transferring the contents of what's in an individual's head or in a particular database to another person's head via a book, lecture, or e-mail. It involves both explicit knowledge that is easily codified and tacit, how-to knowledge that is harder to characterize (Nonaka 1998).

Both processes involve workers as active constructors of their own learning and require considerable social, institutional, and technological support to succeed.

In the examples of knowledge management strategies and learning processes we present here, we pay particularly close attention to the way that learners—both expert and novice—play an active role in monitoring their own learning. We also focus on the ways that technology supports this role and builds organizational knowledge within a company. At the intersection of workplace learning and knowledge management can be seen key processes and technologies that help manage the existing knowledge assets of a company while at the same time building up and expanding the existing expertise to meet emerging demands and open up new opportunities for organizations.

3.2 Knowledge Management Processes That Support Newcomer Learning

One of the central ways that companies manage knowledge is by hiring, training, and dismissing personnel (Starbuck 1992). Companies can significantly alter the knowledge available to them by bringing in promising novices and new experts or by training their existing staff in new work processes designed to keep a company's competitive edge. Any time companies bring in new staff, however, they are faced with the challenge of helping newcomers learn about the company's culture and ways of doing business. They are also faced with the challenge of introducing newcomers to their specific jobs—what is expected of them and how they are to relate to other groups within the organization, for example. Third, much of what newcomers will be expected to learn will necessarily be learned on the job, as they are trying to solve problems they encounter as they work. A mixture of formal and informal training is typically needed to ensure that newcomers do not flounder but rather engage quickly in the task of contributing to their company's bottom line.

SPUD: Learning How Expertise Is Distributed

For newcomer learning to be effective, the company's managers need to have some pretty clear ideas about the expertise that newcomers will need to acquire and build that awareness into a comprehensive workplace learning program. One knowledge management tool that may be helpful is a *knowledge map*, graphical representations of the distribution of knowledge in a company. Information mapping may describe location of information, who's responsible for it, what it's used for, and access privileges (Davenport, Eccles, and Prusak 1992). A knowledge map, among other things, is intended to illustrate shortages and redundancies—where there's too little or too much information (Davenport and Prusak 1997).

The SPUD (Skills Planning and Development) Project at Microsoft is an example of a knowledge map aimed at matching system developers to jobs and work teams (Davenport and Prusak 1998). The project involved several steps: developing a structure of knowledge competence types and levels; defining knowledge required for particular jobs; rating performance of people in current jobs; implementing knowledge competencies to online system; and linking to training system. The project identified workers with various kinds of skills labeled anywhere from "foundation" (having skills that most system developers are likely to have) to "universal" (being skilled in a broad range of highly technical tasks) and identified both explicit and tacit kinds of expertise. SPUD allowed newcomers in Microsoft to get a better sense of "who's who" across domains, to identify who might be available to solve a problem in a new area or with a particular kind of software.

What new system developers at Microsoft and newcomers at companies elsewhere must do in order to gain expertise and competence is to develop into full members of the local community of practice at their workplace. To accomplish this aim, newcomers—like all apprentices to communities of practice—need to be able to identify who are experts in the company, where they are located, and how to approach them, something that the SPUD project began to do for newcomers at Microsoft. But they needed more than just a database to learn how to do their jobs.

Newcomers also need opportunities to participate in practice "on the periphery" (Lave and Wenger 1991) while they are learning how to do their work. Practice on the periphery can involve interaction with experts via simulations and modeling tools, where the company's expertise is captured and distributed via training modules to newcomers. It can also involve online assistance to newcomers, where experts provide help in solving problems on the fly. When a record of this learning is kept in common, the problem-solution pairs are made available to other learners in the company (both newcomer and expert) and contribute to the company's management of expertise.

GuSS: Learning How to Do One's Job

One of the problems companies face when designing learning opportunities for newcomers is how to best use experts' time. Experts in companies are always in high demand: using them to conduct regular training sessions with new employees is not always an option. And even if it is an option, the question remains: how best to use their time? Or, from a knowledge management perspective, what is the most efficient way to ensure that knowledge of experts is transferred to novices and distributed widely across the company? No matter what, the use of experts to support learning will be costly, but the cost of failing to give newcomers the foundation they may need to create the next generation of ideas and products for the company may be even greater.

The Institute for Learning Sciences (ILS) has developed a process for gathering what have been called "war stories" (Orr 1990) from experts as a first step toward transferring knowledge from expert to novice in a company. War stories are stories told by experts, often to one another, that capture the interesting and unusual problems faced by people on the job—the missed opportunity, the intractable customer service problem, and so forth. What is particularly useful about war stories as a knowledge management strategy is what also makes them such a good learning tool—war stories provide insight about how experts handle real problems on the job. To be sure, gathering stories is no easy task itself: it requires the kinds of skills anthropologists bring to the task of describing cultural practices. One needs to have a good idea of what different communities of practice are up to when they are working. The collector of war stories must "restore the work," making visible what is often invisible or tacit for even the practitioners themselves (Star 1995). And most important, one must know when a particular story should be told and in what situations.

ILS has developed processes for companies that employ scenarios and simulations for use in formal training environments that incorporate the use of war stories of the kind just described (Star 1995). The ILS approach calls for intensive data gathering on the part of trainers—acquiring some knowledge of the domain, interviews with experts, and the identification of both typical and atypical failures of workers on the job—at the beginning of the process. Interviewers ask specific questions about unusual problems workers have had to face or inventive solutions to problems, and try to identify how experts label and store the war stories they tell for their own use in practice. Based on this information, trainers construct a set of *scenarios*, or possible situations that provide opportunities for workers to gain skill in the target domain.

Two software tools, GuSS (Guided Social Simulation) and SPIEL (Story Producer for InteractivE Learning), are available to trainers to help recontextualize the war stories into the new scenarios that have been created. GuSS is a program designed to teach complex social skills such as coaching, supervision, and selling. GuSS presents learners with the constructed scenario, possible sequences of action, and feedback on how they are performing as they respond to the evolving situation in the scenario.

The war stories pop up in GuSS as users perform some action that is inconsistent with what an expert might do. For example, in one simulation created by trainers at Ameritech, account executives encounter a situation in which they are trying to sell ads in the Yellow Pages to a customer who has bought an ad in the past. The customer's business has been experiencing difficulties in the past year, and getting the customer to buy again or even buy a bigger ad is a tough sell. In the opening scene, the office manager—the wife of the owner—answers the door. If the seller fails to use the opportunity to ask her about what's been going on in the business before her husband arrives (she defers to him when he is present), a headline pops up to warn the seller that a critical opportunity to learn about the business has been lost. A tag line or "bridge" announces the relevance of a war story to follow: assuming that the owner's wife will not have a role in the business may not be wise. A video of an expert seller at Ameritech can then be viewed, in which the seller tells of a story involving a husband and wife team where the wife was responsible for all business decisions. While the seller had made the appointment with the husband, if she had ignored the wife in the conversation, the sale would have been lost.

Within the GuSS architecture, SPIEL functions as the tool that trainers use to specify what story to tell when. In this sense, SPIEL helps restore some of the context of the war stories that are lost when they are videotaped. They key to the success of simulations in GuSS is that the stories being told are *relevant* to the problem at hand. They may function, moreover, not just to warn against possible opportunities missed but in many other ways as well. Stories are categorized in SPIEL as to whether they show alternatives, critique the learner's expectations, project possible results of learner actions, or explain the perspectives of other people to the learner—all functions that stories may have in the workplace (Burke 1998). SPIEL requires designers to create only one index of what the story "means," and it uses the strategy set to determine which stories to use when in a scenario. SPIEL then causes an appropriate story to pop up during the course of the simulation.

Making war stories available to newcomers in an organization through the GuSS and SPIEL tools enables newcomers to learn many aspects of their work practice that might be lost if they were simply given a training manual and a list of instructions on how to do their jobs. First, the war stories help to characterize *noncanonical practice*, that is, events that are anomalous, unusual, or surprising (Brown and Duguid 1991). Describing the noncanonical helps workers understand what can't be written down in policy guidelines, procedures, or other kinds of directive documentation. It gives them clues about what to pay attention to, about what kinds of tacit knowledge they will need to perform skillfully on the job.

The Answer Garden: Learning Opportunities within Ongoing Practice

There are a number of tools that have been designed to help workers locate the information and expertise they need just in time. Databases are certainly one source of information that many workers consult, especially if they are actively maintained and there is a culture within the company that invites writing down expertise in a database and then using it. The success of any such database depends on this culture and on the way information and expertise are represented within it. It is possible to design learning environments that help newcomers and experts come together and that augment a traditional discussion or problem-solving database with some specific tools to help make learning problems and their solutions visible to newcomers.

The Answer Garden is a tool designed to support the growth of organizational memory through the creation of databases of commonly asked questions (Ackerman 1994). It is designed especially for organizations that provide technical hot lines to customers, since these companies need to answer recurring (and novel) questions quickly and accurately. To use the Answer Garden, users respond to a hierarchically ordered set of multiple-choice questions. The order and questions are set by the experts, who use a tree-branching strategy to help users identify their problems and locate answers. Users can see the "tree" at any time, and thus they can see the expert's picture of the array of possible problems users might face. If they don't find an answer to their question, they can press a button with the label "I'm unhappy." Users can then send an expert an anonymous e-mail with their question. New questions and answers are immediately fed into the database, which grows as users and experts interact. Experts can also redesign the tree-branching structure as new questions arise or to clarify parts of the knowledge structure that may be confusing to users. The database grows organically, producing useful knowledge just in time, as users need information to solve problems at hand in their work (Ackerman and Malone 1990). The expertise that is captured in the Answer Garden is different from training manuals and other directive documentation developed ahead of time by planners, because it is formed online, as problems are being solved. The advantages of Answer Garden are that it is available anytime and that the information is likely to be perceived as more reliable, since companies identify experts to answer the questions posed by users. The experts, in turn, don't have to answer many simple questions that recur but can instead concentrate on more interesting problems.

A field study of Answer Garden showed some of its promise and also some of the limitations of the current design. A group of software engineers at Harvard and MIT used Answer Garden for a semester to help solve problems they encountered using the X Window System and its toolkits. This field of work practice is an ideal test bed for an organizational memory tool like Answer Garden: there is no body of knowledge that all software engineers share, and the constant change in the field requires engineers to be developing expertise constantly, just-in-time. Experts in using the system were also available to help by responding to e-mails sent by engineers who could not find the answer to their question in the Answer Garden.

Usage of the system was fairly consistent over the semester. Over half the software engineers used the system at some point during the time. Of these, half used the system intermittently or more than ten times during the semester. These data and interviews from users suggest that the software engineers saw the usefulness of the system in principle: they were comfortable using the Answer Garden as an intermittent source of expertise in solving problems they had with the X Window System.

The Answer Garden is a potentially powerful tool for supporting newcomer learning because it provides newcomers with access to experts in real time and to the ways they have helped other novices in the past. The e-mail system allows newcomers to ask questions without feeling incompetent, and it allows everyone to see a visual representation of the problem spaces that other newcomers have inhabited as they have progressed in learning the X Window System. Its record of problems and solutions contributes to an organization's memory of what problems have been solved and thus helps to manage the expertise in a particular domain in which the Answer Garden is employed. The Answer Garden, then, could be said to be a just-in-time learning solution where the learning is not lost but is maintained as part of the organization's history of learning opportunities.

3.3 Knowledge Management Processes That Support Expert Learning

Supporting learning among experts requires a somewhat different set of processes than those required for newcomers. Experts in today's economy do not remain experts simply by holding onto what knowledge they have; they, too, must be involved in learning and the creation of new knowledge. What makes them experts today may in fact be that they can learn quickly to solve new, never-before-anticipated problems on the job.

The expert is fundamentally an innovator, problem creator as well as problem solver, engaged in supporting the company's ongoing efforts to position itself as a leader within a particular field.

To function in this way, experts need to operate within larger learning communities or learning organizations. They need opportunities to encounter other experts who are in areas remote from them or who share different perspectives from them, or who come from other enterprises altogether. Their learning depends on gatherings of diverse experts, encounters with others that may force them to rethink their approaches to defining and solving problems they encounter on the job. By encountering diverse perspectives, experts become less likely to remain blinded by their own professional biases, and by conducting a dialogue with experts from different domains, experts come to see new and challenging problems as opportunities to apply what they know to engage the company's emerging problems and opportunities.

Gatherings of diverse experts are occasions for *knowledge creation* within companies. They are fundamentally opportunities for companies to invent new work processes, create new products, and identify new markets. Knowledge management among experts is a problem of organizing learning resources and opportunities in such a way that experts have new venues for talking with each other. That talk must take place within a culture of risk taking and innovation that encourages them to develop projects and products that force them to pull together expertise from different disciplines or fields. In this way, learning and knowledge management come together to support both individual expert and organizational learning across the company.

Revisiting the Denver Project: Expanding Expertise beyond Individual Skill

The process of gathering experts together to talk with one another is illustrated by the photocopier repair technicians described in a review article by Penuel and Roschelle (1999).

The Denver Project involved giving technicians portable radios to allow them to talk with one another to solve difficult problems they encountered at client work sites (Orr 1993). The project was successful (from the technicians' point of view) because technicians were able to share stories and problems with each other on the go. The radios reduced their reliance on face-to-face meetings at the beginning or end of the work day and made sharing of expertise a regular part of their jobs.

The technicians were using their own "war stories" in ways that were different from the way ILS used its war stories in designing simulations for newcomers. For the technicians, the war stories served to build an emerging community of practice among expert repair technicians: the stories that were told about particular machine repairs, client relationships, and their own mistakes were a means of developing and demonstrating their competence as technicians and a means of collective remembering. This collective remembering preserved knowledge of different repair situations, which could be applied to diagnose new, unanticipated problems. Technicians used the old knowledge—passed on through stories shared and reconstructed by technicians—when they recognized familiar patterns emerging in a new situation. Over time, experts became even better at diagnosing problems (Orr 1990), and through telling and listening to stories the technicians came to construct interpretive communities that shared ways of relating events, interpreting situations, and diagnosing and solving problems (Brown and Duguid 1991). Ultimately, they developed a shared company database that captured their war stories and made them available to all technicians. Technicians' stories thus acted as "repositories of accumulated wisdom" (Brown and Duguid 1991) within the company, helping to achieve the fundamental goal of the creation of knowledge about new and as-yet-unsolved problems.

Today there are increasingly sophisticated ways that technologies can support the kind of expert-expert learning that integrate people, processes, and technology into integrated knowledge management–expert learning solutions. These technologies distribute company expertise broadly at the site of problem solving and help create new knowledge among experts that can help identify new products and markets. The technologies draw on the power of the Internet and company intranets, a backbone that supports remote collaboration. These technologies also scaffold expert learning by providing specific ways for experts either to develop a broader understanding of the expertise available to them to solve a particular problem or to dialogue with one another in the course of solving a problem.

The CILT Knowledge Network: Solving New and Emerging Problems
Just as stories help accomplish goals of individual and team workplace learning and knowledge generation, so too do representations and models. Among other things, shared models can establish a common language for collaborating across and within communities of practice. Problems in communication are typical when, say, engineers, contractors, and architects collaborate to build an office building (Engestrom, Engestrom, and Karkkainen 1995). Shared representations provide experts with a means to see what experts are around them and available to solve problems. Knowledge networks, like knowledge maps, are tools that allow workers to learn more about the expertise around them. Some knowledge networks, like the one we describe here, are specifically geared toward helping experts learn from one another and create new learning technologies at the edge of their own expertise.

The Center for Innovative Learning Technologies is an innovative collaborative that brings together industry and expert researchers in learning technologies. The CILT Knowledge Network is a continually updated database of resources about the learning technology research community available to any CILT member. The database includes description of CILT members, projects, and papers. Within the database is a demonstration tool developed by AT&T called ReferralWeb for creating knowledge maps that help the user visualize the connections between people in CILT as shown by who co-authored publications with whom. ReferralWeb lets expert researchers begin to see the networks and connections among other experts as evidenced by prior collaboration, not just institutional affiliation. What makes the CILT Knowledge Network useful, however, is not just the mapping tools and database but the processes that surround the network and motivate collaboration. Members of CILT participate in an annual conference at which they present the latest tools in one of four areas: visualization and modeling, community tools, ubiquitous tools, and assessment. Researchers from across organizations—including across industry and research organizations—

can collaborate to develop minigrants to explore the edges of learning technology. Funded minigrants have included product development proposals that could lead to commercialization, and the researchers involved have all testified to the success of CILT in promoting these kinds of cross-institutional collaborations to support innovation.

CALL: Making Problems and Solutions Visible
The aim of the Center for Army Lessons Learned (CALL) is to gather information about U.S. Army operations and convert it into knowledge that improves the effectiveness of troops in the field. CALL is unusual in that it sends teams of experts into the field to observe missions at first hand and then works with line and staff organizations to distribute knowledge in the form of "lessons learned" both vertically and horizontally within the organization. In recent years, as the army has performed functions that it has been ill-prepared to carry out, such as peacekeeping, the CALL's ability to provide best-practice knowledge rapidly to field operations staff has become a critical component of army operations (Henderson, Sussman, and Thomas 1998).

Conditions within army operations certainly support organizational learning. Widespread information sharing is valued because withholding information costs lives. Good ideas are implemented not because someone demands it but because they are useful in saving people's lives. The army consistently reviews its operations using the after-action-reviews process. After missions and trainings, officers meet to discuss what went wrong or what was successful, and they are therefore used to reflecting collaboratively on their experiences as a means to enhance organizational learning.

CALL is particularly successful in supporting expert learning. CALL relies on communities of experts from different fields to structure a process for observing missions in action, to actually go on missions, and to synthesize information into lessons learned. Teams who go into the field are composed of eight to twelve "guest experts" from across the army with different specialist roles. CALL selects one leader for the team from within its organization, and one of the guest experts serves as a co-leader for each team, ensuring that CALL itself is able to learn continuously from its observations.

The team members' job is to identify systematic problems and also successful solutions or best practices. In the field, they act as vertical and horizontal information sources. When they are faced with new problems, they may offer to local units lessons they have culled from previous missions. They may also watch as leaders in charge of the mission come up with solutions to unanticipated problems, and document those for review. In this way, the CALL team members gain trust by contributing their expertise, and in exchange they get inside information about how the operation is working from the viewpoints of participants in the operation.

CALL team members in the field submit their information daily to the CALL headquarters, where it is entered into a database in the form of thick descriptions. It is also posted on bulletin boards and distribution lists in order to get feedback from a diverse group of experts across the country. The descriptions circulated by CALL keep communities of experts updated on new developments in their particular area of expertise and also serve as the basis for the creation of lessons learned. The ideas they generate are turned around to the ground team within five days and developed into simulations, training manuals, and videos for use by troops in the operation.

The interaction among diverse experts is critical in the transformation of thick field descriptions into lessons learned that can be used in the field. Through discussion among experts on bulletin boards and listservs, and through feedback with experts in the field, common interpretations are developed by hashing out divergent views and by attempting to identify bias in information gathering. These cross-functional teams help to distribute best practices quickly while at the same time supporting expert learning. The technology supports the rapid distribution of information to experts across the organization, enabling them to participate collaboratively to create useful knowledge for staff in the field. The experts who participate in CALL are constantly challenged to update their expertise, and their interaction with experts from outside their specialization to develop useful interpretations of events for operations staff enable individual expert learning and organizational learning to happen simultaneously.

3.4   Conclusion

In this chapter we have described several processes and technologies that can help companies work more effectively to leverage the knowledge they have to solve new problems while at the same time supporting workplace learning among individuals and teams working on those problems. In each of the examples, we saw exemplary practices in knowledge management, supported by tools that help meet the learning needs of workers, whether they be novices or experts.

There are three critical points of intersection between workplace learning and knowledge management that can be identified in the three examples (table 3.3). First, *workers learn and manage knowledge within communities of practice.* Both learning processes and knowledge management processes are embedded within communities of professionals, whether they be experts or novices. In the Microsoft SPUD project, novices learned about the distribution of expertise within the extended professional community of a large company distributed across a wide geographical area. Novices could also become participants in a trajectory of expertise development that was aligned with the knowledge map created by the company. In the Denver Project, it was experts learning from each other through stories they shared about difficult problems they faced on the job. The result of both interventions was that novices and experts alike became more knowledgeable about where and how to access expertise within the company.

A second common thread is that *learning and knowledge management are most effective when focused on actual problems.* In the simulations designed by ILS, novices learned how to solve the kinds of problems they would face on the job, becoming expert through practicing a variety of problems in their target domain. Via the CILT Knowledge Network, researchers and business developers came together to apply what they already knew to innovate and address emerging problems, generating new expertise through creative solutions to new problems. Knowledge transfer and knowledge generation were key outcomes in both projects, as novices and experts both had occasion to become active in their own learning by engaging with core problems within their field or organization.

Table 3.3
The Intersection of Knowledge Management and Workplace Learning

Point of Intersection	Example	Learning Principle	Knowledge Management Outcome
Workers learn and manage knowledge within communities of practice	*Novice learning:* Microsoft SPUD Project *Expert learning:* Denver Project	Learning takes place within communities of practice	Novices and experts alike know where and how to access expertise within the company
Learning and knowledge management are most effective when centered on actual problems	*Novice learning:* Yellow Pages Sales (ILS) *Expert learning:* CILT Knowledge Network	Novices learn to become experts through practice in solving a variety of problems in a domain Becoming an expert means applying learning to new contexts	Expertise is effectively transferred from expert to novice; new expertise is generated through creative solutions to new problems
Effective knowledge management involves leaving visible traces of the learning process	*Novice learning:* Answer Garden *Expert learning:* CALL	Prior knowledge mediates (can enhance and inhibit) learning. Learning is enhanced through reflection	Individual learning is transformed into organizational memory, a resource for companywide learning

A third important intersection is that *effective knowledge management involves leaving visible traces of the learning process.* The Answer Garden leaves a "trace" of every problem faced by novice programmers and its solution provided by an expert. The CALL team leaves visible traces in the form of databases of thick descriptions and lessons learned that are used by operations staff in the field. In both cases, experts' and novices' prior knowledge is transformed. Learners use their prior knowledge, but they transform it in the process of taking advantage of learning opportunities embedded within ongoing practice. The result is that their expertise is expanded, and by the technology's leaving a trace of their learning, individual learning becomes organizational memory, a resource for companywide learning.

A final word of caution: the examples that show the intersection of workplace learning and knowledge management should be viewed as unusual and distinctive. It is easy to conflate learning and knowledge management as concepts and strategies, and tempting to believe that by designing an effective knowledge management strategy, one has solved the problems of workplace learning. The examples within the points of intersection, however, do point to the promise and potential of creating an integrated solution, the key to which is rooted in both principles of learning and the collaborative technologies that support the solution. Our future as learners and as designers of learning depends upon an understanding of the limits and possibilities of this intersection.

References

Ackerman, M. S. 1994. Augmenting the Organizational Memory: A Field Study of Answer Garden. In *Proceedings of the ACM Conference on Computer-Supported Cooperative Work (CSCW '94)*, 243–252.

Ackerman, M. S., and T. W. Malone. 1990. Answer Garden: A Tool for Growing Organizational Memory. In *Proceedings of the ACM Conference on Office Information Systems*, 31–39.

Armstrong, J. S. 1985. *Long-Range Forecasting: From Crystal Ball to Computer.* 2d ed. New York: Wiley.

Brown, J. S., and P. Duguid. 1991. Organizational Learning and Communities of Practice: Towards a Unified View of Working, Learning, and Innovation. *Organization Science* 2 (1): 40–57.

Burke, R. B. 1998. Representation, Storage, and Retrieval of Tutorial Stories in a Social Simulation. In *Inside Multimedia Case-Based Instruction*, ed. R. C. Schank, 175–284. Mahwah, N.J.: Erlbaum.

Cohen, A. L., B. Penuel, E. Trondsen, and K. Patton. 1999. *New Workplace Learning Technologies: Activities and Exemplars.* Cambridge, Mass.: Lotus Development Corporation.

Davenport, T. H., R. G. Eccles, and L. Prusak. 1992. Information Politics. *Sloan Management Review* 34 (1): 52–65.

Davenport, T. H., and L. Prusak. 1997. *Information Ecology: Mastering the Information and Knowledge Environment.* New York: Oxford University Press.

———. 1998. *Working Knowledge: How Organizations Manage What They Know.* Boston: Harvard Business School Press.

Engestrom, Y., R. Engestrom, and M. Karkkainen. 1995. Polycontextuality and Boundary Crossing in Expert Cognition: Learning and Problem Solving in Complex Work Activities. *Learning and Instruction* 5: 319–336.

Henderson, J. C., S. W. Sussman, and J. B. Thomas. 1998. Creating and Exploiting Knowledge for Fast-Cycle Organizational Response: The Center for Army Lessons Learned. *Advances in Applied Business Strategy* 5: 103–128.

Lave, J., and E. Wenger. 1991. *Situated Learning: Legitimate Peripheral Participation*. New York: Cambridge University Press.

Nonaka, I. 1998. The Knowledge-Creating Company. In *Harvard Business Review on Knowledge Management*, 21–46. Boston: Harvard Business School Press.

Orr, J. E. 1990. Sharing Knowledge, Celebrating Identity: War Stories and Community Memory in a Service Culture. In *Collective Remembering: Memory in Society*, ed. D. Middleton and D. Edwards, 169–189. Newbury Park, Calif.: Sage.

———. 1993. Ethnography and Organizational Learning: In Pursuit of Learning at Work. In *Organizational Learning and Technological Change*, ed. S. Bagnara, C. Zucchermaglio, and S. Stucky. New York: Springer-Verlag.

Penuel, B., and J. Roschelle. 1999. *Designing Learning: Cognitive Science Principles for Innovation*. Cambridge, Mass.: Lotus Development Corporation.

Prusak, L. 1997. Introduction to Knowledge in Organizations. In *Knowledge in Organizations*, ix–xv. Boston: Butterworth-Heinemann.

Senge, P. 1990. *The Fifth Discipline: The Art and Practice of the Learning Organization*. New York: Doubleday.

Star, S. L. 1995. The Politics of Formal Representations: Wizards, Gurus, and Organizational Complexity. In *Ecologies of Knowledge: Work and Politics in Science and Technology*, 88–118. Albany: SUNY Press.

Star, S. L., and J. R. Greisemer. 1989. Institutional Ecology, "Translations," and Boundary Objects: Amateurs and Professionals in Berkeley's Museum of Vertebrate Zoology, 1907–1939. *Social Studies of Science* 19: 387–420.

Starbuck, W. H. 1992. Learning by Knowledge-Intensive Firms. *Journal of Management Studies* 29: 713–740.

II

Studies of Expertise Sharing in Organizations

This part of the book contains five case studies that describe the sharing of expertise in a variety of organizations: a political unit, a steel mill, a virtual organization, a software maker, and an airplane producer.

Case studies in real organizations are of central importance in understanding expertise sharing because expertise is socially arranged and organized. Studies that examine a site over time allow one to identify factors affecting expertise sharing. Moreover, studies from different organizational settings help identify similarities and differences.

When tools are introduced into organizations, it is important to evaluate the effects of their use within specific organizational contexts. Special attention must be paid to the way the technologies are introduced and the social interventions that go along with them.

In this part Fitzpatrick describes expertise sharing within a branch of an Australian state government that develops strategies and plans policies. This organizational unit is interesting because it operates in a large, complex, politically charged environment. Its policy and strategy work implies networks of external relationships with other people, departments, industry bodies, different levels of government, and multiple information sources. The branch is also interesting because it was only recently formed. The workers do not know each other well, and there are no long-established patterns and conventions to draw upon. The study explores the nature of expertise as embodied knowledge, the implications of this for expertise sharing, and consequently how better expertise sharing could be facilitated.

Pipek, Hinrichs, and Wulf compare two case studies of expertise sharing. In the first case the authors observe how expertise is shared within the maintenance engineering processes of a steel mill. Special attention is given to the role the central archive plays in sharing knowledge on the current state of the mill. The second case looks at expertise sharing within a network organization of consultants and trainers. A lack of formal structures and a huge degree of volatility require mechanisms to make the members aware of one others' expertise. A comparison of the two sites shows differences in the distribution of expertise between human actors and shared technical artifacts. While repository-based approaches are problematic in both cases, the nature of the knowledge to be exchanged and the organizational context lead to considerably different effects in sharing. The authors also report on the use of expertise locators, systems to help find expertise, within the organizations.

Ehrlich focuses more explicitly on the design requirements for expertise locator systems. She reports on an empirical investigation to garner the design requirements for an expertise locator system. Working with a focus group of scientists and associated professionals, Erhlich develops an enumeration of the attributes that need to be included in an expertise locator system. The sources the attributes can be derived from are presented, and specific design issues are discussed. One of the findings from her study is how critical it is to co-design the expertise locator and the data it requires, and she provides an in-depth discussion of the trade-offs and issues surrounding these data.

Ackerman, Boster, Lutters, and McDonald argue that finding the data for an expertise locator system may be difficult. Their concern is finding new methods of uncovering the data required. To determine the knowledge distribution among the workers, the authors develop an instrument that can be made organization-specific at relatively low cost. The chapter describes their instruments and a prototype tested at a medium-sized medical software company that develops applications for practice management. By comparing the results gained by the instrument with estimations of workers' expertise provided by colleagues (yet another instrument), they argue for the success of discount data collection methods.

Finally, Haas, Aulbur, and Thakar describe the approach Daimler-Chrysler Aerospace Airbus has taken to support expertise sharing within communities of practice. Communities of practice are seen as people across different organizational units who have a common interest, interact to share information, and solve problems in their area of expertise. The chapter takes the management perspective of those responsible for stimulating expertise sharing within a huge distributed organization. The organizational, motivational, and technical activities to establish and support communities of practice are described, as well as lessons learned. It is interesting to note that approaches to encourage expertise sharing are transferred across product lines and cultures to different parts of the multinational organization.

4

Emergent Expertise Sharing in a New Community

Geraldine Fitzpatrick

This chapter provides an empirical account of emergent expertise sharing within the Strategy and Policy (S&P) branch of a department involved in the business of state government.

The S&P branch is interesting because, while small in terms of numbers of employees, it operates in a large, complex, politically charged environment. Its policy and strategy work involves networks of external relationships with other people, departments, industry bodies, different levels of government, and multiple information sources. Hence it has large-community needs but small-community cost-benefit constraints.

The S&P branch is also interesting because it was only recently formed. There is no long-established history or tradition to draw upon. The role of the branch is still being evolved and negotiated. Many of the members of the branch do not know each other well, having been drawn from other departments.

The case study captures a period of intensive bootstrapping in which the foundations of a shared knowledge base are established.[1] This bootstrapping involves identifying and locating the shared expertise of the group and making visible the sorts of information that will later be taken for granted or become part of a shared history and context for the group—the necessary background information that will likely underpin its ongoing expertise-sharing practices.

Some of these bootstrapping activities were explicit and directed toward the *content* basis of the work of S&P, e.g., establishing appropriate information stores and pushing information flows. Content, while necessary, was only part of the story. Putting content to work most effectively was critically dependent on knowing relevant *context* information.

Having a good network of *contacts* was also critical to getting the work done.

The members of S&P brought with them a wealth of information that could potentially be valuable to the rest of the group if it were known. However, this information tended to arise from deeply *embodied knowledge*, that is, information uniquely and integrally a part of who the person is. Such embodied knowledge is the essence of expertise. For this reason, it was often hard for people to make explicit or even anticipate that something they knew would be useful for others, and vice versa. Also, the potential value of any single piece of information depended on its being embedded into networks of other embodied information.

In contrast to content information, the bootstrapping of shared context and contact information from embodied knowledge tended to happen relatively unself-consciously as the members of S&P went about their jobs—mostly via tacit strategies triggered in the context of interpersonal relationships.

Various examples are presented in this case study that highlight the sorts of information needed by the members of S&P and the emergent processes by which that expertise was initially shared.

Because expertise is about embodied knowledge, facilitating better sharing of embodied knowledge cannot rely on being able to make explicit and codify the necessary information. While it might be possible to codify some information, such as that contained in a curriculum vitae (this larger-grained, more public information I call *information in the large*), much of the sharing is about smaller-grained information (*information in the small*) that is only triggered in the context of interpersonal relationships and only makes sense when interconnected and put to work with preexisting knowledge. Strategies to facilitate more effective expertise sharing have to necessarily complement codification and storage approaches with approaches that support social processes enabling communication and information flow. It is for this reason that I choose to talk about *expertise sharing* rather than expertise management; sharing implies an interactional process; management implies to some extent that such sharing can be anticipated, documented, and controlled.

The following section introduces the case and the study method. In the next section, the nature of S&P's work is described, noting its mix of longer-term projects and ad hoc demands that occur in a network of complex relationships. To get the work done, the members of S&P employ an underlying strategy of *satisficing*.[2] Their information-gathering strategies can be characterized as *just-in-time* (JIT) and *just-in-case* (JIC), targeting not just content but context and contact information as well.

Focusing on context and contact information, the next section explores the different things that people wanted to know in this regard and the ways in which they discovered this information. Specifically, I discuss the bootstrapping of expertise sharing in terms of various *finding-out* processes—finding out information in the large, finding out information in the small, finding out what people do now, and finding out what people are like.

I then explore the nature of expertise as embodied knowledge, the implications of this for expertise sharing, and consequently how better expertise sharing could be facilitated within this group. Before concluding, I also reflect on how such approaches might also have a place in larger-scale communities via intermediaries.

4.1 The Case

Strategy and Policy (S&P) is one of the many branches of a division of a department, which in turn is one of many departments constituting the structure of a state government. It is a relatively new branch with a relatively new role; at the beginning of the study, the S&P branch had only just been formed some two months previously with a brief to develop policies and plan strategies for a statewide information technology and communication agenda on behalf of its department. The details of what this brief meant on a day-to-day basis, and what, if any, power the branch had to implement the brief, were under continual negotiation within the branch itself, within the broader department, and across other departments.

As with many governments, reporting structures are bureaucratic and hierarchical. The branch director reports to the divisional manager, who reports to the director general of the department, who reports to the minister, who reports to the state premier. The minister and premier are elected politicians. The others are public servants.

The makeup of the branch, in terms of numbers, roles, and individuals, continues to be in a state of flux. Generally there are about fifteen people, mostly transferred or seconded from disparate branches and departments. Some of the people had worked together previously. Others knew little of each other, others knew colleagues by reputation or from contact at previous interdepartmental activities.

The location of the branch was also in a state of flux. During the course of the study, it occupied an island of space surrounded by other branches of its department with whom it shared meeting rooms and kitchen facilities.

The three senior officers and the director each had private offices. The others were in twin-share offices. The four administration staff members were distributed among the offices. All offices were located on either side of a small section of corridor.

Staff members had no discretion in reconfiguring their space to better meet needs—their space was regarded as temporary, and there were rumors that eventually they would be moved to another building. They also had little discretion in their information technology (IT) infrastructure; they used the common hardware and software platforms provided at the discretion of the IT branch of the department.

Method
The study took place intermittently over approximately six months at the request of the branch. As part of an ongoing relationship with our research center, the branch asked for help with its communication and information flow issues.

We began the study with a one-day workshop involving the whole S&P group; this was co-facilitated with two colleagues. Prior to the workshop, we conducted on-site interviews with the director and two senior members. During the workshop, we used the locales framework (Fitzpatrick 1998) as a vehicle to understand the scope of their work and to help identify general issues of concern.

Following a preliminary report and consequent discussions, I undertook five days of intensive study at their workplace over a period of two weeks. Because of the previous interactions, I was able to go into the workplace with a relatively rich understanding of the group and its issues. This enabled more focused observations and interactions with the group.

Data were collected using qualitative methods, including direct observation of work, attendance at group meetings, collection of related documents and artifacts, situated discussions with individuals, and semi-structured interviews. The analysis followed grounded theory principles (Glaser and Strauss 1967).

This was followed by a further written report that was to serve as a discussion document with the group to make visible some of the internal group processes, identify issues of potential concern, and outline a set of possible discussion and action points around each issue. I conducted a second half-day workshop with the group to discuss and prioritize the issues raised in the report and to plan for further action.

The advantages of engaging in a cycle of activities over a six-month period—interviews, initial workshop, preliminary report, discussions, study, detailed report, and follow-up workshop—and having regular feedback from the group meant that study findings could be triangulated and verified across time and circumstances.

The account in this chapter discusses the S&P branch to this point. Since the last workshop, there has been a significant change in management in the department and the branch. Further action from this study has been put on hold.

Scope

The contribution of this study is to provide an empirical account of a particular type of community or group that is small but interdependently embedded in a network of relationships, and the emergent expertise-sharing practices that characterized the early phase of its life cycle. In particular, it makes visible and explicit the sorts of information that will later become part of the givens, the shared history, and the knowledge foundations of this group—necessary background information that will likely underpin its ongoing expertise-sharing practices. We can talk of these emergent practices as bootstrapping expertise sharing for a new community.

4.2   The Work

As a new branch, the role of S&P is highly emergent. Members of S&P have little prior history or tradition to draw upon, apart from general government procedures. Its focus area of information technology and communications is also rapidly changing, with new ground being broken at an increasing rate.

Dual Strands of Work
Even so, at a general level there are clearly two *concurrent strands* of work that members have to weave into their day-to-day jobs.

Assigned Projects and Policy Responsibilities   People are given specific projects or policy areas for which they are responsible. These constitute the more predictable and stable aspects of work because they are long-running activities. The foci of project and policy areas mirror general industry trends and include topics such as electronic commerce, networking infrastructure, and technology skills training.

Ad Hoc, Unpredictable, Event-driven Demands   These tend to be more short-lived, unpredictable activities interspersed into the working day, which every member has to contend with. The most frequent ad hoc demand is for an updated or new briefing note for the minister so that he can be prepared for questions in parliament or from the media. Such ministerial requests are particularly important and frequently have to be attended to within strictly defined and often pressurized time frames. Other examples include requests for information from peers, the public, or industry via the phone; people dropping in; organization of one-off events; and attendance at miscellaneous meetings, workshops, and conferences.

Complex Network of Relationships
These two strands of work take place within a complex web of relationships. While S&P is only a small group, its policy and strategy work has far-reaching implications. The branch is defining whole-of-government and whole-of-state directions for information technology and communi-

cations as well as the infrastructure and types of services to be provided by the government to the general community via that infrastructure. As such, there are a number of interested stakeholders. These include the IT industry and community bodies as well as the other internal government departments that will be delivering those services. The members of S&P also need to be cognizant of, and contributing to, national standards and policy efforts, making relationships with relevant federal government departments important as well.

S&P has no mandate, though, to enforce the uptake of, or compliance with, the standards, policies, and strategies it defines. It also has no role in their implementation. As such, S&P can only make an impact if it gets buy-in from all stakeholders. This necessitates wide consultation and the enlistment of key players as stakeholder champions.

Strategies

By definition, the work of the people in S&P is highly information-intensive, complex, and often time-critical.

Satisficing is their primary underlying strategy for coping in such an environment. Working with time constraints, with limited resources, and with potentially unlimited information, the branch director states that his team "cannot know everything about everything." The team therefore operates explicitly within a framework where "good enough" is good enough. At the same time, the director is acutely aware that he and his team are new at this role and have a lot to learn. He is concerned that they have yet to find the right balance between pragmatic compromise and optimizing strategies to sufficiently yet effectively satisfy work needs. At the first workshop, the group characterized its own problems in this regard as being about communication and information flows. Such flows are at the heart of expertise sharing.

Within this satisficing framework, there are two other strategies that characterize S&P's approach to work. The first strategy I call *just-in-time* access to relevant information as a need arises, e.g., to write a briefing note. Examples include targeted information search, asking for help, sending out requests over e-mail, and so on. The second strategy can be called *just-in-case*, the intentional, accidental, or incidental activities for gathering, filtering, or archiving information just in case it is useful at a later time. Because S&P was very much in the early phase of its life cycle, much of the information gathered via JIT and JIC strategies served to bootstrap the shared knowledge base that would underpin the ongoing work of S&P.

Information Types

In carrying out the work of S&P, different types of information are required. These can be broadly characterized as content, context, and contacts.

Content Information   Content information is factual topical information central to the policy work and for ad hoc briefing notes, and so on. In particular S&P needs up-to-date information about trends, technologies, and standards: What are the current trends in electronic commerce? What networking infrastructure currently exists in the state?

The usefulness of content information in the S&P work is often inversely proportional to its age: the more recent the information, the more potentially useful it is. For example, a press cutting discussing the latest advance in networking technologies is more valuable for policy development than a fuller but older journal article on the topic.

It is not surprising that the main sources of content information tend to be the following hard and soft sources. Hard sources include magazines, newspapers, past briefing notes, filed paper documents, and circulated notices. Only occasionally do any of the branch members access library resources such as books or journals. Soft sources are those in electronic form, including personal and shared file directories, online indexes to hard-copy sources such as contents of filing cabinets, the Internet, push-information services, and online search tools.

Context Information   Context information is most critical for the staff members' success and for their career trajectories. This is the contextual information within which content is interpreted, used, and communicated. People talk about it in terms of "knowing the business" and "having a feel for the bureaucratic process." Depending on the situation at hand, this could involve knowing current and historical context as well as political and environmental issues: What is the sort of information needed right now and how can it be accessed? Who is around now to help with this issue? What is the party political line on this issue? What has the minister said in the past? Who are the personalities involved and what are their agendas? Which industry people currently "have the minister's ear"? What are the minister's advisers saying? What are the electoral ramifications? Is there an election pending? Who will read this? Has anyone done work in this area before?

Contextual information is rarely written down in any form. There are a number of different reasons why this seems to be the case: people often don't know that they know something relevant for someone else; or they think the information is peripheral to the core information/event; or they believe it will be politically unwise to record it; or on its own it is not considered worth recording; or there is no place for it to be recorded.

Because it is not generally recorded, context information usually has to be known already or else found out in discussion or inferred from other information. As such, the main sources for context information are "warm" people resources. The value of context information is often only realized when it is interconnected with other pieces of information. In the subsequent section Bootstrapping Through Getting the Work Done, there are many examples that illustrate the value of context information in practice.

Contact Lists   Contact lists are another highly valued information resource closely related to context. Having a good network of contacts is a critical factor in obtaining context information and in managing S&P's many external relationships. Organizational directories exist, but these are the least preferred source of contact information. Members invariably prefer to have a known or named contact person for consultation and for encouraging buy-in to their strategies and policies (remembering that they have no mandate to enforce compliance). Such contacts are perceived as providing entry points to their areas and as potential allies to co-opt to the agenda at hand. Contacts are also perceived as being trustworthy, and there is a sense of mutual obligation in helping one another out.

Focus on Sharing Context and Contacts

During the course of the study, the most explicit and organizationally visible bootstrapping activities were focused largely on the codified external content information sources, supporting aspects of both JIT and JIC strategies. Having good access to quality information is fundamental to the work of S&P. These activities were directed at trying to improve the availability and quality of information, both hard and soft, via improved discovery, storage, and retrieval mechanisms.

For example, the group was evaluating various industry push-information services. It was also evaluating a content-based search tool for accessing online directories. S&P hired temporary staff to code and file the backlog of paper folders from legacy departments and to update the online index to the hard-copy folders. The branch developed tracking systems for the production of briefing notes. It revised the way in which clippings from a media-monitoring service and other notices were circulated around the group to avoid bottlenecks.

My focus here, however, is on issues around the context and contact information and the group processes by which this shared tacit knowledge was built up. In contrast to the explicit attention and planned action around content information, the identification and sharing of context and contact information largely happened serendipitously as an undercurrent to ongoing activity. Yet it was this information that proved to be most critical for expertise sharing underpinning both JIT and JIC strategies.

For example, the success of JIT strategies depended not only on quality information stores and search/retrieval tools available at the time but also on more ephemeral information, such as knowing who is around at the time, who is likely to be able to help, knowing that the information and tools exist, knowing how to interpret the content information and put it to work, and so on.

Similarly, the quality of information returned from the media-monitoring service and other push-information services played only a small part in the success of JIC information gathering and filtering. Often the more useful JIC information was picked up implicitly or accidentally by accumulating a particular set of past experiences and histories, and while going about everyday activities such as flicking through a news-paper, seeing a new notice on the information board, happening to see another's document on the printer, chatting with colleagues, attending meetings, finding out who knows what, who, and so on. Sometimes people were aware of tuning in to the information at the time. Often they only realised it after the fact when some other event reminded them of what they had previously heard or seen.

The significance of context and contact information was heightened in this group because of its relative newness—it did not have an established history; it did not have established processes for even small things, such as leave applications; it did not have shared stories; and many of the staff members did not know each other well.

On the other hand, each brought a diverse and very current set of skills, experiences, networks, and knowledge from previous postings. One thing clear from the start of S&P was that the success of the group would be determined by members' shared expertise in their policy and project areas, and by the effectiveness of the information and communi-cation flows by which this expertise was discovered and shared.

This time in the life cycle of S&P, then, was an intensive period for uncovering or creating this information, whether implicitly or explicitly. This same level of activity was unlikely to be so evident when the group became more established and so much more information was taken for granted or became part of a shared history and context for the group.

The following section presents various examples that highlight the sorts of context and contact information needed by the members of S&P and the processes by which that information was shared to bootstrap expertise sharing within the group.

4.3 Bootstrapping through Getting the Work Done

In bootstrapping a computer, the necessary code is intentionally loaded into the computer first before other programs. S&P did not have the same luxury—the bootstrapping of a shared knowledge base in the group had to happen in parallel with getting work done day-by-day, and the facilitation of expertise sharing *in practice* tended to be more acci-dental than intentional.

In the following discussion I highlight some of the emergent expertise sharing that occurred in the course of getting the work done. Specifically, I discuss the ways in which expertise-sharing foundations were laid in terms of various finding-out processes—finding out information in the large, finding out information in the small, finding out what people do now, and finding out what people are like. Much of this finding out was directed toward uncovering basic information to support expertise identification and expertise selection when later needed; McDonald and Ackerman (1998, 324) suggest that these are "the two crucial problems that must be solved for individuals to satisfy their need for expertise."

Finding Out "In the Large"

To bootstrap expertise sharing in a new community, some of the basic information that people wanted to know was information in the large— by this I mean information that is of relatively course grain and likely to be relatively easy to find out. It is information that people are more likely to self-report or that is more amenable to being recorded in some form or to being publicly available.

For S&P this included such information as who knew what, who knew whom, where people had worked, what people had worked on before, who is working on what now, what people are like, and so on. People often came across this information through previous knowledge or in general conversation, e.g., asking "Where did you come from?", although rarely as a strategic move.

The arrival of a new staff member highlighted the value of this type of information. Some months after the group had started, Mary was seconded to S&P for a special project. She was an extroverted person and asked for time at the first branch meeting she attended to introduce herself. She talked about what her skills and interests were and what projects and roles she had previously worked in—the type of information one might also find in her curriculum vitae. She also talked about what she understood about her new role at the branch, and more interestingly, she gave the group a sense of what her work values were. She invited any help people were willing or able to give, saying that this was a new area for her. She also talked about her attitude to e-mail, saying that she liked to use e-mail to send out interesting pieces of information to the group or to ask for help and was more than happy to receive similar e-mails. If people had a problem with this, they could let her know.

While not everyone in the group would feel comfortable doing the same thing, Mary's introduction proved highly valuable. She gave them a strong feeling for the sort of straightforward honest person that she was. People were also able to infer a significant amount from her background description, different people picking up on different things. Ann, who had an ongoing concern about library access, hoped to find an ally in Mary because of her librarian background. Tony, who had responsibility for developing some regional programs, inferred that Mary would likely have excellent contacts in the rural sector that he could make use of when the project was more advanced and "filed that snippet of information away for future use."

The main value in Mary's introduction was in giving general pointers to the types of detailed expertise she was likely to have. One person talked explicitly about the value of this information for "getting a sense of what you can get out of people" and then being able to "make instinctive use of their talents when you need them later."

Finding Out "In the Small"

A lot of other potentially useful information in the small would never emerge in an introduction such as Mary's—information at a much finer level of granularity that people would rarely think to self-report because they would not deem it relevant or important at the time. There were many instances within S&P where people did not know there was something to be known, or did not know they knew something of interest to another. Most of the time, this information was only discovered and shared by accident in the course of casual conversation. In the following sections finding out in the small is described as happening by processes such as finding out accidentally, finding out by "snooping," finding out incidentally, finding out incrementally, and finding out the real story.

Finding Out Accidentally   Kate and Ann shared an office and were engaged in their normal morning banter when Kate happened to mention she was reading the minutes of a meeting she had attended the previous evening. Ann's interest was immediately piqued, and she started asking more detailed questions. It turned out that what Kate was saying helped Ann identify some contacts that would help her solve a problem she had been working on for days. Even though they shared an office, Kate had had no idea this would be relevant to Ann—a case of not knowing that you know something useful to someone else, and not knowing what others need to know.

There is also the case of not knowing what you yourself need to know, as illustrated when four of the members were sitting in an office waiting for a teleconference to begin. A general conversation started up about a particular company and the contract work it was doing for the government. Kevin had been involved in setting up this contract in a previous job, and he started telling the story of how it had come about and what were the issues going on at the time. Dave said afterwards that he had never heard any of this before but that it was particularly relevant background to something he was working on now and helped him understand why another department was not being very cooperative. The value of such story telling has long been recognized as an important mechanism for expertise sharing (Orr 1990; Fagrell and Ljungberg 1999).

Finding Out by "Snooping"   Such accidental information discovery can happen in other ways as well. During her introduction Mary had sheepishly confessed to taking someone else's document from the printer because it looked interesting. The group laughed and agreed she wasn't the only one who did this; they talked generally of happening to notice "interesting" things on the printer tray or on people's desks. Mary also discovered things for herself, for example, "by snooping around the shared drive," where she found a template for writing briefing notes. No one had mentioned it to her, and she hadn't really thought about asking whether one existed.

Finding Out Incidentally   In many instances, people made discoveries incidental to their core activity. Scott was a new administrative assistant in the group. He was young and shy, and even though he had been there some weeks, he hadn't really chatted to many people except for work reasons. He was then given the task of helping everyone install a search engine to be evaluated by the group. Part of the job was helping people set up their keyword lists. Scott said later that he really liked doing this because it gave him an opportunity to chat to people he hadn't spoken to before. He also learned more about their interest areas and what they were working on by noting what they put in their keyword lists. This information was especially useful for when he took incoming queries over the phone and had to decide the best person to forward them to.

Another administrative assistant also made explicit use of the keyword lists of the people in her subgroup, subscribing to the same push-information service that they did to get a general sense of what they were interested in and what they were reading.

Finding Out Incrementally   Often people found out about something incrementally, not appreciating what they had previously seen until it was interconnected with further information that gave it context and relevance. This was the case for Scott, who had come across the term AGILS[3] for the first time when he was looking at formatting some online searches; he hadn't understood it and so had ignored it. A couple of days later Leigh asked him whether the new search engine being installed supported the AGILS metadata categories. Scott said he only realized that he had seen it and that it was related to metadata when Leigh had asked this. Leigh had been involved in the working group that had developed the standard, so she then proceeded to explain how it had come about and how far the adoption process had got.

Now Scott could not only recognize the term but also knew what it related to and understood some of the history of how it came to be—a case of incremental JIC knowledge acquisition that embedded the term into increasingly richer networks of other information.

Finding Out the Real Story   Finding out what people called the "real stories," the "gossip," the "reasons why," as Dave did while waiting for the teleconference, was invaluable for doing a good job in S&P. This is because S&P operated in a highly charged political and bureaucratic environment where common sense and logic did not always win and where content information often had to be cleverly interpreted and applied within the realities of the circumstances at the time.

Finding out the real story around a briefing note, for example, the event that triggered the request, was particularly important for being able to decide how best to update an existing note or write a new one. One of the problems, however, was that briefing notes were handled in very formal ways and had to adhere to strict formatting guidelines—the author of the note was never recorded in the final stored version, nor was the initial written request included. As a historical artifact (Mc-Donald and Ackerman 1998), the briefing note was only accounted for as a depersonalized, decontextualized archival document and so failed to provide support for actually locating the artifact in its political-historical context.

To find out the real (hi)story, one had to find the initial author or someone who had been around at the time the note was written. The older the note, the more difficult this was, especially as some of the notes were legacy from preexisting departments. The briefing notes would still be revised or written as requested, but potentially lacking important contextual information that could make the effort more worthwhile.

Kevin talked about how he had made good use of such background context information, together with "having a good sense of the minister," "to influence government policy on the fly." He had been asked to draft a speech for the minister on a particular topic that came under his responsibility area. Kevin was aware of the hot topics in the media at that moment and could also guess at what impact the minister wanted to make in his speech. While the speech included all the expected statements, Kevin was able to "slip in" a statement about one of his pet topics. He was surprised but delighted that this statement made it to the final version, and he now had the minister making a public commitment to a project that would have taken significantly more work to put on the political agenda by other means.

Finding Out What People Do Now

Apart from general background context information, people often stated that they didn't feel they had a good enough sense of what everyone in the group was currently working on and hence what potential expertise they held, and what potential points of overlap and collaboration existed between their projects. An instance of this has been illustrated already in the case of Kate and Ann, despite the fact that they shared an office.

This problem of not knowing what others are working on was exacerbated by the newness of the group and the evolving definition of their role—several individuals stated they were only just starting to get a sense of what they were doing themselves. Knowing what other people were also working on was important because interests often overlapped without people realizing it, or often people had expertise, prior experience, or contacts in the area that they would have been willing to share had they realized the need.

Finding out what people do now tended to happen by finding out what people were doing within their own teams, finding out what people were doing across teams, and finding out via information brokers.

Finding Out within Teams   A branch initiative that helped people better understand what others were doing was the breaking of S&P into three teams, each with their own team leader and responsibility for a particular area. Most people commented that the smaller groups proved to be a useful way of containing the problem of needing to know what others were doing in that they only had to keep up with a few people in more detail.

The real effectiveness of the groups varied, however. One of the most effective groups had a relatively high degree of interdependence and cohesion among the members' projects. The team also had the good fortune to be sent to a conference where they were able to spend three days getting to know one another better, and getting to hear and discuss the same content information. There was unanimous agreement that this was invaluable.

The team leader was also a good communicator, quick to come into people's offices to discuss issues and responsive to people's dropping into his office. He initiated a team planning meeting at the beginning of each week where everyone reported on what they had achieved the previous week and discussed plans for the coming week.

Carmel, the administrative assistant for the group, commented that these meetings helped her learn about their work and prioritize her time.

She often found herself in the position where two people would both come to her with urgent requests and she found it hard to know what to do first. Now seniority did not confer an automatic right of priority, and all the team had a better appreciation of how their work fitted in with others'.

Finding Out across Teams   Knowing what people in other teams were doing was still a problem. While there was some general indication by virtue of group membership, this knowledge often lacked important detail around which expertise-sharing could happen.

The value of whole-branch meetings for facilitating engagement in the details of work and cross-team sharing depended on the type of meeting. The whole branch did meet weekly, but mostly for reporting activities or dealing with administrative matters. As stated by the director, these were important forums for generating a certain level of cohesion and for getting agreement around shared values, for example, that it is a "good thing" to keep circulated documents moving around in trays.

At one very different branch meeting, however, Mary presented preliminary ideas on her project, a significant one for the branch, and asked for feedback. What followed was a lively discussion around the issues, bringing a broad range of views. This one meeting served multiple purposes: Everyone was informed about the state of Mary's work; Mary received input she needed to advance the work; and everyone generally had the opportunity to hear and learn from what others contributed. This was illustrated by the comment of one person after the meeting: "I was surprised by what some people said. I hadn't realized that Jenny was interested in X." This was despite the fact that he and Jenny had worked together for some months now.

By accident of history, office sharing by people from different groups also proved to be valuable[4] for facilitating interteam information flow, either through casual discussions, as in the case of Kate and Ann, or through overhearing conversations, phone calls, and so on.

Finding Out via Information Brokers   An unofficial but crucial role in facilitating information flows and networking of contacts was that of information broker. This is very similar to Nardi and O'Day's (1999) mediator role: "Mediators—people who build bridges across institutional boundaries and translate across disciplines—are a keystone species in information technologies." McDonald and Ackerman (1998) and Ehrlich and Cash (1999) similarly talk about "expertise concierges" and "intermediaries," respectively.

The team leaders played pivotal roles as information brokers both within their teams and in facilitating cross-group interaction. Because they met weekly with the director, they had a good sense of who was doing what. There were many instances in which a team leader identified that different people should talk together because they were dealing with overlapping concerns. The team leaders also played a pivotal role in facilitating network and contacts sharing, for example, by making conscious efforts to bring relevant team members along with them to interdepartmental meetings or meetings with industry groups.

A key person for all the teams, however, was Kevin: "Kevin knows everything," it was said frequently. Especially for the ad hoc, time-critical work, Kevin was the person they all went to for help to find out what they should do, whom they should talk to, what information currently existed, and where to find it.

Because of his eclectic mix of interests and experiences, Kevin was also the person who ended up doing most of the difficult "left field" briefing notes that came to the branch. This is effective for producing good briefing notes but not for giving others the opportunities to expand their skills. For this reason, the branch was in the process of changing to a more random allocation of briefing notes. Kevin then expressed concern that he would be asked to contribute his expertise but without any formal recognition of his role in the process. This concern is similarly reflected by Nardi and O'Day (1999): "Ironically, [the mediator's] contributions are often unofficial, unrecognized, and seemingly peripheral to the most obvious productive functions of the workplace."

Finding Out What People Are Like

The value in getting to know people better and building workable interpersonal relationships conducive to expertise sharing should not be underestimated. Having a good sense of others, their skills, status, personalities, current work load, and so on, makes for better targeted, more effective JIT information access, for instance, by knowing who can help right now, and the psychological cost of asking (Allen 1977). In a new community such as S&P, opportunities for building relationships need to be bootstrapped just as much as the content information base.

Casual corridor chats or serendipitous meetings at the printer or drinks together after work were commonly used opportunities for chatting to people, getting to know them better, and finding out what people were doing. More formally organized activities such as meetings also proved useful, as indicated by the comment about "not realizing Jenny was interested in X" and by other comments after Mary's self-introduction at a branch meeting.

An indication of the effects of not knowing people well, especially "in the small," involved Mary and Kevin, with whom she shared an office. Being a person of strongly held beliefs and a dry sarcastic sense of humor, Kevin had made a statement to the effect of "Never ask the stakeholders what they think—too much trouble!" which of course meant the opposite. It wasn't until a branch meeting discussion some days later that Mary realized she had totally misinterpreted the comment because she did not know him well enough to recognize it as a facetious remark about one of his "hobby horses."

This is not the sort of information that one would retrieve from a skills database or that would be told in introduction: "Hi, I'm Kevin, I have a dry wit and I'm passionate about community consultation!" It was only uncovered over time through opportunities to chat and observe. In Mary's eyes, knowing this information transformed Kevin from a detractor to an ally whose expertise could have a critical impact on the success of her project.

Finding Out—In Summary

Many different finding-out processes have been reviewed by which the members of S&P were able to discover and share expertise as part of building up a shared knowledge base in the group, especially with respect to context and contact information. This sharing of expertise in practice happened in the course of getting the work done, and largely via interactional processes. The next section discusses the nature of this expertise as embodied knowledge, the implications of embodied knowledge for expertise sharing, and how sharing embodied expertise can be better facilitated.

4.4   Expertise as Embodied Knowledge

The main contribution of this case study is to point to issues around bootstrapping expertise sharing in a new community. For S&P this bootstrapping had to take place concurrent with the doing of work. It is not surprising, then, that satisficing—doing something well enough to satisfactorily suffice—is an accepted underlying strategy. The concern of the director, however, was that they could always be doing "well enough" better.

The more visible and organizationally supported activities to improve their satisficing strategies were directed toward establishing the explicit codified (hard and soft) information—its discovery, retrieval, storage, access, and flow. Such content information, however necessary to the core work of S&P, is not sufficient in its own right.

In the previous section I discussed the types of information needed by the people in the group, and the processes by which this information was uncovered and shared, issues that were accentuated because of the relative youth of the group and the evolving definition of their role.

There is the basic information that people wanted to know about each other by way of background, such as where someone had previously worked, what their interests were as captured by keywords, and so on. I have called this information in the large. But it is only the tip of the iceberg. Much of the information that was exchanged in the study vignettes was more subtle and finer-grained, the information in the small. People also needed to know the how, why, where, and who in order to put the content—the what—to work when required. It was this knowledge of context and contact, as previously lived or as able to be gathered or inferred, that made the difference.

This finer-grained context and contact information arose from deeply embodied knowledge, that is, information that is uniquely and integrally embodied in the person's personality, creativity, intelligence, perceptions, experiences, and relationships. Embodied knowledge is the essence of expertise.[5]

The sharing of this information was not formally planned and discussed, as was the case with content information. Rather the members of S&P uncovered and shared much of this information relatively unselfconsciously as they went about their jobs via tacit JIC strategies triggered in the context of interpersonal relationships.

Implications of Expertise as Embodied Knowledge

What are the implications of embodied knowledge for expertise sharing?

First, embodied knowledge is *difficult to make explicit*. Because it is so much a part of who they are, people were often unaware of what they knew and consequently were unable to anticipate a priori that it could be useful to others to articulate it. That is why people often didn't know that they knew something. By the same token, it is also why they didn't know what they didn't know or that they needed to know something.

Even if such information could have been made explicit, it was unlikely to be recorded. In S&P sometimes the information was too politically sensitive. More frequently, it would be because a piece of information wouldn't seem important enough on its own merit to make explicit. If there were to be conscious efforts to make information explicit, which of the myriad things that people know, that are part of who they are, should be extracted?

Second, embodied knowledge often *needs triggering* in order to be shared, that is, contextual information is itself more likely to be shared in context. While it might have been difficult to anticipate a priori what expertise could be shared, it seemed to come naturally in the course of a conversation, in the telling of stories, and in response to hearing or seeing a connected theme and choosing to contribute or divulge related information.

Third, embodied knowledge is *deeply embedded*, gaining value synergistically as it is increasingly interconnected with other knowledge. In being communicated, any single piece of contextual information often had limited value in its own right. It was only when it was taken up by another and embedded and interconnected with their own embodied knowledge that it gained value, for example, by being able to infer new knowledge. Further, by virtue of being uniquely embodied and embedded, the same piece of information could be taken up and put to work in different ways by different people and useful at different times.

Fourth, as a consequence of being deeply embodied and embedded, expertise knowledge is *continually evolving* and changing by virtue of ongoing doing, living, experiencing, and being.

Further, as a group becomes more established and builds its own history, much of the context and contact information that is being uncovered now will become taken for granted in the group (in the way that the bootstrapping program is when using a computer). In this way, embodied knowledge can take on a *group embodiment* by virtue of a lived shared history, culture, and relationships.

Facilitating Better Expertise Sharing
In parallel with the explicit efforts for bootstrapping content information, this case study points to ways in which expertise sharing from embodied knowledge could also be facilitated to better promote the bootstrapping of context and contact information.

For S&P suggestions for facilitating expertise sharing had to take account of a number of constraining factors. The members of S&P were extremely busy doing their jobs and would need to perceive significant benefit before committing any extra time and effort to making information available to others, if that information could even be made explicit. The branch had little autonomy over its own technology, relying instead on a centralized IT department outside of its control. The staff members occupied temporary offices that they were not allowed to alter. They had to conform to ministerial requirements, for instance, for depersonalized and decontextualized documents in the official archives.

The existing career structures and reward systems in a public service environment encouraged some but discouraged others to share expertise. For example, the visible success of the team leaders was predicated on the success of each person on their team; hence it was to their own advantage to be effective information brokers and to share contacts and networks. Kevin's career path, on the other hand, depended on his being able to differentiate himself as having good knowledge and contacts. It was against his best interests to share this information, even though he was "the person who knew everything."

Any efforts to promote better expertise sharing in the group need to take account of these constraints and aim for maximum benefit for minimal effort. Further, given these constraints, and the embodied nature of expertise and the ways in which it is shared, "whole of environment" approaches are needed that are not solely reliant on technological solutions. Instead they should try to create and exploit synergies between technological, organizational, social, and spatial factors.

At the second workshop we discussed a number of proposals to facilitate better ways of finding out information and laying the foundations for expertise sharing in practice. These proposals included the following:

• *Promote finding out in the large*   by making existing online personal information available in a shared directory.

Examples could include curricula vitae, meeting schedules, contact lists, keyword lists, and to-do lists. This is predicated on continued use of the content-based search engine to enable easy searching over the online documents. A tool such as Yenta (Foner 1997) that creates and shares personal profiles based on text content analysis could also be useful for providing "in the large" pointers to potential sources of expertise. For these information sources to be made use of, parallel efforts would be needed to evolve the culture to encourage people to look in the shared drive for information. It is not clear whether people would make this effort because they underutilize the information that is currently available to them, preferring instead to ask someone or to work with what they already know. More traditionally, information can also be made available by posting relevant paper copies to notice boards, where they can be accessed by others or noted serendipitously in passing.

• *Promote finding out in the small*   by increasing opportunities for effective interaction and relationship building, and engendering a culture where it is good to talk.

More casual or organized social events are good in this regard; inclusion of people from beyond the branch at different times would help expand contact networks. Online tools such as Tickertape (Fitzpatrick, Mansfield et al. 1999), BABBLE (Bradner, Kellogg, and Erickson 1999), or ICQ can enable more opportunistic chat and JIT questions than does e-mail. Erickson and Kellogg (2002) and Fitzpatrick, Kaplan et al. (2002) give illustrations of how such tools enable expertise sharing.

Revised meeting styles (or providing for a mix of meeting styles) that promote discussion of motivation and content, not just administrative process, can facilitate focused sharing of expertise around issues. Creating gathering spaces, such as a notice board in the corridor with changing content or a coffee/reading area (remembering that this group does not have its own tea room space), can enhance opportunities for serendipitous information exchange and relationship building.

• *Promote finding out what people do* by increasing the visibility of work. Making schedules and to-do lists shareable are steps in this regard. These could be augmented by event notification mechanisms that push the relevant information to people who register an interest (Segall and Arnold 1997). Keeping a parallel local store of documentation, such as briefing notes that include annotations such as author name and other background information, would also be useful in promoting the notes' role as historical artifacts (McDonald and Ackerman 1998).

• *Promote sharing and collaboration* as valued activities by addressing career advancement criteria and finding ways to make the sharing of expertise more visible and accountable. This addresses concerns similar to those raised by Orlikowski (1993)—that success of technology in fostering collaboration depends on appropriately aligned organizational culture and structures.

These proposals were aimed at facilitating emergent expertise sharing in practice in the following ways: increasing people's JIC store by implicit absorption so that they would know more than they realized; making JIT access better targeted because people would have a better idea of the who, where, why; increasing the contextualization of content information by providing opportunities for the richer embedding and augmenting of existing information; enhancing peer networks; and thus promoting more optimal satisficing processes within S&P.

Is Expertise "Sharing" Only for Small Communities?
As stated earlier, the S&P branch is interesting because it operates in a large, complex, politically charged environment where a constantly evolving network of external relationships is critical to achieving its policy outcomes. As such, S&P shares many of the informational needs of a large community but has the cost-benefit constraints of a small

community; technological approaches to expertise management have to be carefully considered because there is limited scope for making such investments for the small numbers of people involved.

Being a small group, however, is also to their advantage. If we accept that expertise is largely about embodied knowledge, and access to expertise happens mostly in the context of interpersonal relationships and localized interactions, then S&P is an ideal size for fostering better interactionally based processes in order to foster better expertise sharing.

What does this mean for larger communities then? Technical solutions are more often the first approaches to expertise management in larger groups, and understandably so. There are significant cost-benefit advantages to deploying technology-based solutions that enable access to large databases of information or large numbers of people via some communications medium such as e-mail. It is also unrealistic to consider the notion of interpersonal relationships with a large number of people who may not even be geographically accessible.

What this study suggests, however, is that the more interactionally based sharing of expertise might still have a place in larger-scale communities via intermediaries or brokers across subgroups. While S&P is a small group, it is also part of a much larger group: the state government and the other bodies it interacts with, such as community agencies and other government agencies. Even though the staff had access to many resources such as directories, the most effective strategy for the members of S&P to engage with other groups was to rely on a known contact that could be their own or borrowed from a colleague. Access to expertise and sharing of expertise, even at this larger group level, happened via interpersonal relationships between individual members of subgroups. Whether political ally or local champion or someone who owed a favor, this contact person became an intermediary to a much larger group of expertise.

4.5 Conclusion

Because expertise is deeply embodied knowledge, strategies directed to supporting expertise sharing, even in large-scale communities, cannot discount the interactional human-to-human processes through which this expertise is triggered and shared in a local setting or across settings. This socially situated nature of expertise sharing is becoming well accepted.

While expertise sharing will be ongoing throughout the life of a community by virtue of being dynamically embodied, this case study highlights some of the core information that needs to be exchanged in order to bootstrap this as an ongoing process especially in smaller-scale groups, information from which working relationships are built to form the foundations for further sharing.

But will the bootstrapping of expertise sharing become a focus of planned activity for future new groups? Experiences more generally in CSCW literature (e.g., Bowers, Button, and Sharrock 1995; Suchman 1987; Wastell and White 1993) suggest that it will be a difficult case to argue, and herein lies a cautionary note. Expertise sharing has much in common with other work that has been described as "invisible work" (Star 1991). Invisible work is often socially situated, involving communication and interaction-based activities. In describing their own work, people consistently leave out these activities because they do not regard them as part of the "real work" (Forsythe and Buchanan 1992; Forsythe 1993).

This tendency to render social and communicative work invisible has significant implications for the future support of expertise sharing. Because it is embodied, because it is mostly triggered in interactional contexts, expertise sharing can similarly be ignored or deleted, and its importance down-played.

The potential to reduce knowledge and expertise to codified information stored in a database is understandably seductive, just as workflow diagrams are seductive for rendering ordered accounts of work that is in reality messy, situated, contingent, and continually evolving. But they only tell part of the story. Invisible work will be needed from all of us who accept the implications of embodied expertise to keep the reality of expertise sharing on the knowledge management agenda.

Acknowledgments

This work was undertaken while the author was working at the Distributed Systems Technology Centre, The University of Queensland,

Australia. I wish to thank the members of the S&P branch for their co-operation and openness during the course of the study; also Simon Kaplan and Tim Mansfield, who were involved in the first workshop. The work reported here was funded in part by the Co-operative Research Centre Program through the Department of Industry, Science, and Resources of the Commonwealth Government of Australia.

Notes

1. I borrow the term *bootstrapping* from its more technical use—to boot (or bootstrap) a computer is to start a computer by first loading the operating system and other basic software. For expertise sharing in groups, I use the term *bootstrapping* in the sense of the group's building its own initial shared knowledge base as the foundation for ongoing expertise sharing when it is needed.

2. Coined by Herbert Simon (1960), in the sense of sufficiently satisfying rather than optimal strategies.

3. Australian Government Information Locator Service.

4. This is a statement of what happened, not a preferred position. I acknowledge that there are trade-offs between people from different teams sharing an office versus people from the same team sharing an office.

5. This is a position also taken by McDonald and Ackerman (1998): "The term expertise assumes the embodiment of knowledge and skills within individuals."

References

Allen, T. J. 1977. *Managing the Flow of Technology*. Cambridge, Mass.: MIT Press.

Bowers, J., G. Button, and W. Sharrock. 1995. Workflow from Within and Without: Technology and Cooperative Work on the Print Industry Shopfloor. In *Proceedings of the European Conference on Computer-Supported Cooperative Work (ECSCW '95)*, 51–66.

Bradner, E., W. A. Kellogg, and T. Erickson. 1999. The Adoption and Use of "Babble": A Field Study of Chat in the Workplace. In *Proceedings of the European Conference on Computer-Supported Cooperative Work (ECSCW '99)*, 139–158.

Ehrlich, K., and D. Cash. 1999. The Invisible World of Intermediaries: A Cautionary Tale. *Computer-Supported Cooperative Work* 8: 147–167.

Erickson, T., and W. A. Kellogg. 2002. Social Translucence: An Approach to Designing Systems That Support Social Processes. Forthcoming in *ACM Transactions on Computer-Human Interaction*.

Fagrell, H., and F. Ljungberg. 1999. Exploring Support for Knowledge Management in Mobile Work. In *Proceedings of the European Conference on Computer-Supported Cooperative Work (ECSCW '99)*, 259–275.

Fitzpatrick, G. 1998. The Locales Framework: Understanding and Designing for Cooperative Work. Ph.D. diss., University of Queensland, Brisbane, Australia.

Fitzpatrick, G., S. Kaplan, T. Mansfield, D. Arnold, and B. Segall. 2002. Supporting Public Availability and Accessibility with Elvin: Experiences and Reflections. *Forthcoming in Computer Supported Cooperative Work*.

Fitzpatrick, G., T. Mansfield, S. Kaplan, D. Arnold, T. Phelps, and B. Segall. 1999. Augmenting the Workaday World with Elvin. In *Proceedings of the European Conference on Computer-Supported Cooperative Work (ECSCW '99)*, 431–451.

Foner, L. N. 1997. Yenta: A Multi-Agent, Referral-Based Matchmaking System. In *Proceedings of International Conference on Autonomous Agents (Agents '97)*, 301–307.

Forsythe, D. E. 1993. The Construction of Work in Artificial Intelligence. *Science, Technology, and Human Values* 18: 460–479.

Forsythe, D. E., and B. G. Buchanan. 1992. Nontechnical Problems in Knowledge Engineering: Implications for Project Management. *Expert Systems with Applications* 5: 203–212.

Glaser, B., and A. Strauss. 1967. *The Discovery of Grounded Theory*. Chicago: Aldine.

McDonald, D. W., and M. S. Ackerman. 1998. Just Talk to Me: A Field Study of Expertise Location. In *Proceedings of the ACM Conference on Computer-Supported Cooperative Work (CSCW '98)*, 315–324.

Nardi, B. A., and V. O'Day. 1999. *Information Ecologies: Using Technology with Heart*. Cambridge, Mass.: MIT Press.

Orlikowski, W. 1993. Learning from NOTES: Organizational Issues in Groupware Implementation. *The Information Society* 9: 237–250.

Orr, J. E. 1990. Sharing Knowledge, Celebrating Identity: War Stories and Community Memory in a Service Culture. In *Collective Remembering: Memory in Society*, ed. D. Middleton and D. Edwards, 169–189. Newbury Park, Calif.: Sage.

Segall, B., and D. Arnold. 1997. Elvin Has Left the Building: A Publish/Subscribe Notification Service with Quenching. In *Proceedings of Queensland AUUG Summer Technical Conference*, Brisbane, Australia.

Simon, H. 1960. *The New Science of Management Decision*. New York: Harper and Row.

Star, S. L. 1991. The Sociology of the Invisible. In *Social Organization and Social Processes: Essays in Honor of Anselm Strauss*, ed. D. Maines, 265–283. New York: Aldine.

Suchman, L. A. 1987. *Plans and Situated Actions: The Problem of Human-Machine Communication*. New York: Cambridge University Press.

Wastell, D. G., and P. White. 1993. Using Process Technology to Support Cooperative Work: Prospects and Design Issues. In *CSCW in Practice: An Introduction and Case Studies*, ed. D. Diaper and C. Sanger, 105–126. New York: Springer-Verlag.

5

Sharing Expertise: Challenges for Technical Support

Volkmar Pipek, Joachim Hinrichs, and Volker Wulf

Knowledge is an important resource in the economy these days. It is typically distributed among different actors and embodied in various artifacts (Saloman 1993; Hutchins 1995; Ackerman and Halverson 1998). So, on the level of national economies as well as on the level of individual organizations, it is important to find innovative ways to stimulate learning by sharing knowledge among people. There are mainly two, often intertwined, ways of sharing knowledge. In the direct way, human actors of different kinds of expertise can communicate and help each other to construct new knowledge. In the second, mediated way, the actors with a higher level of expertise can create artifacts that may initiate and facilitate knowledge construction processes of others.

People in need of learning usually face the problem of either finding the appropriate material or the right expert. For tackling these problems, networked computer applications can play an important role. They can support the finding of and communication with an expert as well as allow the creation of artifacts that represent and give access to information with the aim of stimulating learning.

Within the field of computer-supported cooperative work (CSCW), learning processes in organizations have been studied both empirically and with regard to the design of information systems (Lees 1997; Stahl and Herrmann 1999; Bierens de Haan et al. 1999; Fagrell and Ljungberg 1999). Of these design-oriented approaches, the Answer Garden (Ackerman 1994; 1998; Ackerman and Malone 1990; Ackerman and McDonald 1996) is an early example that tries to bridge the gap between the sharing of learning material and the search for experts.

In this chapter we challenge certain assumptions on which computer support in knowledge and expertise sharing is typically based. We look at two companies that represent opposite ends of the organizational spectrum and show how their work practices prevent the assembly and sharing of knowledge that is key to the company. Our first case study looks at a traditional industrial firm whose physical infrastructure has been maintained for a century. The division of labor involved in plant maintenance within this firm ensures that a comprehensive database of maintenance documentation would be opposed to the individual interests of most of the involved employees. A second case study looks at a progressive network of high-powered consultants, collaborating virtually. There, a key knowledge domain involves the distribution of expertise so that the right people can be connected with potential projects. However, here too the widespread documentation of such expertise as well as the open sharing of knowledge artifacts that these experts develop would be opposed to the interests of most members of the network, particularly the leaders. Personal control over artifacts like training materials and over knowledgeable ties to potential consulting partners is considered essential in this business, even within a network explicitly designed for sharing.

Computer support for work, whether in industrial or service domains, is generally conceptualized as a technical problem of collecting all the relevant information in an electronic repository and then making it available for systematic searching and browsing. However, our case studies indicate that such an approach is based on a number of implicit assumptions that are often not valid within the social practices that exist in real workplaces:

• Much critical knowledge is never made explicit in materials that can be computerized, e.g., plant facilities are often changed without changing the corresponding blueprints so that only the workers who were involved can recall the changes.

• Data may exist in electronic form but be inaccessible for practical purposes because it was catalogued according to a system that has no relation to potential needs for that information.

· Knowledge of various kinds and local work practices have subtle social roles within the fabric of a company, not just the straightforward purposes that are explicitly acknowledged.

· People are often only willing to share information based on interpersonal relationships, and with some guarantee that they will retain some ownership of that knowledge, if only in principle.

Such interactions between social and technical considerations present important challenges to the design of computer support for cooperative work. We discuss these after first presenting our two case studies: a steel mill, and a network of trainers and consultants.

5.1   Expertise Sharing in Maintenance Engineering

We investigated knowledge and expertise sharing in the maintenance engineering of a major German steel mill in the Ruhr area. The investigations took place in the context of the OrgTech project (Organizational and Technical Development in the Context of the Introduction of a Telecooperation System in Small and Medium-Sized Engineering Companies) (Wulf et al. 1999). The project aimed to support the cooperative work processes within and between two engineering firms and the steel mill as one of their customers. The two engineering firms take on subcontractual work for the steel mill, such as the construction and documentation of steel furnace components. A construction department inside the steel mill coordinates the planning, construction, and documentation processes, and manages the contacts with external offices at the steel mill. We gave special attention to a specific problem: finding out about the actual state of a certain part of the plant. Because of the complexity of the plant and its long history of over one hundred years, this was a difficult problem. It required extensive access to documents and drawings as well as to people.

Research Methodology

The OrgTech project follows an interventionist research approach: the Integrated Organization and Technology Development (OTD) framework (Wulf and Rohde 1995). The OTD process is characterized by a parallel development of workplace and organizational and technical systems, the management of (existing) conflicts by discursive and negotiative means, and the immediate participation of the organization members affected. Within this change process the question of how to support the sharing of knowledge among the different experts involved in the maintenance of the steel mill became a focus of concern. The results presented here come from a variety of different sources:

• *Analysis of the work situation.*   By means of numerous semistructured interviews, workplace observations, and further questioning about special problem areas, the field of application was examined in a comprehensive and detailed way.

• *Analysis of the documents available.*   By looking at the given documents, especially the drawings, system descriptions, and literature about the topic, the relevant artifacts were investigated.

• *System evaluation.*   On the basis of task-oriented examinations like usability tests and software-ergonomic reviews, the given systems were examined according to the criteria of ergonomic design, especially with regard to task adequacy.

• *Project workshops.*   During various workshops with the application partners, organizational and technological interventions were discussed to improve the maintenance engineering processes.

Field of Application

The maintenance engineering department in the steel mill deals with repairing and improving the plant. It is a distributed process in which different organizational units of the steel mill and the external engineering offices are involved. Figure 5.1 gives a schematic overview of the maintenance engineering process.

In general, the starting point for a maintenance order is the plant operator, who controls the production equipment and machinery in a plant and supervises the steel production. When maintenance is necessary, the maintenance department of the plant operator asks the company-internal construction department for further processing. Depending on the type of order and the measures required, the transaction is handled internally or passed on to external engineering offices. An external order is pre-

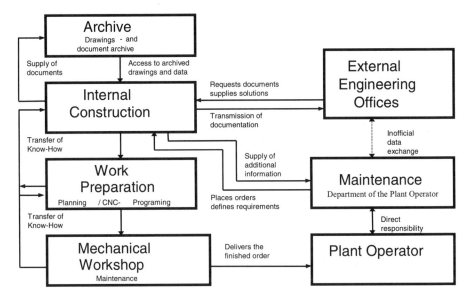

Figure 5.1
Diagram of order processing.

pared and surveyed by the responsible contact person in the internal construction department. For this reason, the necessary drawings and documents are compiled and passed on to the engineering office for further processing. Usually, the order specifications contain errors and need further clarification right from the beginning. So, discussions and extensive reordering of drawings often become necessary. These must be expressed in a comprehensive way and returned to the construction department of the steel mill. Once again drawings and documents must be found, coordination work done, and contacts with other departments initiated. This process of reordering requires a high level of work and expenditure of time for all participants.

After the external offices finish the construction planning, the internal construction department has to check it, place the new construction plans into the archive, and initiate the production process of the spare parts required. Finally, the spare parts are assembled into the plant. While this is the general process scheme of maintenance engineering, various sorts of informal communication and self-organized variations of the process can be found, and they add to the complexity of the problems.

In the following we investigate in detail the problem of knowledge and expertise sharing of one specific aspect of the process of maintenance engineering. In this case, the problem to be solved is to find out the actual state of those parts of a plant that are relevant for a design problem. For more than one hundred years the different plants of the steel mill have been continually modified, destroyed, and replaced with other plants. The knowledge about this process is distributed among different actors in the plant and several archives containing drawings of the plant, which are stored in various media. The central drawing archive contains (Hinrichs 2000)

• about 300,000 technical drawings,

• about 2,500 DIN A4 files with technical descriptions, part lists, statics information, and calculations,

• about 500 DIN A3 files with plans of electronic and hydraulic devices.

A large portion of these documents is filed in conventional paper form and saved on microfilm. The electronic drawing data consist of scanned drawings, which are saved in raster format (TIF) and CAD data (DWG). The electronically archived document stock contains

• about 5,000 CAD drawings,

• about 20,000 raster format drawings and 30,000 scanned drawings on microfilm files,

• about 90,000 documents describing the plant, maintenance processes, and drawings.

In order to handle the large number of drawings and documents, in 1995 an electronic archiving system was implemented to archive and provide the technical documentation. This system allows finding drawings by numbers or keywords. Drawings are identified by numbers, which are specified by the filing clerk. For classification reasons these drawing numbers can be allocated to so-called basic numbers. These basic numbers refer to plants and components existing within the company. They were created for the purposes of the accounting and controlling departments of the steel mill.

The electronic documentation is stored on a data jukebox, which is equipped with magneto-optical disks. Descriptions of the documents are stored on an Oracle database and may be retrieved via the archiving system (called ADOS) programmed in Microsoft Access. At present, conventional and electronic archiving methods are used in parallel because conversion from conventional to electronic archive would take too much time. However, continual conversion of all relevant data is the goal.

Finding out about the actual state of a certain plant in the steel mill is a central problem in maintenance engineering. In our work with the plant operators, we investigated how this problem could be tackled.

Central Repository: The Problem of Completeness
The information stored in the central archive is incomplete, for several reasons. First, there are information losses due to the physical properties of the storage media. Over one hundred years, paper documents have turned out to be transitory. So, a large number of drawings are of bad quality or have to be reconstructed in order to provide the required information.

Second, drawings are stored on different media: paper, microfilms, and electronic storage devices. The drawings contained in electronic storage represent only a subset of all existing drawings. If an information seeker does not find the relevant information in the electronic archive, he has to proceed with the paper and microfilm archives.

Third, the central archive does not contain all information on the actual state of the steel mill. Certain modifications of the state of the plant cannot be found in the drawings at all. During the handling of accidents, plants may have been modified instantly without prior planning and without the creation of drawings. At the end of a budget year, certain works are carried out instantly to use the still available funds of the associated departments. These modifications typically are not documented in drawings either, although they are "known" by the staff members involved. Finally, even well-planned and documented modifications of the plant may have been made in a slightly different form than shown on the drawings. This can result from inadequate plans that had to be adapted to the given environment. Sometimes the final modifications completely disregarded the given plans.

We discussed different approaches to increase the completeness of the central repository. We suggested improving the completeness of the electronic repository by scanning all drawings into the database. Such an approach would require much time and effort. Because of high costs and the fact that the long-term future of the steel mill is unclear, this option was not viable from the point of view of the management. A more complete documentation of the actual modifications would be possible, but this would require additional labor and the commitment of the different plant operators and construction firms. In certain cases, the lacking documentation reflects missing permissions to do what has been done. In these cases the plant operators and the construction firms are very unlikely to document modifications even if the resources for that should be provided.

Central Repository: The Problem of Categorization Schemes

While the electronic drawing store suffers already from being incomplete, additional problems are due to missing or problematic patterns of categorization. This makes the retrieval of drawings difficult. The main way to retrieve documents in the database is via their basic number. This classification scheme divides the steel mill into cost centers. It was set up by the accounting department to allocate costs. However, it is not very intuitive for engineers because its concepts do not follow a technical perspective. The drawing numbers, another index, are rather arbitrarily assigned. They partly represent a temporal order for the creation of drawings. However, this order can be pretty distorted because the drawing numbers are allocated to engineering offices when getting an order. Typically the engineers do not use up all the drawing numbers allocated to them for a certain order. In these cases, they reuse the already allocated numbers for future orders.

In addition to these categorization schemes being problematic, they are not applied consistently. Approximately 20 percent of the drawings stored in the central repository do not have any classification; a direct assignment to plants or their location is not stated. Their categorization can only be processed with in-depth system knowledge. Approximately

25 percent of the drawings are not categorized according to the correct basic or drawing number, or are stored without keywords. Such drawings can only be found by the description used in the ADOS system or by search via indirect paths (e.g., asking knowledgeable colleagues). These problems are mainly due to the fact that the transition from paper to electronic archive was carried out by an external service provider. For cost reasons, it was students who scanned and categorized the drawings. They lacked motivation and understanding for the complex categorization task.

Finally, the existing archive system does not offer extended search functions. Drawing numbers and basic numbers (both of which are not self-explanatory) are the main attributes to search for. Moreover, the interface to specify queries is not very intuitive (Hinrichs 2000). So, retrieving documents in the archive database requires quite a bit of experience.

We discussed different approaches to improve the retrieval of drawings. First, one could (re)classify the documents in the electronic drawing archive. Such an approach would require a large amount of time of experts familiar with the particularities of the steel mill. Because of high costs and the fact that the long-term future of the steel mill is unclear, this option was not viable from the point of view of the management. Considerations to save costs had already led to the engagement of an external service provider who did not categorize the drawings appropriately. Another approach could make more attributes of the drawings available for retrieval. For instance, one could apply pattern recognition or optical character recognition (OCR) algorithms on the scanned drawings to make the legend on each drawing available for keyword search. These extensions of the database scheme would require considerable labor input because they could not be implemented automatically. Again, because of high costs involved, this was not acceptable to management.

Central Repository: The Problem of Competing Decentralized Stores
Because of the problems with the central archive, a couple of local archives are maintained by the different actors involved in plant maintenance. Drawings are distributed among individuals in the maintenance

departments of the local plants. These individuals often have built up their private paper-based archive of those aspects of the plant they are responsible for. These archives contain up to five hundred sketches and often occupy several shelves in the offices. Often drawings within these private archives are annotated to document changes in the state of the plant. So these private archives are often more accurate than the central one.

Seen from a central perspective, these paper artifacts are not easily retrievable because they are distributed among various locations of the steel mill. Their owners, who know best how to find the relevant documents, regard them as private property.

So the knowledge about the actual state of the steel mill is distributed between different drawing archives and human actors. The workers of the local maintenance departments of the mill typically best preserve the knowledge about the actual state of their plant.

Updating Repositories: The Problem of Inappropriate Division of Labor
The maintenance of the drawing archive and especially of the database is the responsibility of the archive group. This group is like the maintenance construction department of the central support division of the steel mill. Between this central division and the different plant operating divisions, there is an ongoing rivalry for power and resources. The competition for resources has led to a strict division of labor between these organizational units. Only the archive group has the right to modify the central database. The construction department has to send drawings to the archive group after their job is finished. Afterwards they have only read access to the central database. They cannot modify missing or incorrect classifications or update documents. The workers in the local maintenance departments, who have built up their own local archives based on paper drawings, do not use the electronic drawing database very much.

The restrictive access rights make it difficult to gain the benefits of a shared repository. Only the central archive group is allowed to reclassify or update the drawings. In case of a more flexible division of labor and corresponding access rights, the maintenance department of the plant operators and the internal maintenance engineers could both update the database. When discussing this issue with the workers of the different plants, they were not very eager to improve a database they had neither been responsible for nor used much. The given division of labor and the existing conflicts between the organizational units prevented activities that would have improved the quality of the central database.

5.2   Expertise Sharing in a Network of Trainers and Consultants

In the previous section we looked at an industrial setting where the documentation of the knowledge on the steel mill's state can draw on a long professional tradition of formalizations and categorizations. However, we saw problems in sharing knowledge because parts of the data requested and even parts of the shared repository are not digitized and are distributed among different actors. Now we look at a setting from the service industry. SIGMA is a network organization of trainers and consultants. This field of application seems to be especially well suited for technical tools to support expertise sharing. The network is equipped with a technically well-working infrastructure. However, our study shows a number of problems in supporting the sharing of expertise technically.

Research Methodology
The primary goal of this study was to get to know the pattern and problems of knowledge sharing in SIGMA. In our research, SIGMA serves as a prototype of a network organization in which autonomous entities form alliances to market complex services. For this study, we conducted twelve narrative interviews with network members of different kinds (hierarchical level, level of expertise, length of network affiliation). The interviews took between 45 and 120 minutes. Most of them were recorded on tape. The interviews consisted of a free narrative part ("Please describe your work within SIGMA") and more focused questions on knowledge acquisition and knowledge transfer.

The narrative interviews were complemented by unstructured interviews with key role players (managing director, project manager). Additionally, several regional and administrative meetings as well as several annual meetings of the associates were observed. The interviews were part of a long-term research effort within this network organization (Rittenbruch, Kahler, and Cremers 1998).

We analyzed the material along three lines of interest: media used for information transfer and storage, problems seen regarding the organization of information flows within SIGMA, and how new members are successfully introduced to the network standards.

Field of Application

SIGMA is a training and consulting company distributed all over Germany. It is a network, consisting of more than two hundred entrepreneurs and freelancers, that has the legal form of a limited liability company. Apart from a few employees whose work contributes to the infrastructure of the network (e.g., administration and secretaries), the network does not employ members on the basis of traditional labor contracts. Instead, the individual members are freelancers with a variety of payment modes. The network offers several financial, infrastructure-related, or administrative services to the associates, who in turn contribute 10 percent of their turnover to fund the network services. Another 20–25 percent of the turnover has to be given to the "client owner" who established a project for SIGMA. All the members can offer their skills under the umbrella of the brand "SIGMA."

About two-thirds of SIGMA's turnover (about $10 million) comes from training. The services cover a wide range of issues from teaching basic computer skills via specialized programming classes to leadership courses. SIGMA's clients range from the labor exchange administration to the upper management of Fortune 500 companies. Further business activities are in the fields of consulting and software development (especially groupware configuration and computer-based training applications).

Besides the four managing directors, SIGMA has no organizational hierarchy and understands itself as a self-organizing network. While there are project managers and regular project members, a network member's position may vary over time. The high level of self-organization and the flat formal hierarchy allows SIGMA to act flexibly within dynamically changing markets.

However, despite this value of free self-organization, SIGMA developed some structures within the network. Informal hierarchies are omnipresent and strongly structure the organization and the activities of its members. The four founders of SIGMA are managing directors and represent SIGMA in more general cases. They still have the client ownership of some of the biggest and most important customers of SIGMA. Because of their experience and their familiarity with the network and its members, they are also very important network nodes. Their work and status are usually confirmed by the annual meeting of all associates.

Around forty network members are managers, a status that normally can be gained when the turnover of the projects acquired reaches a certain level. The manager forum meets four times a year to discuss conflicts as well as more strategic issues within SIGMA.

Other structures developed along geographical and market-related aspects. In some cities members of SIGMA share office space (usually for representation and meetings, not as a workplace; only one office has a secretary), and members with similar business interests united in business field groups to coordinate their activities. Sometimes the latter developed into limited liability companies, which now also are nodes in the network. The structure of SIGMA is highly volatile.

Figure 5.2 illustrates this by trying to give a snapshot of the approximate structure of SIGMA. Germany has been divided into four business areas with one managing director acting as network node for each of them ("west" has been further divided). Members can build regional nodes/offices, and members group in business fields to coordinate services, which can also be one important customer or key account. On the right are the institutional members of SIGMA, which are in most cases limited liability companies themselves. The bottom represents the network itself, the members as well as the different service divisions. Some of them also exist in the legal form of a limited liability company. The picture is neither complete nor consistent (e.g., Is the regional node in Dresden more associated with the "west2" area then with the "east" area, where it geographically belongs? The managing director of the "south" area decided to establish a limited liability company for this area. There is also a business filed that insists on not belonging to an area.), but this heterogeneity is possible and tolerated as long as it does not affect the sales.

From the very beginning, SIGMA tried to maintain the "spirit of SIGMA" as a cultural background for its members and as a guiding line

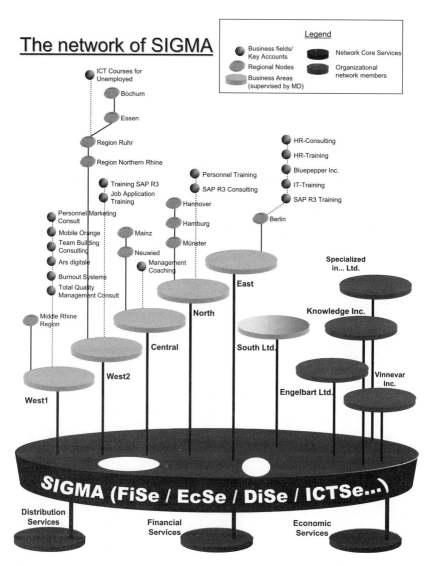

Figure 5.2
The network of SIGMA.

for newcomers. SIGMA regards itself as a business community open to everyone who complies with the business model and the standards and conventions of the network. The community acts as a network of cooperative entities, which are self-organizing according to market demand and concrete projects.

SIGMA always relied on a common technological infrastructure. In 1995 an intranet based on a bulletin board system (with a messaging system and file-sharing areas) was introduced, and in 2000 it was replaced by a Lotus Notes–based intranet. Only the intranet server service is included in the infrastructure service of the network; all other infrastructure costs are borne by the network members themselves, as are any costs related to training, software, and communication (phone/ Internet). Almost every member of SIGMA possesses a personal computer (most of them with Internet access) and a mobile phone.

Working with Sigma means providing one's own workplace, typically a home office with telephone, personal computer, Internet access, a variety of software programs, fax, and other technical equipment. The overwhelming majority of communication activities happen via (mobile) phones. E-mail (via SIGMA's intranet infrastructure or an external Internet service provider) is in most cases only used for document transfer. Fax and mail communications usually occur only if legally relevant documents are transmitted. Paper and folders still are the most frequently used storage media, although personal computers and laptops are very common.

Electronic Repositories: The Problem of Organizational Awareness
When asked whether they would give away (e.g., teaching) material they had produced, almost all interviewees said they would give it to anybody in the network. But when asked for details, several expectations were expressed concerning that knowledge transfer:

• "I want to know what the material is used for." This is meant to informally control whether the material is used in the right context and whether some kind of financial compensation can be expected.

• "I want to have feedback on whether the material served its purpose." This helps the creator of the material to improve the quality of the material or how it can be modified for different contexts.

• "If the material is being modified, I want the modified material to flow back." This turns the information transfer into an act of collaboration.

• "I want a trustworthy handling of my material." This especially addresses whether and how material should be forwarded to third parties. Material forwarding is socially controlled. In general, forwarding is tolerated if the author is notified.

Sometimes material is reused by its content, and sometimes only by its structure (e.g., training concepts). Some material becomes a "public good" within SIGMA after some time because it serves as a good example; some material is forwarded with the explicit condition that it not be used or cited literally (usually training concepts and material developed for a client who now has the copyright). And, of course, all this is a matter of trust; personal recommendations and informal guarantees help to navigate through SIGMA for finding material and easily getting it. For all the material, it is important that it circulate only within SIGMA. These are not generally known conventions. They are not explicit, and all of them were described by different network members.

For most interviewees, it was a conscious decision to be the "portal" of their own information and material. The request for material (usually via mobile phone; material is then provided by e-mail) was considered a valuable act of communication and an opportunity to get news on new projects, rumors, and initiatives within SIGMA. The person who is asked for material gains knowledge on new projects (or new clients) or new persons in SIGMA, since these are the typical situations in which material is being requested (to prepare for a new training). The requesting person can get information on how to approach the new project, where to find additional information or material in SIGMA, and who can be valuable to talk at regarding further projects.

However, one interviewee thought a repository would be a good idea. This interviewee worked very close to a managing director (and important network node). So requests for material as an opportunity to communicate were not that important to him. Other interviewees clarified that the request for material not only serves this purpose but also becomes a valuable opportunity to inform on current events in SIGMA. Additionally, an electronic repository approach would not allow for an access control pattern to teaching material as flexible as the "social control" described here.

Expertise Profiles: The Problem of Updating

Those network members who frequently acquire new projects have problems in determining what competencies are actually in the network (important for not accidentally denying client requests that could be satisfied by means of the network) and who in the network has which competencies (important for team composition). Approaches to tackle these problems technically failed.

A profile database (in form of an Excel sheet) was issued and reissued several times. Even when a collaborative effort to produce a current version of the personal profiles succeeded (e.g., on manager meetings or the annual meeting of associates), it soon became outdated because almost nobody maintained his or her profile.

Different problems occurred in an approach to tackle the problem by means of internal home pages. Network members used those for "social communication" (anecdotes, cartoons, links to "fun pages"), although management had planned to make them available to clients as well. Like the profiles, the home pages were not maintained very well and soon became outdated.

The basic conflict, in our view, is that the business model of SIGMA leaves all the infrastructure work to the individual, who is at the same time forced to be as productive as possible. Maintaining one's profile is not directly productive. Profiles are usually updated when sending a proposal to clients, but the update is always very content-specific to meet the information requirements of the client. Together with the high degree of autonomy of SIGMA members, this leads to a low priority for the task of updating the expertise profiles.

Expertise Profiles: Hiding One's Own Corona

Another problem with explicating expertise profiles is the existence of "colleague ownership." Senior network members with their own client ownerships have a corona of network members with whom they conduct their projects. Many of them were introduced to SIGMA by the senior network member. They consider this corona to be their own human resources (see the next section, on mentorship). Though the senior member can claim a kind of informal ownership of his or her corona, any member of SIGMA can of course autonomously decide whom he or she is working with. However, senior members with bigger clients rely on their local infrastructure. Consequently, senior network members tend to hide the competencies of their corona unless there is an explicit agreement on team-building priorities.

Mentorship: Participating in a Legitimate Peripheral Way

SIGMA has a mentorship model to familiarize new members with the network. Typically, a mentor introduces a newcomer to the formal rules and conventions of the network and introduces her to other members. Although the SIGMA mentorship model is an official model of the mentor's responsibility for the new member, its realization often has similarities with the process of legitimate peripheral participation, as described by Lave and Wenger (1991). New members work in minor roles in projects together with experienced members. They acquire the knowledge and the skills necessary for working in SIGMA during their time on these projects. Other anchors of introduction are the intranet and, in most cases, different regional meetings, which usually have a formal part and an informal part. A brochure for new members was produced in spring 2001, but it is not yet clear to what degree it increases the transparency of SIGMA for new members. It seems unclear how technical tools could replace or even augment the mentorship model, which allows for legitimate peripheral participation in real projects.

5.3   Discussion

There are some commonalities between the two case studies. Expertise shared among individuals plays a crucial role, access to shared repositories is important but insufficient for knowledge construction, and organizational micropolitics can hamper knowledge and expertise sharing. However, the particularities of the two fields of application lead to differences in the process of expertise sharing.

Shared Repositories

For centuries, engineering has developed conventions on how to represent complex technical facts. In their professional education engineers learn how to document their knowledge in a mutually understandable way. Building on these professional conventions, it is much easier for an organization to build up repositories of shared documents. By contrast, in the domain of consultancy there are fewer common formalisms and conventions for documentation. These differences influence the ability of the actors to document and access knowledge in shared artifacts.

We also see differences between repositories in organizations that have a long history relevant to current problem solving, and repositories in organizations, like SIGMA, that have a short history. Many problems of central repositories can best be observed in organizations that have a long history of document-related knowledge sharing. We assume that young organizations may face similar problems at a later stage of their history.

Another difference comes from the infrastructure support the organization offers for the production and maintenance of shared repositories. While the steel mill created a specific organizational group to document the knowledge on the state of the plants, in SIGMA there is no central organizational unit to support the documentation and sharing of know-how. In the case of SIGMA this is due to the rather low percentage each associate pays for the common infrastructure. Because there is no central repository, sharing of knowledge-related artifacts has to be decentralized between peers. The artifacts are still contextualized by the reference to their producer, and by the interaction that precedes their exchange. In the steel mill, organizational procedures are established that regulate how to modify and access the information in the central repository. However, use of the central repository leads to a decontextualization of the knowledge-related artifacts. The effect of this phenomenon is compounded by the problematic categorization schemes. However, two facts ease the recontextualization of the drawings in the steel mill. The professional conventions ease the reinterpretation of the drawings. Moreover, there is a stable mapping between specific plants of the mill, the drawings documenting the current state, and the maintenance workers who have additional and up-to-date information.

With regard to the problems of classifying and retrieving artifacts in a large shared repository, the steel mill gives an account of the complexity of the task. The long history of changing classification schemes and the different professional perspectives of engineers and accountants add to the complexity of the problem. The graphical nature of the drawings and the different electronic formats make search algorithms difficult to specify.

Clearly, the steel mill is a case where not all the relevant material is accurately digitized. But both cases indicate that this is not just a legacy issue but also a matter of work and communication practice within the organizations. Although in both cases evidence existed that improvements were possible (an external engineering office maintains a *complete* archive of its projects done for the steel mill; one business group in SIGMA has built up a repository with restricted access), it also became clear that because of certain aspects of the organizational culture (spontaneity of building in the steel mill; side benefit of communication among the autonomous actors of SIGMA), there would never be a complete and accurate repository of all drawings or all teaching material.

Expertise Locator Software

The location of expertise is very different in the two cases. In case of the steel mill, we look at rather stable tasks and clearly defined responsibilities. Locating the appropriate expert to find out about the current state of a plant does not pose a big problem to the members of the organization. Exceptions from this rule are newly employed staff and apprentices who do not yet know the structure of the organization well. So the algorithms and the data necessary to locate experts in the steel mill are rather straightforward. The efforts to maintain the profiles are rather limited; one has to follow mainly job changes within the steel mill. Moreover, such a traditional organization is equipped with means to maintain these data. So technical support for expertise location is rather easy to build, but its utility is rather limited as well.

By contrast, SIGMA has a great need for expertise location support. SIGMA's tasks change dynamically; so does the relevant expertise of its members. The mutual understanding of each other's expertise is much lower in SIGMA than it is in the mid-size software development organization described by Ackerman and colleagues (see chapter 7). We assume this is mainly due to the decentralized nature of the network organization and its bigger size.

(Re)defining the scheme to describe the expertise profiles is as big a task as updating the individual members' profiles. It is difficult to create a common understanding of the scheme as well as of the individual attributes. Moreover, the ongoing modifications require efforts that are not directly productive. Additionally, any explicit model would show not only competence but also lack of competence, especially when it would be coupled with a locator system. Both types of information are sensitive, and not everybody within SIGMA would like it to be published within the whole network.

Shipman and Marshall (1999) describe other examples where users do not consider the necessary standardization for ontology building helpful. Rice et al. (2000) showed in their study of a virtual organizations how even simple keyword usage in a collaborative tool of a virtual team degenerated over time.

At present, expertise localization is in most cases a task of social navigation. Asking colleagues is a desired access control mechanism working in both directions. For the expertise seeker, it is important to get informed recommendations on where to look further, and for the experts, it is important to ensure that requests are not arbitrary but come through selective channels. Another benefit is that this system of expertise location inherently uses up-to-date information. While these mechanisms help contextualize requests for expertise, they do not satisfy the needs for efficiently building project teams. So, software support for expertise location is needed (see chapter 6). However, networked organizations pose high demands on expertise locators.

The Role of Micropolitics

The sharing of expertise is hindered in both fields of application by micropolitical considerations. Competition for human or financial resources reduces the flow of knowledge in both organizations. In the steel mill, this fact is manifested by the problematic state of the central repository and the nonintegrated local storage for drawings. In SIGMA, the phenomenon of "colleague ownership" reduces the organizational visibility of certain actors' expertise. This lack of visibility of expertise can be seen as a partial substitute for boundaries derived from formal organizational structures. The coexistence of competition and cooperation ("co-opetition"—Brandenburger and Nalebuff 1996) may also play an important role in explaining why members of SIGMA prefer to be the "portal" to their own sharable material: they can control the reciprocity of mutual favors much better than by placing all their material into a central repository.

While it is well known that micropolitical considerations hinder the flow of knowledge-related artifacts within an organization (Argyris and Schön 1996; Senge 1991), the study of SIGMA indicates that these considerations can also affect the visibility of expertise. The design of expertise locator systems must take this fact into consideration.

Creating Knowledge Work Support: Awareness of Implicit Assumptions
The descriptions we gave from our application fields also stress that designers should be cautious when applying an idea for supporting knowledge work to an application field. Often implicit assumptions of approaches to support knowledge work do not hold:

• Not all knowledge artifacts are digitized (e.g., drawings in the steel mill).

• Not all knowledge artifacts can be digitized (e.g., economic reasons in the steel mill).

• Not all digitized knowledge artifacts are public goods in an organization (e.g., teaching material in SIGMA).

• Knowledge artifacts that are supposed to represent the current state of a real object or situation (e.g., drawings of plants in the steel mill) do not always do that.

• Work practice and documentation processes (as a process of knowledge artifact creation) are not always coordinated appropriately (e.g., the documentation process in the steel mill does not cover the spontaneous building processes).

• Individually created "private" knowledge artifacts are—though extremely helpful sometimes—not always known and easily accessible (e.g., "private" artifacts in both fields: local construction drawings in the steel mill, and teaching material in SIGMA).

• Not all digitized knowledge artifacts can be stored in a public repository even when they are somehow accessible for everyone in an organization (e.g., cultural obstacles in SIGMA).

• Accessing knowledge artifacts via social navigation is not always replaceable by an automatic query-based approach because the social aspect of social navigation may be considered too valuable to lose (e.g., communication culture in SIGMA).

• Explicating expertise is not always appreciated in an organization (e.g., in SIGMA, for organizational and cultural reasons).

We believe that the creation of computer support for knowledge work and expertise sharing is a task of organization and work design, as we know from research in computer-supported cooperative work. The discussion of the case studies helps us to find and validate design requirements for tools supporting expertise sharing.

5.4   Conclusion

In this chapter we discussed the results of two studies of knowledge artifacts and their handling in very different fields of application. On the one hand, we had a steel mill with its conservative organizational structures, where we looked at the handling of construction drawings for plant maintenance processes. On the other hand, we had SIGMA, a networked community of trainers and consultants, and an extremely decentralized type of virtual organization, where we observed expertise sharing regarding teaching materials. Our studies addressed repository-based approaches to support knowledge work and "locating expertise" approaches, and documented the obstacles found.

Repositories are not always complete. Economic and cultural reasons may even hinder their creation and maintenance. Examples were the cost of digitization in the steel mill, the history of drawing categorization in the steel mill, and the desire for social access control in SIGMA.

While the importance of "private" knowledge artifacts and archives at SIGMA was no surprise, the importance of the local "private" archives of plant operators and other staff members for the maintenance process in the steel mill was interesting to note. Knowledge workers tend to create their own "memory system," and this can be a valuable (in our case even indispensable) complement to any organizational memory.

This also shows a case where social navigation is superior to formal query-oriented navigation to find expertise. Social navigation also explores those private archives, and it adds context to a request for expertise. This can be advantageous for the knowledge seeker, since he may get help in applying the knowledge to the problem context, and it can be advantageous for the knowledge provider, since she gets information on the context the knowledge is being applied in, and on how the knowledge develops in different contexts. Additionally, the act of communication itself can be considered valuable, especially in distributed organizational contexts, since it helps maintain a picture of the current state of the organization.

For "locating expertise" approaches, we learned that expertise explication or its maintenance is not always welcomed. Individual and organizational aspects of work organization complicated approaches to expertise explication at SIGMA.

The results of our studies gave valuable insight on how tightly the functioning of an organization's knowledge infrastructure and its work culture (practice, tradition, and communication) are connected. It teaches us as designers that the design of software tools to support knowledge-intensive organizations is always also a process of designing knowledge work.

Acknowledgments

We would like to thank our colleagues from the OrgTech, the InkoNetz, and the OlViO projects for supporting our research efforts, which led to the results presented here. Special thanks goes to Helge Kahler, Eva Meyer, Markus Rittenbruch, Meik Poschen, Bettina Toerpel, Stephan Thimm, and Markus Won for their work within SIGMA. Gerry Stahl gave us valuable feedback on an earlier versions of this chapter.

This research was supported by the European Commission, the German Ministry of Research and Education, and the State of North Rhine–

Westphalia. We are very grateful to the employees of the two fields of application for their active participation in the three research projects.

References

Ackerman, M. S. 1994. Augmenting the Organizational Memory: A Field Study of Answer Garden. In *Proceedings of the ACM Conference on Computer-Supported Cooperative Work (CSCW '94)*, 243–252.

————. 1998. Augmenting Organizational Memory: A Field Study of Answer Garden. *ACM Transactions on Information Systems* 16 (3): 203–224.

Ackerman, M. S., and C. Halverson. 1998. Considering an Organization's Memory. In *Proceedings of the ACM Conference on Computer-Supported Cooperative Work (CSCW '98)*, 39–48.

Ackerman, M. S., and T. W. Malone. 1990. Answer Garden: A Tool for Growing Organizational Memory. In *Proceedings of the ACM Conference on Office Information Systems*, 31–39.

Ackerman, M. S., and D. W. McDonald. 1996. Answer Garden 2: Merging Organizational Memory with Collaborative Help. In *Proceedings of the ACM Conference on Computer-Supported Cooperative Work (CSCW '96)*, 97–105.

Argyris, C., and D. A. Schön. 1996. *Organizational Learning II*. Reading, Mass.: Addison-Wesley.

Bierens de Haan, C., G. Chabré, F. Lapique, G. Regev, and A. Wegmann. 1999. Oxymoron—A Non-Distance Knowledge-Sharing Tool for Social Science Students and Researchers. In *Proceedings of the International Conference on Supporting Group Work (GROUP '99)*, 219–228.

Brandenburger, A. M., and B. J. Nalebuff. 1996. *Co-opetition*. New York: Doubleday.

Fagrell, H., and F. Ljungberg. 1999. Exploring Support for Knowledge Management in Mobile Work. In *Proceedings of the European Conference on Computer-Supported Cooperative Work (ECSCW '99)*, 259–275.

Hinrichs, J. 2000. Telecooperation in Engineering Offices: The Problem of Archiving. In *Proceedings of the Conference on Designing Cooperative Systems (COOP '2000)*, 259–274 . Amsterdam: IOS Press.

Hutchins, E. 1995. *Cognition in the Wild*. Cambridge, Mass.: MIT Press.

Lave, J., and E. Wenger. 1991. *Situated Learning: Legitimate Peripheral Participation*. New York: Cambridge University Press.

Lees, D. Y. 1997. An Analysis of Knowledge Work and Its Implications for the Design of Information Artifacts. Ph.D. diss., Faculty of Computer Studies and Mathematics, University of the West of England, Bristol, U.K.

Rice, R., A. Majchrazak, N. King, S. Ba, and A. Malhotra. 2000. Computer-Mediated Interorganizational Knowledge Sharing: Insights from a Virtual Team

Innovating Using a Collaborative Tool. In *Knowledge Management and Virtual Organizations*, ed. Y. Malhotra, 84–100. Hershey, Pa.: Idea Group.

Rittenbruch, M., H. Kahler, and A. B. Cremers. 1998. Supporting Cooperation in a Virtual Organization. In *Proceedings of the International Conference on Information Systems (ICIS '98)*, 30–38.

Saloman, G., ed. 1993. *Distributed Cognition: Psychological and Educational Considerations*. New York: Cambridge University Press.

Senge, P. 1991. *The Fifth Discipline*. New York: Doubleday.

Shipman, F. M., and C. C. Marshall. 1999. Formality Considered Harmful: Experiences, Emerging Themes, and Directions on the Use of Formal Representations in Interactive Systems. *Computer Supported Cooperative Work* 8: 333–352.

Stahl, G., and T. Herrmann. 1999. Intertwining Perspectives and Negotiation. In *Proceedings of the International Conference on Supporting Group Work (GROUP '99)*, 316–325.

Wulf, V., M. Krings, O. Stiemerling, G. Iacucci, M. Maidhof, R. Peters, P. Fuchs-Fronhofen, B. Nett, and J. Hinrichs. 1999. Improving Interorganizational Processes with Integrated Organization and Technology Development. *Journal of Universal Computer Science* 5 (6): 339–365.

Wulf, V., and M. Rohde. 1995. Towards an Integrated Organization and Technology Development. In *Proceedings of the Symposium on Designing Interactive Systems (DIS '95)*, 55–64.

6

Locating Expertise: Design Issues for an Expertise Locator System

Kate Ehrlich

In most business settings, individuals have access to a wealth of information, sufficient to address most business problems. Yet, there are many occasions when the best answer comes from finding the right person rather than the right information. Because finding a trusted adviser is so important, most individuals build up a set of personal connections that they can call upon at short notice for momentary or extended joint work (e.g., Nardi, Whittaker, and Schwarz 2000). In companies where people stay in the same job for many years, employees have time to develop these connections. But in the current climate of mergers and acquisitions, downsizing and outsourcing, many people don't remain in the same job for long. When an employee leaves a company, he or she may stay connected with the same people, but those connections are no longer effective for internal proprietary work.

Although personal connections are likely to remain the preferred method of finding trusted people, there is a need to use technology to scale from personal networks to the larger community of people within the organization. Technology used to find people, variously called a people finder, an expertise locator, corporate yellow pages, or a skills inventory, provides a way to represent people so that any individual can find the right person—and be found themselves—based on what the person knows, not just whom they know. An expertise locator stores information about a person in a profile, which can be browsed or searched to find a person, based on skills, experience, or background as well as by name.

This chapter describes a design analysis for an expertise locator, based on several years of research and development. The chapter departs from some other approaches by proposing that an expertise locator be regarded as a communication vehicle—a way to initiate a conversation with the right person—rather than merely as a search tool. The conversation itself takes place in a social and organization setting, which governs such conventions as who can talk with whom and what information can be shared. As such, the design of the expertise locator must take into account social and organizational elements as well as technical ones as part of a sociotechnical system (e.g., Bikson and Eveland 1989). Before describing the design analysis, the chapter looks at the benefits of an expertise locator, as a tool for individuals to find people and as part of a knowledge management initiative.

6.1   Leveraging Knowledge in an Organization

Benefits for the Individual

In the hands of an individual, an expertise locator provides benefit beyond simply finding people. As part of the research that led to the design of the expertise locator described in this chapter, a small market research study was done with people who had developed and deployed some version of an expertise locator in their organization.[1]

Some people liked to use the system to increase their awareness of activity in the company. "When I get an e-mail with an attached distribution list, I often will use [our expertise locator] to find out what group they're in," says Ward Clark of Open Market, an Internet commerce company. "I do a little data mining on my own. When [our expertise locator] had pictures, one of my favorite uses was to remind myself of what people looked like. I can remember names and I can remember faces, but this kept the association."

Other people found that the system helped them tailor their own responses to people they had yet to meet. "When I get correspondence or e-mail from someone I don't know, I go [to the expertise locator] to see who they are before I respond," says Michael Telljohann of Procter & Gamble. "This way I have some perspective on where they're coming from. There's a big difference between what I say if they are new to the company and if they've been here for thirty years."

Expertise locators can link people who might never have an opportunity to meet face to face. "Procter & Gamble is North American–centric," explains Telljohann. "We've built a new technical center in China with several hundred people, two-thirds of whom are new Chinese hires. It is of extraordinary value for them to plug into the mainstream of our research community. At the same time, people who go to China from our North American operations lose the daily personal contact with colleagues they knew, and they don't stay aware of new hires in the organization." For these researchers, too, Telljohann argues, P&G's system makes a significant difference in their ability to contact people with the expertise they need.

Benefits for the Organization: Using Conversation to Retrieve Tacit Knowledge

An expertise locator, by representing the experience and skills of the employees, is a way to represent tacit knowledge. Many companies develop knowledge management programs to codify and store explicit knowledge so that it can be easily distributed to and accessed by people who need it in the organization. But new knowledge gets generated faster than it can be codified. And a lot of information does not readily lend itself to codification. For these reasons, knowledge management also depends on getting access to tacit knowledge, that which is not amenable or ready to be codified.

An expertise locator benefits companies in two ways. The first is that by mapping the tacit knowledge it helps individuals develop better awareness of "who knows what," as illustrated in the previous examples. But just knowing the location of knowledge is not enough. The real value for the organization comes when the knowledge gets applied to a problem (e.g., Davenport and Prusak 1998). Having "more" knowledge, by having, say, a large number of experts, is less valuable than having fewer experts who have learned to apply what they know. Faraj and Sproull (2000) studied the performance of software development teams as a function of the "quantity" of expertise in the group and the degree to which the expertise was available to be applied to problems. They found that teams were more effective when members knew who were the experts, knew when it was necessary to call on an expert to solve problems, and had access to the experts. Teams who could make effective use of the expertise performed better than teams who had "more" expertise but were less effective at finding and accessing it. Thus, an expertise locator has to do more than just represent tacit knowledge; it needs to represent the knowledge in a way that facilitates retrieval and application.

One way to retrieve tacit knowledge is through conversations. If search tools are the way to retrieve explicit knowledge, then conversation is the mechanism for retrieving tacit knowledge. A study by Ehrlich and Cash (1994) emphasized the benefits of a conversation-based model of retrieval. They studied the dialogue between customers and support analysts working for a software company. While some customers found it less work to call the support desk than to look up the documentation to find the answer, the analysis of the dialogue revealed that additional, more subtle, factors were also operating. It was apparent that customers, even those who were highly technical, would find the right document but fail to interpret the content to understand the connection to their problem. It was also clear that customers did not always interpret their problem correctly. A good support analyst would detect when the problem as presented didn't make sense and help the customer reinterpret the symptoms. The value of the conversation was in reframing the problem as well as in finding a good solution. Similar advantages come from conversations with people who act as intermediaries between information sources and the people who seek solutions (Sasson and Sharon 2000; Ehrlich and Cash 1999; Allen 1977; Gladwell 1999).

Extending Social Networks: Strong and Weak Ties

The second benefit that accrues for a company is that an expertise locator helps to build social capital by strengthening the ties between people who know each other and facilitating conversations between people who don't know each other. Social capital depends on a rich social network of connections. According to Putnam (2000, 19), "Social capital refers to connections among individuals—social networks and the norms of reciprocity and trustworthiness that arise from them."

Cohen and Prusak (2001) argue that increased social capital benefits an organization through a higher level of commitment and cooperation amongst employees, which in turn benefits the organization through increased talent retention and more intelligent responses to customer needs.

Expertise locators don't build these personal networks, but they can help augment them by fostering connections with people outside an individual's personal network but inside the same corporation. Social scientists talk of the strength of weak ties that bind us to people we don't know personally but who may reside within the same social unit such as an organization. Granovetter (1973) talks of the strength of weak ties for bridging from the people we know to those we don't know within the same company. Weak ties are beneficial because they provide access to a larger pool of resources and expertise. While strong ties can provide more social support—emotional aids, goods and services, companionship and a sense of belonging, weak ties connect people who are more socially dissimilar and who belong to other social worlds (Constant, Sproull, and Kiesler 1997).

A study by Constant, Sproull, and Kiesler (1997) of employees in a technical company, illustrates how weak ties benefit the organization. It is common in large distributed organizations for people to solicit advice and help from the community at large by using the company e-mail system to broadcast requests for information. These e-mail messages often begin with "who knows ..." and continue with a request for the name of a person, document, or information. These requests are frequently answered even though the person sending in the response may not be personally acquainted with the person asking the question. As Constant and colleagues found, broadcasting these messages to a broad yet unknown audience can bring back good answers because the sender is getting the benefit of drawing from a pool of people who are senior, knowledgeable, and often more advantageously placed in the organization. Although asking relative strangers for help can be risky for the information seeker, who has no way of verifying the information provider's reliability, experience, or even willingness to provide a thoughtful answer, Constant et al. reported that the seekers found the answers they got back to be useful and worth the time spent reviewing the responses. These kind of weak ties between people who belong to the same organization but don't know each other are beneficial because they provide information seekers with access to a large pool of skills and talent. But some degree of reciprocity is required to make these weak ties work. In the technical culture studied by Constant et al., there was a shared recognition that anyone solving a difficult problem needs to reach out to others for information and advice. In other organizational cultures, reciprocity might be part of a "gift exchange" in which a person helping someone today can legitimately ask that person a favor in the future.

An expertise locator, as defined in this chapter, is also an example of a system that relies on weak ties because the intended use is to connect people who don't know each other. If the system is appropriately designed, a seeker can expect to accrue the benefits of accessing the larger pool of expertise and talent in the organization. The key to the success of the expertise locator system lies in its design.

6.2   Requirements for the Design of an Expertise Locator

There are certain technical requirements for the design of an expertise locator. It must be easy for users to search or browse for people with particular skills, knowledge, or background, and to have confidence in the search results. The system needs to be fast and easy to use. And the system should scale to include the whole enterprise. These are not trivial issues, but they are reasonably well understood. What is less well understood is how to design and deploy a system that will deliver on the promise of connecting people who don't know each other. This section describes three key issues for that design.

Representation and Maintenance of Profile Data

At the heart of an expertise locator is the issue of how to represent what someone knows. Anyone using an expertise locator to find, say, "someone who understands titanium wing structures" whose expertise is needed to complete a design, needs to be confident that a person found using an expertise locator does indeed have the necessary credentials and credibility.

There are various ways to represent skills and knowledge (e.g., Stewart 1997). One approach is to develop or import a taxonomy to represent the different areas of knowledge. For instance, British Petroleum lists over fifteen hundred areas of expertise in its system (Lotus Institute 1999). However, it can be challenging to develop a taxonomy that applies broadly in an organization. Issues include determining what level of granularity is appropriate for each descriptor. For instance, a skills taxonomy could include high-level descriptors such as "knowledge management" or be more granular and include specialties within knowledge management like "expertise location." In addition to issues of granularity, the selection of descriptors in the taxonomy must be part of the common language of the organization. Because of these and other difficulties in developing useful, manageable taxonomies some organizations turn to outside consultants (e.g., Teltech) to help develop a taxonomy that fits with the culture and structure of the organization. Another approach is to develop a simple taxonomy that uses descriptors and structure that are broadly used and understood. In some organizations a person's title is a good indicator of their level of knowledge or expertise, although title is by no means a universal code of competence.

A related issue is whether to include ratings to indicate the degree of knowledge or level of expertise. Although this might be a worthy goal, in practice it is sufficiently onerous and unreliable to have questionable value. Davenport and Prusak (1998) report a conversation with an executive at Mobil who found that when the oil company's employees were asked to rate their own skill levels, "experts were modest about their capabilities and neophytes overstated theirs." Getting others, such as supervisors, to do the ratings, say, as part of the annual performance review can be cumbersome and also not very accurate.

Whatever decision is made about how to represent skills and knowledge, the data must be easy to collect and keep up-to-date. Perhaps the biggest challenge for the acceptance of an expertise locator system is compliance—being able to maintain the accuracy and reliability of the data over time. Individuals are reluctant to do the work to keep their profiles up-to-date, especially because it appears to be a lot of work for little or no perceptible reward. Some companies develop incentive programs or processes to encourage people to keep their profiles current. Another approach is to automate the data collection and update so that there is less work for the individual. In practice most successful expertise locators require a combination of the two (Lotus Institute 1999).

Responsiveness

When an individual finds and contacts a person after using an expertise locator, there are social and pragmatic issues that govern whether the person will respond, especially if it is a "cold call." In some types of organizations, such as consulting, it is common to seek information from other people because all the knowledge needed to serve a client is unlikely to be contained within the project team. The commonality fosters a type of reciprocity in which an individual who answers a question one day is just as likely to be the questioner at a later time. In these types of organizations there are few barriers to making or receiving calls from strangers. But in other types of organization calls from strangers might have to follow more formal protocols. For instance, junior members of an organization might be discouraged from making unsolicited calls to senior members.

The notion of responsiveness also relates to a person's accessibility. Several people have pointed to the importance of accessibility for an expertise locator system. McDonald and Ackerman (1998; 2000) developed an expertise location system for a small software company that builds, sells, and supports medical and dental practice management software. The system separates out three components relevant to finding people: identification of the knowledge that is generated automatically from contextually derived heuristics; selection from this list based on filtering for people most likely to respond; and interaction management, which lets people control their accessibility to others. An initial user study revealed that, all other things being equal, employees preferred to connect with people who are physically or organizationally close. The three factors together help the system be sensitive to the differences between, say, an administrative assistant who might score high on identification of knowledge based on frequent exposure to key documents and an engineer who is well known as a practitioner of the particular knowledge.

Organizational Culture

An expertise locator is an example of the kind of weak tie mentioned earlier. As in the earlier example of the "who knows ..." kind of question, whether the person responds to an unsolicited call on their time and knowledge will depend on whether the organizational culture is one that supports information sharing. But it is more complicated than that: the organization and the expert must be willing to give up time, often for no immediate reward or benefit.

In organizations where there are strict separations between departments, there may be resistance to letting an expert spend time helping someone in another department, especially if the expert is already in high demand in his or her own department and there is no visible benefit for helping. A department must be willing to let its employees give time to another part of the organization for the system to work.

Each employee must also be willing to be part of the system. Some people, especially those with valuable skills or knowledge, already feel overwhelmed with demands on their time. They view a system like an expertise locator as representing an uncontrolled increase in those demands and so may be reluctant to participate. In terms of the overall acceptance of the system it is important to make sure enough senior people participate early. Their participation endorses the system and "seeds" it with valuable profiles.

6.3   Expertise Locator Design

This chapter describes the design of an expertise locator system, paying particular attention to the three factors just outlined: representation and maintenance of data; responsiveness; and organizational culture.[2] The intent was to address the organizational issues through a carefully managed rollout of the system, which is briefly described later in this chapter. The data representation issues, especially those related to establishing credentials, and some of the issues of responsiveness are addressed through the technology design, which is the focus of this section.

First, I describe the results of a small focus group that was run with twelve representatives from the intended end-user population. In the study the participants were given several questions to be answered individually or as a group to better understand their social practices for establishing credentials and engaging in conversations with strangers. The focus group was part of a larger initiative that included gathering requirements of several large multinational companies, internal system design, and development—all in the context of other knowledge management projects.

User Study

Credentials   I asked the focus group to tell us how they would respond in the following situation: "You are at an internal conference and find yourself in the coffee line next to someone you don't know. What are the top five questions you would ask to ascertain who the person is, his level of knowledge, his credibility, and what kind of conversation you want to continue to have?"

The answers I got back indicated what was important:

• *Establishing personal and political context*—which part of the company the person is from; relationships with other parts of the company; size, funding, and status of current project

• *Establishing personal credentials*—what the person does, where he has been, what he has worked on; is he the person doing the work (how people talk indicates level of knowledge, familiarity and competence on a particular topic)

• *Establishing reputation*—what online forums does the person participate in (people who participate a lot or in many different forums are perceived as more knowledgeable and more involved)

• *Learning about the person*—what they do rather than what they know

• *Creating connections for the future*—described by one respondent as "parking" information for potential future connections, but can also be thought of as a way of being more aware of other people in the organization

Responsiveness   I also wanted to learn about the social norms of responsiveness, a willingness to call a stranger or respond to a call from a stranger. To get at this norm, I asked each person individually to answer the following question: "Under what circumstances would you be willing to call someone you didn't already know?" I also asked, "What factors would make you more likely to engage in conversation when someone you don't know contacts you?"

The answers implied that people in this group were clearly used to getting "cold calls" from people seeking information, and they were generally very willing to respond. The kind of things that made it easier to respond were the following:

• *Reciprocity.* It is important to know the other person's areas of expertise and interests before making the call, and also when receiving a call. This information establishes the relevance and validity of the request. People were also more likely to respond to requests that caught their interest or to requests where there was a common interest (see also work on communities of interest, e.g., Wenger 1998).

• *Relevance.* These people didn't mind responding to calls for help provided that they were confident that they were the right and perhaps the only person who could help. There was a strong sense of not wanting to waste their own time or the other person's time, and for the questioner to demonstrate the relevance of the question to the skills and interests of the person being asked.

• *Third-party introduction.* An introduction or reference from a known third party is the preferred method of getting or making a "cold call," but it is not required.

• *Urgency.* People were more likely to respond to urgent or important questions or to questions for which there was a strong business need.

• *Attitude.* The tone of someone's voice and the way the person introduces herself and the problem influence whether the question will be answered (see also Galegher, Sproull and Kiesler 1998).

The data from this user study illustrate some of the social norms that this group used to establish credentials and engage in conversation with strangers. The data emphasize context, reputation, and a person's history as important elements for establishing credentials. They also point to the need for the seeker to be aware of common interests or common experiences with the expert before engaging in conversation, and for the expert to have access to as much information about the seeker as the seeker does about the expert.

An expertise locator should facilitate conversations between people, known and unknown. This section highlighted some of the social factors that govern those conversations. These conclusions must be considered preliminary. But based on other fieldwork (e.g., Lotus Institute 1999; McDonald and Ackerman 1998) they appear to capture plausible and salient dimensions for design. Individual organizations and groups may differ in how they emphasize and interpret these dimensions, however.

The conversations themselves take place in "social space" outside the confines of the expertise locator itself. But the system can facilitate the conversation by representing key information that allows the seeker to determine credentials and responsiveness. This representation is addressed in the next section.

Design Analysis for an Expertise Locator

The heart of an expertise locator is the profile, which stores information about each person. To the extent that a profile is a way to find out about other people, it needs to represent the information a seeker would need to know about another person to establish their credentials, find common ground, and understand the pragmatics of the person's availability. A profile should represent the context and history of a person as well as what they know and how well they know it. In other words, the three key factors a seeker should be able to extract from a profile are a person's credentials, the likelihood of her responding to an unsolicited query, and accessibility. From this viewpoint, we can usefully think of a profile as being made up of five primary sources of information. First, expertise is embedded in an organizational context. For this reason it is important for a seeker to have information about where and how the expert resides in the organization, called *demographics*. Second, a person's credentials are established through a combination of *credibility*, observed *behavior*, and *reputation*. Finally, *accessibility* acknowledges the need to represent information about availability and preferred modes of communication as well as general access to the person. These labels are an explanatory convenience to describe the key elements of an expertise locator and would not appear in the profile.

This section describes how to operationalize each of the five categories in a way that lends itself to automatic generation and update of the content. It is assumed that any of the information could also be entered manually. For each category, I describe what information might be included, how and where that information might be collected, and issues associated with the content or collection method.

Demographics   Demographic information refers to the factual elements that define the person's relationship to the company and organization where they work. In addition to basic information about name, address, and phone numbers, this category might include information about office location, years with the company, the name of the organizational unit, the project, the name and contact information of a backup person (e.g., administrative assistant), and possibly the name of a manager or supervisor. This kind of information places a person in an organizational context.

Sources   Demographic information can be found in personnel or employee records. Some companies also maintain records of each employee's office location.

Issues   There may be limited access to data in personnel records for privacy and security reasons. However, the data to be used in the expertise locator are generally already shared and so may be available elsewhere if they cannot be retrieved from the primary source. The more troublesome issue in getting the data, however, is matching the entry in the expertise locator system with the entry in the employee record. Most systems require an exact rendition of a name before the information associated with that name can be retrieved. Thus "George Bush" may be different from "George W. Bush" or "George H. W. Bush." A bigger issue is the accuracy of the source data. A simple example is information about an employee's office location. When employees move offices frequently, the system recording the change may lag well behind the actual move. To the extent that an expertise locator pulls its data from other sources, it is only as accurate as those sources. This is a common issue for automated data collection, especially when the source data are informal and unstructured.

Credibility Credibility refers to the characteristics that help an information seeker determine what someone knows, how they know it, and how well they know it. The kind of information used to determine credibility is similar to what a person might put in a resume. The important elements include areas of knowledge, professional background, professional history inside and outside the company, and professional interests.

The information used to establish credibility varies from profession to profession. For instance, researchers establish credibility by reference to attended universities, published papers, talks and professional affiliations, and public recognition in the form of patents and awards. In consulting, credibility is established with respect to which clients the person has worked with, in what capacity, in what geography, and perhaps the length of the engagement. For lawyers it is different again. Each profession has its own set of credentials. These credentials would be identified as part of the process of customizing the expertise locator for the organization and the people who will be using it, which is described later in this chapter.

Sources Information about credibility comes from resumes, project listings, project descriptions, status reports, and internal and external proposals, patents and patent filings, awards and recognition.

Issues The electronic sources for projects, project descriptions, and status reports are often incomplete, unreliable, or inconsistent, which hampers automation efforts. As the organization becomes more aware of the need and importance of maintaining electronic records of project work, the quality of the information may improve. We know anecdotally that expertise locators fail when individuals don't keep their profiles up-to-date. Hence, the benefit of shifting the burden of updates to an automatic process is to alleviate that problem. But that process needs to be fed from other sources. If an organization uses incentives to encourage compliance, those incentives could be applied to ensuring that project information is kept current, which would serve the project as well as the expertise locator.

Behavior   Information from resumes and projects provides a formal validation of a person's credentials. But as I learned from the focus group, when we observe our colleagues' behavior online and offline, we also glean valuable insights into their professional and personal interests. We infer a level of interest or even expertise, for instance, when someone in a meeting asks a lot of in-depth questions on a particular topic. And we notice when someone posts a lot of documents or responses in online discussion groups. By associating the person doing the posting with the topic of discussion, we may infer that the person is interested or knowledgeable about that topic.

The more we know or think we know about someone else's interests, the more we are in a position to judge whether their interests overlap with our own. As indicated in the user study, someone contacted by a stranger might be more inclined to respond if the stranger indicates what interests they have in common.

Sources   There is active research on metrics that can be used to infer a person's areas of expertise and interest from their online behavior. For instance, the Discovery Server from Lotus keeps track of subject matter experts by analyzing and categorizing unstructured information from online discussions and documents. Tacit Systems performs statistical analysis on e-mail to extract keywords that can be inserted into a person's profile.

Issues   The main challenges are those of developing the right metrics to make legitimate inferences about people's interests or intent from their behavior. For instance, if someone responds to a lot of postings in an online discussion on knowledge management, is that necessarily an indicator of interest or expertise in the topic? The person posting the messages could be an administrator or a facilitator of the discussion rather than a subject matter expert. A high frequency of postings could also occur from a novice who is trying to acquire knowledge in the subject area. A detailed analysis of the content of the messages could, in principle, clarify these two interpretations, although in practice most analytic systems are not that sophisticated.

Reputation   Reputation provides an independent verification of a person's skills, interests, and credentials. Operationally, aspects of reputation can be computed from the frequency and context in which a person's name appears in a document. Someone else would have written the document. For instance, a person who is regarded as an expert in titanium wing structures might be frequently mentioned by name in internal memos or technical specifications written by that person's peers or supervisors.

Not all reputation is positive. Just because someone's name appears in a document, even if it appears frequently, does not automatically mean that the references are positive. For instance, a corporate executive might be mentioned by name in the business or technical press, but the article could be critical of the executive, the company, or the subject area. Only a very good content analyzer could tell the difference.

Reputation is inferred through metrics that record the frequency with which a person's name appears, where the name appears (e.g., in header information or in the body), the subject matter of the document, and the valence of the document (whether the document takes a positive or a negative slant on the subject). The metrics also need to verify that someone other than the expert has written the document.

Reputation can also be garnered through ratings by an information seeker of the value of the response from the expert. In practice, ratings are more valuable in systems, such as Abuzz, that route written questions to the best expert available rather than endeavoring to set up conversations between seeker and expert.

Sources   Reputation can be extracted from an analysis of internal documents or external news stories.

Issues   The main issue is the quality of the tools that generate the metrics and the content analysis. As in the case of inferring interests from online behavior, it is easy to generate wrong inferences if the metrics or tools are not well tuned. There are many reasons in addition to subject matter expertise why someone's name might appear frequently in a document. For instance, legal documents might include frequent mention of a clerk or other administrator. A person looking at the document would have no difficulty distinguishing between the real expert and someone who is not an expert but whose name appears often for other reasons. It is another matter to develop a program that can perform as flawlessly.

Accessibility   The fifth and final category of a profile is accessibility, which has three elements: practical, organizational, and functional.

Practical accessibility refers to a person's current availability and her preferred method of contact. Is the person in town or on vacation? Does the person prefer to be contacted by phone, mobile phone, e-mail, instant messenger, or fax? Is the person willing to accept unsolicited calls? People who already have many demands on their time might choose, for a period of time, to be unavailable to people outside their personal network but may still want to remain in the expertise locator system.

Organizational accessibility acknowledges any organizational barriers that might prevent or inhibit contacting a person whose profile is found. For instance, a high-level executive might have the desired expertise, but depending on the role and responsibility of the seeker, and the organizational culture, that executive might not be the most appropriate person to call upon.

Functional accessibility refers to the value of the conversation. Even if a person with the right knowledge and organizational equality can be found, the conversation might not be successful. For instance, even with the best of intentions, the person might not respond in a timely fashion. Or, the person's style of response doesn't fit the problem because she provides answers that are too long or too complex for the seeker to understand, or provides answers that are too short to be valuable. Some of these issues might be negotiated through conversation. Nevertheless, it can be useful to be aware of another person's communication style prior to initiating the conversation.

Sources   The primary source for information on accessibility is office location and contact information that has been annotated to indicate preferred mode and time of contact. Organizational accessibility can be inferred from information about a person's organizational role and title.

Expertise locators may include a photograph as part of the profile to help seekers associate names with faces, although there are privacy issues associated with distributing photographs.

Some aspects of accessibility are highly subjective and might not be amenable to codification. An alternative way for an individual seeking advice to get qualified information about another person is to do so through a third party, preferably one who is known to both the seeker and the expert. In that case, the seeker might use an expertise locator to narrow the search and then contact a reference of the person who is found to vouch for him. Making connections through other people is colloquially referred to as six degrees of separation (Gladwell 1999).

Issues   A major issue in establishing contact preferences is keeping the information up-to-date as people move around and as their preferences change.

Organizational Issues
The success of an expertise locator system depends on a mix of social, organizational, and technological factors. These factors are manipulated primarily through the design of the technology—the infrastructure, application and content, and the organizational design—the way the application is rolled out to the organization. As with other kinds of knowledge management technologies, there are practices associated with rolling out an expertise locator (e.g., Davenport and Prusak 1998).

An expertise locator might be rolled out to the organization in two phases. The goal of the first phase is to assess the organizational and technical readiness of the organization. The organization must be ready to invest time to ensure that its employees maintain their profiles either by verifying any information that is updated automatically or by manually editing the profile. The organization and individuals must be willing to spend time helping others.

The goal of the second phase is to customize the expertise locator to the organization so that it is aligned with the norms, terminology, and sources of information that prevail in the particular group where it is to be deployed. The content issues described earlier provide a design analysis for an expertise locator. The details of the data fields in the profile would need to be defined by each group to map to such things as the particular terms in common use and the elements that compose the credibility of each professional group. The tool would also need to reflect the norms about availability and accessibility. Many of these details would be specified through a structured deployment program, which might include the development of training materials and identification of a group of early adopters who could be co-opted to provide trial runs of the system as well as provide initial data and act as ambassadors for additional users. The deployment would also include a communication plan to inform stakeholders and others in the organization of progress and perhaps a key event at which the expertise locator could be announced. Good key events include internal conferences that bring a lot of people together in person. A conference is also a good time to take pictures of people that can be included in their profiles.

6.4   Discussion

An expertise locator provides a valuable tool for individuals to develop awareness of "who knows what" and to reach out to people across the organization. As a way of mapping tacit knowledge it complements many knowledge management programs, especially those that focus on codifying explicit or documented information. When an expertise locator is combined with other search mechanisms, it simplifies the process of finding people or documents related to a particular topic of query.

This chapter departs from other approaches by arguing that an expertise locator is a tool for initiating conversations, especially with people outside an immediate set of personal connections, rather than just a search tool. This approach brings into focus the social and organizational issues that are as intrinsic to the successful deployment of an expertise locator as the technical design. The social issues govern conventions around who talks with whom, when, where, and about what. Organizational issues include how much the organization is willing to share of people's time, what expertise means, how it is valued in the organization.

As a conversational tool, the user of an expertise locator has three primary goals: establish credentials of the person who is found, increase the likelihood that the person will respond to an unsolicited query, and establish the accessibility of the person. The main focus of this paper has been to translate these goals into a design analysis for thinking about how to populate profiles, which are the core of an expertise locator system. It was argued that the content reflects five sources of information about a person: demographics, credibility, behavior, reputation, and accessibility.

Many forms of expertise locator have been developed for internal use. Some succeed; many fail, especially when the information in the system is not kept current. This chapter also suggested ways in which u, ates could be automated. But that introduces a different set of issues. In particular, automating the process of collecting and maintaining the data in a profile, rather than relying on an individual to keep it up-to-date, depends on the existence of reliable, complete, available sources. Although companies keep a lot of information online, many of the sources, especially for unstructured data such as projects, are incomplete and inconsistent.

This chapter has only touched the surface of many of the issues involved in the development and deployment of an expertise locator and has asked more questions than it has answered. Nevertheless, by positioning an expertise locator as a conversational tool, it is hoped to provoke further inquiry and exploration into the role and representation of tacit knowledge in organizations.

Acknowledgments

Many people were involved in the research and development of the expertise locator, notably Barbara Kivowitz, Matthew Simpson, and Dan Gruen, my collaborators on the focus groups and deployment strategy. The ideas in this chapter were influenced by the exceptional thinking in the knowledge management research community at Lotus, including Lotus Institute under Chris Newell, Lotus Research under Irene Greif, and the IBM Institute of Knowledge Management. I also extend appreciation to all the people who provided their patience and support throughout the early stages of the pilot.

Notes

1. These stories were also reported in Lotus Institute (1999).

2. The expertise locator described here was designed for a distributed group of scientists and associated professionals. There was to be an initial pilot rollout to a group of about three hundred people. Unfortunately, because of unexpected personnel changes, the pilot was stopped just prior to deployment.

References

Abuzz. http://www.abuzz.com/.

Allen, T. J. 1977. *Managing the Flow of Technology.* Cambridge, Mass.: MIT Press.

Bikson, T. K., and J. D. Eveland. 1989. Technology Transfer as a Framework for Understanding Social Impacts of Computerization. In *Proceedings of the Third International Conference on Human-Computer Interaction,* 28–37.

Cohen, D., and L. Prusak. 2001. In *Good Company: How Social Capital Makes Organizations Work.* Boston: Harvard Business School Press.

Constant, D., L. Sproull, and S. Kiesler. 1997. The Kindness of Strangers: On the Usefulness of Electronic Weak Ties for Technical Advice. In *Culture of the Internet,* ed. S. Kiesler. Mahwah, N.J.: Erlbaum.

Davenport, T. H., and L. Prusak. 1998. *Working Knowledge: How Organizations Manage What They Know.* Boston: Harvard Business School Press.

Ehrlich, K., and D. Cash. 1994. Turning Information into Knowledge: Information Finding as a Collaborative Activity. In *Proceedings of Digital Libraries Conference.*

———. 1999. The Invisible World of Intermediaries: A Cautionary Tale. *Computer Supported Cooperative Work* 8: 147–167.

Faraj, S. A., and L. Sproull. 2000. Coordinating Expertise in Software Development Teams. *Management Science* 46: 1554–1568.

Galegher, J., L. Sproull, and S. Kiesler. 1998. Legitimacy, Authority and Community in Electronic Support Groups. Technical Report 98-12. Cambridge, Mass.: Lotus Development Corporation.

Gladwell, M. 1999. Six Degrees of Lois Weisberg. *New Yorker,* January 11, 52–63.

Granovetter, M. 1973. The Strength of Weak Ties. *American Journal of Sociology* 78 (May): 1360–1380.

Lotus Discovery Server. http://www.lotus.com/home.nsf/welcome/discoveryserver.

Lotus Institute. 1999. *Leveraging Expertise: People-Finder Systems.* Internal Report.

McDonald, D. W., and M. S. Ackerman. 1998. Just Talk to Me: A Field Study of Expertise Location. In *Proceedings of the ACM Conference on Computer-Supported Cooperative Work (CSCW '98)*, 315–324.

———. 2000. Expertise Recommender: A Flexible Recommendation System Architecture. In *Proceedings of the ACM Conference on Computer-Supported Cooperative Work (CSCW '2000)*: 231–240.

Nardi, B. A., S. Whittaker, and H. Schwarz. 2000. It's Not What You Know, It's Who You Know: Work in the Information Age. *First Monday* 5 (May 1).

Putnam, R. 2000. *Bowling Alone: The Collapse and Revival of American Community*. New York: Simon and Schuster.

Sasson, L., and J. S. Sharon. 2000. Knowledge Stewards: On the Trail of Tacit Knowledge. *Knowledge Directions* 2 (2): 22–31.

Stewart, T. A. 1997. Does Anyone Around Here Know . . . ? *Fortune*, September 29, 279–280.

Tacit Systems. http://www.tacit.com/.

Teltech KMS. http://www.teltechkms.com/.

Wenger, E. 1998. *Communities of Practice: Learning, Meaning, and Identity*. New York: Cambridge University Press.

7
Who's There? The Knowledge-Mapping Approximation Project

Mark S. Ackerman, James S. Boster, Wayne G. Lutters, and
David W. McDonald

Within knowledge-intensive organizations, one of the most fundamental
tasks is expertise location, or locating others with relevant expertise for a
problem at hand within an organization.

· Sarah, a new employee, wants to find someone who can help her ship a
computer to an international trade show. She wants to know what ship-
pers are best for this and what problems she may encounter. She has
asked around her group, but everyone had left this to the previous assistant. Sarah would like to find another assistant in the company who can
help.

· Paul wants to find someone who has used JavaSound on a new mobile
platform. The software does not work properly, and he needs help. Paul
is unable to tell whether the problem arises because he does not understand how to use the software package, or because the package has bugs,
or because the package is a new release and conflicts with some of his
existing system software.

Both of these people will likely find answers through one of a small
number of ways. If unable to find the answer in printed documents, an
information seeker may search for someone with the required expertise
through mutual associates and gatekeepers (Allen 1977), paper directories and references, communication technologies (Sproull and Kiesler
1991; Finholt 1993; Constant, Kiesler, and Sproull 1994), or more
recently, computer-based systems.

Expertise finders, or expertise recommenders, are a form of recommendation system (e.g., Resnick et al. 1994; Konstan et al. 1997). Recommendation systems typically point the user toward books, movies,

or other objects of interest, but expertise finders point people to other people. An example is Expertise Recommender (ER) (McDonald and Ackerman 2000). It attempts to point the user toward people who know the most about a software module under repair. In general, an expertise finder's intention is to augment the seeker's typical search strategies by including individuals outside of the immediate social environment or daily experience.[1]

For these expertise finder systems to be of significant assistance, however, they must effectively point at the relevant people for any given problem. Therefore, the expertise finders must reasonably reflect an understanding of the greater knowledge network within the organization. While people are adept at knowing at least local portions of the knowledge network, this knowledge must be built into computer-based recommendation systems.

Trying to provide these data is directly analogous to the well-established problem of knowledge elicitation for the development of expert systems. We call our problem *expertise mapping*, and the required effort to be expertise or knowledge *elicitation*. In expertise mapping, one needs to inventory the organization's knowledge as well as to map the information flow within the organization. Common approaches to this have involved assessment interviews, skills inventories, and extensive surveys (Hoffman et al. 1995). Key limitations of these methods are their high cost (as measured in time for the organization's members) and their tendency to significantly disrupt daily work. They also tend to collect only fairly flat, one-dimensional assessments of expertise and expertise topics. Most important, because of the dynamic nature of expertise networks, these assessments are nearly obsolete the moment they are collected and are very difficult to maintain over time. Maintenance of the data over time becomes a critical issue.

In this chapter, we report on the Knowledge-Mapping Approximation (KMA) project, which concentrates on the problem of providing systems with the type of data needed to adequately determine the people most likely to be able to answer a given question. While it is relatively common to consider system prototypes to find others, less research has been pointed toward finding adequate data for these expertise finders. As Ehrlich points out (see chapter 6), generating the requisite data to feed computer-based recommendation systems is a daunting task. Because of the difficulty of this problem, we have bracketed off other significant issues, such as how people understand the context surrounding finding someone to help. (This issue is addressed by Fitzgerald in chapter 4.) We focus here only on the first steps in finding adequate data; this chapter discusses the initial steps in the KMA project.

7.1 The KMA Project: Looking for Approximation Techniques

Since the initial assessment of a knowledge network is unwieldy, the ongoing maintenance prohibitively costly, and the results relatively superficial, the KMA project has examined a new approach. Our goal has been to not completely capture the knowledge network but instead to find reasonable first-order approximations. As with any approximation technique in engineering, the motivation is to more easily compute and assess the phenomenon while staying within known error rates. For example, the famous bin-packing problem in computer science is NP-complete: One cannot determine the optimal placement of a substantial number of three-dimensional items in a pack or two-dimensional items to be cut from a metal sheet in computable time. For real applications, one must use an approximation. The approximation will not provide the optimal solution, but it will provide a satisficing solution within a known tolerance.

Our goal in the KMA project has been to frame the collection and maintenance of expertise data as a critical research problem. There are probably a myriad of possible ways of mapping the distribution of knowledge in an organization; here we only wanted to establish the feasibility of a rough approximation. However, any means of approximation had to fit within important organizational constraints: the initial data should be easily collected (e.g., requiring no more than one hour of each employee's time), the database should be simple to maintain (e.g., via continual capture of relevant digital artifacts), and its resultant measures should correlate well with the understanding of expertise in the site itself (high face validity).

With these constraints in mind, we designed three data collection techniques that together would generate our rough approximation (fig-

Knowledge Mapping Approximation Project Overview

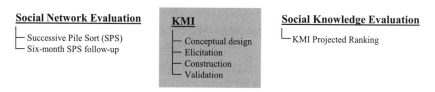

Figure 7.1
Overview of the Knowledge-Mapping Approximation (KMA) instruments.

ure 7.1). The first involved collecting social network data to augment organizational structure and working relationship data we had already collected. To do this, we used the successive pile sort (Boster 1986; 1987; 1994). The second was the construction and administration of a Knowledge-Mapping Instrument (KMI) to produce a snapshot of the current distribution of knowledge within the group. This snapshot would yield both an understanding of the location of expertise in the organization and a sense of the flow of information through the organization's knowledge network. The third was a survey of group members' evaluations of each other's levels of expertise. For this we asked each participant to guess the likely KMI scores of colleagues.

7.2 Pilot Study Site

This pilot study was conducted at a medium-sized software development company, Medical Software Corporation (MSC),[2] a company that builds, sells, and supports medical and dental practice management software. MSC is a medium-sized company, with just over one hundred employees. The pilot study was performed in conjunction with a larger field study at the site that was examining expertise location behavior and developing an expertise recommendation system (McDonald and Ackerman 1998).

A short description of MSC's business and products is critical to understanding the types of knowledge that are important to the organization and the employees. MSC has been in the practice management business for over twenty years. Practice management software is primarily concerned with appointment scheduling, treatment planning, patient recalls, insurance billing, patient billing, and payment reconciliation. While these functions are closely related to the clinical management (treatment) of the patient, practice management is often considered the business side of medicine. MSC is the dominant player in the group medical and group dental markets.

MSC sells several software packages, ranging from text-only systems running on high-performance Unix servers (mostly used by large medical practices) to graphically oriented Windows systems (mostly used by smaller medical and dental practices). The MSC text-oriented system is older and written in a proprietary form of BASIC. Thus, most software engineers must acquire knowledge of fairly arcane details of the MSC systems, the language, and the system platforms. For example, the top-level menu of the medical program has over one hundred specifically identifiable features, and often there are submenus. Moreover, the features are spread through more than two hundred medical system specific programs, with numerous programs that are shared by the medical and dental systems. Moreover, the standard application is highly customizable, and many files have client-specific customizations. Customization is often handled with a large number of customization flags that are not always mutually compatible.

The software is in a relatively constant cycle of new feature development and maintenance. New feature development is often the result of requests from existing clients. When enough new features have been added to the software, they are integrated into a complete system, and that new system is declared the next version. This new version is then offered to any client for minimal cost. A client is never forced to upgrade to a new version of the software. This development strategy means that many different versions with different customizations are in the field and supported all at the same time.

While there are many idiosyncrasies in the MSC products, MSC is representative of many technical organizations:

• While there is a constant hum of improvements, bug fixes, and new features, the basic product architecture, underlying feature set, and a substantial code base have been stable for over five years.

• Only a handful of technical architects in the company can understand the entire product line and know most of the code base. Other software engineers and support engineers know only bits and pieces of the systems.

The participants in this pilot study worked in three departments: product development (the software engineers and administrative personnel responsible for the MSC products); system development (the software engineers and administrative personnel responsible for supporting the various system platforms, including networking); and technical support (the support engineers and administrative personnel responsible for solving customers' problems). Each department included entry-level, senior, and management employees.

7.3   Data Collection

In the following sections we chronicle KMA development through the stages of design, elicitation, construction, and validation of the instruments. These sections highlight specific lessons learned in our pilot study at MSC about our prototype approximations.

Social Network Structure

The structure of the social network was elicited with the successive pile sort (Boster 1987; 1994). In this task, the names of all the members of the social group are written on cards. Participants are asked to sort the members into as many subgroups as they like, based on their judgment of the intensity of interaction of group members. After this initial free pile sort, participants are asked to successively merge their groups and then split the groups. The complete order of merges and splits is recorded. The resulting data can be represented as a binary tree expressing the relative social proximity of all members of the group. This method has the advantage of eliciting members' judgments of all the interactions in the group (rather than just those involving ego) and of rank-ordering their intensity. Although the successive pile sort technique is generally used on small groups (groups with twenty-five members or less), it was applied in this study to a group with forty-three members.

Knowledge-Mapping Instrument

To apply the Knowledge-Mapping Instrument (KMI), it is necessary first to discover what is important for members of the group to know (*elicitation*), next to develop an instrument that tests for that knowledge (*construction*), then to assess whether the constructed instrument succeeds at its purpose (*validation*), and finally to document which members of the group know those things (*administration*).

Elicitation

The knowledge management, decision support system, and expert system literatures all describe what is often a very difficult process of eliciting knowledge from people (e.g., Davenport and Prusak 1998; Liou and Nunamaker 1993). Hoffman et al. (1995) provide an excellent review of the literature for the various elicitation techniques. All of the techniques have significant, known limitations, especially in the cost of obtaining the original data for an inventory.

With the KMI, we wanted to avoid formally eliciting the knowledge important for members of the group. Our goal, instead, was to have the group members tell us what they know and what they think others around them ought to know. This was important for two reasons. First, what counts as expertise depends on the specific needs of the organization (Orr 1996). Since the content of the KMI is provided by the participants themselves, we believe we are assured of an instrument with a high degree of relevance and validity. Second, we wanted to avoid acquiring domain expertise ourselves in order to write the instrument because this would have been too costly for a rough approximation. We reduced the cost of pulling out the "know-how that cannot be verbalized" from group members (Polanyi 1967) by having group members write the KMI themselves.

Thus, an important part of our research was figuring out the best way to prompt group members to assess expertise in order to obtain the requisite tacit "knowledge of knowledge." We wanted an elicitation procedure for the KMI that was brief (taking no more than fifteen minutes of a participant's time), easy to understand, and specific to the knowledge that was important to group members. With these three criteria in mind, we elicited what knowledge was important to the participants by telling them that they were helping to create a trivia game, similar to Trivial Pursuit. The result was the KMI described here. By framing the instrument for assessing the distribution of knowledge through the group as a trivia contest, we were able to reduce the psychological cost to the participants. For this pilot study, the trivia game assessed participants' knowledge of the ongoing development, support, and use of MSC's flagship medical practice management system. Drawing from the three technical departments (product development, system development, and support), we recruited thirty-five participants.

We asked each participant in the study for help in generating questions and answers. Asking them to consider their co-workers as future players of the game, we requested questions that would vary from mildly challenging through very difficult to virtually impossible (questions to which "only you would know the right answer"). Our goal was to have the participants tell us what they think they are best at and what they think others ought to know about their work. We were also hoping to elicit questions that showed significant differentiation in expertise among the three groups.

In general, the prompting metaphor of constructing a trivia game provided a meaningful frame of reference for the elicitation process, and it motivated participants. However, we did need to develop prompting aids, and the elicitation task was still difficult for many participants.

Following are some important lessons we learned from this procedure:

• We were able to obtain with modest effort nearly seventy questions. Each elicitation interview took approximately fifteen minutes. The entire collection effort required eight days of interviews.

Moreover, in asking for trivia questions, we located additional resources at MSC that could generate even more questions. These included system documentation, questions in training manuals, and questions generated for user group meetings. However, in this pilot study we did not use these resources, preferring to test the KMI elicitation process alone.

• While less tasking than standard knowledge elicitation techniques, the elicitation of trivia questions was nonetheless demanding for our participants. Participants did not have equal facility in composing three good multiple-choice questions. For example, writing multiple wrong answers (so that they are clearly but not obviously wrong) is quite difficult. This was compounded by time and social pressures (fifteen minutes with the researcher audio-recording the process). We asked each participant to produce three trivia questions together with possible answers. Twenty-one of the thirty-five participants gave us at least one usable trivia question, and seven supplied two or three times the number of questions requested.

• As we began collecting data, we found that we needed to create a formalized interview and a form to prompt participants. We developed sample trivia questions with slots for the question and the multiple-choice answers—one correct answer and four challenging incorrect answers. After brainstorming about a particular question, we used this form to prompt the participant, ensuring a completed trivia question and answers at the end.

• In retrospect, we realize we made a mistake in asking participants to generate the trivia questions in a conference room instead of in their offices. This decontextualized setting provided limited environmental cues to prompt question generation and limited local resources to verify the correctness of answers.

• We needed to have a researcher present during the elicitation process. Attempts at having participants generate questions on their own, replying either by e-mail or in person on our next visit, were futile. When we were present, we could maintain motivation, prompt in the case of partial responses, and provide supportive feedback for the iterative improvement of questions.

• We attempted to get participants to rank the difficulty of their questions. Almost all were unable to do so, noting that they could not rank in the absence of a specific task or referent group. That is, they saw questions as difficult only in relation to specific circumstances—difficult for Support but not Product Development, or easy for people who had carried out specific system tasks.

Construction
We validated the aggregate set of questions using a three-step procedure. Our goal was to develop a method that would provide results without

needing domain expertise, but for our initial pilot study we had to understand the quality of the questions we received. Therefore, initial validation was performed by McDonald, who had spent a total of eighteen months observing expertise and knowledge processes at MSC (McDonald and Ackerman 1998). He reviewed and categorized each card according to the following criteria: knowledge domain (areas of specialization such as users, developers, support, and system administration), perceived difficulty (on a five-point scale), and clarity ("clear," "ambiguous," or "does not make sense").

After repairing the questions to the best of our ability and removing any questions that were too similar, there remained 22 questions (from 13 participants) that were not sufficiently clear. For each of these we returned to the participants for further clarification or expansion. Of the 22, 14 were revised, 6 were removed, 1 was replaced, and 1 remained unchanged.

This clarification occurred after a two-month hiatus. An interesting observation from these return visits is that most participants did not recognize their own questions, suggesting that the material may seem relatively fresh if it is presented to participants with some time delay.

After randomizing the order of the questions to evenly spread the topic domains and difficulty levels throughout the instrument, we administered the instrument to two test participants at MSC. They found the instrument clear, easy to take, challenging in content, and most important, enjoyable and engaging. Most of the question-answer sets were acceptable as they were or required only minor refinement.

Validation

At the completion of the construction phase, we had selected fifty-eight well-formed question-answer sets for the final version of the KMI. We then administered this to twenty-six participants.[3] The data gathered were from a majority of all three departments as well as key management and technical members. Participation was voluntary, occurring over the lunch hour in small groups of two to eight participants.

At the conclusion of each session, we asked participants for feedback on the KMI, particularly whether they had any problems with any specific questions. In addition, after all data had been collected, we asked technical experts to evaluate our answer key. Through both of these methods, we found some additional problems:

• Some questions had minor wording errors (e.g., the name of a program was not FINANBAL, but FINANCBAL). In all cases, it was clear from the question what was meant, and the key was not changed.

• One question asked about an organizational process that involved an employee who no longer filled that role. However, the responsibility had not been assigned to another person, and the key was not changed.

In both of the preceding situations, participants did not seem confused.

• Five questions touched on differences between acceptable organizational practice (work-arounds and alternative methods of acting) and official practice (Suchman 1983; Suchman and Wynn 1984). In these cases, the correct answer was ambiguous, since participants could have interpreted either practice as "best." In all of these situations, we allowed multiple correct responses on the answer key.

• Two other technical questions also had more than one correct answer. In both of these cases, there existed an obscure way to produce the desired result in addition to the usual way. For these two questions as well, we allowed multiple correct responses on the answer key.

• One question that concerned a data entry procedure based on a form external to the organization was removed. The form had been changed four months prior to the administration of the instrument, and participants were uncertain to which version of the form the question referred.

As with the test participants, the rest of the participants found the KMI engaging, challenging, and enjoyable. The average time to complete was just over thirty minutes (longer than our target but not prohibitive). Participants scored a mean of 35.19 out of a possible 57, with substantial variation among participants ($SD = 9.85$). Interestingly, there was significant agreement among participants on the answers even if they were incorrect.

To examine the robustness of the KMI, we compared participants' scores with and without the problematic questions noted earlier. (The rejected question was not included.) We found no statistically significant difference in participants' scores. This suggests that after due diligence in the construction phase, a small number of ambiguous questions (nearly 15 percent in this instance) can be tolerated. The KMI, as developed in our pilot study, appears to be a very robust instrument.

7.4   Findings from the Pilot Study

Social Network Structure

The social network structure of the group is shown in figure 7.2, top. There are three fairly distinct clusters: the support group, the system development group, and the product development group. Two individuals (H and S) are recent arrivals and are not clearly identified with any of the groups. Thus, the overall structure of the group clearly reflects the working groups within the organization: network ties are closer among the members of the support, system, and product groups than they are between members of different groups.

This structure can also be represented as a hierarchical cluster diagram (figure 7.2, bottom). This is perhaps a more appropriate representation of the data, because a tree diagram more nearly corresponds to the way that the data were collected in the successive pile sort (as an ultrametric). Again, there are three main clusters, corresponding to the three work groups at the organization. (One can think of this as an inductive way of eliciting the organization chart.)

Knowledge-Mapping Instrument

We had originally expected that the pattern of agreement on the KMI would show the division of intellectual labor in the organization—that, by and large, the support team would know a great deal about support and little about development, while the development teams would know a great deal about development but little about support issues.

Instead, we found that expertise was spread fairly evenly through all groups, and was determined not so much by group membership as by the number of months that the individual had been in the organization. This may reflect a situation in which success in the organization depends on integrative knowledge—individuals cannot afford to become too specialized and lose sight of what other members of the organization know and the problems they need to solve. Figure 7.3, top, shows the rela-

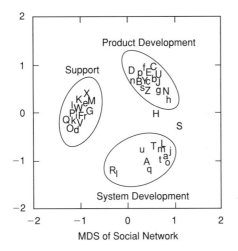

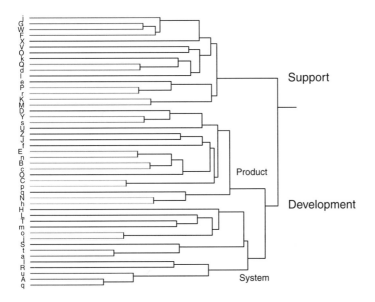

Figure 7.2
Social network structure in MSC (top); the same structure represented as a hierarchical cluster diagram (bottom).

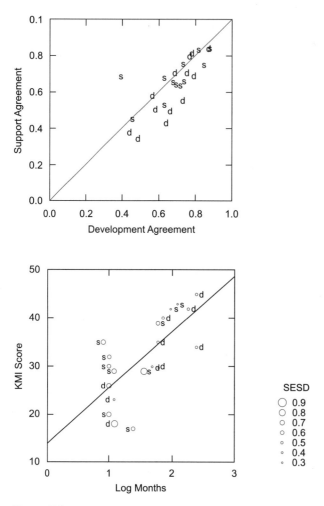

Figure 7.3
Knowledge agreement among groups (both development groups aggregated)
(top); Knowledge-Mapping Instrument (KMI) scores ranked by experience
(bottom).

tionship between knowledge of development issues on the KMI and knowledge of support issues.

In general, support knowledge and development knowledge at MSC are highly correlated ($r = .75$, $p < .001$). However, the outliers make sense in terms of work group membership. Although in general knowledge of the two domains go hand in hand, if there is a marked difference in an individual's knowledge of support and development issues, it reflects his or her work group membership. Figure 7.3, bottom, shows the relationship between overall score on the KMI and the number of months at the organization. (We used a log transformation of the number of months, given that there appears to be a learning curve—learning is rapid at the beginning of one's employment in the organization and slower later.) This figure illustrates three findings: performance on the KMI is moderately correlated with the duration of employment at the organization ($r = .44$, $p < .03$); there is no tendency for support people to perform better than development people on the KMI, or vice versa; and there is much greater variation in the KMI scores of individuals who have only been at the organization a short time than those who have been there longer. We do not know whether this reduction is due to individuals with long experience at the organization becoming "saturated" (reaching the asymptote of the learning curve) or whether it reflects the selective retention of those who are quick learners and the letting go of those who are slower.

The social evaluation scores do *not* show a similar pattern—individuals who have been at the organization longer do not agree on the knowledge of others any more than do recent arrivals.[4] There is no relationship between agreement on the social evaluation of others and length of time at the organization ($r = .08$, $p > .6$). Although the regression line has a positive slope, it is not significant.

It is the case that individuals who have been at the organization longer are presumed to have greater knowledge than the recent arrivals ($r = .5$, $p < .005$). It is likely that people are using the length of employment of others as a heuristic for guessing others' expertise, as reported in McDonald and Ackerman (1998). Figure 7.4 shows the relationship between performance on the KMI and perceived knowledge by other members of the group.

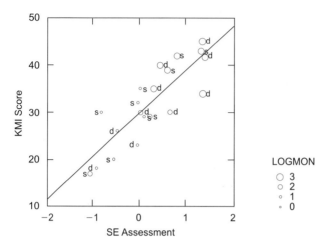

Figure 7.4
Scores on the Knowledge-Mapping Instrument (KMI) and Social Knowledge Evaluation (SE).

Nonetheless, use of this experience heuristic alone does not explain how participants evaluate each other's knowledge, because in the aggregate they are much better at it than would be explained by use of only the experience heuristic. In general, the social evaluation of others very accurately predicts their KMI scores; the correlation is .85 ($p < .001$), much higher than the .5 correlation of social evaluation with duration of employment. Nevertheless, use of the expertise heuristic is evident in an examination of the outliers; the individuals who score lower on the KMI than they were expected to are uniformly those with long experience at the organization, while the overachievers (those who scored higher on the KMI than expected) are those with relatively short experience at the organization.

Managers show slightly higher agreement in the social evaluation of their employees than do nonmanagers, perhaps because they have been in the organization for a longer period of time or because their job responsibilities require them to assess the expertise of their employees. Given the strong expectation that managers should be exceptionally skilled at social evaluation, perhaps the more interesting result is that the difference is relatively small. In fact, we ran a monte carlo simulation that randomly drew groups of engineers and computed how closely their aggegate approximated the whole. We found that, on average, seven engineers provided as robust an estimator of expertise as did aggregating the evaluations of the three top managers.

7.5 Conclusions and Future Work

Our prototype approximations as developed in the pilot study reported here show considerable promise. We were able to obtain a rough estimate of how much each participant knew and also of how others assessed group members' knowledge. The fact that the instrument was essentially developed by the participants themselves and was rated by them suggests that our approximation not only captured the critical aspects of the distribution of knowledge in this organization but also may serve as a prototype for a valuable class of approximation techniques. We were able to uncover a knowledge map, with some limitations at limited expense—this is precisely the beginning of finding adequate approximations. Indeed, we believe that we developed two expertise approximations in this pilot study: one based on directly assessing the knowledge of the group members (the Knowledge Mapping Instrument) and the second based on indirectly assessing that knowledge through the evaluations of others (the Social Knowledge Evaluation).

Several important issues remain for future investigation. For use as an expertise locator in companies similar to MSC, it may not be worthwhile to develop a full-fledged KMI to directly assess group members' knowledge. The KMI in this pilot study was closely approximated ($r = .85$) by the Social Knowledge Evaluation. In this organization, people had a good understanding of what other people know—at the least, they had a good understanding of other people's expertise levels for the kinds of knowledge that were valuable to MSC. The fact that the three top managers or seven lower-rank engineers could provide similar evaluations potentially provides another approximation technique that could be valuable, although this needs to be examined in future studies. This might be valuable in any size of organization, but especially valuable in larger organizations. If this finding holds, we could collect essentially similar data using far fewer people than we did in this pilot study.

Second, to help people within similar-sized organizations beyond what they already know, effective routing of questions may require more detail. That is, if people already know a fair amount about one another, what they lack when they are looking for someone with the required expertise is detailed knowledge of what others know—what they need to find answers to specific questions. It may be that the size of this organization may be the maximum size where one might know everyone else's expertise, since, with about fifty people, it is a very large small group.

If this is the case, the KMI approximation may be more suited for larger organizations, as might be expected. While we needed to pilot these approximations within a medium-sized company (in order to have a tractable field study), these methods, particularly the KMI, may offer more substantial help when the organization is large and heterogeneous. We can expect that group members' ability to adequately rate one another will not hold across larger organizations. In larger organizations, one person would not be able to personally evaluate more than a fraction of the other people. In fact, those other people would likely be within the same part of the organization and therefore know many of the same areas of expertise. In a very large organization (for example, a transnational company), a person might not even know what groups have expertise within a given area. Still, by systematically aggregating these local evaluations one might be able to develop a robust global expertise locator.

Finally, the technique used in this pilot study cannot distinguish whether participants were rating one another based on the details of their anticipated expertise or their overall sense of expertise. That is, it is possible that raters, especially in a group this small, knew one another's areas of expertise and rated people precisely. Alternatively, group members may have had a sense of how good someone is technically without knowing the details of their expertise. From experience on projects, comments in hallways, and random conversations over lunch and near water coolers, one may come to feel that someone is technically solid without knowing the exact areas of his or her expertise. More work is required to understand how people were rating one another.

In sum, the Knowledge Mapping Approximation project described in this chapter developed and piloted two promising classes of approximations for finding the data necessary to drive expertise finder systems. These approximations both require additional refinement but offer promise for helping solve the data collection problem for sharing and managing expertise.

Notes

1. We use the term *expertise* instead of *expert* because these finders may wish to identify a range of expertise. For example, Paul might need someone with substantial knowledge of the software systems, whereas someone with more superficial knowledge may be able to help Sarah.

2. All names and identifiers have been changed.

3. While we gained two new participants after the start of the project, we were unable to obtain KMI results from nine of our original thirty-five because of staffing changes and general unavailability.

4. For the Social Knowledge Evaluation, we asked each participant to provide the anticipated KMI score for each colleague, providing a rough ranking.

References

Allen, T. J. 1977. *Managing the Flow of Technology*. Cambridge, Mass.: MIT Press.

Boster, J. S. 1986. Exchange of Varieties and Information Between Aguaruna Manioc Cultivators. *American Anthropologist* 88 (2): 428–436.

———. 1987. Agreement Between Biological Classification Systems Is Not Dependent on Cultural Transmission. *American Anthropologist* 84 (4): 914–919.

———. 1994. The Successive Pile Sort. *Cultural Anthropology Methods* 6 (2): 7–8.

Constant, D., S. Kiesler, and L. Sproull. 1994. What's Mine Is Ours, or Is It? A Study of Attitudes About Information Sharing. *Information Systems Research* 5 (4): 400–421.

Davenport, T. H., and L. Prusak. 1998. *Working Knowledge: How Organizations Manage What They Know*. Boston: Harvard Business School Press.

Finholt, T. A. 1993. Outsiders on the Inside: Sharing Information Through a Computer Archive. Ph.D. diss., Carnegie-Mellon University, Pittsburgh, PA 15213.

Hoffman, R. R., R. Nigel, A. Shadbolt, M. Burton, and G. Klein. 1995. Eliciting Knowledge from Experts: A Methodological Analysis. *Organizational Behavior and Human Decision Processes* 62 (2): 129–158.

Konstan, J. A., B. N. Miller, D. Maltz, J. L. Herlocker, L. R. Gordon, and J. Riedl. 1997. GroupLens: Applying Collaborative Filtering to Usenet News. *Communications of the ACM* 40 (3): 77–87.

Liou, Y. I., and J. F. Nunamaker, Jr. 1993. An Investigation into Knowledge Acquisition Using a Group Decision Support System. *Information and Management* 24 (3): 121–132.

McDonald, D. W., and M. S. Ackerman. 1998. Just Talk to Me: A Field Study of Expertise Location. In *Proceedings of the ACM Conference on Computer-Supported Cooperative Work (CSCW '98)*, 315–324.

———. 2000. Expertise Recommender: A Flexible Recommendation System Architecture. In *Proceedings of the ACM Conference on Computer-Supported Cooperative Work (CSCW '2000)*: 231–240.

Orr, J. E. 1996. *Talking About Machines: An Ethnography of a Modern Job.* Ithaca, N.Y.: Cornell University Press.

Polanyi, M. 1967. *The Tacit Dimension.* London: Routledge and Kegan Paul.

Resnick, P., N. Iacovou, M. Suchak, P. Bergstrom, and J. Riedl. 1994. Group-Lens: An Open Architecture for Collaborative Filtering of Netnews. In *Proceedings of the ACM Conference on Computer-Supported Cooperative Work (CSCW '94)*, 175–186.

Sproull, L., and S. Kiesler. 1991. *Connections: New Ways of Working in the Networked Organization.* Cambridge, Mass.: MIT Press.

Suchman, L. 1983. Office Procedure as Practical Action: Models of Work and System Design. *ACM Transactions on Office Information Systems* 1 (4): 320–328.

Suchman, L., and E. Wynn. 1984. Procedures and Problems in the Office. *Office: Technology and People* 2: 133–154.

8

Enabling Communities of Practice at EADS Airbus

Roland Haas, Wilfried Aulbur, and Sunil Thakar

8.1 Knowledge Management

A practical definition of knowledge management demonstrates that it is, despite suspicions to the contrary, a well-defined business objective. To manage knowledge means to know what is known, who knows it, how it has been applied, and how it can be further leveraged and shared (Wilma D. Abney, DaimlerChrysler Corporate University). The task at hand for managers and employees alike is to enable the access to and sharing of information, to leverage expertise, and to control information pollution. Key elements of knowledge management are the management of intellectual property (patents and rights), the gathering of information in databases, and the establishment and support of communities of practice (Drucker 1998).

Communities of practice (CoPs) consist of people with a common interest who interact to share information and to solve problems in their area of expertise. Communication, both formal and informal, is the main driver of success in a community of practice. Communities of practice are not static but evolve and adapt continuously to changes in their knowledge domain. With time, CoPs not only generate their own identity but also shared artifacts. An example of this is the Electronic Book of Knowledge (EBOK) in the Chrysler Group. The EBOK is an important component in the CoP process that documents the knowledge of the CoP members in the form of "lessons learned" or "best practices" (Wenger and Snyder 2000).

The establishment of strong CoPs and the efficient management of corporate knowledge are vital for companies in knowledge-intensive businesses, particularly in the face of fierce international competition and in the context of multinational mergers and acquisitions. This is true in particular for EADS Airbus (European Aerospace, Defence and Space Corporation) in the context of recent and future mergers (Daimler-Benz and Chrysler to DaimlerChrysler; DaimlerChrysler Aerospace, Aerospatiale Matra, and CASA to EADS).

The reuse of lessons learned and the adoption of best practices can lead to significant cost savings and process simplifications. Chrysler (now DaimlerChrysler Auburn Hills—DC-AH) is an outstanding success story for the consistent reuse of lessons learned and best practices. The Chrysler concept of communities of practice, which Chrysler engineers refer to as Tech Clubs, and the introduction of EBOKs has given them a significant advantage over competitors (figure 8.1). Time-to-market for new models was cut by a factor greater than 2, development costs were slashed by an increase of first-time-right engineering, and the time needed for training new engineers was cut in half. Yellow Pages, which contain the names and competence profiles of company experts, greatly

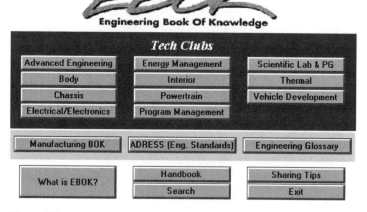

Figure 8.1
Entry page of Chrysler Group's Tech Clubs/CoPs (Lotus Notes version).

improved the access to experts and the networking capabilities of new employees.

The Origins of Communities of Practice at Chrysler

Before 1988, Chrysler Corporation employed a traditional, sequential, and component-based approach to the production of vehicles. Design used to pass the work on to Engineering, which transferred its results to Procurement, and so on. Owing to "stovepipe" thinking and insufficient communication and collaboration between the different functions, plenty of costly re-do loops used to occur. For example, manufacturing engineers might have discovered late in the process that the design of a particular part could not be manufactured and hence rejected the part. As a consequence, the Design department had to redesign the part. Clearly, these re-do loops led to significant increases in time-to-market. Not surprisingly, the overall time-to-market for Chrysler vehicles was about sixty months in the mid-1980s, which was not tenable in the face of stiff Japanese competition.

Chrysler's response to the Japanese threat was to move to a platform-based model for vehicle production. The basic idea was to bring together all development stakeholders of a vehicle in teams. Designers, engineers, representatives from Procurement and Supply, marketing experts, and advanced manufacturing representatives would be co-located and work cross-functionally on a product, thereby reducing re-do loops and discovering inconsistencies early on. As a result of the platform concept and subsequent developments such as the Tech Clubs and the EBOKs, time-to-market of Chrysler vehicles was cut in half.

After a few years, the platforms were in danger of themselves developing into lateral stovepipes, and it became apparent that knowledge was not flowing easily enough in the original functions for optimized production. An example demonstrating the lack of communication was the fact that a moisture barrier was left out of the door of one model during early engineering tests.

To close strategic gaps in knowledge flow, informal communities of engineers who formerly worked together in the stovepipe organization but who were separated because of the platform reorganization started to appear. Their initial agenda was an informal exchange of best practices and lessons learned at the different platforms, in the engineers' respective areas of expertise. Management immediately recognized the importance of these communities to ensure a two-dimensional matrix structure for knowledge flow. Communities were soon institutionalized to form the so-called Tech Clubs. The concept was imitated in functional departments other than Engineering and, after the merger of Daimler-Benz and Chrysler Corporation in 1998, within parts of the European organization of DaimlerChrysler.

The Origins of Knowledge Management at EADS Airbus

The complexity of high-tech products such as a commercial aircraft results in a flood of detailed information on processes in Engineering, Manufacturing, and Sales, for example, in the form of lessons learned and best practices (Tzafestas 1993). Information technology is an essential enabling tool to evaluate and preprocess the corresponding data. A variety of information technology (IT) products, technologies, and concepts such as intelligent agents, search algorithms, portals, and case-based reasoning are available today to help individuals sift through databases, customer reports, and other forms of electronically available data.

EADS Airbus Engineering realized the need to preserve and manage its knowledge assets. The drive to structure and preserve corporate knowledge was motivated by several factors. Downsizing during the Dolores project (Dollar Low Rescue, mid '90s) led to significant loss of knowledge. In addition, the competitive climate in the aerospace industry forced EADS Airbus to focus on knowledge management. For example, Boeing realized significant support cost savings through online access to information related to repairs and maintenance. Also, Boeing managed its intellectual assets efficiently, leading to a large number of new patents.

The mission of the knowledge management group at EADS Airbus Engineering was to build communities of practice, to support them in documenting their core knowledge, and to consolidate existing knowledge management initiatives, where available, into a coherent knowledge management strategy. The knowledge management core team was established about two years ago.

Figure 8.2
Work shares and partners within EADS Airbus.

If the highly distributed nature of the engineering work done is considered (figure 8.2), knowledge management also becomes a key feature for integrating distributed engineering and design-build teams.

The adaptation of Chrysler's Tech Clubs and EBOKs to the business context of EADS Airbus Engineering is currently an important thrust area of the knowledge management group. We would therefore like to start this report of our experiences with an introduction to the CoP/ EBOK process at EADS Airbus Engineering and in the light of newly formed DaimlerChrysler knowledge management CoPs.

Challenges and Solutions
The knowledge management efforts at EADS Airbus Engineering follow a two-pronged approach. We build the infrastructure and support mechanisms for the creation of effective engineering CoPs. At the same time, we play an active role in the newly formed CoPs for knowledge management within DaimlerChrysler Corporation. The DaimlerChrysler Corporate University (DCCU) leads the knowledge management CoPs. The community itself includes knowledge managers from all business units. Within the community, Airbus Engineering is responsible for IT-

related questions. Chrysler's knowledge management efforts are accepted as best practice within and will be implemented throughout the CoPs. In the following account, we describe the challenges and solutions that we face in establishing the knowledge management CoPs and the engineering CoPs.

8.2   Communities of Practice

The identification and establishment of communities of practice can benefit a great deal from the answers to a few basic questions that help to break down the complexity of the task and to structure the knowledge and the people associated. The questions follow an approach suggested by Drs. Etienne Wenger and William Snyder, who support the DCCU and the knowledge management CoPs as consultants.

Key Questions to Be Answered

What is your knowledge domain?   Given the context of the knowledge management initiative within DaimlerChrysler, the knowledge domain is defined by the following question: How can we transfer the Tech Club/ EBOK process from Chrysler to the business units? All processes and people that are vital for answering this question are part of the knowledge domain and of the CoPs, respectively. The motivation to form a CoP stems from the fact that DaimlerChrysler faces global competition in a knowledge-intensive business. Continuous improvement and innovation supported by the CoP/EBOK process is a must and enjoys companywide management support.

Within Airbus Engineering, three prototype CoPs exist, each of which has a different structure to cater to different customer requirements. The Composites CoP centers on composite materials and their use in Engineering, Manufacturing, and Sales (figure 8.3). A somewhat unstructured environment for the EBOKs was required: three books, one each for Engineering, Manufacturing, and Sales, are used currently. No structure was identified for the chapters. A second CoP focuses on avionic systems and is structured according to ATA specifications. Finally, a methods

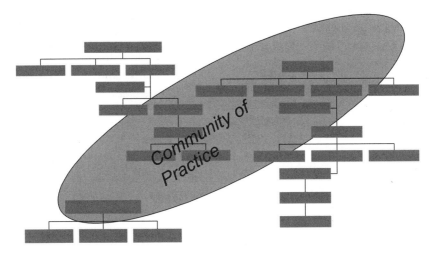

Figure 8.3
Communities of practice across functional boundaries, bringing together experts with a specific area of interest.

and support CoP acts as a standard Chrysler-type Tech Club. Its books are organized around topics such as standardization and configuration management.

The motivation for starting these communities of practice varies. For example, in avionics, which is a book in the Systems CoP, the business need is to cut down on the training time for incoming engineers and to document existing knowledge (Bach, Vogler, Oesterreich 1999). Other books are being written to homogenize processes and to increase first-time-right engineering.

Who will participate in building the community?   The knowledge management initiative at DaimlerChrysler began with the DCCU's identifying key knowledge management leaders. A kick-off meeting formally started the CoP. The CoP includes representatives from Human Resources, Research and Technology, Finance and Controlling, and Quality Management in addition to knowledge management leaders from all DaimlerChrysler business units. Subgroups that target specific topics were formed, such as IT under the leadership of Airbus Engineering.

At Airbus Engineering, key account managers interview business unit leaders and experts to identify possible CoPs and useful EBOKs that could have a real impact on performance. The key account managers draw upon the information gathered in interviews and on additional information such as knowledge maps, which exist for specific areas of expertise (Drucker 1998).

An initial CoP and EBOK structure is presented to leading managers and experts and redefined as needed. A kick-off meeting initiates the process and identifies CoP coordinators and book owners. The key account manager continues to be involved with the CoP and provides support as and when it is needed.

What should the community of practice do?   One area of priority for the DaimlerChrysler knowledge management community of practice is to review the different knowledge management efforts throughout the company to identify best practices, such as the Chrysler Tech Club/EBOK process, and to harmonize knowledge management efforts throughout the company. For example, at the IT level, an overview of technologies used will be needed. Do IT implementations meet criteria such as user-friendliness, security, flexibility, scalability, and platform-independence? If IT has been outsourced, how competent are the suppliers? How do they perform on price? Which technology is outdated? To answer these questions and to prevent reinvention of the wheel, a J2EE-compliant IT platform was chosen. Based on this technology, the DaimlerChrysler Research Centre India in Bangalore implemented a modular knowledge management infrastructure.

The task of the Airbus Engineering CoPs is to improve business performance. Since the establishment of CoPs is only recent, no results regarding their performance are available yet.

Practical Considerations

Once the basic questions are answered, two practical problems still remain unsolved: How does one encourage the formation of CoPs, and what support will they need? How does one quantify the benefits of a CoP? We describe our approach to these questions using the example of Engineering CoPs at Airbus.

Encouragement and Support   Enabling a knowledge-sharing culture in a large organization is a highly complex task (Bach, Vogler, and Oesterreich 1999). Here is a possible approach that describes different areas in which encouragement and support are needed:

Leadership   Leadership of a CoP is a distinction that has to be earned. Choosing the right Tech Club leader is vital for the success of a Tech Club. The leader needs to create and communicate a vision for the Tech Club. In collaboration with carefully chosen experts, he or she needs to identify Tech Club deliverables, chair and manage regular meetings, and monitor progress on the EBOK. Open communication must be continually encouraged.

Management Support   Active participation in a CoP implies a work load of about 20 percent for a CoP leader and about 10 percent for a CoP member. Employees will make such a large time commitment only if it is sanctioned by or even required from management. Support from leading executives for the CoP/EBOK process is a must.

Motivation   Several incentives can be used to generate employee buy-in for knowledge management efforts. An important motivator is the fact that shared knowledge increases the respect for and the influence of the expert (listing in Yellow Pages, identifying the "knowledge management employee of the month"). Knowledge sharing should also be part of every employee's performance evaluation and thereby directly affect pay raises and promotions. Other motivating factors can be a reduction in work load to compensate for additional work done in documenting knowledge and premiums such as recognition lunches and additional holidays.

Behavior   Organizational behavior must change to create a knowledge-sharing work environment. Such a change means accepting employee mistakes and failures as part of a learning process. Admission of failures should not automatically threaten an employee's job. Active support must be given to create a strong group identity.

Education   Employees must be convinced of the benefits and payoffs of knowledge management and must learn to use its tools. Ways to achieve this goal are tutorials and seminars, especially for new employees, since the benefit that comes from using, say, the EBOKs is potentially large in their case. Also, results of the EBOK have to be used in internal training seminars.

Help Desk Support   Support during normal business hours is needed to register and act on customer complaints pertaining to the functionality of the EBOKs, message boards, and other means of CoP communication. Help in clarifying Tech Club access rights for supplier personnel and, if need be, help for authors with the editing of complex documents are also needed. In addition, support in the areas of conducting efficient meetings, motivating CoP members, and teaching authors how to write EBOK chapters is essential.

Marketing   Employees have to be made aware of the concept and potential of communities of practice. Ways to achieve this awareness include presentations to management and employees, road shows, and articles in the company newsletter. Referring potential customers to the results of successful CoPs is especially helpful.

Measurement of Performance   Objective measurement of the success of knowledge management initiatives is crucial for ensuring continued management support. At Airbus Engineering, knowledge management initiatives are evaluated against five different criteria. While the first two criteria are the easiest to measure, the last three generate the greatest value addition.

Generated Knowledge   Generation of knowledge can be measured by the number of CoPs, EBOKs, chapters (initialized and published), experts listed in the Yellow Pages, and discussion groups. A further indicator that measures generated knowledge is the number of best practices/ lessons learned in comparison with the total number of projects. Similarly, the number of interviewed employees who leave the company in relation to the total fluctuation rate is a good indicator of generated or retained corporate knowledge.

Distributed Knowledge The distribution of knowledge can be measured by the number of downloads and reads for EBOK chapters, and the number of CoP meetings and their attendance. The number and activity of discussion groups is also a good measure of knowledge distribution, as is the number of workshops on special EBOK topics. Finally, the number of tutorials by experts given to new or less qualified employees also directly measures knowledge distribution.

Applied Knowledge The number and quality of reader feedback commenting on the relevance of lessons learned and best practices in their work environment clearly measures the application of knowledge. Other measures include the homogenization of processes through the adoption of best practices, more efficient training of employees, and a reduction in the number of suppliers.

Efficiency and Quality of Knowledge Distribution An important measure is the user's attitude towards the CoP/EBOK process, which is revealed by the results of questionnaires and the ratio of positive to negative reader feedback. Indicators for an efficient knowledge distribution are also the time spent between the generation (e.g., end of a project) and the documentation of knowledge, or the number of days spent for documenting and distributing knowledge. Further parameters to be considered are the average age of chapters in the EBOK and the time it takes for new employees to come up to speed.

Indirect Parameters The CoP/EBOK process has a variety of indirect consequences. For example, increase in productivity per employee should be observable, as well as an increase in first-time-right engineering and in innovation. Measurement parameters could be, for instance, the percentage of new products and services in terms of the total product portfolio, the average number of project days per person in research and development, the percentage of products designed with customer participation, and improved response times in customer support.

An Example: The Composite Materials Tech Club

The composite materials community of practice (Composites CoP) at Airbus faces the following business challenge: the quality of the materials must be improved and errors in handling composite materials must be reduced.

In particular, this requires close communication and efficient information exchange between Manufacturing, Engineering, Quality, and Services. Manufacturing, Engineering, and Services are located in different cities (Stade, Bremen, and Hamburg), which further complicates communication.

In addition, competencies have to be managed, for example, in the form of Yellow Pages that list experts, their areas of expertise, and contact information.

The Composites CoP eventually will link all people within Airbus who work on composite materials, driven by strong management support.

The Electronic Books of Knowledge of this knowledge-sharing community mirror its communication needs (figure 8.4): one each for Manufacturing, Engineering, and Services. The different chapters of these books

Figure 8.4
Knowledge sharing and functional roles within a community of practice.

typically discuss different technologies, aircraft programmes, standardization practices, and so forth. The lessons learned and best practices are entered by means of a Web-enabled application that is easily accessible throughout the plants and engineering offices.

Any member of the CoP (reader status) can access documents; however, no changes can be made. Writers take a more active role as they write down best practices and lessons learned. The book owners (Composite Manufacturing, Engineering, and Services) are responsible for the book's overall validity, the specific focus, and the approval of content. For the latter, they rely on a peer review process—members of the CoP cross-check all information and approve it.

Let us look at a simple example of how this works.

Sometime ago Quality, Services, and Engineering noticed some problems with the compaction of composite materials that had been produced. For small components, there is a simple, nondestructive solution to quickly check the compaction. This was written down as a best practice in the following form:

Compaction of sandwich parts shall be checked after manufacturing by dipping them in warm water. Increased porosity of CFRP sandwich parts may cause water ingression in service. Sandwich parts may suffer defects after manufacturing. Before delivery, water-tightness shall be checked. This test can be done by dipping these parts in warm water; air bubbles will show possible defects. This test can be combined easily with NDT (nondestructive testing) done in final inspection. If water soaking is not possible, X-ray is an option to detect water after NDT.

The message spread quickly. Soon after the best practice was published in the engineering section of the CoP's EBOK, the method was routinely applied within Manufacturing.

8.3   A Web-Based System for Collecting and Distributing Knowledge

Information technology is an essential enabler of the knowledge-sharing process. This section describes a Web-enabled knowledge portal, based on Engineering's EBOK, that allows writing, storing, and searching for best practices and lessons learned. The documents are discussed and reviewed by peers and, if finally approved, stored in the knowledge repository.

A successful IT infrastructure must satisfy customer needs, which is why we started with a prototype that is constantly improved and adjusted to meet customer requirements (see figure 8.7, later). Six criteria must be satisfied by an efficient IT tool for knowledge management:

- User-friendliness
- Security
- Efficient search
- Flexibility
- Scalability
- Platform independence

For example, user-friendliness is achieved by using simple Web pages to read and upload best practices and lessons learned. Using a tool like the EBOK should not require additional skills beyond the navigation of the intranet. Full text search of all documents should be possible.

The Basic Functionality

To enter the knowledge pools the user has to log in. This is based on a single sign-on philosophy: the user needs his user ID and password only once to get access to the specific community of practice with the books, chapters, and subchapters. The user will get access to only those areas (knowledge books) that he is allowed to see.

There are three basic ways of using the knowledge repository:

- The user can browse the books and their substructures, reading best practices and lessons learned in a random manner.
- The user can use the structure to navigate through specific books and chapters.
- Information on a specific topic can be retrieved through a keyword search.

By clicking on one of the book icons, the user enters the next level of detail, where he finds substructures like chapters and subchapters and then finally reaches individual documents. The documents have a simple structure containing meta-information (author, date of creation, CoP membership), the title, keywords, a brief abstract, and the core information (figure 8.5).

Figure 8.5
Exploring the knowledge space.

While exploring the CoP the navigation tree is of great help. The following search functions are part of the system:

· Full text search

· Keyword search

· Search for authors and groups

Submitting the Documents   When a member of a CoP wants to document a specific lesson learned or best practice, he only needs to push a button. An input mask pops up.

After the title, name, and some keywords have been filled in, the text can be entered directly into the browser window. The text should be short and descriptive. Using copy-and-paste, it is easy to fill in information from other text documents.

Workflow   All documents should be reviewed by peers. This process is directly supported by a workflow engine built into the system.

A document starts as a draft version under review. Readers and reviewers add comments, and the author refines his work. Finally, the document is approved by one of the reviewers, typically the book owner, who is responsible for the content, and published (status set to "final").

Readers can provide feedback on any chapter or subchapter by filling in comment sheets attached to the documents.

Help and Statistics   A variety of help and information is available online:

· FAQs for troubleshooting

· Instructions on how to use the different features of the tool (e.g., search module, editing module)

· General philosophy and value addition for the knowledge management process (what is it, what are the lessons learned and best practices, what does the company gain?)

System Architecture

The system is a pure Java-based implementation built on the Java 2 Enterprise Edition (J2EE). The user interface front end uses JSPs (Java-Server Pages) and Servlets. The main functionality, that is, the business logic, is implemented by EJBs (Enterprise JavaBeans). The system consists of different modules for

· Administration (knowledge structuring and user management)

· Document management (to handle documents and meta data)

· Search

· Workflow (peer review for validity and consistency of the knowledge base)

· Help (on-line help and training)

· Statistics (reads/writes, feedbacks)

The system architecture comprises three tiers (figure 8.6):

· Tier 1: client with presentation logic (Web tier)

· Tier 2: application logic (EJB tier)

· Tier 3: database server (back end)

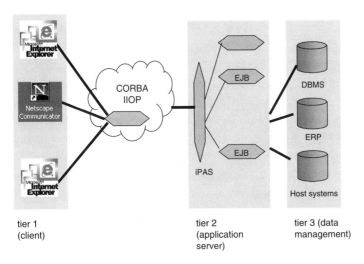

Figure 8.6
Multi-tier system architecture.

The third tier consists of an Oracle 8i enterprise server for data management; the middle tier utilizes IONA's iPortal application server for providing the Web and EJB container. The EJBs model event-triggered business logic.

The Web tier consists of a Servlet that acts as the client's (browser's) single point of entry to the system. Depending on the number of users and the backup strategy, the application can be distributed over several servers, each server running one or more CoP components.

By utilizing J2EE technologies it is possible to build a flexible, purely object-oriented, scalable system that can serve large numbers of users.

8.4 Lessons Learned and Experiences Gathered

Figure 8.7 shows the roots of knowledge management within Chrysler's platform teams and the EBOK road map for EADS Airbus. By initiating, encouraging the growth of, and supporting CoPs at Airbus, we made a couple of important observations that led to the following lessons learned:

• *Top Management attention is crucial to overcome internal resistance.*
Fortunately, our knowledge management initiative had the support of

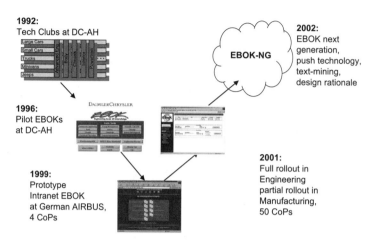

Figure 8.7
History and future plans for the EBOK.

Airbus's former Head of Engineering, Dr. Wolfgang Schneider. This turned out to be a key factor when it came to the day-to-day implementation of knowledge management processes.

• *Marketing and story telling are important.* To convince people about the ideas of knowledge management one has to be prepared to do a lot of marketing. Storytelling is an important part of that. At Airbus it was very helpful when members of our first CoPs could tell their success stories.

• *CoPs need a well-defined structure, but one should be careful not to formalize too much.* A well-defined knowledge structure helped the CoPs to gain momentum. However, some CoPs tried to formalize too much, which led to a decline in participation.

• *Avoid getting stuck in a tool discussion.* Some groups at Airbus spent a lot of time looking for the best tool to use for their documentation processes, which led to lengthy discussions on document management systems, groupware, and product data management. These groups lost their focus.

• *Use open software standards.* CoPs and knowledge management initiatives are very dynamic. Their needs change with time. A knowledge management tool should integrate seamlessly with different knowledge sources, both structured (relational data) and unstructured. Look for interoperability standards and connectivity.

• *Align knowledge management with the major business processes.* At the beginning many CoPs felt that knowledge management was just something over and above their daily business, with no immediate value addition. One needs to show how to integrate knowledge management initiatives into daily operations. Many CoP meetings, discussing the current status of the knowledge repository, could be aligned with the regular expert group meetings.

• *Treat people's concerns seriously.* Knowledge is power, and to document one's knowledge, that is, to "give it away," made some people very uneasy. They felt that it would be easier now to replace them. We found it extremely important to treat these concerns seriously. A knowledge-sharing culture does not emerge overnight—it has to be developed step-by-step.

8.5 Summary

EADS Airbus Engineering realized the need to preserve and manage its knowledge assets. The knowledge management process was driven by the establishment of communities of practice that actively shared knowledge. The chapter introduced a Web-based system, called the Electronic Book of Knowledge, that helps groups of people share and discuss their knowledge. The system is a pure Java implementation based on the J2EE platform.

Figure 8.7 summarizes the development phases, from the first communities of practice at Chrysler to the first prototypes at Airbus and the release of the Web-enabled EBOK. This system will be further enhanced to become a powerful knowledge portal that includes advanced search features, knowledge push, advanced personalization, and connectivity with other knowledge sources (guidelines, digital libraries, enterprise resource planning, engineering systems).

References

Bach, V., P. Vogler, and H. Oesterreich, eds. 1999. *Business Knowledge Management.* New York: Springer-Verlag.

Drucker, P. F. 1998. The Coming of the New Organization. In *Harvard Business Review on Knowledge Management*, 1–20. Boston: Harvard Business School Press.

Fishwick, P. A., and R. B. Modjeski, eds. 1991. *Knowledge-Based Simulation*. New York: Springer-Verlag.

Flanagan, D. 1997. *Java in a Nutshell*. Cambridge, Mass.: O'Reilly.

Haas, R. 1999. Java Technologies for Internet/Intranet Applications and Embedded Systems. In *Proceedings of the HiSys-Conference*, Sindelfingen, Germany.

———. 2000. Corporate Intranets: Applications and Technologies. In *Proceedings of the International Conference on Concurrent Enterprising (ICE2000)*, Toulouse, France.

Haas, R., W. Aulbur, and A. Stautz. 2000. A Web-Based System for Distributing and Sharing Engineering Knowledge. In *Proceedings of the Euromedia Conference*, Antwerp, Belgium.

Haas, R., and M. Dotter. 2000. Design Rationale in Computational Fluid Dynamics. In *Proceedings of the European Simulation Symposium (ESS2000)*, Hamburg, Germany.

Lee, J., and K. Lai. 1996. What's in Design Rationale? In *Design Rationale: Concepts, Techniques, and Use*, ed. T. P. Moran and J. M. Carroll. Mahwah, N.J.: Erlbaum.

Moran, T. P., and J. M. Carroll. 1996. Overview of Design Rationale. In *Design Rationale: Concepts, Techniques, and Use*. Mahwah, N.J.: Erlbaum.

Orfali, R., and D. Harkey. 1998. *Client/Server Programming with JAVA and CORBA*. New York: Wiley.

Tzafestas, S., ed. 1993. *Expert Systems in Engineering Applications*. New York: Springer-Verlag.

Wenger, E., and W. Snyder. 2000. Communities of Practice: The Organizational Frontier. *Harvard Business Review* (January–February): 139–145.

III

Exploring Technology for Sharing Expertise

In this part of the book we focus on the question of how information technology can support the sharing of expertise. The seven contributions found here address a wide variety of application fields and use cases. And although all the systems described approach the problem of expertise sharing from different viewpoints, we can see how research traditions as different as those of artificial intelligence and computer-supported cooperative work (CSCW) join forces to find innovative solutions for different situations of expertise sharing.

When looking at the tools it also becomes very clear where this kind of research goes beyond earlier approaches to design tools for knowledge management. None of our contributors was satisfied by a repository solution. The designers of all systems here were very much aware of the fact that not all the knowledge needed in a problem situation can be made explicit or stored in a knowledge base. All the systems offer access to knowledgeable people; some of them directly support communication. The work to recontextualize abstract knowledge, to apply it to the current situation, is not left to the knowledge seeker but is seen as a collaborative process.

This kind of knowledge communication happens all the time whenever people work together. CSCW systems are meant to support cooperative work, and that is why we start this part of the book with a CSCW perspective. Greenberg and Roseman describe how the quality of collaborative work can be increased by using a room metaphor as the central idea around which to develop a groupware system—a steady place to find particular expertise. They also describe how this consistent use of a metaphor eases the sharing of expertise.

Fagrell takes an approach to mobile expertise sharing in a very interesting setting. Supporting journalists on location with knowledge on an issue about which they are not experts is a tough challenge for expertise-sharing systems. Besides providing a lucid example for the dynamics journalists work in, Fagrell also shows that expertise sharing is not a matter of information quantity but of information quality. Considering the tight time frames journalists work in, it is important to provide the right anchors to information and expertise, not extensive amounts of the information itself.

It is interesting to note that the journalists mentioned by Fagrell prioritized material and expertise provided by other journalists. This indicates that besides an appropriate information transfer itself, it is helpful if there is a shared understanding of the basic conditions in which a journalist works. This type of knowledge is hard to transfer, but it is very important for the efficiency of expertise sharing. This is why Eales aims at supporting those often informal communities of practice within organizations. Starting from Lave and Wenger's well-known theory of expertise sharing in "communities of practice," Eales develops requirements for a collaborative support system that supports efficient expertise sharing in organizations.

Whereas Eales works with communities in the sense of informal structures that are orthogonal to other organizational structures, Erickson and Kellogg put their work in the context of communities that do not necessarily share an organizational background and whose one and only goal is to share knowledge. They designed a tool for such "knowledge communities" that aims at supporting communication and—what makes their work special—at providing visualizations of communication as additional means for orientation. One could also imagine expertise marketplaces, places where people could find and sell specific kinds of expertise.

With the contributions we have described so far, we slowly left the safe harbor of organizational structures like roles, responsibilities, and departments. These structures provide orientation and also a cultural background on how to proceed when in need of expertise. But the less defined a work or problem context is, the more difficult it becomes to actually find an expert who can help. The solutions developed for the expert-finding problem usually analyze existing material (e.g., profiles, documents) in an organization or community to deduce the expertise of its members. Yimam-Seid and Kobsa give us a thorough analysis of earlier approaches to solve this problem. They show which design decisions have to be made when implementing an expert-finding tool and where some approaches fall short. They describe a framework for expert-finding tools that helps avoid the shortcomings of other approaches.

Yimam-Seid and Kobsa focus on an abstract level of tool design, but Maybury, D'Amore, and House present two particular expert-finding tools that have been developed, implemented, and evaluated. Besides an expert-finding tool in the sense of the previous contribution, they describe a tool to visualize affinity groups built along shared skills and interest. This is useful for social navigation in the context of expertise finding, for instance, when we are able to contact someone closely related to an expert currently out of reach.

As noted throughout this book, not all knowledge is explicable. Sometimes knowledge can only be gained by observing the practice of knowledgeable people (we all remember Nonaka's famous example of the design of a bread-baking machine, where an engineer only succeeded because she went to work at a local bakery to learn about making bread). In the last contribution, Linton addresses the problem that, especially in the virtual sphere in which computer-supported work usually takes place, sometimes practice is not observable. The tool he presents aims at visualizing the use of functions in an application to enable users to find out about possibly interesting functions they have not as yet used.

Although all the work presented in this part supports expertise sharing in various ways, we can distinguish two traditions of thinking in the approaches. One tradition (e.g., chapter 10) establishes a perspective on the specific setting in which expertise sharing occurs, and it aims at providing appropriate means for that setting. The second tradition (e.g., chapter 12) tries to generalize (partial) problems that are typical for expertise-sharing processes and to find applicable solutions. In our view, the future of research on knowledge management or expertise sharing lies exactly in establishing a mutual understanding of these two traditions and in finding approaches that unite both perspectives in analysis as well as tool design.

9

Using a Room Metaphor to Ease Transitions in Groupware

Saul Greenberg and Mark Roseman

There are many perspectives on how expertise can be managed and shared by people. For example, from an artificial intelligence perspective, key challenges include how we can get experts to articulate their knowledge (via knowledge elicitation techniques), how that knowledge can be encoded on a computer system (perhaps as an expert system), and how people can query and verify that knowledge. From an organizational memory perspective, challenges include how knowledge collected by members of the organization can be captured in an ongoing fashion (e.g., frequently asked questions), structured within the computer (e.g., as a tree), and searched in a meaningful way.

Our own perspective considers expertise sharing as a fundamental part of everyday collaboration. When people collaborate, they often communicate their knowledge or are coordinating ways to share their knowledge. Our premise is that if we can provide people with groupware systems that support and enhance their collaborations, then the same systems will naturally support expertise sharing and management.

Unfortunately collaboration is awkward in today's groupware systems. In this chapter we describe one of the reasons why groupware is awkward: it contains gaps that make it difficult for people to move easily between different styles of work. After introducing the problem, we describe why systems based upon a room metaphor can ease people's transitions across these gaps, allowing them to collaborate naturally and thus making it easier for them to share and manage their expertise.

9.1   Gaps in Groupware

In 1987, DeSanctis and Gallupe proposed a typology of group decision support systems that indicates how particular technologies bridge time and space. This typology was then applied to groupware by Johansen (1988) and subsequently propagated in almost every introduction to computer-supported cooperative work (CSCW) (e.g., Nunamaker et al. 1991; Shneiderman 1997; Dix et al. 1993; Baecker 1993; Preece 1994; Baecker et al. 1995). Table 9.1, for example, shows a typical space/time matrix and its quadrants.

Various authors have extended this typology to include further dimensions (Baecker et al. 1995) such as

• differences in group size (DeSanctis and Gallupe 1987);

• whether there are multiple individual versus group sites (Nunamaker et al. 1991);

Table 9.1
A Typical Space/Time Matrix

	Same Time	Different Times
Same Place	*Face-to-face interactions* Conference tables with embedded computers Public displays Dedicated tools for, e.g., voting and brainstorming	*Ongoing tasks* Team rooms Group displays Shift-work groupware Project management
Different Places	*Distributed real-time interactions* Chat systems Transparent sharing of single-user applications Collaboration-aware groupware Video conferencing Media spaces	*Communication and coordination* Unstructured or semi-structured e-mail Electronic bulletin boards Asynchronous conferencing List servers Workflow systems Schedulers Collaborative hypertext

Source: After Baecker et al. (1995).

• whether the time and place are predictable or unpredictable to participants (Grudin 1994);

• informal versus formal encounters (Preece 1994);

• refinement of same time/different times to distinguish access to a system and its objects as concurrent synchronized, serial, mixed, or unsynchronized, as well as to distinguish the "granularity" of sharing in terms of the object chunk size and the frequency of update (Dix et al. 1993).

The problem is that these taxonomies, while useful for classifying CSCW issues and technologies, do not reflect the ways people work together in practice. In the real world, people move continually and effortlessly between different styles of collaboration: across time, across place, across formality, and so on. Unfortunately, many groupware technologies were designed to handle only the limited collaborative activity or situation indicated by a single cell within the matrix, as can be seen by the examples in table 9.1. Consequently, when people move between styles of collaboration, they must switch from one groupware application to another. This introduces a barrier, or gap, that interferes with people's normal collaborative patterns. More formally, *gap* is defined as a physical or perceptual boundary within groupware that either distracts participants from the work they are doing or blocks them from crossing the spatial, temporal, or functional boundaries inherent in collaborative work (Ishii, Kobayashi, and Grudin 1993).[1] To move across these gaps, people now make fairly heavyweight and disruptive transitions within and between software. Alternatively, they may decide that the personal cost is too great and do without groupware support.

There are many other gaps in groupware, and some of those identified in the literature are raised here:[2]

• The gap between individual and shared work, where people have difficulty moving themselves, their working styles, and their artifacts between a personal working area and the group's working area (Ishii, Kobayashi, and Grudin 1993; Baecker 1993, ch. 14)

• The technology gap that exists when groups use both conventional software and groupware (Baecker 1993, ch. 14) and when groups work in heterogeneous computer environments

• The gap between synchronous and asynchronous work, where either different-time or same-time interaction is supported, but not both (Baecker 1993, ch. 14)

• The gap between different phases of a collaborative activity, where people need to move between different work tasks for instance, the movement between pre-, during-, and post-meeting activities, where people move between meeting preparation, the actual meeting, and meeting cleanup (Dubs and Hayne 1992; O'Grady and Greenberg 1994)

• The gap between the desire to collaborate and actually establishing a groupware session (Cockburn and Greenberg 1993)

• The gap between same place and different places, where part of a group that is trying to meet are co-located in a single room, another part in another room, and the rest in their own offices (Nunamaker et al. 1991; Baecker 1993, ch. 14)

• The gap between informal and formal activities (Nunamaker et al. 1991; Preece 1994)

• The gap between computer and desktop tools, where physical artifacts and tools (such as paper documents and pencils) cannot interoperate with electronic artifacts and tools (such as a paint program) (Ishii 1990)

One goal of modern groupware research is *seamlessness*, defined as mitigating or "eliminating unnecessary obstructing perceptual seams" or gaps (Ishii, Kobayashi, and Grudin 1993). Other authors have expressed similar views. Some assert that gaps must be bridged if groupware is to be effective (Baecker 1993, ch. 14), and others have called for any-time, any-place groupware (Baecker et al. 1995).

In this chapter we argue that groupware systems supporting a room metaphor can nurture a wide range of collaboration styles within a single environment. The affordances of a room metaphor imply functionality that helps mitigate or remove technical gaps, and that supplies users with a conceptual model which reduces perceptual seams. Consequently, the transitions that people make as they move between their styles of collaboration are eased. Technology that supports this wide range of collaboration styles will also support how people naturally share and manage expertise.

We begin by briefly listing some basic features of the room metaphor and how it affords individual and collaborative work. Then, we use the

TeamWave Workplace system as a case study of a groupware system designed around a room metaphor.

In sections 9.4 to 9.7 we introduce four different gaps and discuss how the room metaphor as realized in TeamWave Workplace can ease people's transitions across these gaps. In section 9.4 we show how rooms are equally suitable for supporting individual and group work. In particular, the transition between individual and group activity is just a function of the way a room is used and of the number of people in a room. In section 9.5 we show how making room artifacts persistent lets people move fluidly between synchronous and asynchronous work. People can leave messages, artifacts, and annotations for others, or work on them together if they occupy the same room at the same time. We illustrate this with an example that shows how people move through the pre-, during-, and post-meeting processes of a formal meeting. In section 9.6 we show how rooms ease the difficulty of establishing real-time connections by providing awareness of who is available for real-time interaction and by automatically making connections when they enter a common room. In section 9.7 we discuss how a technical space can become a social place by the way people craft meaning into particular rooms. In each section we discuss how these activities relate to the sharing and management of expertise.

9.2 Features Inherent in a Room Metaphor

The crafting of physical space and how it can be used by people is well known in the field of urban planning and architecture (e.g., Alexander 1979). Similarly, the crafting of virtual space is being studied in human-Computer interaction (e.g., Henderson and Card 1986; Kuhn and Blumental 1996; Harrison and Dourish 1996; Benford et al. 1996). In this section we extend that work to develop an (incomplete) list of features suggested by a room metaphor. We concentrate on features that afford both individual and collaborative work, and their implications for the design of electronic rooms.

A room metaphor is a particular type of spatial model whose features afford a natural way to provide people with good collaborative opportunities (e.g., Kuhn and Blumental 1996). The rooms we consider are analogous to physical rooms used by teams within an organization. Such rooms typically include (Covi, Olson, and Rocco 1998)

• personal offices;

• shared rooms available to several teams, where a room's use may be scheduled and there is an expectation that the room be returned to its former state after use, e.g., breakout rooms and conference rooms;

• live-in dedicated project rooms, which (usually) contain open offices housing a team of three to six people and a shared space where people can work together and leave artifacts in it, e.g., skunk works and team rooms;

• non-live-in dedicated project rooms, which are similar to the previous example except that team members have their offices elsewhere, e.g., war rooms;

• public spaces for social interaction and casual work, e.g., coffee rooms, foyers, and commons.

The features described in this section and summarized in the first two columns of table 9.2 arise from particular properties inherent in physical rooms. Rooms are bounded spaces; they act as containers; items within a room have spatial locations; and people can inhabit a collection of rooms. Later sections describe how particular features can be represented electronically, as summarized in the rightmost column of table 9.2.

A Room as a Bounded Space
The first property of a room is that it is a *bounded space* and affords the features of partitioning, containment, and permeability.

Walls can *partition* a large space into a collection of rooms. Because of partitioning, the distance and barriers (walls) between rooms can separate or bring people and their artifacts together (Harrison and Dourish 1996). Individual rooms act as *containers* (Kuhn and Blumental 1996). They contain people, furniture, tools for work and communication (e.g., telephones, overhead projectors), documents, and other artifacts that can support both individual and group activities. Finally, rooms are *permeable*. People can enter and leave them (Kuhn and Blumental 1996), and items can be brought into them or can be removed from them. People can also look into a room, perhaps because the door is open or because there is a window in it.

Table 9.2
Features of Physical Rooms and How They Are Supported in TeamWave Workplace

Feature	Description	How Supported in TeamWave
Bounded Space		
Partitioning	Rooms are collections of bounded spaces, separated by walls.	The space is partitioned as a set of discrete rooms, individually presented within a large window. Individuals and objects can be in only one room at a time.
Containment	Rooms can contain people, tools, and artifacts.	Rooms contain generic tools for communication (e.g., chat) and work (e.g., shared whiteboard and the drawings created on it). They also contain any number of applet instances and the artifacts created within them.
Permeability	People can enter and leave rooms, look inside them through doors and windows, and bring things in and out of them.	People can navigate between rooms. Doorways to other rooms can be placed within a room. People can also see who is in other rooms and their levels of activity but cannot see what is going on in a room unless they enter it. People can only copy items to other rooms.
Container		
Persistence	Objects left in a room persist over time in the same spatial location.	All rooms and their current states persist over time, even when the server is shut down and restarted. This includes marks on the whiteboard, and applets and their contents. However, for privacy, people can only see the chat text typed while they were in the room.

Table 9.2
(continued)

Feature	Description	How Supported in TeamWave
Customization	People can bring in their own artifacts and arrange them in the space.	People customize a room by creating it, marking the wall, adding applets to it, setting access controls, and using the applets. Customizations persist over time.
Privacy and ownership	The way a room is customized often indicates its ownership and who is allowed to be in it.	Rooms are given names and have an owner. Access control rights can be set explicitly. Door states can be set to indicate how public or private a room is.
Spatial Location		
Spatial relations	Objects can be organized within a room when a person spatially relates them to one another.	Applets in a room can be placed close together, and their positions persist until they are moved. Marks on the whiteboard can also be situated next to applets.
Proximity and action	Collaborators can interpret each other's actions by how close they are to one another and to the objects in the space.	People's position in a room, its whiteboard marks, and its applets and contents are indicated by telepointers and radar overviews.
Common reference and orientation	People see and reference the room, its objects, and its inhabitants from a similar orientation.	A room appears identical to all people in it, but through scrolling, they can have different views into it. Even though they may see different portions of the room, all have a small radar overview that provides a bird's eye view of the entire room.
Reciprocity	Collaborators know that others can see their actions and objects in the same way.	When people are in the same part of a room, all objects and the fine-grained actions taken over them appear immediately on all displays.

Table 9.2
(continued)

Feature	Description	How Supported in TeamWave
Inhabitation of the Space		
Presence and awareness	People sense each other's presence and activities as they navigate between rooms and glance into doorways.	A peripheral window shows all the people present in the space, and which room they are in. Another window shows a list of rooms and who is in them.
Encounters	People meet and initiate encounters as they navigate between rooms and as others enter inhabited rooms.	People can send a message to others seen in these windows. Or they can enter the room, which automatically initiates communication channels.
Habitation	Different rooms can be inhabited by one or more people, or be empty.	Different rooms can be inhabited by one or more people, or be empty.
Real-time meeting definition	A meeting occurs merely by having two or more people in a room.	A meeting occurs whenever two or more people are in the same room. Communication channels are automatically opened, and people can collaborate over all the items in the room.
Asynchronous definition	Asynchronous collaboration occurs when people leave things for others in a room.	Asynchronous collaboration occurs whenever a person leaves a note or artifact in a room. Because items persist, anyone who later enters the room can see them.

A Room as a Container

Second, rooms are containers that afford the features of persistence and customization. Objects left in a room *persist* over time. Consequently, people can place and store objects in it (Kuhn and Blumental 1996). When people leave a room, they expect its objects to remain undisturbed in the same spot on their return, unless someone else had entered the room in the interim. As a persistent container, a room can be *customized* by people's bringing in their own artifacts and by manipulating artifacts already within the room. The way a room is customized often indicates its *ownership* and its *privacy*, that is, who is allowed in it (Kuhn and Blumental 1996). For example, Covi, Olson, and Rocco (1998) studied the way cognitive artifacts are used in dedicated project rooms. They noticed that these rooms contain flip charts and whiteboards as well as items taped to the walls. These act as shared visual displays that display work in progress, current status of tasks, reference materials, and so on.

Spatial Locations of Objects within a Room

The third property of rooms is that objects occupy spatial locations within them, which affords the features of spatial relations, proximity and action, common reference and orientation, and reciprocity.

The *spatial relations* between items in a room are indicated by their spatial location relative to one another. Consequently, people can organize a room by associating, aggregating, and ranking its objects (Kuhn and Blumental 1996). For example, Covi, Olson, and Rocco (1998) noticed that software developers using flip chart sheets in their dedicated skunk works room moved and clustered the sheets at various times, for instance, sheets were placed side by side so that people could look for similarities between the software requirements shown on them. As another example, teams collaborating over a whiteboard or table top often specified relations of text and graphics by clustering them together (Tang 1991). Yet again, Leiva-Lobos, De Michelis, and Covarrubias (1997) mention "the physical arrangement of the work space makes the historical and spatial context of the project visible to its participants." Next, collaborators use *proximity of actions* to interpret each other's activities by seeing how close people are to one other and to the objects in the space (Harrison and Dourish 1996). Because objects are fixed in a common location, people within the room can have a *common reference and orientation* to one another and to the objects within the space (Harrison and Dourish 1996; Benford et al. 1996; Tang 1991). They all see and reference the room, its objects, and its inhabitants from a similar orientation. Similarly, collaborators can expect *reciprocity* because they know that others can see their actions and objects in the same way (Harrison and Dourish 1996). In essence, the objects and their arrangement within a room becomes part of a shared visual display (Covi, Olson, and Rocco 1998). However, the degree of common reference, orientation, and reciprocity around the display depends on where people are directing their attention (Gutwin and Greenberg 1996).

Rooms as an Inhabited Collection

The final property of rooms is that people can inhabit them. Combined with other properties, this affords the features of presence and awareness, encounters, and the way rooms can be inhabited. It also defines both real-time meetings and a limited form of asynchronous interaction.

People inhabiting a collection of rooms show *presence and awareness.* Habitation means that individuals are present in the space and that others can sense their presence and activities as they move between rooms and as they glance into them. Consequently, people meet and occasionally initiate *encounters* with one another as they navigate between rooms and as they enter rooms with other people in them (Kraut, Egido, and Galegher 1988; Kuhn and Blumental 1996). These encounters can become many different kinds of conversations: short social banters, informal status reports, opportunistic discussions, and of course opportunities to request and share expertise. Next, different rooms can be *inhabited* by one or more people, or be empty. However, the size and layout of particular rooms can restrict how many people can be reasonably accommodated. The way people use the space also defines different types of interaction. A *real-time meeting* can be defined as merely having two or more people inhabit the same room, as they can now communicate and collaborate with one another. In contrast, *asynchronous collaboration* occurs when people leave things for others in a room: they know that the other people will be inhabiting the space sometime in the future.

Summary

Physical rooms have features that imply how people can use them for both individual and collaborative activities, which include how people naturally share expertise. For example, people inhabiting a room often request help from other people within a room, either by explicit questions like "Do any of you know how to get the printer to work with transparencies?" or by implicit out-louds (Heath et al. 1995), where people say what they are doing to keep others informed, for instance, "I can't seem to get this thing to print transparencies." As another example, the persistent nature of artifacts in a room means that people can exchange their expertise over time, for example, contributing experts may work (perhaps asynchronously or synchronously) on a blueprint left on a drafting table over several days. Artifacts can also help manage expertise, for instance, notes left in a room (perhaps in a visible place or as something attached to an artifact that it is talking about) can indicate specific requests for help, list what one has done, or note what one is about to do. A third example is that rooms are natural repositories for formal expertise. Documents developed by a group are collected, and the group knows where this collection is stored and how to access it. Adding and modifying this collection is easy because it is within the inhabited space.

While providing collaboration features in a room may make sense, most groupware systems do not support the features and corresponding collaboration opportunities suggested here, or do so in an awkward manner. To contrast, we suggest that the reader juxtapose the offerings of typical systems based on the notion of "groupware as tool" (e.g., a shared whiteboard application or an audio/video tool) with the offerings of groupware based on a room metaphor.

One example of such a room-based system is TeamWave Workplace, which is used as a case study in this chapter.

9.3 TeamWave Workplace

TeamWave Workplace is a commercial Internet groupware product based on a room metaphor.[3] TeamWave was originally based on a research prototype called TeamRooms, developed at the University of Calgary (Roseman and Greenberg 1996a; 1996b; 1997; Roseman 1996). In turn, TeamRooms was influenced by our earlier work developing the

GroupKit groupware toolkit (Roseman and Greenberg 1996c). The features and user interface of TeamWave Workplace described here reflect an early version of TeamWave (released in early 1997) that was very similar to the TeamRooms prototype. Later versions of TeamWave (detailed at the TeamWave Web site) differ significantly from the version presented here.

In this section we briefly describe the interface and features of Team-Wave Workplace. Figures 9.1 and 9.2 illustrate the main components of the TeamWave user interface. The large window at the bottom of figure 9.1 shows a user (Carl) sharing a room called TeamWave Demo with two other users (Saul and Mark). The bottom window in figure 9.2 shows the same room as seen by another user (Saul), who is looking at a different part of the room. The top windows in figures 9.1 and 9.2 show various peripheral windows.

Startup Features

Setup TeamWave uses a client-server architecture, where a server on the network maintains a set of rooms for a community. Administrators set up the membership of a TeamWave community by specifying which users are allowed to connect to the server. Administrators may also define subgroups and their membership, which allows an end-user to assign access control rights to a room by specifying a group's name.

Starting Up Through a traditional login dialogue, users connect their client to the TeamWave server that maintains the set of rooms for their community. They are then placed in a default room, and their screen will look similar to the one shown in figure 9.1 (except for the business card window). Before detailing the contents of the rooms window, we describe how users can navigate between rooms and create new ones.

Entering Other Rooms Figure 9.1 displays the Rooms on This Server window (a), which lists all rooms currently available to the community. A user enters another room by selecting it from this list. Though primarily used for navigation, the list also displays which users are in each room. For example, Adam is in the Foyer while Saul, Mark, and Carl are in the TeamWave Demo room. The door icons are primarily social

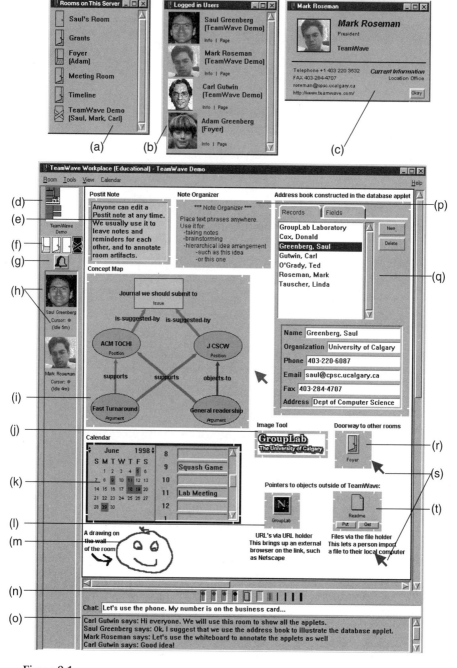

Figure 9.1

TeamWave Workplace user interface, showing a room and peripheral windows as seen by user Carl.

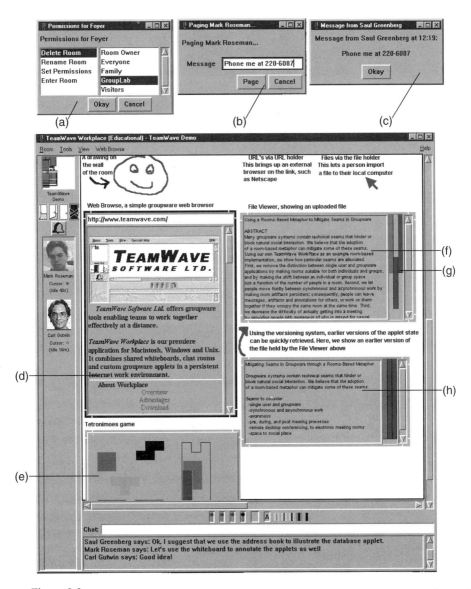

Figure 9.2
Another user's (Saul's) view of the same room, in which he has scrolled to a different position. Other peripheral windows are also illustrated.

indicators; open doors suggest public rooms, and closed doors suggest private rooms. The icons also reflect system access rights, for instance, a locked door prevents users from entering the room.

Creating New Rooms   Users create new rooms by choosing a command from the Room menu, specifying a name for the room. By default, anyone in the community can enter, change, or even delete a room. If desired, the room's creator can limit these actions to specific subgroups (figure 9.2(a)).

Seeing Other Users   Users also see a Logged in Users window that lists all people currently connected to the group's server as well as the room each user is currently working in. For example, in figure 9.1, we see that four people are currently logged on (b). Each person's image is normally a scanned-in picture provided by the user. In one experimental version of TeamWave, the still pictures could be replaced with video snapshots taken several times per minute.

Seeking Information About Other Users   More information on users can be found by double-clicking a person's image or by selecting Info from the Logged in Users window (figure 9.1). This will display a business card window (c) that includes phone and fax numbers, e-mail addresses, personal home page URLs, and people's physical locations.

Standard Communication Features
Though each room in TeamWave can be customized to suit the specific needs of the group and their task, certain generic facilities are provided that are useful for a wide range of groups and activities.

Paging   A user can send a message to another logged-in user, even if they are in different rooms, by selecting Page from the Logged in Users window (figure 9.1). This raises a dialog box allowing the user to compose a short message (figure 9.2(b)). The message will appear in a pop-up window on the other person's display (figure 9.2(c)).

Chat   A simple text-based chat tool (figure 9.1(o)) is provided that allows users to type messages to each other when they are in the same room. While digital audio or video conferencing can provide an excellent complement to TeamWave, the system does not require such facilities, thereby accommodating users without the necessary hardware or bandwidth.

Shared Whiteboard   A shared whiteboard occupies the "wall" of each room. Users select different colored pens or the eraser from the pen tray (figure 9.1(n)) and can produce freehand drawings on it (m). They can also add text to the wall, as shown by the labels in the room.

Awareness Features
TeamWave provides several facilities for maintaining awareness of other team members in the room. These facilities provide both a general awareness of who is around and a more fine-grained awareness of others' actions in the room (Gutwin and Greenberg 1996).

Room Users   Each room displays a list of users in the current room (figure 9.1(h)). The local user is not shown on the list, which is why the images in figures 9.1 and 9.2 differ. The user list also shows idle times for each user, which indicates how long it has been since that person was active in the room (since they last typed or moved the mouse).

Telepointers   Within the workspace itself, telepointers—one for each user—communicate gestures to provide a fine-grained sense of awareness of the actions of other users (figure 9.1(s)). Telepointers are colored, and each person can see the color of the other people's telepointers on the user list (h).

Room Overview Radar   Because the room is larger than will fit on a single display, a radar view (figure 9.1(d)) provides a stylized miniature overview of the entire room. The radar shows the locations of all applets in the room, the position of each user's viewport into the room, and miniature telepointers to show the location of their mouse cursor. As users move around the room and manipulate applets, the radar tracks their actions. Because users can scroll independently to different parts of the room (see figure 9.2 and figure 9.3 [later], where only a small part overlaps), the radar lets each person track where the others are and what they can see.

Applets

While the communication and awareness features provide fairly generic support for collaboration, applets in TeamWave are designed for more specific needs of the group. Each applet is in fact a special-purpose groupware application, which team members can include in their rooms as needed by selecting them from the Tools menu. For example, a room used to manage a software project may have applets for task lists, bug-reporting forms, a pointer to an online version of the project's specification, and so on. In contrast, a "coffee room" might have applets for a card game, online comics, or electronic postcards left in the room by traveling colleagues. As another example, the particular room illustrated in figures 9.1 and 9.2 was set up to display and annotate all TeamWave applets for a demonstration.

As shown in figures 9.1 and 9.2, each applet is embedded in its own frame within the room, in a similar fashion to OpenDoc or OLE/ActiveX components (Orfali, Harkey, and Edwards 1996). At any time, users may select new applets from the Tools menu, choosing from a list of available groupware applications. Users can move, resize, and delete applets. All such changes are immediately visible to all users in the room. Applets can also add commands to the global menu bar (e.g., there is a Calendar menu label in figure 9.1 because the Calendar applet has the focus).

TeamWave supports any of the types of applications that could be constructed in GroupKit (Roseman and Greenberg 1996c), including text editors, drawing tools, card games, meeting tools, groupware Web browsers, sticky notes, doorways providing direct portals between rooms, pointers to documents that will be displayed in external applications, and so on. Applets are fully group-aware, allowing shared views, immediate updates of fine-grained actions, and simultaneous editing.

Group Memory

TeamWave keeps a version history of the state of each room and each applet. Versions are automatically saved when the last user in a room leaves or when a user explicitly saves a snapshot. Users can browse and retrieve earlier versions. If a user asks for a previous version of a room, the complete state of the room is replaced with the earlier version. If she asks for a previous applet version, a new instance of that applet is created in the room that holds the earlier version. This allows users to compare two versions of an applet, for example, to review earlier stages in a project. In figure 9.2 a group has used the File Viewer applet (f) to view a paper that was being written by a group member. Through the versioning mechanism, group members retrieved a much earlier version of the paper (h), allowing them to compare the differences.

Lowest Common Denominator Technology

Because groupware must be accessible to the entire group, TeamWave requires only a modest technology infrastructure. First, TeamWave works with low bandwidth networks, including 14.4 modem links. Second, TeamWave runs on most popular systems, including Windows 95/NT, MacOS, and several flavors of Unix. Thus people in a TeamWave community can use quite different platforms yet still collaborate with each other.

9.4   Transitions between Individual and Group Work

Sharing and managing expertise appear, almost by definition, to be activities that require collaboration between people. Consequently, we envision and design systems for expertise management that assume collaboration as the starting point. Unfortunately, this view is naive, for it does not recognize that expertise begins with individuals whose concern is to develop and use their own expertise over time. The need to share expertise can come after the fact, perhaps when others demand it, or by serendipity, or perhaps as a side effect of a group's need to coordinate and share their knowledge over a developing project.

Everyday working styles of people, which include the ways people share expertise, shift regularly and easily between individual and group activity. This implies that software should support both individual and group needs. Unfortunately, most systems are categorized either as single-user applications or as multi-user groupware. Forcing people to switch tools introduces a gap for those who want to move between individual and group activities.

Single-user applications offer little or no explicit support for people who want to work together through computers. While people do often use single-user systems collaboratively (Nardi and Miller 1991), much effort is required to do so across time and distance barriers. Nardi and Miller's (1991) study of spreadsheet users, for example, clearly describes how co-located people share expertise over spreadsheets: one person developing the content of a spreadsheet is helped by another who understands how to program spreadsheets. This style of interaction is far more difficult when people are geographically distributed. On the other hand, groupware built to fit only group needs is often inadequate for supporting individual work. The gap between these two categories often means that people cannot use the same tools for conceptually similar tasks that cross over individual and group work (Ishii, Kobayashi, and Grudin 1993; Baecker 1993, ch. 14). People must take on the additional work load of shifting between tools and learning how to use new tools. They must translate common artifacts, such as documents, into formats amenable to both single and groupware systems.

In this section we show that the gap between these two categories is unnecessary and that a room metaphor can naturally support the light-weight transitions between single and group activities.

Considering Individual Work as Cooperative Work

Cockburn and Thimbleby (1991) suggest that CSCW environments can be problematic when there is a disparity between systems used for personal work and those used for cooperative work. They argue for a *reflexive perspective* on CSCW that blurs the distinction between personal and group work, claiming that an individual often behaves in ways that resemble a group's behavior. They suggest that cooperative environments must not only support group activity but also cater to individual requirements. If these environments are useful for personal work, they will become familiar and predictable, which in turn minimizes the extra effort usually associated with learning a dedicated groupware tool.

The reflexive perspective of CSCW suggests that individual work has properties of group behavior, where individuals adopt at least two roles when working:

• In a *personal management role*, a person coordinates and schedules personal activities, such as creating to-do lists, leaving reminders for oneself, and so on. As part of this, people can easily share expertise with their future selves. For example, programmers recognize that a technique just mastered is easily forgotten; if they anticipate using this technique again, they may write an example program to demonstrate it and store it away for later referral. Similarly, people often look at ways they have previously done something to help them reconstruct how they did it.

• In a *worker role*, a person actually carries out the steps of the activities.

When there is more than one project and more than one working environment, such as when the physical work is spread over several machines in different locations, people spend much time communicating and coordinating with their future selves, almost as if their future selves were actually different people.

TeamWave and Individual Work
The room metaphor in TeamWave Workplace has been used in exactly this reflexive manner. For example, consider the personal room shown in figure 9.3, which is stylized from an actual room created and used by one of the authors. We see room artifacts created for personal management, such as the to-do list, a calendar for personal scheduling, and a note that reminds the room's creator about urgent actions. The room also contains ongoing work that the owner can review and work on whenever he is in the room. This includes the concept map of interface methodologies being developed for a course and a partially completed paper review. In a sense, these artifacts acts as a working memory that contain the person's developing knowledge; they act as the means to manage that knowledge within a person over time. Finally, the room contains pointers to objects not visible in this room. These include a file titled "teamwave.txt" (a paper being written) that can be uploaded and downloaded, and a doorway pointing to the Grants room, which contains documents relevant to current grant applications.

TeamWave implements several features of a room metaphor (table 9.2) that make it a suitable environment for supporting an individual's personal management role and worker role: persistence, customization and ownership; spatial relationships of objects; and machine-independence.

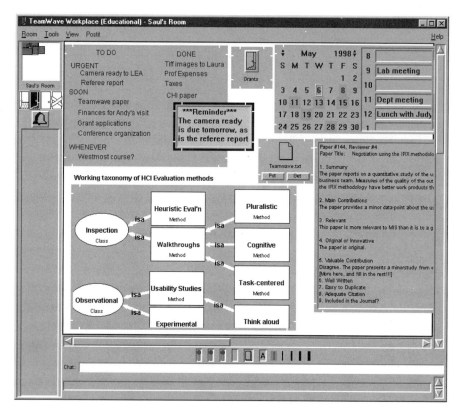

Figure 9.3
A TeamWave room that supports individual work. Personal management tools include the to-do list, the calendar, and the reminder as well as the immediate visibility of ready-to-hand work artifacts. These artifacts include pointers to other rooms, documents, and ongoing work.

First, the persistent nature of a room and the fact that it can be customized creates a sense of personal space, context, and ownership. When its owner enters it, all items are exactly as they had been left. Multiple rooms means that people can create multiple contexts to reflect different tasks and that personal task switching is quickly accomplished by moving to the appropriate room (Henderson and Card 1986; Card and Henderson 1987; Card, Robertson, and Mackinlay 1991). In contrast, users of traditional graphical environments must reestablish their context by remembering relevant files, opening them, positioning and sizing them on the screen in a meaningful way, and moving to the correct portion of the file.

Second, relationships between personal management activities and work artifacts can be made by spatial proximity and by annotation. As an example, a note (figure 9.3) reminds the room's owner that both the camera-ready copy of the paper and the referee report are due tomorrow. The note's appearance and position on top of the to-do list suggests urgency. It is also close to the artifacts being referred to. The paper ("teamwave.txt") is next to the note, and the paper review is clearly visible. (Alternatively, the owner could have used the whiteboard to draw lines between the note and the items.) The positioning of doorways to other rooms next to some relevant information is yet another way to link related items. In contrast, traditional systems do not link personal management tools with work artifacts.

Third, TeamWave is not tied to any individual machine, which means that people can access their rooms anywhere, anytime, and from most platforms (e.g., Macs, PCs, Unix). Unlike pages on the World Wide Web (which are also accessible anytime, anywhere), all room artifacts are editable. People can also make non-TeamWave objects accessible within a room by uploading them into the room as a file. For example, a person can import a Microsoft Word file into the room and then download it onto a different machine later. In this case, the file is viewed and edited outside of TeamWave.

In summary, the notions of persistence, customization, ownership, and spatial relationships inherent in the room metaphor; the anytime, anyplace access to work artifacts; and the cross-platform capabilities of TeamWave support the tenets of reflexive CSCW by providing personal coordination, management, and expertise sharing.

Flow between Individual and Shared Work

The next step is to see how rooms facilitate people's smoothly shifting between individual and group work, which includes how expertise held by one person can be shared naturally.

Physical rooms can be empty, or occupied by a single person, dyads, small groups, and (space allowing) large numbers. People can bring items into a room, either for their own use, to leave for others, or to work on together with others. For example, Covi, Olson, and Rocco (1998) observed that physical rooms afford easy transitions from individual to group work, where team members report "being co-present during individual work provided opportunities for interruption at a moment's notice for important interactions." The room itself is passive; what determines whether the room (including its contents) is a group or individual space and whether a meeting is occurring (see table 9.2, real-time meeting definition) is simply the entry and departure of people, and social convention.

The room metaphor in TeamWave Workplace is similar to its physical counterpart. The system makes no technical distinctions between single-user and group rooms, or between single-user and groupware applications and artifacts contained by a room. We have already seen that a room can provide a good personal management and working space for individuals. The same facilities make it a good group management and working space. The same room becomes a group space whenever a second person enters it. If a person enters an already occupied room, the room and its applets behave as fully functional real-time groupware, and synchronous collaborative work can be pursued. If a person enters a previously occupied room, he can see what items others have left. That is, the room's persistence can cause it to behave like asynchronous groupware that supports group management activities.

In summary, people can make the transition between individual and shared work smoothly because rooms make no technical distinction between individual and group tools. The same tools for personal management, expertise sharing, and work become tools for group management, group expertise sharing, and group work. As in real life, it is the individuals and groups that determine how the space is used, rather than the technology.

9.5   Transitions between Synchronous and Asynchronous Collaboration

Most groupware supports either synchronous or asynchronous collaboration, but not both. In this section we briefly review the major styles of groupware within these categories, show how a room metaphor lets people move fluidly across the synchronous/asynchronous gap, and illustrate through a scenario a group's blending of asynchronous and synchronous activities over an entire meeting process.

Groupware for Synchronous and Asynchronous Work

There are several major categories of asynchronous systems (table 9.1, right side). People can send messages to one another with electronic mail, and to groups with list servers and bulletin boards (Sproull 1991; Sproull and Kiesler 1991). Group members can carry on lengthy but focused conversations with asynchronous conferencing systems that maintain conversational threads about specific topics (Turoff 1991; Sproull and Kiesler 1991). They can also negotiate and schedule activities on group calendars (Lange 1992). Managers and workers can coordinate commitments through semistructured and structured messaging systems (e.g., Object Lens by Malone, Lai, and Fry 1992; the Coordinator by Flores et al. 1988; Lotus Notes). Teams can track activities through workflow systems (Abbot and Sarin 1994). Organizations can also post and retrieve documentation comprising a repository of organizational memory and expertise through hypertext systems (Conklin 1992; Ackerman and Malone 1990; Ackerman 1994).

Similarly, there are different categories of synchronous systems (table 9.1, left side). These support real-time communication ranging from textual chat systems, to audio channels, to video phones. Recent advances in communication systems increase the sense of tele-presence, where interpersonal cues are transmitted, such as body language, gaze direction (Ishii, Kobayashi, and Grudin 1993), gestures (Tang 1991; Greenberg, Gutwin, and Roseman 1996), and spatial relations between participants (Buxton 1992). Other systems support real-time collaboration over work artifacts. These include application sharing (Greenberg 1990), groupware drawing systems (Greenberg, Hayne, and Rada 1995), groupware text editors (Baecker et al. 1993), live presentation tools, and business meeting tools for brainstorming and idea organization (Valacich, Dennis, and Nunamaker 1991). All these systems encourage interaction, which in turn acts as a natural conduit for sharing expertise through conversation and discussion.

For group members to switch between asynchronous and synchronous interaction, they must switch the tools they are using. This is a heavy-weight transition. Applications must be found and started, communication channels must be established, documents created in asynchronous tools (e.g., an e-mail attachment) must be imported into a groupware application that allows them to be shared and edited, and so on.

How Rooms Permit Asynchronous and Synchronous Activity

A room metaphor offers a simple way for a group to move between asynchronous and synchronous work. First, when team members are present in a room at the same time, they are automatically working together synchronously. Unlike groupware applications that require people to create and establish separate connections between each tool and communication channel, a room acts as a single connection point. The act of entering a room immediately connects all people within it, both for communication (e.g., the chat tool) and for work (e.g., all applets and the background whiteboard).

Second, when people work in the room at different times, they can work asynchronously just by leaving things in the room. In a study of real project rooms, Covi, Olson, and Rocco (1998) observed that teams leave coordination documents for each other: to-do lists, action items, telephone logs, vacation schedules, and so on. TeamWave supports this type of asynchronous activity through the same features that support reflexive CSCW. Persistence allows work artifacts and annotations to be left in a room for others to review or change at a later time. Spatial proximity can link these messages and artifacts. For example, notes, reminders and comments can be left on the whiteboard or written on Post-its next to a relevant work object.

Third, the same artifacts work for both asynchronous and synchronous work. All room objects can be used either by a single user or by several users at the same time. Team members can work on tasks individually and then share task artifacts with others, either asynchronously or synchronously. The transition between asynchronous and synchronous activity becomes a function of how people use the rooms and its tools, rather than a function of system constraints. Of course, this same capability also helps ease the transition between single-user applications and groupware.

Scenario: Flow through the Pre-, During-, and Post-Meeting Process
This section illustrates through a scenario how a group using TeamWave can blend asynchronous and synchronous activities over the different phases of a meeting life cycle.

Formal meetings are organized ahead of time. One example is a committee meeting, consisting of up to ten people and usually arranged for a formal exchange of information, for making decisions, or for delegating responsibilities (Jay 1976). Dubs and Hayne (1992) and Jay (1976) see this style of meeting as a process that cycles through three generic phases: pre-meeting setup, during-meeting activities, and post-meeting activities (which could lead into the next meeting). Each phase in turn contains a variety of subactivities, as detailed by Dubs and Hayne (1992) and shown in table 9.3. In unrelated work, Poltrock and Engelbeck (1997) describe several meeting scenarios that closely match these phases.

Most groupware systems typically support only a single phase or activity within the meeting process. Scheduling software, for example, only schedules people and resources as part of the pre-meeting process. Similarly, e-mail supports "informing" participants in the pre-meeting (which may include attaching documents to bring people up to speed as part of expertise sharing) and "communicating next steps" in the post-meeting. Most real-time groupware provides single tools that support only particular tasks and processes in the during-meeting phase. Existing groupware contains considerable gaps that inhibit people from moving through the synchronous and asynchronous phases of the meeting process.

The room metaphor, in conjunction with e-mail, can ease a group's transitions across many (but not all) of these gaps. Consider a scenario inspired by a real-life situation. Saul and Judy are co-chairs of the technical track of a conference, and Adam and Jeremy are the conference chairs. Saul is charged with setting up the first meeting for this team. Figure 9.4 illustrates how Saul can configure several rooms as part of the pre-meeting process. Saul begins by creating a room called Meeting Room. Using the Roster applet, he then jots down the meeting goal and the roster of potential attendees. With the note organizer, he notes agenda points. He indicates the time of this and subsequent meetings on the Calendar applet. Saul then collects information relevant to the agenda items; these are critical for expertise sharing, to make sure people come into the meeting sharing a certain level of knowledge. For agenda

Table 9.3
Phases and Activities in Formal Meetings

Phase	Activity	Examples
Pre-meeting	Set goals	Review previous meetings to understand the status of ongoing process.
		Describe meeting goals that establish a purpose for the meeting.
	Get participants	Develop a roster of appropriate potential attendees.
		Inform participants of meeting.
	Collect materials	Develop and gather necessary documents, including the agenda.
		Circulate background material ahead of time.
		Select and reserve equipment, e.g., presentation tools or process aids.
During meeting	Start-up	Revise meeting objectives.
		Review and revise agenda.
		Revise tool selection.
	During	Monitor activities to see how they conform to constraints, e.g., time.
		Follow particular processes and perform meeting tasks as required.
		Record events as required.
	Wind-up	Summarize the meeting.
		Determine the next steps.
Post-meeting	Document	Create and distribute documents.
	Communicate	Communicate next steps to participants.

Source: Compiled from Dubs and Hayne (1992).

item 1, he creates another room, Timeline, and adds relevant information to it. A doorway to this room is included in the main meeting room, with an arrow attaching it to the agenda item. For agenda item 3, he uploads an external document (the ACM budget) so that others can retrieve and read it ahead of time. For agenda item 4, he includes a URL pointer to the old call for papers produced for the previous conference. (Alternatively, he could have used the groupware Web browser to include the call for papers directly in the meeting space.) He then uses the Database applet to create an "action item" tool, where action items as well as who is responsible for carrying them out can be added quickly

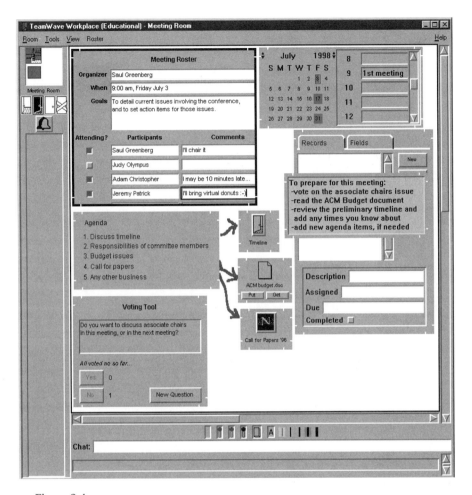

Figure 9.4
A TeamWave room configured for a formal meeting. As part of the premeeting process, the chairperson has indicated the meeting goals and the roster of participants, and has brought in materials and tools necessary for the meeting.

during the meeting. Also included is a voting tool, which in this case is primed with a question about a potential agenda item but which will also be used throughout the actual meeting. He then tells participants by e-mail to look into this new room and leaves a Post-it note in the room telling them what to do before the meeting. (Instead of e-mail, the Roster applet could conceivably be extended to automatically inform people about the meeting.)

At this point, other participants can enter the room, review the information already in place, and add their own contributions (e.g., agenda items, tools, documents) in preparation for the meeting. The room in figure 9.4 shows the roster partially filled in by participants who have indicated asynchronously that they will attend. In terms of expertise sharing, individuals may modify the information (e.g., if they notice it is incomplete or inaccurate), or annotate it with supplemental information, or even bring in new information that they feel should be included as part of the meeting.

When the meeting actually begins, participants see one another "walk through the door" as their icons become visible on the room users' list and as their images and telepointers appear within the room. Participants then work together synchronously. They review the agenda and move onto particular agenda items, using information that has been brought into the room ahead of time. For example, they move into the Timeline room when it is time to work on the conference schedule. Of course, new tools and information can be brought in as needed to support particular processes and tasks. Salient meeting points can be easily recorded, perhaps by inserting notes into the room and by adding action items to the previously prepared database. Participants can then review these points and action items, and summarize the meeting during the windup phase.

The post-meeting process, which is mostly asynchronous, is straightforward as well. The state of the room becomes part of the meeting record, and the versioning system attached to rooms and applets allows people to review the evolution of meeting artifacts. Any participant can go into the room and retrospectively add any documentation and information that further summarizes the meeting and that leads into the next one. The room becomes the medium for the group to communicate asynchronously with each other. In essence, the state of the room at the end of the meeting reflects the current state of expertise held by the group, which can still be modified as required.

The room metaphor portrayed by TeamWave can only go so far to support formal meeting processes. Unlike many group decision support systems (Nunamaker et al. 1991), a room does not impose any meeting process. Nothing dictates that rosters and agenda items be prepared, that relevant information be brought into the room ahead of time, or that action items be recorded. As with a physical room, it is the discipline and social structure of the team as well as the affordances of the space that create a sense of a formal meeting room. Of course, formal protocols *could* be encoded into a room, where the software would insist that participants follow a particular meeting protocol.

In summary, this scenario shows how people using TeamWave rooms can move smoothly between synchronous and asynchronous activities within the meeting life cycle. Because TeamWave artifacts persist, a room supports asynchronous activity. Participants can configure a meeting room ahead of time with necessary information and tools, leave messages for others, and add information retrospectively. Because all items in a room have real-time groupware capabilities, TeamWave supports real-time conferencing just by having more than one person in a room. Participants can meet in a room and use it to review information, to bring up tools to support particular tasks, and to record items for posterity. Because TeamWave rooms are persistent and versioned, the room becomes a repository for all meeting artifacts and tracks how they evolve over time.

9.6 The Transition from Being Aware of Who Is Around to Working Together in Real Time

In the real world people regularly and serendipitously encounter one another and use these encounters as opportunities for further conversation. This is difficult to do in most groupware; there is a gap between knowing who is available in the electronic community and using that knowledge to establish a real-time groupware session.

Successful teams rely on regular contact between their members, and this contact is often informal and unplanned (Kraut, Egido, and

Galegher 1988; Root 1988; Cockburn and Greenberg 1993; Poltrock and Engelbeck 1997). In physical environments informal interaction occurs regularly: people bump into each other in hallways; they see each other in the coffee room; they happen to be waiting together by the printer for their printouts; they reside in a live-in project room. While conversations may only last for a few seconds or minutes, much can occur within them. People coordinate actions ("I need to see you. When are you free?"); exchange information; share expertise (e.g., requests for help; Poltrock and Engelbeck 1997; Ackerman and Starr 1995); or offer opportunities ("Come to our demonstration"). People can also see what others are doing, which lets them monitor progress and learn how things are done (Covi, Olson, and Rocco 1998; Poltrock and Engelbeck 1997). While it is hard to draw the line between sharing expertise, social banter, and communication, it should be clear that casual interaction is an excellent way to manage and supply opportunities for lightweight sharing of expertise.

Yet the barrier to rich spontaneous interactions is distance (Kraut, Egido, and Galegher 1988), and users of wide area networks will be at a disadvantage unless a prosthesis that overcomes distance barriers is available. Many mundane factors interfere with making contact over computers. People must know electronic addresses and even machine names. People must ready software, equipment, and each other well in advance for real-time remote conferencing. With video conferencing and media spaces, people must be in the (usually few) conference rooms that have the media equipment available. Yet, for informal interaction, people must find each other with minimal effort.

People must also select one or more of the many communication channels and applications that may be available to the group. From a technical perspective, sites may not have the same software; workstations may not support the necessary media (e.g., digital audio); specialized equipment may not be available (e.g., video cameras); poor networks may limit interactions; applications must run across platforms; and so on. From a human perspective, the communication channel or groupware must match a group's task (e.g., real-time text editing) and accommodate how people are available (e.g., asynchronous vs. real-time). If people cannot make contact, then groupware systems—no matter how elegant—cannot be used.

How Rooms Support Lightweight Real-Time Encounters

The room metaphor mitigates the transition of entering into a groupware conference. Because rooms are an inhabited space, they afford presence and awareness, encounters, habitation, and real-time meetings (table 9.2). TeamWave also includes features that minimize technical hurdles, such as cross-platform compatibility.

Being Available   As mentioned previously, people can pursue their single-user activities in TeamWave. As in a physical room used for both individual and group activities, people will be around more often and thus available for real-time encounters (Covi, Olson, and Rocco 1998). This is quite different from most groupware, where the only reason to be in a groupware session is for an explicit meeting.

Knowing Who Is Around and Available for Interaction   When people populate a spatial setting, they sense who else is around in their local community as they walk through the corridors, glance into offices, and see others in public spaces. People judge other's availability for conversation by seeing if their door is open, by seeing how busy they look, and by a variety of other cues. A room metaphor can provide a similar sense of presence and awareness by displaying who else inhabits the rooms that constitute the electronic community, as well as status information about each person.

Identifying who else is around in the community encourages informal interaction. TeamWave does this in several ways: a user list, idle indicators, and periodic video snapshots. *User lists* are shown in the Logged in Users window (figure 9.1(b)) and include only the people who are currently logged on to a community's server and thus reachable through TeamWave. Following the room metaphor, this is equivalent to wandering down the halls and seeing who is in their offices. Of course, being logged on to TeamWave does not guarantee that people are actually present; they may be away from their computers. To compensate, an *idle indicator* located beneath each person's image indicates how long it has been since that person has used the keyboard or mouse. With short idle times, the person is almost certainly reachable. Longer idle times only estimate presence: the person may be away or just not actively working on the computer (Greenberg 1996). In essence, the idle indicator tries to approximate the difference between someone's being out of their office (and unavailable) even though the door is open, and someone's being in their office. Next, in one experimental version of TeamWave *periodic video snapshots* were used to provide people with a better feel for the availability of others. The still images were replaced with snapshots taken several times per minute. This provides useful information (while still using very modest bandwidth) about whether other people are actually present and available for collaboration. These snapshots bring a person's real room and environment into the virtual rooms and serve a function similar to those found in the Portholes system (Dourish and Bly 1992).

Other cues help decide availability. The presence of a person in a particular physical room, and the degree to which the door is open, can indicate how interruptible that person may be. In TeamWave, this is mimicked by allowing people to see which room a person is in via the Logged in Users window (figure 9.1(b)). More explicitly, one of the four *door states* of a room, which can be set by a room's occupants, is visible on the Rooms on This Server window (a). As in real life, a wide open or partially open door icon indicates a willingness to accept interruptions, whereas a barred door suggests that the room and the people in it are inaccessible.[4]

Finally, special rooms can be set aside as informal meeting places. For example, one site had a lounge that used the Image applet to point to popular daily comic strips available on the Web, such as the "Dilbert of the Day." This became a popular room, which afforded accidental encounters.

Establishing Contact   Once a person determines that someone is available, there are several ways of actually establishing contact with him. Congruent with the room metaphor, one could just barge into a room. This is, of course, subject to the group's norms and social mores as it relates to the room and the people in them. As in real life, the other room occupants see that a person has entered a room because his picture appears (figure 9.1(h)). They can start talking to one another through the chat facility available in every room (o). Though we would hardly expect a lengthy meeting to be carried out in a room without the benefit of an audio channel, text can be useful for short or sporadic interactions, or where it is impractical to provide an audio connection. If a person would rather initiate a conversation before entering a room, she can page anyone (figure 9.2(b)) on the user's list. This displays a note on the other person's screen (c), which can be quickly answered to, say, invite that person in. Any person's phone number can be found on his business card (figure 9.1(c)), allowing phone calls to be made quickly before a room is entered, or afterwards. Once in a room, a person can attract the attention of others in the room (who may not be looking at the computer screen) by ringing a bell (figure 9.1(g)), which plays a sound on all computers.

Of course, one person may want to establish contact with others who are not currently logged on to TeamWave. In this case, she can revert to the asynchronous tools mentioned in previous sections, such as leaving a note in a room to suggest a meeting time and place.

Working Together   The power of the room metaphor is that, once in a room, the working context is immediately available. All tools and room artifacts are ready to hand, and new tools are easily added. In Team-Wave the back wall is a whiteboard, so people can augment their conversation at any time simply by sketching new artifacts or annotating existing ones (Greenberg, Hayne, and Rada 1995). Thus "back of the envelope" style conversations are easy. Similarly, the ever-present chat tool means that conversation (albeit low-bandwidth) is always possible. As well, the applets within a room can quickly become the focus of conversation.

Rooms also replace the rigid concept of a meeting enforced by most groupware systems. Many such systems have session managers, where people create real-time meetings and attend them (Greenberg and Roseman 1999). In contrast, a meeting in TeamWave is a social phenomenon created by the group simply by being in the same room at the same time (table 9.2).

Example: A Serendipitous Encounter
A simple but real example serves to illustrate how all these features work together. We had hired a student to work in our laboratory part-time for a month. Because of summer vacations, scheduling differences, and the part-time nature of the student's work, the laboratory supervisor

(Greenberg) had not actually had a chance to talk to the student. While Greenberg was tele-working in his TeamWave room from home one day (which is 110 kilometers from the laboratory), he noticed through the awareness facilities that the student was working in another room. Because she was in a room actively used by the team, he felt free to enter it. They then had their first conversation. It began with social banter but progressed to the student's discussing and presenting the work she was doing. This included a tour of her working contributions to the room and its work artifacts. Greenberg then commented about this work, including suggestions about how it could be done more effectively. In effect, they were sharing expertise, one about work in progress, the other about applying his experience to this work. After the conversation, they both went back to their individual work in their separate rooms.

In summary, TeamWave's room metaphor affords opportunistic and lightweight interaction, as illustrated by the example and summarized in table 9.2. The social opportunity to meet can be by circumstance and serendipity rather than by intention and planning. We saw in the example that both people were around (habitation) because they were pursuing their individual work; they were aware of one another through the awareness tools (presence and awareness); one person easily initiated the conversation just by entering the room (encounters); and both found it easy to incorporate the room context and artifacts into the discussion and expertise sharing (meeting definition). Everything was extraordinarily lightweight: the only "required" action to initiate the transition to a real-time interaction was a single mouse-click by Greenberg to enter the room.

9.7   The Transition from a Technical Space to a Social Place for Work

So far, we have seen how the room metaphor lets us apply characteristics of physical spaces to virtual spaces. Yet thinking about the characteristics of space alone does not capture all the richness of these environments. In the physical world a space is often adopted by a group and transformed into a *social place* for their interactions. For example, a house becomes a home when a family lives in it; a generic office becomes a personal one when its occupant hangs pictures on the walls, clutters the desk, and occupies it while he does his work; a room becomes a project room when a group uses it as a place to pursue its activities and to develop project artifacts (Covi, Olson, and Rocco 1998). In this section we show how the room metaphor can serve as a basis for forming such social place.

The Difference between Spaces and Places

Harrison and Dourish (1996) argue that designers who think only about the features of physical spaces are missing a crucial aspect of collaboration. Whereas *space* provides a physical venue giving opportunities for collaboration, it is the group's understanding of how the space should be used that turns the venue into a *social place*. Places extend spaces by including the social meanings of actions within a space, the cultural norms and mores that set convention, as well as the group's cultural understandings of the roles played by the people and artifacts that inhabit the space. Harrison and Dourish (1996) reason that a group forges a sense of place over time as its members actively participate in the space and appropriate objects within it. Places are thus social constructs, the "understood reality" of the group that derives (in part) from the opportunities afforded by the space. Benford et al. (1996, 81) also agree with this distinction; they define space as "a context which provides a consistent, navigable and shared spatial frame of reference (e.g., Cartesian space)" and a place as a "basic containing context for participants."

Fitzpatrick, Mansfield, and Kaplan's (1996) *locales framework* uses Strauss's (1993) theory of social worlds to distinguish social places from technical spaces. In this framework a *social world* is a group of people with some common purpose, a site for collaboration, and some means to communicate. A *locale* is the actual site in which a group collaborates, the actual means by which people communicate, and the actual means by which the work is achieved.[5] For example, a team with the goal of designing a software system would form the social world. If the team met in a meeting room, the room and all its artifacts—its visual and auditory communication, its whiteboard, its table, and the paper within it— would form a *physical locale*. If instead the team met through a groupware system in conjunction with a telephone, then that would form a *virtual locale*. While a virtual locale may not be actually realized in physical space, it still provides the site and means for the social world to collaborate.

More formally, the locales framework comprises five aspects, as summarized here (Fitzpatrick 1998; Fitzpatrick, Mansfield, and Kaplan 1996):

• *Locale foundations* define a collection of people and artifacts (tools, objects, information) in relation to the central purpose of the social world. A locale within a social world is best considered as a center of collective purpose that is part of a dynamic and continually evolving system. Locales are fluid places with social meaning that may be mapped onto physical spaces, although care must be taken that the structure of the physical space does not conflict with the dynamic social structures.

• *Mutuality* considers those interactions within locales that maintain a sense of shared place. Mutuality includes "presence" information that people and artifacts make available to others, and how people maintain awareness of that information. It also includes "capabilities" that entities have to transmit and receive information, and how entities choose from these capabilities to create a particular presence awareness level.

• *Individual view over multiple locales* acknowledges that individuals can be participating in many locales. Each person's individual view is an aggregation of his views onto his particular locale. People also manifest a *view intensity* onto particular locales as they vary their focus and participation across locales.

• *Interaction trajectories* concern how courses of action evolve over time. In essence, people come into locales and social worlds with past experiences, plans, and actions. The trajectory describes how these move through time, for example, as people negotiate plans and actions with each other.

• *Civic structures* concern how interactions fit within a broader communal level. Civic structures can be considered a meta-locale that describes how social worlds and locales relate to one another, how people find their way between them, and how new locales are formed and old ones dissipated.

All aspects of the locales framework describe characteristics of what makes a social place. From these characteristics, we can then consider how these aspects are afforded by technical spaces such as TeamWave's room metaphor.

Constructing a Social Place within TeamWave Workplace Rooms

Fitzpatrick, Mansfield, and Kaplan (1996) argue that groups can create a social place that is not bounded to a physical space. While this is true, we suggest that the room metaphor and its spatial properties can assist the distributed group in fashioning a social place within an electronic medium. In essence, a newly formed TeamWave Workplace site is a space that lacks social context. However, the affordances of TeamWave rooms (table 9.2) and the way rooms can be customized mean that the individuals composing a social world can conveniently craft the rooms into locales that act as their social place.

Community Membership and Formation   The TeamWave administrator controls community and group membership. The act of deciding who is allowed to enter a particular TeamWave site defines (albeit in a technical manner) who belongs to that community. This may comprise predefined groups (e.g., all members of a department), distributed special-interest groups (e.g., people with interests in a particular topic), goal-oriented teams (e.g., members of a conference committee), or some ad hoc membership (e.g., individuals interested in visiting a particular site).

Of course, a community is more than an access control list. In practice, formation of the initial community may require some champion or subgroup to motivate other members to actually enter and participate within the TeamWave site. This could include hand-holding to make sure that the software is correctly installed and configured, some training, and probably a strong motivating factor. For example, we saw a community form itself when one member of a TeamWave mailing list offered to set up a TeamWave site for other list members. He motivated others by offering hands-on experience for early TeamWave adopters as well as visits by TeamWave experts who could provide the group with guidance. Essentially, this person wanted to share expertise both by having the community explore the system together and by bringing in outside experts who could guide the learning process and react to what people were doing. In his own words,

I don't know if there is anyone else in this list who is currently in the learning/ investigating stage of working with collaborative software, but I thought I'd offer this idea. I recommend that [we] establish a periodic, ongoing "conference" hosted by an experienced TeamWave developer/facilitator where potential users could log in and participate in a way that would exercise all of the capabilities of TeamWave.

After positive responses were received, the TeamWave site was set up and other list members were invited to attend. Some rooms were created ahead of time (preliminary locales), and notes were sent around that included explicit suggestions on how they should be used (which could be considered the initial formation of a civic structure). Part of this structure included an explicit way to set up meeting times, a way to increase mutuality:

When you first log in, you will find a reception area or lounge, with doors to other offices. Each of you will have an office for your own investigations. There will be a door to a meeting room, too. I will make the lounge the default and leave a group-scheduling calendar and some notes. Please use the calendar to indicate your dates and times online to assist others in working with you. May I suggest using the meeting room for meetings to keep the lounge uncluttered and faster-loading. The meeting room could be used for your feedback to Mark and his group.

What is particularly interesting about this example is that much of the correspondence involved the social construction of a place, who would belong to it, and the initial social rules and conventions. Indeed, the community and its social place were in some sense established well before anyone actually entered the TeamWave space. Even so, the room metaphor began to come into play. It gave the group a space to meet that they could call their own. Because rooms could be customized, the initial structure was tailored to fit group needs. As well, rooms provided a context for the expected behaviors and the mores of the group.

Using Rooms to Create Locales   Rooms are just bounded spaces. Their physical entities are their walls and tools, the applets, and the information contained in the applets. Their personal entities are the people that come and go in them. A person or group can use a room as a bounded center of a social world. We have already seen examples of this. The personal room of figure 9.3 is a locale for an individual, although its membership can be expanded as people are invited into the place. The meeting room of figure 9.4 becomes the locale for a specific group's on-going meeting activities. One could argue that the set of rooms used by that group is a locale, in which individual views shift as the focus of the group changes. The point is that it is a room's users who craft the meaning of the room as a social place. Much of this is done by manipulating the room artifacts and by customizing its contents to fit the social needs of the group.

Other aspects of rooms afford other criteria included in the locales framework. Mutuality is afforded by the various awareness widgets, by telepointers, and by the immediate feedthrough of changes when several people are in a room. Interaction trajectories are afforded by the persistence of artifacts within a room as well as by the ability to revisit previous versions. Civic structures are afforded by the ability to leave notes within a room that spell out the terms of engagement and that directly reference objects within the room by proximity or explicit pointers.

Herlea gives an example of how a multiroom locale can be created (Herlea 1997; Herlea and Greenberg 1998). Her goal was to create a locale for iterative requirements engineering, based on the soft systems requirements methodology, where the group's collective purpose would be loosely structured by the locale. Figure 9.5 illustrates this. In this top-level view we see a room that contains a set of doorways to other rooms. Those rooms are configured to support various aspects of the methodology. At the top left, we see three rooms stepping through phases of requirements discovery, including rooms for scope definition, brainstorming, and end-user requirements. The actual rooms are preconfigured with tools and documentation appropriate for the work. Other room sets include requirements refinement, viewpoints analysis, and solution selection. At the center are social rooms, including a meeting room, a coffee room, and an agenda room. The preconstructed locale becomes a guiding structure that supports the social world. That is, the locale helps the group pursue its collective purpose of requirements engineering. As individuals navigate this space, they are changing their view intensity.

A caveat regarding TeamWave rooms as locales is that rooms are at best only approximations of locales (Greenberg et al. 1999). Because the boundaries of a room are fairly rigid, they act as a container rather than

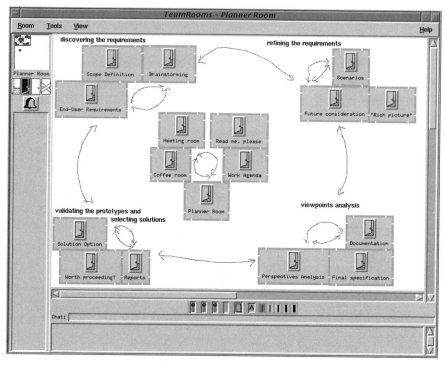

Figure 9.5
The LoReN environment. Rooms are configured to support the iterative requirements engineering cycle. *Source:* Herlea (1997). Used with permission.

as a center. People cannot be in more than one room at a time, even though they may have an individual view that perceives a locale as a union of several rooms. To capture the full richness of the locales framework, rooms would have to be more fluid and permeable than they are. While people can copy applets and their contents from room to room, the physical space is fairly static and somewhat heavyweight compared to the dynamics of a social place.

In summary, the room metaphor can help a group form a social place. Rooms serve as a destination where people can agree to meet and work together. Because rooms can be customized and because they persist, they can be crafted into a locale that evolves over time. Proximity and action imply that people are aware of what others are doing in a room, which affords mutuality. Because rooms are often related to one another, locales can span a series of rooms. Because rooms are revisited over time and because "rules of engagement" can be posted in a room, civic structures will develop over time. All these ease the transition from electronic spaces to social places.

9.8 Related Work

The values of spatial metaphors are well known and have long been used as a foundation for interface design (Kuhn and Blumental 1996). In 1986, for example, an elegant room-based system called Rooms was built to support task switching, where each room acted as a container for a particular set of tasks (Henderson and Card 1986). There are a now variety of collaborative systems that rely on some sort of spatial metaphor. We briefly describe a few of the approaches and systems here, loosely categorizing them as meeting points, social spaces, and working spaces.

Meeting Points
Several systems use the concept of place or room as a gathering point for collaborators. The idea is that when several people congregate at the same virtual point, other tools are automatically invoked to connect them.

With media spaces (e.g., Abel 1990), physical rooms are connected via always-on video and audio channels. From one physical room a person can look into another physical room, greet the people located there, and start conversations. This combines their physical spaces, albeit in a limited manner.

Virtual rooms as meeting points are also popular. The CAVECAT media space (Mantei et al. 1991) used the idea of walking into a virtual room occupied by another user (as displayed on a screen) as a mechanism to initiate an audio/video connection. The DIVA Virtual Office Environment (Sohlenkamp and Chwelos 1994) and GroupKit's Rooms session manager (Roseman and Greenberg 1996c) used virtual rooms to gather and organize people and their documents. Users in these rooms launch external groupware editing tools, these tools are separate from the room itself and run in their own windows.

However, these types of systems do not act as an integrated bounded space. Rather, they mostly afford contact facilitation, informal conversation, and application launching. In contrast, TeamWave integrates the communication channels, the tools, and the way persistent artifacts are created as part of the meeting place by using rooms as containers for all these activities.

Social Spaces

Other systems create social spaces for conversational interaction. The simplest of these are chat rooms, where users connect to a room and can chat to others in the room with typed messages (Turkle 1995). Recent chat rooms found on online services have added rudimentary graphics, but the interaction is still entirely text-based. Another popular class of social space is multi-user domains (MUDs and MOOs). Born of text-based adventure games, traditional MUDs are text-based systems where users connect to a central server. The server hosts a variety of different rooms, each with a unique description and set of objects. As with chat rooms, people can enter any number of different rooms and chat with other people in those rooms. However, they can also type commands to create and modify objects in the rooms.

Several systems have augmented MUDs with nontextual tools. For example, the Jupiter project (Curtis and Nichols 1993) added MBONE audio and video conferencing and graphics capabilities through shared whiteboards. Multi-user virtual environments (MUVEs) create a graphical world, either in two or three dimensions, where people can navigate the world and encounter others (e.g., DIVE; Carlsson and Hagsand 1993). People are often represented as avatars—graphical automations that may even include a video face—that can be seen by others. Text or audio connections to others are often triggered by proximity. If one person's avatar is close to another's, they can hear each other.

While MUDs and MUVEs have been used in limited ways to support collaborative work, most of their appeal is for social interaction. They tend to support large, loosely knit virtual communities where anyone can enter the space, rather than smaller, goal-oriented working groups. Essentially, this is the difference between software supporting virtual communities and teamware products (including TeamWave), which are oriented toward modest-sized teams and organizations (Wong 1998).

Working Spaces

A variety of systems have been developed around a rooms model that contains artifacts directly supporting work activities of small groups:

• *CoLab* was a face-to-face meeting support system that gave a group several meeting tools (Stefik, Foster et al. 1987). After seeing some problems in the software, the designers discussed what it would be like to embed the tools within a room metaphor (Stefik, Bobrow et al. 1987). While the metaphor was not implemented, this was one of the first efforts that seriously considered the design and implications of a room metaphor for groupware.

• *Mushroom Project* is a software framework that provides a type of room called *Mrooms* (Kindberg 1996). Mrooms contain representations (images) of the users who are in a room, communication tools, and information about objects that users share. Objects, which include whiteboards, documents, and multimedia presentations, are usually displayed in separate windows.

• *Collaborative Virtual Workspace (CVW)*, by MITRE Corporation, divides a building into floors and rooms (Spellman et al. 1997). Rather than building applets from scratch, CVW integrates external tools and services into a single environment, and these are mostly displayed in separate windows. However, CVW developers have created their own tools when necessary.

• *Kansas* is an object-oriented multi-user graphical environment written in the Self language (Smith, Wolczko, and Ungar 1997). Designed as a virtual space for learning, Kansas is a large, flat plane rather than a room. Users can be located anywhere on it, and they will see a local portion of Kansas (but radar overviews let people see where others are). Users can also program and run graphical objects in Kansas. When a user alters the properties of Kansas, all other users feel the effects. Similar to some MUVEs, moving together and apart in Kansas will make and break audio connections among users.

• The three versions of *Orbit* (Mansfield et al. 1997) and its predecessor *wOrlds* (Tolone, Kaplan, and Fitzpatrick 1995) are implemented prototypes that test how the locales theory can be supported by software. These systems try to provide a highly flexible way of viewing and shifting between multiple locales and the shared objects contained by them. This innovative approach differs considerably from the room metaphor, for it eschews the relatively fixed way that rooms contain objects and does not preserve the spatial relations between objects.

• *CommonPoint* was an unreleased collaborative desktop environment from Taligent (described in Orfali, Harkey, and Edwards 1996). The desktop used a "People, Places, and Things" metaphor to provide very rich network places where people could gather and work with shared documents. However, CommonPoint would have required radical changes to the computing environment, a complete replacement of conventional operating systems and their desktop metaphors.

• A variety of commercial groupware products now use the notion of a room as a bounded space: Instinctive Technology's *eRoom 1.0*, *facilitate.com 4.5*, Changepoint's *involv Intranet 2.0*, and Lotus' *InstantTeamRoom 1.0*. They are geared primarily toward asynchronous communication and provide almost no support for real-time collaboration, even when users are working with the artifacts in the same room (Wong 1998).

In summary, while these systems rely on spatial metaphors to some degree, they vary greatly in how they support the features mentioned in table 9.2. For example, because the Mushroom Project and CVW display tools in separate windows on the screen, users cannot relate them by spatial proximity as they can in TeamWave. Orbit and wOrlds stress highly tailorable views against the idea of a room as container. Kansas uses an unbounded space rather than bounded rooms. Some systems support mainly asynchronous collaboration.

9.9   Summary

In this chapter we described how a room metaphor could allow groupware to ease transitions across different styles of work, which includes how expertise could be managed and shared. We listed a variety of features afforded by the room metaphor, and how a group can leverage these for individual and collaborative work (table 9.2). We described

TeamWave Workplace and its particular implementation of a room metaphor. Four groupware gaps were then presented, and we showed how transitions across these gaps can be reduced by the properties of the room metaphor. First, the distinction between single-user and groupware applications is removed by making rooms suitable for both individuals and groups, and by making the shift between an individual or group space just a function of the number of people in a room. Second, people can move fluidly between synchronous and asynchronous work when room artifacts are persistent, and when people work together simply by occupying the same room at the same time. As an example, we showed how people can move through the pre-, during-, and post-meeting processes of a formal meeting by allowing rooms to be configured with appropriate tools and information ahead of time, by having all tools support real-time interaction, and by making artifacts in a room persist over these meeting phases. Third, the difficulty of establishing real-time contact is reduced by providing people with awareness of who is around for casual interaction and by letting them meet by entering a common room. Fourth, we showed how a technical space can become a social place by the way a community is formed across rooms and by the way people within a room craft meaning into it. We also argued that the room metaphor's seamless support of these everyday activities will foster an environment where groups naturally share their expertise.

Our understanding of the room metaphor for group work is impoverished, as research is still in its early stages. For example, we need to evaluate how teams use virtual rooms. Yet this is difficult to do (Grudin 1989). Laboratory and short-term experiments will not reflect the way a team uses and shapes its rooms over time. Neither are we ready to perform field studies: commercial-grade groupware systems using room metaphors are rare, and the few existing ones have been deployed only recently. We also have to recognize that even small design and implementation deficiencies in current systems can greatly affect how teams adopt and use them (e.g., Greenberg et al. 1999).

We have some way to go before realizing the full potential of the rooms metaphor. Still, the benefits of rooms are very promising, as shown and in the TeamWave case study.

Acknowledgments

Many people on the GroupLab team contributed in one way or another to this work. This includes Carl Gutwin and his work on awareness, and Ted O'Grady and his work on flexible toolkit infrastructures. Alex Mitchell (along with Mark Roseman) helped code a very early rooms-based session manager. Intel Corporation and the National Science and Engineering Research Council of Canada funded this research. We are particularly grateful to the support and encouragement provided by Intel's Jim Larson, Kenrick Mock, and Tony Salvador.

Notes

Greenberg leads the GroupLab project, which developed the research foundations leading to TeamWave. Roseman, the founder and director of TeamWave Software Ltd, is the chief technical architect of TeamWave Workplace.

1. *Gaps*, *seams*, and *boundaries* are terms used by various authors to express similar concepts.

2. A similar list is raised in Baecker (1993) in his chapter on the future of groupware for CSCW.

3. Information on TeamWave Workplace, including directions on how to license the software, is available at http://www.teamwave.com/. Information on related research and software (such as the GroupKit groupware toolkit) is available through University of Calgary's GroupLab Web site at http://www.cpsc.ucalgary.ca/grouplab/.

4. Door states also serve to mediate access to rooms that have no one in them: open doors indicate more public rooms, whereas closed doors indicate more private rooms.

5. Definitions and example provided by Tim Mansfield and Geraldine Fitzpatrick, personal communication.

References

Abbot, K., and S. Sarin. 1994. Experiences with Workflow Management: Issues for the Next Generation. In *Proceedings of the ACM Conference on Computer-Supported Cooperative Work (CSCW '94)*, 113–120.

Abel, M. 1990. Experiences in an Exploratory Distributed Organization. In *Intellectual Teamwork: Social Foundations of Cooperative Work*, ed. J. Galegher, R. E. Kraut, and C. Egido, 489–510. Hillsdale, N.J.: Erlbaum.

Ackerman, M. S. 1994. Augmenting the Organizational Memory: A Field Study of Answer Garden. In *Proceedings of the ACM Conference on Computer-Supported Cooperative Work (CSCW '94)*, 243–252.

Ackerman, M. S., and T. W. Malone. 1990. Answer Garden: A Tool for Growing Organizational Memory. In *Proceedings of the ACM Conference on Office Information Systems*, 31–39.

Ackerman, M. S., and B. Starr. 1995. Social Activity Indicators: Interface Components for CSCW Systems. In *Proceedings of the ACM Symposium on User Interface Software and Technology (UIST '95)*, 159–168.

Alexander, C. 1979. *The Timeless Way of Building*. New York: Oxford University Press.

Baecker, R. M., ed. 1993. *Readings in Groupware and Computer-Supported Cooperative Work: Assisting Human-Human Collaboration*. San Mateo, Calif.: Morgan Kaufmann.

Baecker, R. M., J. Grudin, W. Buxton, and S. Greenberg, eds. 1995. *Readings in Human Computer Interaction: Toward the Year 2000*. San Mateo, Calif.: Morgan Kaufmann.

Baecker, R. M., D. Nastos, I. R. Posner, and K. L. Mawby. 1993. The User-Centred Iterative Design of Collaborative Writing Software. In *Proceedings of the ACM Conference on Human Factors in Computing Systems (CHI '93)*, 399–405.

Benford, S., C. Brown, G. Reynard, and C. Greenhalgh. 1996. Shared Spaces: Transportation, Artificiality, and Spaciality. In *Proceedings of the ACM Conference on Computer-Supported Cooperative Work (CSCW '96)*.

Buxton, W. A. 1992. Telepresence: Integrating Shared Task and Person Spaces. In *Proceedings of Graphics Interface '92*, 123–129. Reprinted in *Readings in Groupware and Computer-Supported Cooperative Work: Assisting Human-Human Collaboration* (1993), ed. R. M. Baecker.

Card, S. K., and D. Henderson, Jr. 1987. A Multiple Virtual-Workspace Interface to Support User Task Switching. In *Proceedings of the ACM Conference on Human Factors in Computing Systems and Graphics Interface (CHI '87 and GI '87)*, 53–59.

Card, S. K., G. G. Robertson, and J. D. Mackinlay. 1991. The Information Visualizer, an Information Workspace. In *Proceedings of the ACM Conference on Human Factors in Computing Systems (CHI '91)*, 181–188.

Carlsson, C., and O. Hagsand. 1993. DIVE—A Platform for Multi-User Virtual Environments. *Computers and Graphics* 17 (6): 663–669.

Cockburn, A., and S. Greenberg. 1993. Making Contact: Getting the Group Communicating with Groupware. In *Proceedings of the ACM Conference on Organizational Computing Systems (COOCS '93)*.

Cockburn, A., and H. Thimbleby. 1991. A Reflexive Perspective of CSCW. *ACM SIGCHI Bulletin* 23 (3): 63–68.

Conklin, J. 1992. Capturing Organizational Memory. In *Proceedings of Groupware '92*, 133–137. Reprinted in *Readings in Groupware and Computer-Supported Cooperative Work: Assisting Human-Human Collaboration* (1993), ed. R. M. Baecker.

Conklin, J., and M. L. Begeman. 1988. gIBIS: A Hypertext Tool for Exploratory Policy Discussion. In *Proceedings of the ACM Conference on Computer-Supported Cooperative Work (CSCW '88)*, 140–152.

Covi, L., J. Olson, and E. Rocco. 1998. A Room of Your Own: What Do We Learn About Support of Teamwork from Assessing Teams in Dedicated Project Rooms? In *Proceedings of First International Workshop on Cooperative Buildings: Integrating Information, Organization, and Architecture (CoBuild '98)*, Darmstadt, Germany.

Curtis, P., and D. Nichols. 1993. MUDs Grow up: Social Virtual Reality in the Real World. In *Proceedings of the Third International Conference on Cyberspace*.

DeSanctis, G., and B. Gallupe. 1987. A Foundation for the Study of Group Decision Support Systems. *Management Science* 33 (5): 589–609.

Dix, A., J. Finlay, G. Abowd, and R. Beale. 1993. *Human-Computer Interaction*. Upper Saddle River, N.J.: Prentice Hall.

Dourish, P., and S. Bly. 1992. Portholes: Supporting Awareness in a Distributed Work Group. In *Proceedings of the ACM Conference on Human Factors in Computing Systems (CHI '92)*, 541–547.

Dubs, S., and S. Hayne. 1992. Distributed Facilitation: A Concept Whose Time Has Come? In *Proceedings of the ACM Conference on Computer-Supported Cooperative Work (CSCW '92)*, 314–321.

Fitzpatrick, G. 1998. The Locales Framework: Understanding and Designing for Cooperative Work. Ph.D. diss., University of Queensland, Brisbane, Australia.

Fitzpatrick, G., T. Mansfield, and S. Kaplan. 1996. Locales Framework: Exploring Foundations for Collaboration Support. In *Proceedings of the Sixth Australian Conference on Computer-Human Interaction (OzCHI '96)*, 34–41.

Flores, F., M. Graves, B. Hartfield, and T. Winograd. 1988. Computer Systems and the Design of Organizational Interaction. *ACM Transactions on Office Information Systems* 6 (2): 153–172. Reprinted in *Readings in Groupware and Computer-Supported Cooperative Work: Assisting Human-Human Collaboration* (1993), ed. R. M. Baecker.

Greenberg, S. 1990. Sharing Views and Interactions with Single-User Applications. In *Proceedings of the ACM Conference on Office Information Systems*, 227–237.

———. 1996. Peepholes: Low-Cost Awareness of One's Community. In *Proceedings of the ACM Conference on Human Factors in Computing Systems (CHI '96)*, 206–207.

Greenberg, S., G. Fitzpatrick, C. Gutwin, and S. Kaplan. 1999. Adapting the Locales Framework for Heuristic Evaluation of Groupware. In *Proceedings of the Ninth Australian Conference on Computer-Human Interaction (OzCHI '99)*.

Greenberg, S., C. Gutwin, and M. Roseman. 1996. Semantic Telepointers for Groupware. In *Proceedings of the Sixth Australian Conference on Computer-Human Interaction (OzCHI '96)*.

Greenberg, S., S. Hayne, and R. Rada, eds. 1995. *Groupware for Real-Time Drawing: A Designer's Guide*. New York: McGraw-Hill.

Greenberg, S., and M. Roseman. 1996. GroupWeb: A WWW Browser as Real-Time Groupware. In *Proceedings of the ACM Conference on Human Factors in Computing Systems (CHI '96)*, 271–272.

———. 1999. Groupware Toolkits for Synchronous Work. In *Computer-Supported Cooperative Work*, ed. M. Beaudouin-Lafon. New York: Wiley.

Grudin, J. 1989. Why Groupware Applications Fail: Problems in Design and Evaluation. *Office: Technology and People* 4 (3): 245–264.

———. 1994. Computer-Supported Cooperative Work: History and Focus. *IEEE Computer* 27 (5): 19–26.

Gutwin, C., and S. Greenberg. 1996. Workspace Awareness in Real-Time Distributed Groupware: Framework, Widgets, and Evaluation. In *Proceedings of the Fifth International Conference on Human-Computer Interaction (HCI '96)*, 281–298.

Harrison, S., and P. Dourish. 1996. Re-place-ing Space: The Roles of Place and Space in Collaborative Systems. In *Proceedings of the ACM Conference on Computer-Supported Cooperative Work (CSCW '96)*.

Heath, C., M. Jirotka, P. Luff, and J. Hindmarsh. 1995. Unpacking Collaboration: the Interactional Organization of Trading in a City Dealing Room. *Computer Supported Cooperative Work* 3 (2): 147–165.

Henderson, D., Jr., and S. Card. 1986. Rooms: The Use of Multiple Virtual Workspaces to Reduce Space Contention in a Window-Based Graphical User Interface. *ACM Transactions on Office Information Systems* 2 (1): 211–243.

Herlea, D. 1997. A Groupware System for Negotiating Software Requirements. M.Sc. thesis, Department of Computer Science, University of Calgary, Alberta, Canada.

Herlea, D., and S. Greenberg. 1998. Using a Groupware Space for Distributed Requirements Engineering. In *Proceedings of the IEEE Seventh International Workshop on Enabling Technologies: Coordinating Distributed Software Development Projects (WETICE '98)*.

Ishii, H. 1990. TeamWorkStation: Towards a Seamless Shared Space. In *Proceedings of the ACM Conference on Computer-Supported Cooperative Work (CSCW '90)*, 13–26.

Ishii, H., M. Kobayashi, and J. Grudin. 1993. Integration of Interpersonal Space and Shared Workspace: Clearboard Design and Experiments. *ACM Transactions on Information Systems* (October). Reprinted in *Groupware for Real-Time Drawing: A Designer's Guide* (1995), ed. S. Greenberg, S. Hayne, and R. Rada, 96–125.

Jay, A. 1976. How to Run a Meeting. *Harvard Business Review* 54 (2). Reprinted in *Readings in Groupware and Computer-Supported Cooperative Work: Assisting Human-Human Collaboration* (1993), ed. R. M. Baecker.

Johansen, R. 1988. *Groupware: Computer Support for Business Teams.* New York: Free Press.

Kindberg, T. 1996. Mushroom: a Framework for Collaboration and Interaction Across the Internet. In *Proceedings of the International Workshop on CSCW and the Web.* http://www.dcs.qmw.ac.uk/research/distrib/Mushroom/CSCWWeb.html.

Kraut, R., C. Egido, and J. Galegher. 1988. Patterns of Contact and Communication in Scientific Collaboration. In *Proceedings of the Conference on Computer-Supported Cooperative Work (CSCW '88)*, 1–12.

Kremer, R. 1997. A Concept Map Meta-Language. Ph.D. diss., Department of Computer Science, University of Calgary, Alberta, Canada.

Kuhn, W., and B. Blumental. 1996. Spatialization: Spatial Metaphors for User Interfaces. In *Proceedings of the ACM Conference on Human Factors in Computing Systems (CHI '96), Tutorial Notes.* Also available as GeoInfo 8, Dept of Geoinformation, Technical University of Vienna, Austria.

Lange, B. 1992. Electronic Group Calendaring: Experiences and Expectations. In *Proceedings of Groupware '92*, 428–432. Reprinted in *Readings in Groupware and Computer-Supported Cooperative Work: Assisting Human-Human Collaboration* (1993), ed. R. M. Baecker.

Leiva-Lobos, E., G. De Michelis, and E. Covarrubias. 1997. Augmenting and Multiplying Spaces for Creative Design. In *Proceedings of the International Conference on Supporting Group Work (Group '97)*, 177–186.

Malone, T. W., K. Lai, and C. Fry. 1992. Experiments with Oval: A Radically Tailorable Tool for Cooperative Work. In *Proceedings of the ACM Conference on Computer Supported Cooperative Work (CSCW '92)*, 289–297.

Mansfield, T., S. Kaplan, G. Fitzpatrick, T. Phelps, M. Fitzpatrick, and R. Taylor. 1997. Evolving Orbit: A Progress Report on Building Locales. In *Proceedings of the International Conference on Supporting Group Work (Group '97)*, 241–250.

Mantei, M., R. Baecker, A. Sellen, W. Buxton, T. Milligan, and B. Wellman. 1991. Experiences in the Use of a Media Space. In *Proceedings of the ACM Conference on Human Factors in Computing Systems (CHI '91)*, 203–208.

Nardi, B. A., and J. R. Miller. 1991. Twinkling Lights and Nested Loops: Distributed Problem Solving and Spreadsheet Development. In *Computer-Supported*

Cooperative Work and Groupware, ed. S. Greenberg, 29–52. New York: Academic Press.

Nunamaker, J., A. Dennis, J. Valacich, D. Vogel, and J. George. 1991. Electronic Meeting Systems to Support Group Work. *Communications of the ACM* 34 (7): 40–61.

O'Grady, T., and S. Greenberg. 1994. A Groupware Environment for Complete Meetings. In *Proceedings of the ACM Conference on Human Factors in Computing Systems (CHI '94): Posters and Short Papers*, vol. 2, 307–308.

Orfali, R., D. Harkey, and J. Edwards. 1996. *The Essential Distributed Objects Survival Guide*. New York: Wiley.

Poltrock, S., and G. Engelbeck. 1997. Requirements for a Virtual Collocation Environment. In *Proceedings of the International Conference on Supporting Group Work (Group '97)*, 61–70.

Preece, J. 1994. *Human-Computer Interaction*. Reading, Mass.: Addison-Wesley.

Rein, G. L., and C. A. Ellis. 1991. rIBIS: A Real-Time Group Hypertext System. In *Computer-Supported Cooperative Work and Groupware*, ed. S. Greenberg. New York: Academic Press.

Root, W. R. 1988. Design of a Multimedia Vehicle for Social Browsing. In *Proceedings of the ACM Conference on Computer-Supported Cooperative Work (CSCW '88)*, 25–38.

Roseman, M. 1996. Managing Complexity in TeamRooms, a Tcl-Based Internet Groupware Application. In *Proceedings of the 1996 Tcl/Tk Workshop*.

Roseman, M., and S. Greenberg. 1996a. TeamRooms: Network Places for Collaboration. In *Proceedings of the ACM Conference on Computer-Supported Cooperative Work (CSCW '96)*.

————. 1996b. *A Tour of TeamRooms*. Videotape. ACM Conference on Human Factors in Computing Systems.

————. 1996c. Building Real-Time Groupware with GroupKit, a Groupware Toolkit. *ACM Transactions on Computer-Human Interaction* 3 (1): 66–106.

————. 1997. Simplifying Component Development in an Integrated Groupware Environment. In *Proceedings of the ACM Symposium on User Interface Software and Technology (UIST '97)*.

Shneiderman, B. 1997. *Designing the User Interface: Strategies for Effective Human-Computer Interaction*. 3d ed. Norwood, N.J.: Ablex.

Smith, R., M. Wolczko, and D. Ungar. 1997. From Kansas to Oz: Collaborative Debugging When a Shared World Breaks. *Communications of the ACM* (April): 72–78.

Sohlenkamp, M., and G. Chwelos. 1994. Integrating Communication, Cooperation and Awareness: The DIVA Virtual Office Environment. In *Proceedings of the ACM Conference on Computer-Supported Cooperative Work (CSCW '94)*.

Spellman, P., J. Mosier, L. Deus, and J. Carlson. 1997. Collaborative Virtual Workspace. In *Proceedings of the International Conference on Supporting Group Work (Group '97)*, 197–203.

Sproull, L. 1991. A Lesson in Electronic Mail. In *Connections: New Ways of Working in the Networked Organization*, ed. L. Sproull and S. Kiesler, 177–184. Cambridge, Mass.: MIT Press.

Sproull, L., and S. Kiesler. 1991. Increasing Personal Connections. In *Connections: New Ways of Working in the Networked Organization*. Cambridge, Mass.: MIT Press.

Stefik, M., D. Bobrow, G. Foster, S. Lanning, and D. Tatar. 1987. WYSIWYG Revised: Early Experiences with Multiuser Interfaces. *ACM Transactions on Office Information Systems* 5 (2): 147–167.

Stefik, M., G. Foster, D. Bobrow, K. Kah, S. Lanning, and L. Suchman. 1987. Beyond the Chalkboard. *Communications of the ACM* 30: 32–47.

Strauss, A. 1993. *Continual Permutations of Action*. Chicago: Aldine.

Tang, J. C. 1991. Findings from Observational Studies of Collaborative Work. In *Computer-Supported Cooperative Work and Groupware*, ed. S. Greenberg, 11–28. New York: Academic Press.

Tolone, W., S. Kaplan, and G. Fitzpatrick. 1995. Specifying Dynamic Support for Collaborative Work Within wOrlds. In *Proceedings of the ACM Conference on Organizational Computing Systems (COOCS '95)*.

Turkle, S. 1995. *Life on the Screen: Identity in the Age of the Internet*. New York: Simon and Schuster.

Turoff, M. 1991. Computer-Mediated Communication Requirements for Group Support. *Journal of Organizational Computing* 1: 85–113. Reprinted in *Readings in Groupware and Computer-Supported Cooperative Work: Assisting Human-Human Collaboration* (1993), ed. R. M. Baecker.

Valacich, J., A. Dennis, and J. Nunamaker. 1991. Electronic Meeting Support: The GroupSystems Concept. In *Computer-Supported Cooperative Work and Groupware*, ed. S. Greenberg, 133–154. New York: Academic Press.

Wong, W. 1998. Team-Building on the Fly. *Byte* (February): 106–110.

10

NewsMate: Providing Timely Knowledge to Mobile and Distributed News Journalists

Henrik Fagrell

Knowledge management has been recognized as key to sustaining competitive advantage (Ruggles 1998). This chapter focuses on information technology support for knowledge management, usually called knowledge management systems. This category of systems have been criticized extensively in the literature, in particular, for

• offering a passive repository rather than actively supporting remembering (Randall et al. 1996; Bannon and Kuutti 1996; Hughes et al. 1996; see also Ackerman and Halverson 1998);

• not taking into account how work is actually conducted, relying instead on idealized models of human activity (Brown and Duguid 1991);

• assuming that there is a well-defined problem to be solved through rational choice, which is not always valid (March 1991);

• not mediating knowledge that is distributed between many sources, of which only a few are explicitly known in advance (Ackerman and Halverson 1998);

• promoting an objective view of knowledge, which excludes important aspects like originator and context (Fagrell and Ljungberg 1999).

This chapter argues for a complementary approach to information technology support for knowledge management, in which

• knowledge is actively acquired by the user;

• empirical studies of mobile work inform the design (Fagrell and Ljungberg 1999; 2000);

• the user can be aided in defining as well as solving the problems;

• knowledge from many sources is integrated in a way that is tailored to the local use situation;

• communication links between users and originators of knowledge can be established.

This approach is illustrated with the NewsMate system, a mobile knowledge management system for radio journalists, which aims to provide timely information in a distributed and mobile work setting. The client platform of the NewsMate is a Personal Digital Assistant (PDA) with network access using a mobile phone.

The work domain here is radio news journalism. Journalists "repackage" information to make news in understandable and interesting ways. The pace of such work is usually fast. Little time is available for preparation. Reporting is often conducted away from editorial staff at the radio station. For this reason reporters cannot easily adopt traditional desktop-based systems (see Bellotti and Rogers 1997).

Journalists often have to report events on topics that they are not fully informed about (Fagrell and Ljungberg 2000). For this reason, the knowledge management support is concentrated on the issue of timely knowledge, that is, knowledge that is relevant and pertinent for the task at hand.

The historical rationale of many traditional knowledge management systems is to help people find solutions to problems (e.g., Ackerman 1994). It is assumed that the user has a problem that is not entirely unique. The system is then used to identify an already solved similar problem. A solution for the old problem is then applied to the new problem.

Clearly, the alternative setting of distributed and mobile radio journalism can provide new insight into knowledge management. For instance, there are several conceptual dimensions that describe the novel requirements of such work:

• *Problem to task.*   There is little focus on problems that are external to the task. Accordingly, the goal here is to start with tasks rather than problems. For example, the note-taking and authoring that journalists conduct prior to reporting are used as input.

• *Closed to open.* Traditional systems rely on passively storing information internally in the system. Thus, the present system supports an open architecture that uses sources internal as well as external to the organization.

• *Indirect to direct communication.* Knowledge cannot always be repackaged for distribution without problems (Brown and Duguid 1991). For this reason, direct communication between users and experts is supported.

The next section presents the NewsMate in a use scenario.

10.1 Use Scenario

This section examines a scenario where a user is interacting with the NewsMate and colleagues in a typical work situation (figure 10.1). The results that the system displays are genuine, except for the translation to English, and are taken from a prototype installation at Radio Sweden in Gothenburg.

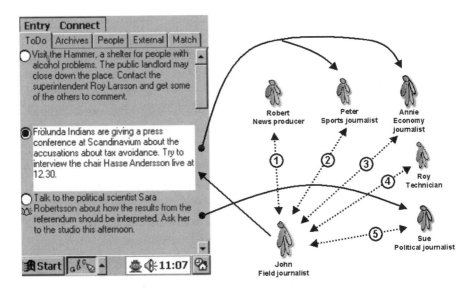

Figure 10.1
The collaboration between the editorial staff in the use scenario.

Figure 10.2
Robert is talking to John while taking some notes on the NewsMate. Note the earphone.

The time is 11:00 a.m., and John, who is working as a field journalist at a radio station, has just finished a report. As he walks to the car, he receives a call on his mobile phone. It is his colleague Robert, telling him that the board of an ice hockey club, Frölunda Indians, has just announced that they are going to give a press conference.

John remembers an article from a morning newspaper, *The Metro*, in which the club was accused of tax avoidance when paying salaries. Robert asks John to go to the press conference and do a report for the 12:30 news. He points out that an interview with the chair of the board would be great. John and Robert discuss the details of the task, and while talking, John uses his NewsMate to make some notes (figure 10.2).

John's task is now to report from the press conference and do an interview with an appropriate framing. He is an expert neither on taxes nor on ice hockey but will be able to do an satisfactory report if the background and framing come into place.

John takes a minute to structure his notes into an entry under the To-Do tab. Then he connects his NewsMate to the server via a mobile phone, activates the To-Do entry, and chooses Send To-Do in the Connect menu (figure 10.3A). A list of keywords is returned, and John chooses the ones that fit and clicks on the Accept button (figure 10.3B). A few seconds later, the results arrive and the mobile phone disconnects.

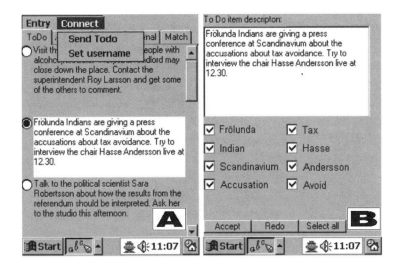

Figure 10.3
A Send To-Do (A); the selection of keywords (B).

John takes a look at the Archives tab, where a list of internal documents is displayed (figure 10.4A).

The titles of the documents give John an overview of what has been done internally on the topic. It seems like tax avoidance in the restaurant sector is common, and John also notes an article about a well-known white-collar criminal. He realizes that perhaps this kind of crime has spread to a new sector. This may be an interesting introduction to the report.

John continues through the tabs and looks at the External tab (figure 10.4B) to see what the newspapers and other competitors have done on the topic. "Just the *Metro* article of value, I suppose," John says to himself when he realizes he already knew about that.

He also checks the People tab (figure 10.4C). Here the names of colleagues who are on duty right now and who have been working on the topic are displayed. The quality of the report is likely to improve if he discusses it with someone with experience on the topic.

When John arrives at the press conference, he plans to contact some colleagues who may help him. Since Erik is at the top of the People list,

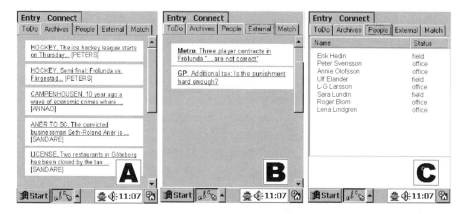

Figure 10.4
Three tabs on the NewsMate: Archives (A), External (B), and People (C).

he is the most appropriate colleague to talk to. Erik is, however, out of the office, and there is no answer on his mobile phone.

Instead, John calls Annie, who answers. John remembers that she has been working on white-collar crime. Annie and John discuss questions like Are there any similar cases? and Does any board member risk jail? Annie thinks the case is not clear enough to be talked about in terms of punishment yet. They agree, however, that he could ask about "bad accounting practice." The communication between John and Annie results in John's becoming aware of some possible angles to report from an accounting perspective.

John hangs up and enters the room where the press conference has just begun. There are a lot of other journalists and people from the ice hockey club there. The chair immediately states, "I will not give any interviews. We're giving the press conference. That's all." The board's main message is that they are not guilty but that they have started an internal investigation. They will not give any further comments until the investigation is finished. John thinks, "Okay, what to do now? I need to have something interesting to report. Let's consult the NewsMate."

John sneaks outside and takes a look at the People tab. The second entry is the sports journalist Peter Svensson. "Oh, Peter, of course," John says, and gives Peter a call. They start a discussion about what has happened. John asks whom else to interview, since the chair refused. Peter mentions that the accountant of the club, Thomas Zetterlund, may accept an interview: "He is the next in line to be the chair of the club." John agrees that he will try to speak to Zetterlund because they really need an interview to complement the report. John asks some more questions: Is tax avoidance common in ice hockey or sports in general? Is this the first case nationally? Through the use of Peter's expertise and John's knowledge of the local conditions, the framing is collaboratively established. This kind of situated knowledge has rarely been accessible in a knowledge management system till now because such systems have lacked the ability to find people. In this case, the time constraint makes direct communication with Peter the best way for John to get the knowledge.

The press conference ends, and John asks the accountant Thomas Zetterlund if he would agree to be interviewed. Thomas accepts, and John contacts Roy, the technician at the studio, to coordinate the broadcast. Roy tells him to be prepared to go on the air in a minute. John waits for Roy to tell him when to start. Roy gives a sign, and John opens by saying, "What we are used to hearing from the real estate and restaurant sectors has now entered the field of professional sports." This framing of the news was derived from timely knowledge provided by the NewsMate. John continues by saying, "Here with us is Thomas Zetterlund, the accountant of Frölunda Indians. Thomas, what do you think about these accusations?" Thomas replies, "We use a lot of agents internationally to contract players, and I cannot say for sure whether they have done anything illegal." He continues, "We are conducting an internal investigation, and I do not want to comment on this further until the investigation is done." After this, John asks about the effect on the sport, and they elaborate a bit on the question. Then he hears Roy in the earphone saying "ten seconds left." John thanks Thomas and ends the interview.

The NewsMate helped John in his efforts to make good-quality journalism. He had not had enough knowledge to be able to ask the right questions and frame the report. When the chair refused to be interviewed, John used the NewsMate to locate someone who could help him find the second-best interviewee. Furthermore, Annie and Peter helped John find an appropriate angle for the report. A traditional knowledge

Figure 10.5
John reads a Short Message Service (SMS) (*left*); the Match tab on the NewsMate (*right*).

management system that focuses on problems would not have given John any of the support he needed to manage his task because he had no actual "problems."

John walks back to his car. On his way the mobile phone beeps to signal that he has received a text message (figure 10.5). Apparently something that may affect John's work has come up. John connects his NewsMate, and a bell is shown on the third To-Do entry (figure 10.1). The entry concerns an interview that John is conducting this afternoon with a political scientist about an upcoming referendum. He becomes aware that his work might not be unique in relation to some other activities at the channel. The channel's repertoire must be considered as a whole: similar reports should not be broadcast without different foci. John activates the entry and checks the Match tab (figure 10.5). It appears as if Sue is planning to do something involving a political scientist. John gives Sue a call, and they agree that two political scientists on the same day is "too much." They agree that the best thing is to drop the political scientist from John's program, because Sue's program is focused on politics. In this case, the NewsMate helped to prevent a potential cross-report. A negotiation had to take place to settle if there was a need to change the focus or content of the reports.

10.2   The NewsMate System

NewsMate is a running prototype system using off-the-shelf technologies in 2000. It was designed this way in order to allow journalists to use it immediately in a field study.

Platforms

All communication in the NewsMate system is done with TCP/IP sockets via a server. The scalability and maintainability relies on the server, which is implemented in Perl with a Berkeley database on the Microsoft Windows NT 4.0 platform. The client-side hardware is a pen-based PDA—Casio Cassiopeia E-105 running Microsoft Windows CE 2.11. The client is implemented in Microsoft Visual Basic for Windows CE. The GSM phone (Nokia 6110),[1] connected to a CompactFlash card (MobiFlash), has Internet access via the Point-to-Point Protocol (PPP). The bandwidth is 9600 bits per second, and the data transmissions are rarely larger than 4 kilobytes. The time required to be online is about one minute.

Users who are not online can be actively contacted using the Short Message Service (SMS). SMS is a part of GSM and makes it possible to send and receive text messages with the mobile phone.

Architecture and Prototype Installation

The architecture is generic but requires integration with editorial systems. The prototype installation described here was implemented at Radio Sweden in Gothenburg.

The server keeps track of all events in the system; very little computation is done on the client. All the communication between the server and the clients are in plain text that is tagged with XML (eXstensible Markup Language). The server also manages all the database calls. The database queries are formatted using a stop-list and a stemming dictionary. The stop-list purpose is to filter out high-frequency and low-content words, for example, *interview* and *the*. The stemming dictionary puts the words in their basic form; for instance, *accusations* and even the misspelled *accusasion* will all be replaced by *accusation*. The stop-list and stemming dictionary are generated from two years of content from the internal archives (about 15,000 text documents of a total size of 10 megabytes). The stemming list is about 300,000 words (4 megabytes) and placed on the server because of its size. The stop-list is 1,500 words (10 kilobytes) and is on the client.

The database of the internal archives is constructed from program reports, proposals for programs, and not-yet-reported surveys, and can be searched with good performance. The database can also provide a list of authors of documents that are related to an entry (see Streeter and Lochbaum 1988). The list of authors will only contain those that are working at this time, that is, logged on to the local area network. The whereabouts of people is also taken into account and based on whether they have checked out a car.

By periodically and automatically gathering the content from the Web edition of local newspapers and a Web service with local news, another database has been constructed. It can be searched in the same way as the internal one, but the original articles are not stored locally. This also includes incoming messages from news agencies.

To find out whether users are working on similar topics, the terms representing the To-Do entries are compared. Furthermore, the overlap in search results from the internal and external archives are compared to find similarities.

Figure 10.6 shows the technical actions of each component:

1. The client filters the To-Do entry through the stop-list.

2. The client calls the server with the formatted query.

3. The server filters the call through the stemming dictionary to put the terms in their basic form.

4. The server queries the external database and receives the results.

5. The server queries the archives/people database and receives the results.

6. The server stores the users' states and checks for overlaps and whether any new or matching messages have arrived.

Figure 10.6
The architecture of NewsMate.

7. If any overlaps or matching news messages are found, text messages (SMS) are sent to the concerned users.

8. The results are returned to the client.

9. The client stores the results as serialized objects.

The user interface is described next because it is critical to how the journalists use the system. The section focuses on the design intentions that were active while creating NewsMate.

User Interface

To-Do   On the To-Do tab the currently active entry determines the content of all the other tabs. It lets the user add, edit, and remove entries. The user updates the text with the pen. The user can choose Send To-Do in the Connect menu, making a list of keywords appear (figure 10.3). The relevant keywords can be selected. If the Redo button is pressed, a new list of keywords is generated. When the user is satisfied, the Accept button is pressed and the results of the other tabs will be returned.

Archives   For each entry that has been sent to the server, a list of ten articles (title and ingress) from internal archives is displayed at the Archive tab (figure 10.4). The user can click on a title and get the full text of the article. The intended use is, however, to remind the user of how the topic had been reported.

External The External tab lists matches from predefined external sources, such as newspapers and new agencies (figure 10.4). By clicking on the entries, the user can browse the full text articles. The intended use here is once again to remind the user of how the topic had been reported externally.

People The People tab displays the names of journalists who have been involved in similar tasks and are currently on duty (figure 10.4). The Status column indicates if a person is in the office or in the field.

Match If there is an overlap between To-Do entries, a notification is issued. The users who are concerned receive an SMS on their mobile phones. The user can then connect, and a bell icon will be displayed beside the entry in question (figure 10.1). When the To Do entry is made active, the matching users name and To Do entry text is displayed on the Match tab (figure 10.5). The match can, of course, also occur when a user has just done a Send To-Do. In these cases, no SMS will be sent.

In some cases, the message will only confirm what the users already know. In other cases, it may be preferable to get into direct contact to resolve the matter. If any new news messages have arrived, which are similar to a registered To-Do item on an offline client, they will be sent in this way as well.

10.3   Related Systems

One of the first systems in the knowledge management category was gIBIS (Conklin and Begeman 1988; Yakemovic and Conklin 1990). The aim was to make the rationale for a design decision explicit by capturing the argumentation in a hypermedia system. The system is partially about getting an overview of complex design problems. There is little evidence of knowledge being reused with this system and the users' tasks except for problem solving. It incorporates other sources of information, such as design sketches and code, by linking to them. There are no connections to present activities, and communication between people is made indirectly through the system. Similar ideas can also be found in a recent system, the RepTool, which includes graphic views and maps to facilitate remembering (Jordan, Goldman, and Eichler 1998).

A similar approach was offered by Terveen, Selfridge, and Long (1993), reporting on a project that created a "living design memory" for software developers. This was accomplished by introducing links to associated information units with the pertinent parts of the products. It can be argued that in a sense facts are placed in the context where they are to be used. The system was integrated with the software development process, which is very different from journalism. It is claimed that relevant knowledge exists in the form of "folklore" and that it should be incorporated in the system. However, to repackage knowledge is problematic (see Brown and Duguid 1991). Instead of getting the "folklore" into the system, our approach is to support people communicating the "folklore." Most of these features can be found in the Project Memory system (Weiser and Morrison 1998). The system also has To-Do lists, but in this case they are in the form of "milestones." This is also the focus of Kreifeldt, Hinrichs, and Woetzel (1993). The To-Do feature of the NewsMate is more like an open resource that is used to reduce the complexity of the task.

Knowledge Pump (Glance, Arregui, and Dardenne 1998) integrates and refines ideas from intelligent information sharing (Malone et al. 1987) and collaborative recommender systems (Resnick and Varian 1997). The system addresses the problem of long-term knowledge interests and is based on user profiles. The NewsMate is mainly used to address short-term knowledge interests linked to tasks. The journalists' user profiles are only based on published records.

Ackerman and Starr (1995) argue for the importance of social activity indicators, that is, it is important to be aware of other people's activities in a collaborative system. In the NewsMate this is addressed with the Match feature, which informs the involved parties in the case of potential cross-reporting.

Answer Garden (Ackerman 1994) aims to help organizations capture and retrieve experiences of their employees. In short, the Answer Garden lets the users browse a network of diagnostic questions to find the answers they want. If the answer cannot be found, the question is routed to experts and later inserted (along with the answers) into the network. The experts can also modify the network; thus the knowledge grows. Answer Garden 2 introduces features that route the user directly to the expert if the solution is not found in the network (Ackerman and McDonald 1996). A collaborative help feature is also added to make the interpretations of deconceptualized information easier. The idea is to remove unnecessary context (Ackerman and McDonald 1996, 103), which can be difficult (Fagrell and Ljungberg 1999). None of the versions of Answer Garden support the user with the task at hand. The system requires additional authoring and support for problem solving.

In a field study McDonald and Ackerman (1998) investigate expertise location. Once again, the focus is on problem solving in software engineering. The identification of potential expertise with the NewsMate is accomplished through the People feature. Furthermore, no matter how experienced a journalist is, a "second opinion" is always appreciated (see Ehrlich and Cash 1999, 162).

Coordination of work and sharing of experiences were the focus of Kristoffersen and Ljungberg (1998) when designing support for a dispersed IT-support group. They focused on tasks, but they were strictly problem-oriented and the communication between people was mainly through the system. The NewsMate is not designed for this purpose; thus coordination and task assignment are done elsewhere.

Finally, Kristoffersen and Ljungberg's system also supports the mobility of the journalists. It has recently been argued that computer-supported cooperative work (CSCW) designers have not taken mobility seriously (Luff and Heath 1998). The main requirement for the News-Mate was that it should move beyond the desktop and into the field.

10.4   Discussion

This chapter introduced the NewsMate, a knowledge management system that supports mobile and distributed news journalists. Our contribution is an approach to knowledge management emphasizing

• that there is a need to step away from the focus on problem solving and instead incorporate knowledge management support in tasks (supported through a To-Do feature in NewsMate);

• that the information architecture should consider records from sources internal as well as external to the organization (NewsMate features that illustrate this are Archives and External);

• that direct communication should be actively favored and based on present conditions (illustrated through the People and Match features of the NewsMate).

According to users, the NewsMate system is useful. I believe that this approach has considered the critique against traditional knowledge management systems:

• Randall et al. (1996), Bannon and Kuutti (1996), and Hughes et al. (1996) have criticized knowledge management for offering a passive repository view of knowledge. The task and direct communication orientation of the NewsMate provides support for active remembering, sensitive to the human conduct that actually takes place in organizations.

• Ackerman and Halverson (1998) show that knowledge is often distributed between many different sources, of which only a few are explicitly known in advance. This is addressed with the open information architecture of the NewsMate in conjunction with the encouragement of direct communication.

However, the massive increase of communication technologies, for example, mobile telephones, e-mail, instant messaging, and PDAs, has led to changes in established work-based communication practices (Nardi, Whittaker, and Schwarz 2000). These technologies are also becoming increasingly common with short-term employment contracts (e.g., freelance journalists). If this is the case, what will the knowledge systems be like? For example, who will "own" the knowledge system? Will there be any central coordination on technical or managerial levels? These are unanswered questions that further research will have to address.

To some extent the approach to knowledge management that is illustrated in this chapter may be useful in future settings. However, a more general version of the NewsMate is under development that includes many technical improvements. For example, improvements of the telecommunication network allows instant connectivity; no dial-up modem connection is necessary. Such technical advances opens new possibilities for the NewsMate.

Acknowledgments

This research is a part of the Mobile Informatics program funded by the Swedish Information Technology Institute (SITI). The author would like to thank the Mobile Informatics group at the Viktoria Institute, especially Fredrik Ljungberg, Kerstin Forsberg, Erik Johannesson, and Steinar Kristoffersen. The author would also like to thank Sofia Eklund, Jens Bergqvist, and the anonymous reviews.

Note

1. The Global System for Mobile communication (GSM), with its 220 million subscribers, is the largest digital wireless communication standard in the world (900/1800 band). The coverage in Sweden is very good, especially in domestic areas. *Source:* GSM Association, www.gsmworld.com (January 10, 2000).

References

Ackerman, M. S. 1994. Augmenting the Organizational Memory: A Field Study of Answer Garden. In *Proceedings of the ACM Conference on Computer-Supported Cooperative Work (CSCW '94)*, 243–252.

Ackerman, M. S., and C. Halverson. 1998. Considering an Organization's Memory. In *Proceedings of the ACM Conference on Computer-Supported Cooperative Work (CSCW '98)*, 39–48.

Ackerman, M. S., and D. W. McDonald. 1996. Answer Garden 2: Merging Organizational Memory with Collaborative Help. In *Proceedings of the ACM Conference on Computer-Supported Cooperative Work (CSCW '96)*, 97–105.

Ackerman, M. S., and B. Starr. 1995. Social Activity Indicators: Interface Components for CSCW Systems. In *Proceedings of the ACM Symposium on User Interface Software and Technology (UIST '95)*, 159–168.

Anderson, R., and W. Sharrock. 1993. Can Organizations Afford Knowledge? *Computer Supported Cooperative Work* 1 (3): 123–142.

Bannon, L. J., and K. Kuutti. 1996. Shifting Perspectives on Organizational Memory: From Storage to Active Remembering. In *Proceedings of the Twenty-ninth Hawaii Conference on System Sciences*, vol. 4, 156–167.

Bellotti, V., and Y. Rogers. 1997. From Web Press to Web Pressure: Multimedia Representations and Multimedia Publishing. In *Proceedings of the ACM Conference on Human Factors in Computing Systems (CHI '97)*, 279–286.

Brown, J. S., and P. Duguid. 1991. Organizational Learning and Communities of Practice: Towards a Unified View of Working, Learning, and Innovation. *Organization Science* 2 (1): 40–57.

Conklin, J., and M. L. Begeman. 1988. gIBIS: A Hypertext Tool for Exploratory Policy Discussion. In *Proceedings of the ACM Conference on Computer-Supported Cooperative Work (CSCW '88)*, 140–152.

Ehrlich, K., and D. Cash. 1999. The Invisible World of Intermediaries: A Cautionary Tale. *Computer Supported Cooperative Work* 8: 147–167.

Fagrell, H., and F. Ljungberg. 1999. Exploring Support for Knowledge Management in Mobile Work. In *Proceedings of the European Conference on Computer-Supported Cooperative Work (ECSCW '99)*, 259–275.

———. 2000. Empirically Informed Knowledge Management Systems in Mobile Domains. In *Proceedings of the Sixth Biennial Participatory Design Conference*.

Glance, N., D. Arregui, and M. Dardenne. 1998. Knowledge Pump: Supporting the Flow and Use of Knowledge. In *Information Technology for Knowledge Management*, ed. U. M. Borghoff and R. Pareschi. Berlin: Springer-Verlag.

Hughes, J. A., V. King, T. Rodden, and H. Andersen. 1994. Moving out from the Control Room: Ethnography in System Design. In *Proceedings of the ACM Conference on Computer-Supported Cooperative Work (CSCW '94)*, 429–439.

Hughes, J. A., S. Kristoffersen, J. O'Brien, and M. Rouncefield. 1996. When Mavis met IRIS: Ending the Love Affair with Organisational Memory. In *Proceedings of IRIS '19*, 767–788.

Jordan, B., R. Goldman, and A. Eichler. 1998. A Technology for Supporting Knowledge Work: The RepTool. In *Information Technology for Knowledge Management*, ed. U. M. Borghoff and R. Pareschi. Berlin: Springer-Verlag.

Kidd, A. 1994. The Marks Are on the Knowledge Worker. In *Proceedings of the ACM Conference on Human Factors in Computing Systems (CHI '94)*, 186–191.

Kreifeldt, T., E. Hinrichs, and G. Woetzel. 1993. Sharing To-Do Lists with a Distributed Task Manager. In *Proceedings of the Third European Conference on Computer-Supported Cooperative Work (ECSCW '93)*, 31–45.

Kristoffersen, S., and F. Ljungberg. 1998. MobiCom: Networking Dispersed Groups. *Interacting with Computers* 10 (1): 45–65.

Luff, P., and C. Heath. 1998. Mobility in Collaboration. In *Proceedings of the ACM Conference on Computer-Supported Cooperative Work (CSCW '98)*, 305–314.

Malone, T. W., K. R. Grant, F. A. Turbak, S. A. Brobst, and M. D. Cohan. 1987. Intelligent Information Sharing Systems. *Communications of the ACM* 30 (5): 390–402.

March, J. G. 1991. How Decisions Happen in Organizations. *Human-Computer Interaction* 6 (2): 95–117.

McDonald, D. W., and M. S. Ackerman. 1998. Just Talk to Me: A Field Study of Expertise Location. In *Proceedings of the ACM Conference on Computer-Supported Cooperative Work (CSCW '98)*, 315–324.

Nardi, B. A., S. Whittaker, and H. Schwarz. 2000. It's Not What You Know, It's Who You Know: Work in the Information Age. *First Monday* 5 (May 1). http:// firstmonday.org/issues/issue5_5/nardi/index.html.

Nielsen, J. 1993. *Usability Engineering.* New York: Academic Press.

Randall, D., J. O'Brien, M. Rouncefield, and J. A. Hughes. 1996. Organisational Memory and CSCW: Supporting the "Mavis Phenomenon." In *Proceedings of the Sixth Australian Conference on Computer-Human Interaction (OzCHI '96).*

Resnick, P., and H. R. Varian, eds. 1997. Recommender Systems. *Communications of the ACM* 40 (3).

Ruggles, R. 1998. The State of the Notion: Knowledge Management in Practice. *California Management Review* 40 (3): 80–89.

Streeter, L. A., and K. E. Lochbaum. 1988. An Expert/Expert-Locating System Based on Automatic Representations of Semantic Structure. In *Proceedings of the Fourth IEEE Conference on Artificial Intelligence Applications,* 345–349.

Terveen, L. G., P. G. Selfridge, and M. D. Long. 1993. From "Folklore" to "Living Design Memory." In *Proceedings of the ACM Conference on Human Factors in Computing Systems (CHI '93),* 15–22.

Weiser, M., and J. Morrison. 1998. Project Memory: Information Management for Project Teams." *Journal of Management Information Systems* 14 (4): 149–167.

Yakemovic, K. C., and E. J. Conklin. 1990. Report on a Development Project Use of an Issue-Based Information System." In *Proceedings of the ACM Conference on Computer-Supported Cooperative Work (CSCW '90),* 105–118.

11

Supporting Informal Communities of Practice within Organizations

R. T. Jim Eales

Informal communities of practice are important for the development and sharing of expertise within organizations. These communities of practice provide the essential context for the creation and dissemination of many areas of expertise that are vital to an organization's success and development. A community of practice is "a set of relations among persons, activity, and world, over time and in relation with other tangential and overlapping communities of practice" and "participation in the cultural practice in which any knowledge exists is an epistemological principle of learning" (Lave and Wenger 1991, 98; see also Wenger 1998). The use of the term *informal* represents a number of different perspectives. It emphasizes informal learning, that is, learner-centered, continuous, local, and context-sensitive learning rather than formal, institutionally sponsored training or e-learning. The term *informal* also represents the hidden or "interstitial" (Lave and Wenger 1991) nature of these communities. Communities of practice do not always, of course, have to be informal; see, for example, Hutchins's account of navigation practice in the U.S. Navy (Hutchins 1995). Although these communities are called informal, they nonetheless represent powerful and authentic learning environments for the development of situated expertise (Billett 1999), expertise for which there is often no other means of development. These communities of practice may, however, vary widely in the efficiency of their support offered to learners and in the level of the expertise at their heart. The technological augmentation or support of these communities can harness the power and quality of their collaborative assistance while offering improved opportunities to distribute and extend the inherent expertise. It would appear to be an opportune time to investigate the technical augmentation of collaborative support. A combination of a collaborative and situated view of expertise development and the potential of ubiquitous networking must present new opportunities for the design of augmented expertise networks.

My interest in expertise management developed out of an initial focus on the development of information technology (IT) skills and a concern to find more effective methods of user support in the area of human-computer interaction (HCI). As computer-based tools become increasingly complex and multipurpose, the skills required from computer users become increasingly specialized and situated. In the workplace, computer users rarely receive adequate training and make little use of printed manuals or online help (Eales and Welsh 1994). Invariably computer users rely on informal collaborative opportunities to develop their situated expertise—a point rarely discussed in user learning and rarely exploited in user support. Collaborative workplace learning has the potential to make a significant contribution to computer-related skills development and to organizational productivity in general, particularly with the right kind of organizational and technical support. IT expertise generally has a wide but shallow profile across organizations. In other words, there is rarely any great concentration of unique expertise, but it does directly influence almost every area of operation. As more and more work becomes computer-based, IT skills are important because they often mediate the development of other areas of expertise. Although some of the design ideas presented here are specific to the development of computer skills, the fundamental basis of the approach is relevant to many other areas of expertise development in the workplace.

The design proposals expressed here are given form in terms of the conceptualization, design, and development of a generic *collaborative support system*. This is a computer-based networked system designed to facilitate and augment the provision of collaborative support for the solution of work-related problems and the general development of expertise among its users. The key to successful design of such a system is to understand the social dynamics of informal communities of practice and collaborative support. A collaborative support system has to be more than just useful and usable—above all *it has to be used*. Workers will not use a collaborative support system just because it exists. The primary design objective is to encourage use of the system and participation in its continuing development. An awareness of the subtle constraints and inducements acting on the collaborative learner in the workplace is required. I have spent a considerable amount of time studying and trying to understand the social dynamics of collaborative expertise development in the workplace (Eales and Welsh 1994; Eales 1996). In many workplaces, mastery appears to be in short supply, and what is required is some kind of collaborative bootstrapping of expertise.

My approach is based on the notion of a sociotechnical system in that it consists of a social subsystem and a technical subsystem. Both subsystems are vital to the overall effectiveness of the system. But as the sociotechnical movement found (Mumford 1987), if the technical system is optimized at the expense of the social subsystem, the results obtained will be suboptimal. The goal, as Preece (2000) neatly summarizes it, is designing usability while supporting sociability. In this instance, a flawed social subsystem is more likely to lead to the nonuse of a system than an inefficient technical subsystem.

11.1 Related Work

Liam Bannon suggested the idea of "helping users help each other" back in 1986 (Bannon 1986). Bonnie Nardi and her colleagues, in particular, presented a number of interesting and detailed studies of collaborative support among various groups of computer users, (e.g., Nardi and Miller 1991; Gantt and Nardi 1992). One interesting approach to user-centerd collaborative skill development, closely related to these studies of cooperation, was the idea of tailorable or customizable systems that actively support users in the development and sharing of customizations (MacLean et al. 1990; Mackay 1990; Nardi 1993). For more recent research on the area of tailorable collaborative artifacts, see Wulf (1999). Although I rarely use the term *organizational memory*, I see my work as also related to research on the technical augmentation of organizational and community memories (e.g., Abecker et al. 1998; Ackerman 1994; Ackerman and McDonald 1996; Ackerman and Halverson 1998; Berlin et al. 1993). In particular, the focus in organizational memory research should be on remembering as an active constructive act rather than on memory as a passive store (Bannon and Kuutti 1996). The spirit of this argument is reflected in the current interest in expertise. I prefer to see my work as a form of computer-supported collaborative learning (CSCL) (Koschmann 1996). Although the area of CSCL is dominated by research focused on formal educational institutions, the application of the CSCL paradigm to the workplace is an important and pressing issue.

11.2   Learning in the Wild

The literature on expertise development relies primarily on laboratory-based cognitive studies, models of learning focused on the individual, and strategies derived from formal instruction. My understanding of informal expertise development has been derived mostly from firsthand investigations of expertise in the workplace. However, I have found two pieces of theory of particular value in interpreting the dynamics of collaborative expertise development. Lave and Wenger's theory of *legitimate peripheral participation* has proved a useful starting point for understanding informal communities of practice, and Hutchins's *distributed cognition theory* has helped to clarify the part played by technical artifacts in these communities.

Lave and Wenger's (1991) notion of *legitimate peripheral participation* is a theory of situated learning described in terms of learning trajectories. In this social theory of learning, learners must be legitimate participants in ongoing practice in order for learning identities to develop into full participation. They suggest that a person's intentions to learn are engaged and the meaning of learning is configured through the process of becoming a full participant in a sociocultural practice, and that this process includes or subsumes the learning of knowledgeable skills. The process can be interpreted as the development of identities and changing membership as a newcomer moves from the periphery to full participation in a community of practice. Although they talk about full participation in terms of identities of mastery, Lave and Wenger suggest that this mastery does not reside in the master, but in the organization of the community of practice of which the master is a part.

For anyone designing a collaborative support system, distributed cognition theory and the work of Hutchins (1995; Seifert and Hutchins

1992) is particularly important. Hutchins presents the notion of a distributed cognitive system and demonstrates the important role played by mediating structures and mediating artifacts. When learning (or developing expertise) in a collaborative environment a person's *horizon of observation* is particularly important. This is the functional work space that a person can monitor or observe. Hutchins points out that technology has a key role here because the horizons of observation of the members of a work group are often defined by technology. Simply being in the presence of other workers does not guarantee that one will learn collaboratively. Hutchins has also drawn attention to what he terms *open tools*, such as navigation charts. He suggests that the design of tools can affect their suitability for *joint use* or for *demonstration*. When a person is performing some activity, the interaction between that person and a tool may or may not be open to others, depending on the nature of the tool. Open tools provide opportunities for the observation of tool use and can contribute to the general spread and development of expertise. Desktop computers, in particular, are not inherently open tools but could more appropriately be described as private tools, in that it is not easy to observe the interaction of a user and a computer other than in a very trivial way.

11.3   Collaborative Support Systems

In attempting to design and develop a collaborative support system, I use a number of basic working principles derived from theories of situated learning and my own and colleagues' studies of collaborative support in workplaces.

• Learning in the workplace is primarily motivated by the everyday dilemmas and needs involved in work activities. Given the right conditions and the right support, these dilemmas can be turned into learning opportunities.

• What is of greatest value to the learner is not "universal" instruction but access to and participation in knowledgeable situated practice.

• The fundamental operational unit of support is the small group. The mutual understanding, mutual commitment, and mutual trust that can develop within these groups are vital resources.

• Even with full collaboration local expertise may be limited. A group should always have ways of extending or improving its collective understanding by learning from the practice of others.

The fundamental argument here is that technological systems can and should be designed to enable and to utilize the potential of collaborative support. A conceptual model of such a collaborative support system has at least two social levels:

• A support group level
• An organizational level

The support group level is conceived as the technological and human support required to facilitate the *sharing* or distribution of expertise *within* a small group of computer users. A *support group* is a small, "closed," and ideally cohesive group of ordinary computer users. This group should be engaged in similar or related work tasks involving the use of the same computer-based tools. Normally, this support group would be based on an existing work group. The thrust of technical augmentation at this level is to make computer use more visible within the support group context, a design motivation that I call *collaborative visibility*. Collaborative visibility is a theoretical concept that tries to link visibility to collaboration and collaboration to visibility. In simple terms, it means that the actions of the individual are visible to the group and the *entire* group must be visible to the individual. Without this mutual visibility (and resulting privacy), essential support group characteristics such as mutual trust, mutual commitment, and the revelation of needs are unlikely to be forthcoming.

The organizational level is concerned with the technological and organizational support required to bind together the various support groups into a network for organizational learning. Perhaps this level can be considered a network of practice (Brown and Duguid 2000). Although the support group is a powerful and valuable basis for expertise development, the closed nature of the group may mean that each support group is in danger of reinventing the wheel. Some method is needed of extending the sum of group expertise and perhaps making valuable expertise available to other groups. It is assumed that a *support person* from each support group will take part in this network along with representatives of the organization, outside consultants, and others, depending on specific circumstances. The support person acts as a gate-keeper to the wider organization, utilizing the resources of a wider expertise network while safeguarding support group privacy.

The importance of social factors in this kind of support system means that the success and effectiveness of the technical subsystem is crucially dependent on factors that cannot be directly addressed by technology. For example, the cohesiveness of the support group, the quality of the support person, and the general organizational climate for learning can all have a significant influence on the success or failure of a collaborative support system. The two social levels of a support system are described in more detail in the following sections.

Sharing Expertise—The Support Group Level

An important method of supporting the distribution of expertise among computer users is to make computer use more visible within a collaborative context. *Individual* dilemmas associated with computer use should be turned into *collaborative* learning opportunities. If technology could make computer-related practice more visible within work groups, this would have a positive effect on the development of computer skills. This is the design principle, mentioned earlier, of *collaborative visibility*.

Generally, privacy of practice is the prevailing situation in most workplaces where computers are used. To illustrate this, I once interviewed an apparently experienced computer user who had never discovered that word processors allow the user to copy between documents, even though this person had worked in an office with several others. When this person wanted to a copy a section from one document to another he printed the first document out and then typed the section again working from the hard copy. The goal of collaborative visibility is to make personal and private tools into collective and open tools, for instance, to make computer use and computer skills more visible *within* a collaborative context. The mutual commitment, mutual understanding, and mutual trust inherent in cooperative work groups are valuable resources for workplace learning. From this perspective, the suboptimal utilization of computer tools can be interpreted not so much as a reluctance to learn but as *isolation* from more knowledgeable practice.

Up to this point the visibility of work activities has been presented as a positive development leading to the spread and evolution of computer-related practice. Visibility, however, also has a negative interpretation. Visibility may well be viewed as an undesirable development by those made visible. One must therefore carefully consider to whom activities are being made visible. Foucault (1977) has presented the notion of *panopticism* based on the historical design of a Panopticon, a circular prison structure of individual cells with a central observation tower. In this structure all inmates are individualized, identifiable, and visible at all times from the central tower, which may or may not be occupied by an unseeable supervisor. Foucault states that the major effect of the Panopticon is "to induce in the inmate a state of conscious and permanent *visibility* that assumes the automatic functioning of power" (201; emphasis added). Zuboff (1988) has highlighted the way in which organizational computer-mediated communication systems can function as a modern Panopticon: "The communications technology with which they had cheerfully elaborated and extended their networks of relationships, access to information, thoughtful dialogue, and social banter had also provided a quantum increase in their *visibility* to DrugCorp's managerial hierarchy" (362; emphasis added). The workers in Zuboff's study were voluntary participants in the organization's computer conferencing system; they could and did cease to use the medium for sensitive communication as management surveillance increased. As more and more work is performed and transmitted electronically, without any possibility for opting out of participation, the threat of an electronic panopticon increases. In a project to equip photocopier technicians with radios so that they could provide mutual assistance and keep each other generally informed, Orr and Crowfoot (1992) found that the possibility of using the radio channel for management surveillance was a major concern for the technicians. "Finally, there was a decision to keep the rest of the organization out of the loop, to make this circulation of information free from interference or even monitoring" (Orr 1993, 11).

Management monitoring is not the only sensitive issue related to the visibility of people's activities. Workers may be sensitive about the particular way they do things and about asking for help, even among their peers. Computer users may be quite aware that they use suboptimal methods to perform common computer-based tasks but do not want this fact broadcast to all and sundry. Revealing ignorance to work colleagues by asking for help can be a difficult and painful process. People generally do not want their ignorance (real or assumed) exposed for all to see. The control of visibility is required to give people the confidence to demonstrate how they use the computer and to ask for assistance in a collaborative support system.

In an attempt to control visibility and encourage participation, it is suggested that participation in a collaborative support system should be *restricted*. That is, all participants in a collaborative support system should be known to each other, and there may be specific conditions for membership and limits on the size of the group. The actual membership of a support group is a tricky issue. It may well be a hard task to decide just who should be inside "the loop" and who should be outside. In the teams of technicians studied by Orr and Crowfoot (1992), managers were only allowed to have a radio if the members of the team voted for it. On the other hand, in the development of computer skills, managers are often active and "equal" members of the end user learning community. From a design point of view, a productive approach to this issue is to ensure that a collaborative support system provides the functionality to be able to restrict and maintain membership, but leave membership decisions to local circumstances.

Collaborative visibility involves the revealing of both activity and the collaborative context. Some ideas for specific technological augmentation are as follows:

• *Make tool use visible.* Making tool use visible to others is the fundamental objective in the quest for collaborative expertise development. However, the idea of visibility goes far beyond the simple notion of being able to physically observe something. One of the most important methods of making tool skills visible is the demonstration.

• *Make the end products of tool use visible.* Under certain circumstances the end products of tool use can be a quick and useful summary of what it is possible to do, in a given situation. They provide a kind of indirect visibility of activities.

• *Allow capture and storage of examples of tool use.*   One of the inherent advantages of technological communication is that it creates the opportunity for the capture of interaction, thus extending visibility by making it possible to relay this information to other places or other times.

• *Support interactive discourse about tool use.*   Participation in the practice of a group is more than just the passive observation of someone doing something. Making something visible also involves revealing the meaning.

• *Allow control of visibility.*   Control over the revelation of practice by the practitioner creates the opportunity for conditions of confidence and trust to develop, and for practice to be revealed in meaningful ways.

The technological augmentation of expertise sharing may, however, create additional problems. Representations of activity or problems, when recorded in some persistent form, can easily cross group boundaries. It may be extremely difficult to control the scope of visibility with any confidence when technology is involved in the communication. The very features of technology that we may perceive as advantages—the ability to support communication across time and space—mean that once something is committed to this form its subsequent visibility becomes hard to control. In face-to-face communication situations, decisions on the revelation of practice can be varied moment to moment depending on all kinds of factors. For example, in the communication between two people, a person may decide whether to communicate or not, how much to communicate, how to communicate, and so on, depending on the particular circumstances of the immediate situation.

The most important design consideration here is that factors such as visibility, monitoring, group membership, group boundaries, and so on, are likely to play a significant part in the acceptance or rejection of a collaborative support system. If one ignores these sensitive issues and imposes visibility by introducing a technological system that takes no account of visibility factors, one can expect the nonuse of the system or the development of elaborate methods of concealment (see Zuboff 1988). Meaningful revelation of practice requires a commitment to, and trust in, those we are assisting or asking for assistance. It also requires confidence in the scope and security of any mediating form of technology. Control over the revelation of practice by the practitioners creates the opportunity for conditions of confidence and trust to develop, and for practice to be revealed in meaningful ways.

Extending Expertise—The Organizational Level

Taking an active and constructive view of expertise development is important. Active engagement in the collective resolution of "owned" problems is the cornerstone of collaborative support. Collaborative support largely takes place in an informal domain. Indeed, the problems and collaborative support are owned by the end users precisely because they are not formal. An informal basis ensures that support is focused on the problems of relevance to the users and utilizes the collaborative commitment and knowledge that is locally available. Informal collaborative support tends to develop in a climate of pressing user needs and organizational neglect (or inappropriate support). To address local problems, informal support generally utilizes a natural division of labor or distributed expertise. Those with specific expertise or interests are used to overcoming problems that are deemed important in a local context. However, largely because this form of support is in the informal domain its quality or availability may be restricted by the influence of various factors:

- *Limited expertise.* Sometimes local expertise may be very limited and no one is prepared to take on the role of unofficial local expert.

- *Restricted communication.* Informal relationships with others are built up largely on an ad hoc basis and may not include those who could be of greatest assistance or who are in greatest need.

- *Restricted time and effort.* The quality of informal support is highly likely to be restricted by the normal time and effort constraints of the workplace.

- *Lack of wider support.* Without some kind of formal recognition, the persons carrying most of the burden of local assistance are unlikely to receive any additional support or information from outside the support group.

• *Lack of technological resources.* The full range of technology may not be available to those engaged in informal support.

Once these limitations are recognized, a possible solution is for the organization to formalize or semiformalize the position of the support person within a work group. A support person requires a combination of technical and social skills. She has to know in detail the tasks of the group, have knowledge of or at least an interest in computer systems, and have a genuine commitment to assisting other members of the group in their various needs. Generally, a support person "emerges" from the group and is then sometimes recognized semiformally by the organization. The support person may be given additional training and organizational support, and allocated time in which to carry out the support role and perhaps the use of some kind of support technology. This recognition may overcome some of the inherent disadvantages involved in informal support, but it may also change the nature of the relationship between the support person and the support group. The move from an informal to semiformal basis of support may be accompanied by a move from a support relationship based on mutual commitment and mutual ownership of the problems to one of dependence on someone with organizational responsibility for local support. My colleagues and I saw evidence of this kind of conflict in our workplace investigations (Eales 1996). A change of perspective may occur from "How are *we* going to overcome this problem?" to "I've got a problem; what are *you* going to do about it?" This may also mark a change from an active to a passive learning approach on the part of the learner. Learning leading to flexible and robust understanding may depend crucially on a feeling of personal (and shared) ownership of the dilemma and an active commitment by the learner to resolve it.

The move to a semiformal support system may also influence the control of visibility. Managers may well consider that the official recognition of the local computer support role entitles them to automatic access to any information associated with the role. Indeed, the support person may have to provide information to management to justify the continuation of his position. Information may be provided in an anonymous form, for example, a list of the most common problems, or it may amount to a report on the competence and problems of each worker.

Such management monitoring may lead to nonparticipation in the official support system, forcing the computer user once again back into informal support relationships. Thus, attempts to move computer support from an informal to a semiformal basis may only result in the creation of a vicious circle. Informal and semiformal methods of support are not necessarily incompatible, however. With careful and sensitive organizational planning the advantages of both kinds of support can be combined. An effectively functioning support group needs to retain the commitment and ownership associated with informal support, while utilizing the organizational and technological benefits that are associated with formal support.

A system developed for use at the support group social level has the advantage that it can also be used at the organizational level with the collaborative support group made up of support persons from different groups and organizational representatives. Use of a collaborative support system at this organizational level supports

· Sharing of practice, problems, and innovations between groups
· Input of specialist organizational expertise
· Communication of support group needs to the organizational level
· Communication of organizational direction to the support groups

Most of the issues relating to the ownership of problems and the difficulties associated with moving from totally informal to semiformal support relationships fall within the organizational rather than the technological sphere. In the design of technology to facilitate the support process, the most important principle related to this informal-formal balance is not to enshrine or incorporate organizational positions of responsibility within the technological system. Channels of communication and assistance must not depend on any one individual for their efficient functioning, thus encouraging use and participation by the whole group. In other words, although the quality of the support person may be an important ingredient in the success of a collaborative support system, the system should still be able to provide useful assistance even when the support person is less than ideal or is nonexistent.

In summary, I want to extend the technology of the workplace to utilize and develop the potential of collaborative support. The driving force in the use and development of such a system is cooperation. Although cooperation is ubiquitous and intrinsically rewarding, it is also a very fragile phenomenon. In the development of computer-mediated collaborative support systems what appears to be required is sensitive design and restrained use of technology. A local and personalized focus on collaborative problem solving appears to be a promising starting point for a collaborative support system. To facilitate this, a method of local interaction between end users is needed that provides a rich illustration of problems and solutions while requiring the minimum of end user time and effort. I believe that the demonstration is of particular significance in the sharing of expertise. The next section discusses the importance of the demonstration in general and considers the particular value of the recorded demonstration for collaborative support.

11.4   The Importance of Demonstrations

Although some kind of collaborative sharing and problem-solving system utilizing collaborative visibility principles will be of great benefit for expertise development, there is a problem of additional user effort required to make such a system function. A collaborative support system is user-driven, and unless the users participate in its development, it will remain "empty" and generally be of little value.

Jim: One section has produced a local procedures manual.

Kylie: I don't see why we should have to write the manual for this section. We could do it, but we don't have the time to sit down and write all these things.

Jim: What if someone comes to you with a problem?

Kylie: But that's different; then they're asking you something, and you're showing them. But to write it down—you don't know what they are going to ask. You would have to write down everything.

   This extract from a transcribed interview comes from a study I undertook into organizational end users and their methods of skill development (Eales 1996). The extract illustrates a number of crucial factors in the design of computer support for collaborative learning in the workplace. In particular, participants need a method of communication that requires little effort to produce (and learn) and yet provides information of high value. In other words, user effort should be minimized while representational value is maximized. Kylie provides a hint of a possible solution, when she says, "But that's different; then they're asking you something, and you're *showing* them."

Ask a colleague how to do something using a computer, and she will invariably *demonstrate* it to you. You are invited into a position where the events occurring on the screen can be clearly seen. The demonstrator then goes through the relevant sequence of operations between the user and machine. The significant events are emphasized, usually by verbal commentary, and you are also able to ask questions if a point is missed or needs clarifying. Demonstrations appear to have particular value for conveying computer-based skills.

Recorded or animated demonstrations are often used as a form of instruction, but the demonstration can also be a very important method of *communication between users* about the way to do things with a computer system. Recorded demonstrations can play an important role in making practice or expertise visible within a collaborative support group. Demonstrations provide a special kind of visibility; they are not just a slice of everyday activity made visible. There are often limitations to what one can learn from merely observing someone doing something when they are not giving a demonstration. I believe demonstrations have specific characteristics that make them particularly valuable in learning:

• *Demonstrations are practical.* Demonstrations have a special importance in learning practical skills. It may be very difficult for the demonstrator or the learner to express the problem or solution in any other way, for example, in speech or written text.

• *Demonstrations are focused.* A demonstration is focused on a specific area. It is not just a sequence of normal activities made visible. It is usually the answer to a specific query or a practical illustration of a problem.

• *Demonstrations are condensed.* A demonstration is a condensed version of significant events. A demonstration normally takes place under time constraints; therefore it tends to feature only events that are significant. The sequence of events in a demonstration may occur over a much longer period of time when performed during normal working conditions.

• *Demonstrations are interactive.*   The interaction between the demonstrator and the learner may be very important. A learner can ask questions or the demonstrator can ask questions. General comments, facial expressions, and body language may also provide valuable feedback for the demonstrator and learner. Interaction may change the whole direction of the demonstration.

• *Demonstrations have a commentary.*   A demonstration normally has an accompanying verbal commentary. A running commentary is not available when someone is merely observing a person's activities. A commentary can serve to highlight significant events or it can contribute additional detail. For example, the commentary may be used to convey conceptual information in coordination with a procedural demonstration.

• *Demonstrations are multilayered.*   A demonstration is normally a rich depiction of situated activities. It represents a variety of information at different levels. A demonstration may be useful in different ways, depending on the level or needs of the learner. For example, initially it forms a simple model of behavior, but later it can be used to glean specific pointers to knowledgeable practice. A learner may also pick up valuable information that was not a part of the original focus of the demonstration. For example, an error may occur during a demonstration that may lead to the discovery of new areas of skill.

• *Demonstrations aid recall.*   In computer use an active demonstration may be useful for the demonstrator because it aids memory recall of the interaction process. Even experienced computer users find it hard to recall the sequences of interactions that occur between themselves and an application when that particular application is not in front of them (Mayes et al. 1988).

Demonstrations can take many forms. I have by and large concentrated on the face-to-face demonstration as the ideal model. Technologically mediated demonstrations can be either synchronous, allowing real-time interaction, or asynchronous, where a demonstration is recorded for later viewing. Some kind of virtual demonstration using avatars is also possible. At the other extreme of the technology spectrum, most printed software tutorials incorporate static text and graphic depictions of how to interact with the system.

The relative ease of recording a demonstration may represent, however, something of a trade-off between representational creation and representational interpretation. Depending on the specific circumstances, there may well be considerably more cognitive effort involved in trying to interpret a recorded demonstration than in the creating that demonstration. The visual and audio complexity that makes demonstrations a rich multilayered representation of practice may make interpretation a difficult task. It may also be difficult for users to generalize the skills represented in a demonstration to their own particular tasks or problems. Unlike well-written textual descriptions, which may require little significant interpretive cost, recorded demonstrations may only have value in a cohesive support group where mutual understanding and a shared situation support interpretation. The mutual understanding built up among group members over time can be a valuable resource in communication and interpretation. It makes it easier for demonstrators to understand the needs of the learners and allows the learners to more easily understand the activities of the demonstrators. The people in a support group can also be expected to use common computer-based tools, to be working on similar or related tasks, and to have to meet comparable standards of practice.

11.5   Outline of a Collaborative Support System

In order to investigate further some of the issues of collaborative support outlined earlier, a minimal experimental prototype of a collaborative support system is required. I began with a very simple conceptual model of the support process, a simple group-based cycle of shared problems and possible solutions. Also, from the outset the recorded demonstration as a significant representational form was incorporated. This section presents an outline of a functional model of a collaborative support system derived from the conceptual model. It is a simple group-based, asynchronous information-sharing system. It uses recorded demonstrations as the principal means of representing expertise and also incorporates a collaborative forum and local memory to support discussion and subsequent storage of local expertise. It should be emphasized that this is intended to be an experimental, minimal, generic model that can be implemented using a variety of different components or technologies.

Recorder Tools

It is possible to create textual and graphical descriptions of problems and solutions for submission to the system. A word-processing package or any other suitable piece of software can be used for this purpose. However, in this system the most important method of representation is the recorded demonstration. The demonstration recorder tool should allow the user to record a demonstration of screen events along with a coordinated verbal commentary. The interface to this recorder tool should be very simple. For example, it could look and work in a similar way to the controls of a cassette recorder. The user selects "record," demonstrates the relevant sequence of screen actions while optionally making comments, and then selects "stop." This creates a file, which can be played back to check the demonstration. The recording can then be either permanently saved or recorded again. The recording can be based on an individual's demonstrating some aspect of computer use, or it can be a recording of an interactive demonstration, that is, what a face-to-face demonstration between two people, with both sets of comments recorded. When a recorded demonstration is selected, it should run automatically.

Many users of this system are expected to be relatively inexperienced and therefore a method of operation is desired that invites participation rather than adding to the learning burden. Perhaps the principal advantage of the recorded demonstration is that it can convey a great deal of information and yet is both easy and quick to create. A recorded demonstration of only 30 seconds' duration can convey a considerable amount of information and yet takes only a short time to record.

The Forum

The term *forum* (a place of public discussion) reflects both collective visibility and interactivity. The forum is the place where interaction, which is a vital part of the sharing and development of practice, takes place. The forum is particularly important in encouraging participation in the support group and the collaborative support system. The development of a support system requires more than passive use from its members; it requires active participation. Computer-related problems are made public in the forum and appropriate solutions are discussed. The forum can also be useful for the support person to communicate organizational issues to the whole group.

The forum is the way in which the local memory grows and develops. Problems, solutions, experiences, and general comments are made public within the group by inserting them in the forum space and inviting responses from other members of the group. When discussion on an area in the forum has reached a reasonably stable state, the core request or problem and relevant responses are transferred to the permanent local memory.

The Local Memory

The local memory is a collaboratively created collection of objects. It is a meta-representational form. Because it is locally created it can contain local methods of manipulating local information. For example, a part of the memory devoted to manipulating a spreadsheet can incorporate demonstrations of operations on the actual spreadsheet models used in the workplace. Initially, of course, the memory is empty. It may be necessary for the support person (or the group as a whole) to submit a range of relevant objects in order to achieve some initial "critical mass." The principal value of the local memory is that it provides a permanent record of solutions to local problems that can be browsed or accessed quickly and easily by members of the group. The demonstrations should be easy to access when someone needs to be reminded of the way to do something. Consequently, speed and ease of access are important structural issues in the organization of the memory. Because the system is user-created, the central design issue is not how it should be structured, but what methods of structuring should be provided for the users.

11.6 Design Issues

I experimented with a number of different prototypes of a collaborative support system (or parts of the system) in a number of different situations (Eales 1996). Practical investigations are never easy. They require real settings with real users and above all real problems, to be able to evaluate how well a system supports the crucial social dynamics of collaborative support. Various practical investigations and experiments have shed light on a number of critical design issues. An important factor to remember is that the effectiveness of a sociotechnical system is always strongly influenced by the inherent characteristics of the specific social subsystem of its use. However, a number of conclusions, relating mainly to technical design, can be drawn:

• The notion of a collaborative support system based on the use of network technology to support situated and collaborative learning appears to meet a particular need for a way to share and develop computer-related expertise within organizations.

• The construction of a basic collaborative support system has proven to be technically feasible with existing widely available software and additional simple utilities.

• The simple collaborative support system functional model with its three elements, recorder tools, forum, and memory, has proved a useful basis for the development of a practical system.

• Recorded demonstrations have proved to be a simple and effective way to communicate computer-related practice.

• User acceptance, indicated by utilization and participation, is the paramount goal to be addressed in the design of a collaborative support system. Without user utilization and participation, all other issues are irrelevant.

11.7   Conclusion

This chapter has argued that informal communities of practice play a vital role in the development and sharing of expertise within organizations. However, these informal communities may have serious limitations. Among other things, they may suffer from a lack of core expertise and restricted opportunities for sharing. Technology can be used to overcome some of these limitations, but the problem requires a balanced sociotechnical solution. I continue to investigate both the social dynamics of collaborative expertise development and the design and development of collaborative support systems. The intricate nature of informal communities of practice and the problems associated with technological augmentation suggest that this will be a long and complex investigation.

Acknowledgments

I would like to thank Jim Welsh for allowing me to legitimately and peripherally participate in his community of practice and the many organizational computer users who shared their sometimes painful experiences with me. I would also like to thank Volker Wulf for his comments on earlier drafts of this article.

References

Abecker, A., A. Bernardi, K. Hinkelmann, O. Kuhn, and M. Sintek. 1998. Towards a Technology for Organizational Memories. *IEEE Intelligent Systems* 13 (3): 40–48.

Ackerman, M. S. 1994. Augmenting the Organizational Memory: A Field Study of Answer Garden. In *Proceedings of the ACM Conference on Computer-Supported Cooperative Work (CSCW '94)*, 243–252.

Ackerman, M. S., and D. W. McDonald. 1996. Answer Garden 2: Merging Organizational Memory with Collaborative Help. In *Proceedings of the ACM Conference on Computer-Supported Cooperative Work (CSCW '96)*, 97–105.

Ackerman, M. S., and C. Halverson. 1998. Considering an Organization's Memory. In *Proceedings of the ACM Conference on Computer-Supported Cooperative Work (CSCW '98)*, 39–48.

Bannon, L. J. 1986. Helping Users Help Each Other. In *User-Centered System Design*, ed. D. A. Norman and S. W. Draper, 399–410. Hillsdale, N.J.: Erlbaum.

Bannon, L. J., and K. Kuutti. 1996. Shifting Perspectives on Organizational Memory: From Storage to Active Remembering. In *Proceedings of the Twenty-ninth Hawaii Conference on System Sciences*, vol. 4, 156–167.

Berlin, L. M., R. Jeffries, V. O'Day, A. Paepcke, and C. Wharton. 1993. Where Did You Put It?: Issues in the Design and Use of Group Memory. In *Proceedings of the International Conference on Human Factors in Computing Systems (INTERCHI '93)*, 23–30.

Billett, S. 1999. Guided Learning at Work. In *Understanding Learning at Work*, ed. D. Boud and J. Garrick, 151–164. London: Routledge and Kegan Paul.

Brown, J. S., and P. Duguid. 2000. *The Social Life of Information*. Boston: Harvard Business School Press.

Eales, R. T. 1996. Design for Learnability: Computer-Supported Collaborative Learning in the Workplace. Ph.D. diss., University of Queensland, Brisbane, Australia.

Eales, R. T., and J. Welsh. 1994. Learnability Through Working Together. In *Proceedings of the Fourth Australian Conference on Computer-Human Interaction (OzCHI '94)*, 27–32.

————. 1995. Design for Collaborative Learnability. In *Proceedings of the Conference on Computer-Supported Collaborative Learning (CSCL '95)*, 99–106.

Foucault, M. 1977. *Discipline and Punish: The Birth of the Prison*. London: Penguin.

Gantt, M., and B. A. Nardi. 1992. Gardeners and Gurus: Patterns of Cooperation Among CAD Users. In *Proceedings of the ACM Conference on Human Factors in Computing Systems (CHI '92)*, 107–117.

Hutchins, E. 1995. *Cognition in the Wild*. Cambridge, Mass.: MIT Press.

Koschmann, T., ed. 1996. *CSCL: Theory and Practice of an Emerging Paradigm*. Mahwah, N.J.: Erlbaum.

Lave, J., and E. Wenger. 1991. *Situated Learning: Legitimate Peripheral Participation*. New York: Cambridge University Press.

Mackay, W. E. 1990. Patterns of Sharing Customizable Software. In *Proceedings of the ACM Conference on Computer-Supported Cooperative Work (CSCW '90)*, 209–221.

MacLean, A., K. Carter, L. Lovstrand, and T. Moran. 1990. User-Tailorable Systems: Pressing the Issues with Buttons. In *Proceedings of the ACM Conference on Human Factors in Computing Systems (CHI '90)*, 175–182.

Mayes, J. T., S. Draper, A. M. McGregor, and K. Oatley. 1988. Information Flow in a User Interface: The Effect of Experience and Context on the Recall of MacWrite Screens. In *People and Computers IV*, ed. D. M. Jones and R. Winder, 275–289.

Mumford, E. 1987. Sociotechnical Systems Design: Evolving Theory and Practice. In *Computers and Democracy: A Scandinavian Challenge*, ed. G. Bjerknes, P. Ehn, and M. Kyng, 59–76. London: Avebury Gower.

Nardi, B. A. 1993. *A Small Matter of Programming: Perspectives on End User Computing*. Cambridge, Mass.: MIT Press.

Nardi, B. A., and J. R. Miller. 1991. Twinkling Lights and Nested Loops: Distributed Problem Solving and Spreadsheet Development. In *Computer-Supported Cooperative Work and Groupware*, ed. S. Greenberg, 29–52. London: Academic Press.

Orr, J. E. 1993. *Ethnography and Organizational Learning: In Pursuit of Learning at Work*. Technical Report SPL-93-040. Palo Alto, Calif.: Xerox PARC.

Orr, J. E., and N. C. Crowfoot. 1992. Design by Anecdote: The Use of Ethnography to Guide the Application of Technology in Practice. In *Proceedings of the Participatory Design Conference (PDC '92)*.

Preece, J. 2000. *Online Communities: Designing Usability, Supporting Sociability*. New York: Wiley.

Seifert, C. M., and E. L. Hutchins. 1992. Error as Opportunity: Learning in a Cooperative Task. *Human-Computer Interaction* 7: 409–435.

Wenger, E. 1998. *Communities of Practice: Learning, Meaning, and Identity.* New York: Cambridge University Press.

Wulf, V. 1999. Let's See Your Search Tool! Collaborative Use of Tailored Artifacts in Groupware. In *Proceedings of the International Conference on Supporting Group Work (GROUP '99)*, 50–60.

Zuboff, S. 1988. *In the Age of the Smart Machine: The Future of Work and Power*. New York: Basic Books.

12

Knowledge Communities: Online Environments for Supporting Knowledge Management and Its Social Context

Thomas Erickson and Wendy A. Kellogg

The issue of how to support the reuse of knowledge—under rubrics such as organizational memory, knowledge management, and expertise management—has received increasing attention over the last decade. In this chapter we take a strongly social approach to the issue, arguing that knowledge (and expertise) is created, used, and disseminated in ways that are inextricably entwined with the social milieu, and therefore that systems attempting to support these processes must take social factors into account.

Our approach to managing knowledge or expertise is to do it online, via multi-user networked environments that support group communication and collaboration. That is, we are interested in designing online environments within which users can engage socially with one another, and in the process discover, develop, evolve, and explicate knowledge relevant to shared projects and goals. We refer to online multi-user environments used in these ways as knowledge communities.

We begin with an example that depicts a number of ways in which the production and use of knowledge is fundamentally entwined with social phenomena. We note that this socially situated view of knowledge is supported by research in a number of disciplines, and also has made its way into the business discourse that surrounds knowledge management. This view raises a challenge for those designing technology: knowledge management systems must take into account, either explicitly or implicitly, the social context within which knowledge is produced and consumed.

One way of addressing this challenge is via the sorts of online multi-user systems that we call knowledge communities. We describe some examples of systems that currently function as knowledge communities and then turn to our own work on designing infrastructures for knowledge communities. Our general approach is to design online environments that, by making users and their activities visible to one another, can enable a variety of social phenomena that support social and work-oriented interaction. We describe a system called Babble, which we have designed, implemented, and deployed to about twenty work groups over the last four years. We report on our experience with Babble, and conclude by discussing some of the general issues we see for designing online environments that support a socially oriented approach to the management of knowledge and expertise.

12.1   Knowledge Work as Social Work

Knowledge management is often seen as an information problem: how to capture, organize, and retrieve information. Given this perspective, it isn't surprising that knowledge management evokes notions of data mining, text clustering, databases and documents. This is not wrong, but it is only part of the picture. We suggest that knowledge management is not just an information problem, but that it is, as well, a social problem.

An Example

One of us once interviewed accountants at a large accounting and consulting firm about their information usage practices. The goal was to find out how they thought they would use a proposed database of their company's internal documents. In the course of the investigation, an unexpected theme emerged: the accountants said that one of the ways in which they wanted to use the documents was as a means of locating people. The accountants' claim—that they wanted to use a *document* retrieval system to find *people*—was, at the time, quite surprising. However, in the course of further interviews, it came to make sense: it was only through the people that the accountants could get some of the knowledge they needed. As one accountant explained, "Well, if I'm putting together a proposal for Exxon, I really want to talk to people who've already worked with them: they'll know the politics and the history, and they can introduce me to their contacts. None of that gets into reports."

For our purposes, there are five important points here. First, as the accountants observed, some types of knowledge tend not to get written down. Sometimes it may be that the knowledge is too politically sensitive: people shy away from recording gossip and innuendo, even though knowledge of it may be very helpful to someone about to do business in that environment. Sometimes knowledge in the form of comments, opinions, or conjectures may not be written down because the resulting records can potentially be subpoenaed. And sometimes knowledge that may seem too trivial to be recorded when first encountered—that a CEO is a teetotaler or a Scotch fancier—can prove quite valuable in the process of establishing a relationship. Because this knowledge is often useful for social purposes, we refer to it by the rubric "social knowledge."

The second point is that the accountants were not just tapping into social knowledge; they were also getting access to *social resources* such as contacts and referrals. One accountant explained that the worst way to approach a company with a proposal was by making a "cold call." It is much better if the accountant, let us call him Charles, can begin a call to a new contact by saying, "My colleague, Jil Smith, suggested I chat with you." Being able to say that one has been referred by a mutual acquaintance is a frequent and powerful facilitator for interpersonal interaction—and this is true even if the relationship is only a few hours old. Charles, by virtue of having permission to assert a relationship with Jil, can draw on Jil's reputation and standing with the person with whom he is trying to open negotiations. Social resources cannot be extracted from a person and embedded in a database: opening the conversation by saying, "I found your name in the corporate knowledge base," isn't the same as saying, "Jil Smith said I should call."

The third point we take from this example is that people don't necessarily need access to an expert. It may be that Jil Smith has had only one previous engagement with Exxon, and that, in terms of facts, she may have far less expertise than an outside consultant. Nevertheless, Jil's experience may be sufficient to provide Charles with the social knowledge and social resources necessary to gain entry into the Exxon environment. In fact, it may be preferable for Charles to talk with Jil, because as a colleague who shares the same work context, she will understand more about what he needs to know, the situations in which he will use the knowledge, and how he is likely to go about using it, than someone traditionally construed as an expert. That is, Jil has social and contextual expertise, in contrast to an outside consultant's factual expertise.

The fourth point we take from this example is implicit in the previous ones: networks of personal relationships, which are created and reinforced through interpersonal conversation, are critical in supporting knowledge sharing. Assuming that Jil's assistance was helpful, Charles has now accrued a small debt or obligation to Jil. When Jil needs assistance, she is likely to come to Charles with questions or requests for social knowledge that fall within his domain. Even if the required information is outside his domain, she may seek to obtain access to his social resources—a referral to one of his contacts, for example. Thus are professional relationships established, and thus do social networks grow. In the long run, if not the short, it may be more valuable for an enterprise if its members seek knowledge and social resources from one another, thus building a web of mutual knowledge and trusted relationships, than if, for instance, employees are given instant access to a top-notch external domain expert.

This brings us to our final point, which has to do with the centrality and importance of conversation in knowledge sharing (see chapter 4). It is no coincidence that both social knowledge and social resources are best shared through talk. It is the time spent discussing apparently trivial social knowledge that suggests that a relationship goes beyond the purely professional, that there is more in play than just a purely instrumental professional exchange. It is the disclosure of politically sensitive information that indicates a degree of trust between two people. It is the ability of one person to take generic information and apply it on the fly to the other's problem that increases the reputation of the giver and creates an obligation for the receiver. This sort of talk—and the exchange of knowledge and social resources it involves—both requires and strengthens networks of personal relationships in workplace.

The Social Construction of Knowledge

This sort of situation is not the exception; it is the rule. A wide variety of research programs, for instance, ethnographies of workplaces, social studies of science, critical theory, organizational memory, the sociology of knowledge, point to the deep connections between knowledge management and social context.

For example, ethnographic studies of workplaces reveal a wide array of social practices implicated in the production and dissemination of knowledge. Lave and Wenger (1991) have developed the notion of a community of practice. They note that one way in which people come to master a body of knowledge is through a sort of apprenticeship or "legitimate peripheral participation" in the activities of a group of practitioners. Wenger (1998) describes the daily work in an insurance claims processing office and shows how it is entwined with social relationships and processes. Similarly, in an ethnography of copier service technicians, Orr (1996) reveals that technical knowledge is socially distributed across a network of technicians, and that it is tapped into and disseminated through oral processes such as storytelling.

A similar sense of the social nature of the production and dissemination of knowledge comes from the field of social studies of science (see Latour and Woolgar 1979; Latour 1987). For example, Traweek's (1988) ethnography of particle physicists examines some of the social phenomena that structure the practice of high-energy physics. She notes the impact of social relationships on the placement of graduate students, the evaluation of experiments, and access to equipment and facilities. Her comments on the role of conversation are particularly interesting:

Talk accomplishes diverse tasks for physicists: it creates, defines, and maintains the boundaries of this dispersed but close-knit community; it is a device for establishing, expressing, and manipulating relationships in networks; it determines the fluctuating reputations of physicists, data, detectors, and ideas; it articulates and affirms the shared moral code about the proper way to conduct scientific inquiry. Acquiring the capacity to gossip, and to gain access to gossip about physicists, data, detectors, and ideas is the final and necessary stage in the training of a high-energy physicist. (122)

At a more general level, Brown and Duguid (1995) note that even documents, which appear to be fixed, immutable public entities whose very purpose is to transcend social contexts, "play an important role, bringing people from different groups together to negotiate and coordinate common practices." Documents, they suggest, in their production, use, and distribution, have their own social life and function as mediators of and catalysts for social activity.

Social Capitalism

An awareness of ways in which work is bound up with social factors has assumed a prominent place in business discourse regarding knowledge management. Often referred to as organizational learning in these contexts, knowledge management in the organization is seen as a collective process in which teams create and share knowledge (e.g., Senge 1990; Nonaka and Takeuchi 1995; Cohen and Prusak 2001; Boone 2001). While proponents typically invoke a systems perspective in thinking about organizational processes, they also emphasize social factors such as relationships, trust, reputation, and commitment in their descriptions of how such processes play out. As a vice president of strategy puts it,

Expertise location is a big issue in companies today. The goal is not only to provide access to information, but to provide access to people who have the information.... I don't want raw data, I don't even want information, I want the judgments of people I trust. (Boone, 22)

Recently the concept of social capital—the "features of social organizations such as networks, norms, and social trust that facilitate coordination and cooperation for mutual benefit" (Putnam 2000)—and the possible role it may play in the networked organization, has come to the fore. Cohen and Prusak (2001) explain the connection:

Social capital makes an organization, or any cooperative group, more than a collection of individuals intent on achieving their own private purposes. Social capital bridges the space between people. Its characteristic elements and indicators include high levels of trust, robust personal networks and vibrant communities, shared understandings, and a sense of equitable participation in a joint enterprise—all things that draw individuals together into a group. This kind of connection supports collaboration, commitment, ready access to knowledge and talent, and coherent organizational behavior. (4)

Elaborating on the connection between social capital and knowledge sharing, Cohen and Prusak point out that exchanging knowledge depends on a social connection: "Without some degree of mutuality and trust, the knowledge conversations will not get started; without some degree of shared understanding, they will not go very far" (86). They also note that the knowledge exchanged in spontaneous conversations "is often social knowledge—shared aims and interests discovered, signals and stories shared that build confidence, trust, and connection—rather than technical or business knowledge that can be directly applied to a product or problem" (86–87).

The Challenge

Thus far we have argued that knowledge management is not just an information problem, but that it is a social problem. That is, we've suggested that effective knowledge management involves networks of people, relationships, and social factors like trust, obligation, and commitment. One can't isolate knowledge from its social context without denaturing it, without stripping it of the social resources and social knowledge that contribute to its utility.

Taking the social nature of knowledge seriously raises a considerable challenge for those interested in designing knowledge management systems. We suggest that rather than thinking in terms of knowledge management it is best to start thinking in terms of supporting the larger social context in which knowledge management is embedded. Our response to this challenge is to explore the role of online multi-user environments. In particular, we are interested in environments within which users can engage socially with one another, and in the process discover, develop, evolve, and explicate knowledge. We refer to online multi-user environments used in these ways as knowledge communities. In what follows we discuss current environments that function as knowledge communities and then turn to our own work on the topic.

12.2   Knowledge Communities

Knowledge communities have a long history, albeit not by that name. The idea that networks of computers might provide a medium within which individuals might come together to share knowledge and expertise dates back to at least 1960. Perhaps the first vision of this nature was offered by Simon Ramo (1961), who wrote of "many millions of human minds ... connected together." Ramo offered a number of scenarios, including one of an attorney consulting an online database that contained more than data:

Even on the nonroutine legal processes, the attorney, in the coming intellectronic age, will be able to consult with the equivalent of a host of informed fellow attorneys. His request to the system for similar cases will yield an immediate response from the central store, together with questions and advice filed by other attorneys on those similar cases—even as he will add his facts and guidance into the system for future use by all. (10)

Over the ensuing decades the idea spread and evolved. From its beginning as a vague if exciting vision, it took concrete form in the special-purpose DELPHI and EMISARI systems pioneered by Murray Turoff in the early 1970s (Turoff 1972; Hiltz and Turoff 1993) and in the PLATO Notes system in the mid-1970s (Wooley 1994). In the late 1970s and early 1980s the idea took off, spreading and evolving, under pressures from application domains such as education and gaming, into a variety of genres of software ranging from bulletin board systems to MOOs (multi-user object-oriented domains).

Some Examples of Knowledge Communities

A complete account of the systems that are used to enable online groups to share knowledge among themselves is well beyond the scope of this chapter. Instead, we look at some representative examples to give an idea of both the types of systems and the forms of use that are current in managing online knowledge. It is important to note that we are not just interested in the software; we are interested in the combination of the software and the way in which it is put to use by its users—we refer to this combination of technology and usage as a knowledge community.

One genre of software that supports knowledge communities is the MOO. MOOs, originally developed as multi-user text-based gaming environments, have been applied to a number of pedagogical and business ends. Examples include MOOSE Crossing, an educationally oriented environment for children aged 8 to 13 (Bruckman 1997); Pueblo, a school-centered MOO in Phoenix, Arizona (O'Day, Bobrow, and Shirley 1996); Tapped In, a distributed community of teachers (Schlager, Fusco, and Schank 1998; 2002); and a MUD (multi-user domain) used by employees at Argonne National Labs for work-related talk (Churchill and Bly 1999).

Another genre of system that can support knowledge communities is the electronic mailing list, or listserv. While mailing lists are used for a variety of purposes, the existence of mailing lists used to share knowledge among cohesive, long-lasting communities is well documented. In one case, a community of about a thousand professional journalists used a mailing list to help one another with technical problems and to find story-specific information sources for over six years (Millen and

Dray 1999; Millen 2000). Another example, the use of a mailing list to support discourse amongst a scholarly community, is described by Ekeblad (1999). And a third example, the use of a listserv by a community of soap opera fans to share knowledge ranging from plot summaries to character background information, is described by Baym (1995; 1997).

In addition to the genres of mailing lists and MOOs, which can be turned to a variety of ends other than knowledge sharing, quite a few systems have been designed with their principal aim being the support of a knowledge community. One example is Answer Garden (Ackerman 1998), a blending of bulletin board and e-mail systems that makes a network of questions and answers available to its users, and uses e-mail to automatically route new questions to appropriate experts whose answers are then incorporated into the network. The Zephyr Help Instance (Ackerman and Palen 1996) has a similar purpose—providing online help information—but uses a synchronous chatlike mechanism to broadcast questions and answers to the user community. Another genre of knowledge community system is the collaboratory. Collaboratories are aimed at the needs of the scientific community and provide real-time access to scientific instruments along with synchronous communication channels ranging from textual chat to real-time audio and video (Olson and Olson 2000). Collaboratories are a highly successful class of applications, with many in existence that have supported dozens to hundreds of users for periods of years.

If one examines these systems and the ways in which they are used to share knowledge, an interesting commonality emerges: virtually all of these systems exhibit a rich array of social phenomena in spite of the fact that most provide only textual communication mechanisms, typically synchronous chat, asynchronous e-mail, or both (as in MOOs). (Even collaboratories, which increasingly support various forms of high-bandwidth synchronous interaction, functioned well when chat was their dominant communication channel.) Examples of the social phenomena found in most knowledge communities range from interpersonal phenomena, such as the negotiation of status and reputation or the development of trust, to the emergence of group norms and conventions. While these systems bear eloquent testimony to the ingenuity of their users in using textual representations to support a rich array of social phenomena, we suspect that we can do better.

This brings us to the question that informs our own work. What would it mean to design an infrastructure for a knowledge community from the ground up? That is, if we take seriously the charge that knowledge management is a social problem as well as an information problem, one response is to ask how we can better support social interaction. How do we go about designing a system that supports not just information sharing but also the exchange of social knowledge and resources, the creation and growth of interpersonal networks, and accompanying social phenomena such as trust, obligation, commitment, and accountability?

To address this question, we developed a system called Babble, which we have used as a test bed for exploring these issues over the last four years. We begin by discussing the rationale that underlies Babble's design: the notion that increasing the visibility of the presence and activity of participants in an online environment can provide a foundation for a variety of social processes and activity. Next we describe the system and discuss the ways in which we have come to use it as part of our daily work practice. Finally, we discuss our experiences in deploying Babble to other work groups.

Supporting Online Social Interaction

In the building where our group works there is a door that opens from the stairwell into the hallway. This door has a design problem: opened quickly, it is likely to slam into anyone who is about to enter from the other direction. In an attempt to fix this problem, a small sign was placed on the door: it reads, "Please Open Slowly." As you might guess, the sign is not a particularly effective solution.

Let's contrast this solution with one of a different sort: putting a glass window in the door. The glass window approach means that the sign is no longer required. As people approach the door they see whether anyone is on the other side and, if so, they modulate their actions appropriately. This is a very simple example of what we call a socially translucent system.

While it is obvious why this solution works, it is useful to examine the reasons behind it carefully. We see three reasons for the effectiveness of the glass window. First, the glass window makes socially significant information *visible*. That is, as human beings, we are *perceptually attuned* to movement and human faces and figures: we notice and react to them more readily than we notice and interpret a printed sign. Second, the glass window supports *awareness*: I don't open the door quickly because *I know* that you are on the other side. This awareness brings our social rules into play to govern our actions: we have been raised in a culture in which slamming doors into other people is not sanctioned. There is a third, somewhat subtler, reason for the efficacy of the glass window. Suppose that I don't care whether I hurt others: nevertheless, I'll open the door slowly because *I believe that you know that I know* you're there, and therefore I will be held *accountable* for my actions. (This distinction is useful because, while accountability and awareness usually co-occur in the physical world, they are not necessarily coupled in the digital realm.) It is through such individual feelings of accountability that norms, rules, and customs become effective mechanisms for social control.

We call systems that exhibit these properties—perceptual salience, awareness, and accountability—socially translucent systems. But there is one other aspect of social translucence that deserves mention. Why is it that we speak of socially *translucent* systems rather than socially *transparent* systems? Because there is a vital tension between privacy and visibility. What we say and do with another person depends on who, and how many, are watching. Note that privacy is neither good nor bad on its own—it simply supports certain types of behavior and inhibits others. For example, the perceived validity of an election depends crucially on keeping certain of its aspects very private and other aspects very public. As before, what we are seeing is the impact of awareness and accountability: in the election, it is desirable that the voters *not* be accountable to others for their votes but that those who count the votes be accountable to all.

We see these three properties of socially translucent systems—visibility, awareness, and accountability—as critical building blocks of social interaction. Notice that social translucence is not just about people acting in accordance with social rules (see Erickson and Kellogg 2000). In socially translucent systems, we believe, it will be easier for users to carry on coherent discussions, to observe and imitate others' actions, to engage in peer pressure, and to create, notice, and conform to social conventions. We see social translucence as a requirement for supporting online communication and collaboration in general, and knowledge communities in particular.

This brings us to the question of how to support social translucence in online environments. How can we provide the cues that allow our socially based processes to operate—and which are so ubiquitous and lightweight in the physical world—in online systems? Two obvious approaches are to use video or 3D virtual environments. However, these have several drawbacks for our purposes. First, they don't scale well: we would like to support conversations among fairly large numbers of people. Second, both approaches are best suited for supporting synchronous interactions, whereas we would like to support both synchronous and asynchronous interactions. Third, they are both relatively demanding in terms of processing power, bandwidth, and display space and characteristics: we would like to be able to support mobile employees working over sub-56K connections and using devices with smaller displays.

As a consequence, we have taken a more abstract approach to supporting social translucence. The abstract approach involves portraying social information in ways that are not closely tied to its physical analogs. Exemplars of the abstract approach include the Out to Lunch system (Cohen 1994), which uses abstract sonic cues to indicate socially salient activity, and Chat Circles (Viegas and Donath 1999), which uses abstract visual representations. This approach also includes the use of text to portray social information; as we have already noted, text has proved surprisingly powerful as a means for conveying social information in knowledge communities.

The Babble System

Babble (Erickson et al. 1999) is an online environment intended to support both synchronous and asynchronous text-based conversations within small to medium-sized groups. The principle goal of Babble has been to serve as a platform for exploring ideas about the social effects of supporting mutual awareness among online groups. However, to do this effectively, we needed to be able to observe real work groups using it as part of the daily work process. As a consequence, Babble needed to be sufficiently robust and lightweight to be usable by groups who don't care about the technology itself.

In terms of infrastructure, Babble is a client-server system with both components written in SmallTalk. Babble stores all data, except for user-specific preferences and state (e.g., the user's last location, last items read, and so forth) on the server and broadcasts them as needed. Babble clients request the data they need from the server (e.g., when a user switches to a new conversation, the client requests the content) and also notify the server of events that it will broadcast to other clients. As this architecture suggests, Babble only works when on a network; when disconnected it has no cache of conversation text. The Babble server runs on a variety of server-class machines; the principle client runs on PCs, though we have had, for varying durations, clients that ran on the Macintosh (in Java) and on the Palm Pilot. Here we discuss only the PC client, since that comprises the vast majority of our experience.

In terms of functionality, Babble resembles a multichannel, text-based chat system in that many users can connect to it and select one of a variety of conversations to participate in (or create their own). However, Babble differs from conventional chat in two ways, both of which stem from our interest in supporting knowledge communities. First, the textual conversation that occurs in Babble is persistent: that is, unlike conventional chat, where newly arriving users only see what has transpired since they've joined a channel, Babble users can see everything ever typed in any existing conversation. These traces give the system the potential to function as a knowledge store, or what we prefer to call a discourse base. Second, Babble makes the presence and activity of the participants visible by a variety of means but principally through what we call the social proxy.

Figure 12.1 shows the Babble user interface. In the upper left-hand corner is a list of names of users currently connected to Babble. In the middle upper pane is the social proxy, which we describe shortly. In the upper right-hand pane is a hierarchical list of the Babble conversation topics (grouped in categories and subcategories). And the pane that occupies the lower half of the window contains the text of the current conversation (whose topic name is highlighted in the topic list); within the pane, each comment is prefaced with the name of the user and the

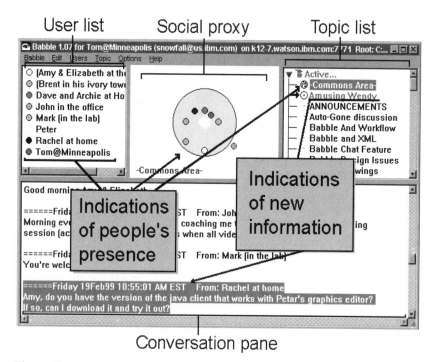

Figure 12.1
The Babble interface. *Clockwise, from upper left:* the list of all users logged on; the social proxy; the topics list; the conversation pane.

date and time of its creation (recall that Babble conversations need not be synchronous; indeed, some are asynchronous, with hours, days, or weeks separating comments). Babble provides a variety of other types of functionality via the menu bar, context-sensitive menus accessed via right clicks, and keyboard shortcuts. These include functions for creating messages, creating, changing, and deleting topics and categories, conducting private, ephemeral chats, and so forth.

The social proxy, in the upper middle part of the window, represents the current conversation as a large circle, and the participants as colored dots, referred to hereafter as marbles. Marbles within the circle are involved in the conversation being viewed; marbles outside the circle represent those who are logged on but are viewing other conversations. What makes the social proxy interesting has to do with the position of the marbles in the circle. When a user becomes active, either "speaking" (typing) or "listening" (interacting with the conversation window by clicking or scrolling), the user's marble moves rapidly to the center ring of the circle. If the user stops interacting, the marble gradually drifts out to the inner periphery of the circle over the course of about twenty minutes. Thus, when there is a lot of activity in the conversation, there is a tight cluster of marbles around the center of the circle. The social proxy shown in figure 12.1 depicts a situation in which five people have been recently active (speaking or listening) in the current conversation, and two others have been idle for a while (and an eighth person is off viewing another conversation).

When people leave the current conversation, their marbles move outside the circle; when they enter the conversation, their marbles move into the circle. When people log onto the system, it creates a virtual wedges for their marbles, adjusting the position of all the marbles in the social proxy; when they depart, the wedges are destroyed and the remaining marbles adjust to uniformly occupy the space. All marble movements are shown with animation, thus making arrivals, movements, and departures visually salient. Although simple, this social proxy gives a sense of the size of the audience, the degree to which the audience is actively listening or contributing, whether people are gathering or dispersing, and who it is that is coming and going.

In addition to the social proxy (which we refer to as the cookie), Babble uses other mechanisms to reveal the presence and activity of users. In the topic list, to the left of the topic names, are minicookies, thumbnails of the social proxy for each topic with a participant in it. So, in figure 12.1, we can see that there is a single person in the second topic, "Amusing Wendy." Babble also highlights information that the user has not yet seen: the names of topics with new material in them are shown in red (e.g., "Amusing Wendy" in figure 12.1), and comments that have been added to the current conversation since the user last "touched" Babble are shown in reverse highlighting.

One of the shortcomings of the cookie is that it only works for synchronous interactions, that is, it shows only the presence and activities of people who are currently logged on to Babble. This is a considerable drawback because the majority of the conversations carried on in Babble are asynchronous, with just a few comments per day (or per week or per

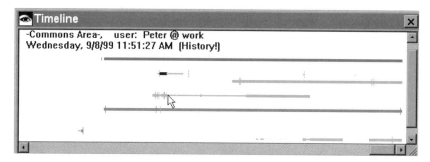

Figure 12.2
The Timeline, showing three hours of activity.

month). As a consequence, we designed a second, asynchronous social proxy for Babble: the Timeline (Erickson and Laff 2001).

The basic goal of the Timeline (figure 12.2) was to provide a way for a speaker to see that people were listening (or not), even when the listening was offset in time. The Timeline proxy works as follows: each user is represented by a row in the Timeline; when he is logged on to Babble, he leaves a flat trace or line, and when he speaks, he leaves a vertical mark or blip on the line. If the line/blip is in color, it means that that user was present/speaking in the conversation currently being viewed by the user of the Timeline; if the user was in a different conversation, the line/blip is shown in gray (and the line becomes thinner). As the user mouses over the Timeline, the name of the topic, the user, and the time being examined is shown in the upper left-hand corner; the user can scroll back through as much as one week of activity. The Timeline also provides access to other functionality via a menu accessed with a right-click on another user's row (e.g., private chats).

For example, in figure 12.2, we can see that nine people have logged onto Babble (shown by the presence of lines) and that all of them have spent some time in the current conversation (shown by the color/ increased thickness of the lines) and that many but not all have spoken (shown by the blips). The line indicated by the cursor shows that the user Peter logged on around 11 a.m., made a couple of comments in the Commons Area conversation, switched to another topic, switched back to the Commons Area about 1 p.m., and then logged off.

How a Babble Is Used by a Group

While one must be wary about drawing conclusions concerning the usability of software when it is used by its developers, our aim here is simply to provide a sense for how Babble is actually used by a group. We begin by describing the group and then move on to discuss how Babble is actually used. In the next section we discuss our deployments of Babble to other groups, and some of the phenomena we have observed across different deployments.

Our group has used Babble for about four years. The group is centered on the software development group ("the lab") that designed and implemented the system, and includes a mix of computer scientists and social scientists (including the authors). The size of the group has varied in number over the years from four to nineteen users. Part of the variance is due to the ebb and flow of people characteristic of groups in large organizations; and part is due to current members of the lab inviting associates—colleagues with whom they have strong social or professional ties—to join Babble.

Geographically, the group of Babble users is about half co-located in New York and half distributed. Most of the lab members are located in the same building, although offices tend to be distributed around the building so actual adjacency is rare. Three members of the lab are telecommuters and spend the majority of their time tens to hundreds of miles away; other members of the lab frequently work at home. Four of the six associated colleagues (those not officially members of the lab, but users of Babble) are remotely located.

Socially, the lab is a cohesive group, with considerable camaraderie. In addition to work-based collaboration, the lab members occasionally socialize, although usually within business hours (e.g., going out to lunch). The associates vary in the strength and number of their ties to the lab members, some being known to almost all lab members and others known only to one or two lab members with whom they have shared interests. Conversation in the Babble system moves fluidly between work and social talk; it is always civil, frequently informal, and joking, teasing, and other ludic behavior is not unusual.

Overall, the Babble system as used by the lab can be characterized as a core of relatively synchronous activity surrounded by a constellation of asynchronous conversations. At the center of activity is a topic called the "Commons Area," a place where co-located and remote members greet one another, share news, engage in banter, and ask general questions. Members of the lab tend to "hang out" in the Commons Area, often remaining logged on for most of the work day. Comments in the Commons Area tend to be short and informal, with relaxed syntax and punctuation, use of paralinguistic expressions ("ummm"), onomatopoeia, emoticons, and playful tropes (for example, the "tossing of cookies" to "a dog" who usually "accompanies" one of the participants—all done via text, of course). The content of conversation in the Commons Area ranges from purely social talk ("good morning"), to the posing of general questions, to reminding people of an impending meeting of general interest, to more technical discussions about work projects. (In theory, more topic-oriented discussion is supposed to take place in specific topics; in practice, work talk often grows out of social discussions, and the recognition that a substantive conversation that "belongs somewhere else" is taking place often does not come until after the fact.) Because of the amount of talk that occurs in the Commons, the content of the Commons Area is automatically archived once a week.

In addition to the Commons Area, there are a variety of other topics or conversation areas in Babble. These have ranged in number from a dozen or so in the early days of Babble to several dozen, the growth being facilitated by the addition of an expandable hierarchical topic list. These topics tend to have asynchronous and mostly sporadic conversation, and they tend to be focused on particular purposes, typically either project-oriented or person-oriented. Examples of topics include personal offices (e.g., "Tom's Office"), project-oriented topics (e.g., "Babble Ethnographies—CB Babble"), and occasional nonwork topics (e.g., "Bad Jokes").

In general, uses of Babble can be grouped into three general categories: social/ludic; informative; and instrumental. Social/ludic activities are those engaged in for social and entertainment purposes, such as the custom of exchanging morning greetings, and the topic devoted to jokes. Informative activities have to do with actions on the system that are addressed to the group as a whole, or to no one in particular, and generally are done without expectation of a reply or responsive action.

These activities include posting announcements and other news believed to be of general interest, commenting on project activity, and keeping online notebooks or offices. The third type of activity is instrumental, that is, activities engaged in with a particular end in mind. These include starting or participating in focused discussions, posting bug reports, holding online meetings, and asking questions. These activities are often, though not always, addressed to a particular participant or group of participants.

Adoption and Social Phenomena across Babble Deployments

Over the last four years we have deployed Babble to about twenty groups. We have studied the deployments using techniques ranging from ethnographic studies (see Bradner, Kellogg, and Erickson 1999 for a study of six Babbles) to studies based on surveys and analyses of log data and conversation archives.

We have had mixed experiences with the adoption of Babble. Sometimes groups try Babble out but fail to adopt it (typically about six weeks pass before it is evident whether or not Babble is going to be adopted by the group). Other times groups use Babble for a period of months and then cease (either because it was for a particular event or period that has ended, or because the composition or needs of the group change). It isn't clear how to operationally define a successful deployment of Babble: the group uses it for its entire existence? the group uses Babble actively for six months? the group uses Babble to carry out a particular activity? If we take, as a rule of thumb, that Babble is successful when it is used on a more or less daily basis by several people for more than six weeks, we can say that about half of our Babble deployments have met with success. As of this writing, we have five Babbles running, all of which are well past the six-week mark, and all exhibiting robust daily activity.

When Babble is adopted by a group, it usually supports a variety of communicative purposes and practices (often similar to those described in the previous section). Here, we describe four social phenomena that we have observed in a number (though not all) of successfully adopted deployments that are most relevant to knowledge communities.

One phenomenon is waylay, in which a user watches for a particular person to become active on Babble (signaled by the movement of their marble into the center of the social proxy) and then initiates a conversation (either publicly within Babble via Babble's private chat mechanism, or by some external means such as the telephone). Because the movement of the marble occurs when the user has just begun an episode of typing or mousing, it indicates a opportune moment for contact (since the user's attention has just shifted to communication with the group). Waylay is used for purposes ranging from asking questions to initiating casual social chat. In general, forms of opportunistic interaction such as waylay permit the same sorts of requests for assistance and transfers of social resources that we have observed in face-to-face knowledge-sharing situations, with the accompanying effect of strengthening interpersonal ties.

Babble also supports the maintenance of group awareness through the exchange of social knowledge. For example, when members of a Babble group travel, many report reading through conversations that occurred in their absence to "find out what happened." For someone who is a member of the group and understands the context, seemingly trivial comments can convey considerable information about what's going on at the individual, group, and organizational levels. Thus, a sign off—"I have to go to the [project] meeting now"—reveals that one participant is still involved in a particular project, and a question—"Does anyone know how to do a screen capture"—indicates that someone is beginning to write a paper. Babble also supports group awareness through the Timeline proxy. Babble participants have reported uses such as looking to see who has visited a topic in which they had posted questions; looking to see whether a colleague who hadn't posted recently had been online; and using the Timeline to get a sense for the activity of the community as a whole.

Another phenomenon that can be observed in groups using Babble is the development of social norms. That is, one participant may develop a particular way of doing something, and others will imitate it. Examples of this include what users include in their online nickname (e.g., some users append "@mylocation" after their name), the types of online conversations created (e.g., some Babbles have categories for "personal places" or "offices"), and naming conventions (e.g., one Babble group uses the term *chit-chat* to signal that a topic is intended for casual conversation. Babble groups also evolve various interactive customs, the most common being to say hello upon logging in (even when no one else is present). Again, the existence of these norms supports social interaction by providing expectations about how to behave.

Finally, we have observed that Babbles are typically regarded as semiprivate, "trusted" places. This became apparent when "strangers" appeared in various Babble systems. Sometimes the strangers were unannounced new members, sometimes they were visitors provided access by an unreflective manager, and in one case the stranger was actually an unannounced conversational software agent. But in all cases the arrival and presence of the stranger (reflected in the social proxies along with the presence of the regulars) was greeted with considerable consternation. In each case, the appearance of strangers provoked concern about how unguarded conversations might be interpreted by those from different contexts, and led to the creation of visitor and membership policies. We suggest that this concern reflects the success of Babble as an online space that is rich in social context.

One issue that is not clear, so far, is the degree to which Babble's social proxies contribute to these phenomena. Analytically, it is difficult to isolate the effects of the social proxies from the effects of purely textual cues. Certainly, there are a number of social practices (such as waylay) that require (or are at least greatly facilitated by) the proxies. It *is* clear that the participants, in general, like the proxies and want them retained as a feature of the system. One user, responding to a question in Babble, writes,

Ah, the cookie ... we love the cookie ... the cookie is good—our colored dots circulate around to "make room" when someone new joins the conversation—that's fun. And when someone's connection dies, they rather dissemble into the ether, angelic like. Which is sort of fun to watch.... Also, when I'm wondering whether my comments have fallen on deaf ears, I can tell when a response may in fact be on its way when someone's dot moves back to the center (happens as soon as someone starts typing). So, yes, we like the cookie—it makes me feel like there are actually people in a room with me....

It is also clear that users are able to "read" Babble proxies, using them to draw inferences about the presence of individuals and the activity of the community as a whole. Another user, commenting on the Timeline proxy, remarks,

It's a little like reading an electrocardiogram, the heartbeat of the community. I noticed that I missed Sandy by an hour on Monday morning.... Pat comes in every so often as a blip. Lynn jumps from space to space....

Nevertheless, although we have compelling anecdotes and a large fund of positive comments by Babble users, analytically separating social benefits conveyed by proxies from those produced by text remains a challenge for the future.

Babble as an Infrastructure for Knowledge Communities

Babble clearly succeeds as a multi-user online environment where sustained social interaction takes place. But does it support knowledge communities? Is the social interaction accompanied with the sharing of information, social knowledge, and social resources, as we claim, a crucial part of knowledge management? This is indeed what we have observed. In the following, we refer to examples and survey results drawn from a Babble group whose membership is composed of a worldwide cross-section of people in IBM and Lotus interested in online communities.[1]

Perhaps the first point to make is that participants do feel as though they are part of a community. This is particularly important to those who are remote teleworkers:

I work remotely and can feel very isolated when I don't travel regularly (as has been the case for the past six months because of travel restrictions). Babble has provided me with a way to feel connected with a group of people outside my basement walls. It is my portal (so to speak) into IBM.

Another says,

As a home office worker, this is perhaps one of the things I miss the most—the ongoing banter I can have with colleagues who are focused on a similar work topic as I am.

This is not simply a feeling of a vague belonging to a group; participants report feeling as though they are hooked into social networks. One participant reports that participation in Babble strengthened an existing network:

Babble has helped me establish a tighter social and professional relationship with all of them—we have much more regular contact with each other, much as we would if we were co-located, via the Babble connection. This in turn has built social capital among us which may be of use in the future.

And these social networks are not just about talk; they can also be tapped for assistance. The participant continues,

I have also contacted Vera about getting her input and advice about setting up a knowledge network, which is part of my "real work." I felt much more comfortable about approaching her with this question as a result of our frequent contacts via Babble than I would have otherwise.

Another Babble member notes,

I like the back and forth.... We have a lot of reflective talk about our own experiences.... At least one case, e.g., a half-joking comment of mine, "anybody want to fund this?" has led to e-mail, phone, and face-to-face meetings and now a serious proposal for funding. I don't know the final outcome yet [the project was funded], but we have found out something significant about another part of the business and have made a serious attempt to propose [a] solution to their problems.

These comments are prima facie evidence that knowledge sharing and expertise management are deeply social processes, that people value informal exchanges with colleagues and may only venture a nontrivial request for information or assistance after a social relationship has been established.

A danger in using the summary remarks of participants to indicate what happens in Babble is that it makes it sound a bit more straightforward and calculated than it is. It is difficult to convey the way in which these effects emerge out of a rich mélange of social and work talk. For example, one instance of the transfer of social resources occurred over the course of a multithreaded, thirty-utterance, seventeen-minute Babble conversation on March 7, 2001. The conversation consisted of two primary participants ("scienceguy" and "Patrick") and was composed of four distinct threads. Two threads were related to work topics (Patrick explaining that he had referred some colleagues to scienceguy, and a discussion of the use of patterns in knowledge management), and two were more social threads (one an attempt to identify an earlier participant's real name, another a request by scienceguy for assistance in developing an Irish accent for an upcoming storytelling performance). The two work-related tasks were treated relatively seriously, even as the two interleaved nonwork threads were used as an excuse for banter. Yet both the social and work threads developed and played off one another throughout the conversation, which concluded with Patrick's revealing the names of the colleagues whom he has referred to scienceguy, and scienceguy's indicating that he would be happy to talk with them. (The situation grows more complex when one recognizes that Babble users are remote from one another and may be simultaneously carrying on other work on their computers, via the telephone, or orally with co-located colleagues.)

12.3   Concluding Remarks

In this chapter we have argued that knowledge management is not just an information problem but is, as well, a social problem that involves people, relationships, and social factors like trust, obligation, commitment, and accountability. This view raises a considerable challenge for those interested in designing systems to support knowledge management. Our approach has been to explore the creation of infrastructures for knowledge communities: online environments within which users can engage socially with one another and in the process discover, develop, evolve, and explicate knowledge.

In our work on Babble, we have begun exploring ways of creating infrastructures that support rich forms of social interaction. We have found that social proxies are a promising development, and we continue to be impressed with the power of plain text as a means of supporting interactions that are both complex and subtle. We believe that one of the most important aspects of a knowledge community is that it can be used as a place for unguarded discussion among people who know one another, who share professional interests, and who understand the contexts within which their remarks are being made.

The notion of a knowledge management environment as a trusted place is an interesting and challenging one. How—technically, socially, and organizationally—can we balance the need for a safe and trusting place with the organizational imperative to share information? One decision facing us as designers is how and to what extent we "design in" norms and social conventions. For example, if we build in technical mechanisms to provide privacy in addition to the usability impact, we also eliminate opportunities for participants to show that they may be trusted or to rely on others to respect their privacy. The Babble prototype has no technical features for controlling access: anyone who has access to the client could, in theory, enter any Babble space. But because Babble makes users visible, this results in groups' noticing, commenting on, and ultimately discussing how to deal with this issue. We believe that a greater understanding of how to design systems that permit social mechanisms to come into play is of great importance in designing future systems for knowledge management.

Acknowledgments

Thanks to David N. Smith for creating the Babble prototype, to Mark Laff, Peter Malkin, and Amy Katriel for implementation work on the Babble server and clients, and to Cal Swart for critical assistance in the deployment of a multitude of Babbles. Thanks, as well, to members of IBM's Social Computing and Pervasive Applications groups for productive conversations, and to the many dozens of Babblers who have shared their insights, responded patiently to surveys, and most important, used Babble in many productive (and often surprising) ways.

Note

1. Identifiers have been changed to protect confidentiality, and comments edited for brevity.

References

Ackerman, M. S. 1998. Augmenting Organizational Memory: A Field Study of Answer Garden. *ACM Transactions on Information Systems* 16 (3): 203–224.

Ackerman, M. S., and L. Palen. 1996. The Zephyr Help Instance: Promoting Ongoing Activity in a CSCW System. In *Proceedings of the ACM Conference on Human Factors in Computing Systems (CHI '96)*, 268–275.

Baym, N. K. 1995. The Emergence of Community in Computer-Mediated Communication. In *Cybersociety: Computer-Mediated Communication and Community*, ed. S. Jones, 138–163. Thousand Oaks, Calif.: Sage.

———. 1997. Interpreting Soap Operas and Creating Community: Inside an Electronic Fan Culture. In *Culture of the Internet*, ed. S. Kiesler, 103–120. Mahwah, N.J.: Erlbaum.

Boone, M. E. 2001. *Managing Inter@ctivity*. New York: McGraw-Hill.

Bradner, E., W. A. Kellogg, and T. Erickson. 1999. The Adoption and Use of "Babble": A Field Study of Chat in the Workplace. In *Proceedings of the European Conference on Computer-Supported Cooperative Work (ECSCW '99)*, 139–158.

Brown, J. S., and P. Duguid. 1995. The Social Life of Documents. In *Release 1.0* (October 11). New York: EDventure Holdings. http://www.edventure.com/. Also at http://www.parc.xerox.com/ops/members/brown/papers/sociallife.html.

Bruckman, A. 1997. MOOSE Goes to School: A Comparison of Three Classrooms Using a CSCL Environment. In *Proceedings of the Third International Conference on Computer-Supported Collaborative Learning (CSCL '97)*.

Churchill, E. F., and S. Bly. 1999. Virtual Environments at Work: Ongoing Use of MUDs in the Workplace. In *Proceedings of the International Joint Conference on Work Activities Coordination and Collaboration (WACC '99)*.

Cohen, D., and L. Prusak. 2001. In *Good Company: How Social Capital Makes Organizations Work*. Boston: Harvard Business School Press.

Cohen, J. 1994. Monitoring Background Activities. In *Auditory Display*, ed. G. Kramer, 439–531. Reading, Mass.: Addison-Wesley.

Donath, J., K. Karahalios, and F. Viegas. 1999. Visualizing Conversation. In *Proceedings of the Thirty-second Hawaii Conference on Systems Science*.

Ekeblad, E. 1999. The Emergence of Multilogue on a Scholarly Mailing List. Paper presented at the symposium "Time and Coordination in a Virtual Community of Learners" at the Eighth European Conference for Research on Learning and Instruction (EARLI), Göteborg, Sweden. Available at http://hem.fyristorg.com/evaek/writings/earli99/multdyn.html.

Erickson, T., and W. A. Kellogg. 2000. Social Translucence: An Approach to Designing Systems That Mesh with Social Processes. *ACM Transactions on Computer-Human Interaction* 7 (1): 59–83.

Erickson, T., and M. R. Laff. 2001. The Design of the "Babble" Timeline: A Social Proxy for Visualizing Group Activity over Time. In *Proceedings of the ACM Conference on Human Factors in Computing Systems (CHI '2001): Extended Abstracts*.

Erickson, T., D. N. Smith, W. A. Kellogg, M. R. Laff, J. T. Richards, and E. Bradner. 1999. Socially Translucent Systems: Social Proxies, Persistent Conversation, and the Design of "Babble". In *Proceedings of the ACM Conference on Human Factors in Computing Systems (CHI '99)*, 72–79.

Hiltz, S. R., and M. Turoff. 1993. *The Network Nation*. Rev. ed. Cambridge, Mass.: MIT Press.

Latour, B. 1987. *Science in Action*. Cambridge, Mass.: Harvard University Press.

Latour, B., and S. Woolgar. 1979. *Laboratory Life: The Social Construction of Scientific Facts*. 2d ed. London: Sage.

Lave, J., and E. Wenger. 1991. *Situated Learning: Legitimate Peripheral Participation*. New York: Cambridge University Press.

Millen, D. R. 2000. Community Portals and Collective Goods: Conversation Archives as an Information Resource. In *Proceedings of the Thirty-third Hawaii Conference on Systems Sciences*.

Millen, D. R., and S. Dray. 1999. Information Sharing in an Online Community of Journalists. In *Proceedings of Esprit i3 Workshop: Ethnographic Studies in Real and Virtual Environments—Inhabited Information Spaces and Connected Communities*.

Nonaka, I., and H. Takeuchi. 1995. *The Knowledge-Creating Company*. New York: Oxford University Press.

O'Day, V. L., D. G. Bobrow, and M. Shirley. 1996. The Social-Technical Design Circle. In *Proceedings of the ACM Conference on Computer-Supported Cooperative Work (CSCW '96)*.

Olson, G., and J. Olson. 2000. Distance Matters. *Human-Computer Interaction* 15 (2–3).

Orr, J. E. 1996. *Talking About Machines: An Ethnography of a Modern Job*. Ithaca, N.Y.: Cornell University Press.

Putnam, R. 2000. *Bowling Alone: The Collapse and Revival of American Community*. New York: Simon and Schuster.

Ramo, S. 1961. The Scientific Extension of the Human Intellect. *Computers and Automation* 10 (2): 9–12.

Schlager, M., J. Fusco, and P. Schank. 1998. Cornerstones for an On-line Community of Education Professionals. *IEEE Technology and Society Magazine* 17 (4): 15–21.

———. 2002. Evolution of an On-line Education Community of Practice. In *Building Virtual Communities: Learning and Change in Cyberspace*, ed. K. A. Renninger and W. Shumar. New York: Cambridge University Press.

Senge, P. M. 1990. *The Fifth Discipline: The Art and Practice of the Learning Organization*. New York: Doubleday.

Traweek, S. 1988. *Beamtimes and Lifetimes: The World of High-Energy Physics*. Cambridge, Mass.: Harvard University Press.

Turoff, M. 1972. Delphi Conferencing: Computer-Based Conferencing with Anonymity. *Technological Forecasting and Social Change* 3: 159–204.

Viegas, F. B., and J. Donath. 1999. Chat Circles. In *Proceedings of the ACM Conference on Human Factors in Computing Systems (CHI '99)*, 9–16.

Wenger, E. 1998. *Communities of Practice: Learning, Meaning, and Identity*. New York: Cambridge University Press.

Wooley, D. 1994. PLATO: The Emergence of Online Community. Available at http://www.thinkofit.com/plato/dwplato.htm.

13

Expert-Finding Systems for Organizations: Problem and Domain Analysis and the DEMOIR Approach

Dawit Yimam-Seid and Alfred Kobsa

Motivated by advances in information technology, organizations are giving more emphasis to the capitalization of the increasing mass of knowledge they accumulate in the course of their business. However, as noted by Stewart (1997), the attempt to put all corporate knowledge on one huge server in the style of the eighteenth-century French encyclopedists is doomed to fail. Stewart continues to assert that the real value of information systems is rather in connecting people to people so that they can share what expertise and knowledge they have at the moment, given that the cutting edge is always changing. Studies into the information-seeking behavior of people working in information-intensive fields also show that people searching for information commonly explore personal communications prior to using formal sources (Hertzum and Pejtersen 2000; Wilson 1995).

Thus, if technology is to foster the effective utilization of the whole range of knowledge in organizations, it has to be able to support not only access to explicitly documented knowledge but, most important, tacit knowledge held by individuals. By enhancing the visibility and traceability of such knowledge, technology can help catalyze collaboration and knowledge sharing among its holders, both within and between organizations. Moreover, the ability to quickly find information on expertise of people can play critical roles in fostering the formation and sustenance of virtual organizations/enterprises, communities of practice, expertise networks, and the like.

The recognition of the need to foster sharing of expertise has lately spawned research efforts in, among others, the knowledge management and computer-supported collaborative work (CSCW) communities.

Concepts like expertise capitalization/leveraging, skill mining, competence management, intellectual capital management, expertise networks, and knowledge-sharing systems are being widely discussed. However, rarely do the discussions go beyond generic assessments and touch concrete design and implementation challenges. Moreover, systems that support such processes are at a very low level of development compared to those that support access to documented information.

In this chapter we investigate the expert-finding problem as well as the various design and development issues and present the solution we are pursuing. We begin with a brief analysis of the expert-finding problem followed by a review of the previous works on expert-finding aids. Then, after contextualizing expert-finding aids in broader organizational information systems, we present the results of our domain analysis, which allows for a more concrete discussion of current shortcomings and possible solutions. Finally, we describe the approach we adopted, followed by an outline of our future work.

13.1   Problem Analysis

A variety of practical scenarios of organizational situations that lead to expert seeking have been extensively presented in the literature (e.g., Mattox 1998; McDonald and Ackerman 1998; Kanfer, Sweet, and Schlosser 1997; Kautz, Selman, and Milewski 1996; Vivacqua 1999; Cohen, Maglio, and Barrett 1998). McDonald and Ackerman (1998) also provide empirical insight into the intricate organizational, personal, and social processes involved in expert seeking. In our extensive survey of the knowledge management literature, we found a widespread acceptance of the fact that an effective knowledge management solution should aim at making accessible not only knowledge that is contained in documents but also knowledge in people's heads (e.g., O'Leary 1998; Hendriks and Vriens 1999). However, still a lot remains to be understood about expert seeking so as to enable the development of effective automated aids.

What Prompts Expert Seeking: Information Need and Expertise Need
Based on interviews we conducted with researchers at a major research institution as well as extrapolation of observations in the relevant lit-

erature, we identified two main motives for seeking an expert, namely, as a *source of information* and as *someone who can perform a given organizational or social function*. This categorization, though fuzzy and sometimes overlapping, proves to be useful in analyzing the goals of automated expert finders.

People may seek an expert as a source of information to complement or replace other sources such as documents and databases. The following cases are just a few possible scenarios that entail seeking experts as information sources:

• *Access to nondocumented information.* Not all information in organizations can be explicitly documented. Much important information can only be transferred through apprenticeship, experience, and informal conversation (Grief 1998). Documented sources can hardly help in novel situations, solutions-in-progress, or situations that are too focused. Besides, there are cases when the needed information is deliberately not made publicly available (in documents or on the Internet) for economic, social, and political reasons (Kautz, Selman, and Milewski 1996).

• *Specification need.* The information that users need to solve a problem is often not well specified and requires a dialogue with an expert to precisely identify it. For example, so as to effectively retrieve information from a retrieval system, a user must be able to convert her problem into search statements. In the information retrieval literature, this conversion is referred to as a transition from the *exploration* phase to the *formulation* phase in the information search process (Kuhlthau 1993a; 1993b). This transition is known to be a pivotal point that is also accompanied by an emotional drift on the part of the seeker from confusion, frustration, and doubt to clarity. Naturally, people resort to seeking experts to painlessly carry them through this drift.

• *Leveraging on others' expertise (group efficiency).* Users often want to minimize the effort and time required to find some piece of information (particularly since frequently what is "lots of work" for the user is "little work" for the expert). This also includes using experts as effective and reliable information filters in selecting the useful information from the huge mass of information available.

• *Interpretation need.* Users are often not interested in a piece of information per se but rather in its situated (contextualized) interpretation or the implications that can be derived from it in the given situation. It might also be the case that the user fails to understand the information even if she manages to find it from documents.

• *Socialization need.*   Users may prefer the human dimension that is involved in asking an expert rather than interacting with documents and computers.

The second category of expert-seeking motives, namely, the need for an expert who can perform a given function, is generally characterized by a more structured search than seeking experts as information sources. In these cases, the need is for someone who possesses a certain type of expertise required to play a role in a particular undertaking. This occurs in cases when either the involvement of the expert herself in a given activity is required, or a continued partnership between the seeker and the expert is intended. Hence, what is involved is more than just acquiring a piece of information. The following are just a few of such cases:

• Seeking a consultant, employee, or contractor
• Seeking a collaborator, team member, community or committee member, or a journal or conference reviewer
• Seeking a speaker, presenter, researcher, promoter, and expert interviewee for media

We can also view these two categories of the expert-finding motives as related to *information need* and *expertise need*, respectively. In the former case, a user is required to specify her information need, whereas in the latter, a more complex specification of expertise need, replete with qualitative and quantitative parameters, is involved. In other words, when seeking experts as sources of information one is mainly interested in the question: Who knows about topic x? When seeking experts who can perform an organizational function, one is equally interested in other questions like How much (well) does y know about topic x? What else does y know? How does y compare with others in his knowledge of x? Search processes for experts who are supposed to perform an organizational function will therefore often be performed more carefully and in a more formalized manner than the search for experts who are supposed to deliver information.

Often, it is difficult to draw a sharp distinction between these two categories of motives because they may occur at the same time or an information need may later turn into an expertise need. For example, someone who served as a source of information may also be needed to act as an ultimate adviser in the correct interpretation of the piece of information as well as the consequences for the concrete problem of the information seeker. Nonetheless, studying these two categories distinctly seems to be useful.

Internal versus External Expert Seeking

In organizations, expert seeking (and consequently, the benefits of finding an expert) can be viewed from internal and external points of view. There are a number of reasons for wanting to know who knows what within an organization (as quickly as possible), including knowledge sharing, team formation, and project launching. An organization also benefits if external entities can easily discern the expertise of its staff because this fosters collaboration, cross-organizational networking, a better image, and so on. For example, many organizations can deliver efficient customer help services if the customers, or their contact points in the organization, can easily trace and direct their queries to the appropriate expert. Similarly, academic and research institutes want the industry, the public, and potential research sponsors and research collaborators to know about and make use of their staffs' expertise.

Lewis (1999) notes that most organizations consider expert-locating services necessary for external expert seeking only, and not for internal expert seeking. This is probably based on the presumption that employees know internal experts well. But, based on a recent survey, Lewis indicates that employees also benefit from support in seeking experts within the organization, as do customers. Internal expert location is more important the larger an organization is, the more geographically distributed it is, and the less homogeneous the composition of its members is (e.g., strict division borders, very different knowledge backgrounds, different histories because of company mergers). All three factors impair informal contacts, which so far are the major ways for disseminating knowledge about others' expertise within the organization.

Automated Support: Traditional Approaches

Whatever their motives, seekers of experts need a range of information regarding people's expertise. They need to know whether a person who can answer their queries or meet their criteria exists, how extensive her knowledge or experience is, whether there are other people who could serve the same purpose, how she compares with others in the field, how the person can be accessed (contacted), and so on. This, in turn, calls for a mechanism that gathers and makes such information accessible. However, doing this manually is obviously a time-consuming and laborious undertaking, making automated aids invaluable.

One way of providing automated assistance is the development of expert databases (knowledge directories, knowledge maps) through manual entry of expertise data. This is exactly what many organizations commonly did in the past. Microsoft's SPUD (Davenport and Prusak 1998), Hewlett-Packard's CONNEX, and the SAGE People Finder are examples of this approach. Similarly, manual data entry is employed in skills inventory systems like Skillview, which are common in the knowledge and human resource management domain.

However, expert databases are known to suffer from numerous shortcomings, including the following:

• Manually developing the databases is a labor-intensive and expensive task.

• These databases usually depend on the willingness of experts to devote their time to initially provide a detailed description of their expertise.

• Because of continual changes in people's specific expertise and skills (especially organization-specific and environment-specific skills), most expert databases are quickly outdated. Updating expert databases manually is resource-consuming for the organization and time-consuming for the experts.

The expertise descriptions are usually incomplete and general. On the other hand, expert-related queries are very fine-grained and specific, and replete with various qualitative requirements (Kautz, Selman, and Milewski 1996). Normally, identifying an individual's specific area of expertise requires a rather detailed analysis of his works, records of activity, and so on.

Personal Web pages, through which individuals provide information about themselves and their expertise, are also used in tracing people with needed expertise. Searching the Web or the organizational intranet by topic may lead us to such Web pages if the experts took their time to maintain up-to-date pages and if the Web pages happened to contain the supplied keywords. While such pages appear to be better sources of information on experts than expert databases, simply using search engines to trace an expert is not normally an effective approach. For one thing, search on a topic returns a large number of various resources, making the selection of personal Web pages currently a time-consuming task. As the search process is general and based on simple keyword matching, it also may not always lead to the relevant experts. Moreover, it is entirely the task of the user to extract and compile all the required data to conduct such analyses as identifying the best expert, determining the accessibility of the expert, her relation with other experts, and so on.

13.2   Automatic Expert Finders

The shortcomings of the approaches described earlier, coupled with the availability of large electronic repositories of organizational and personal records, have led to the suggestion of more helpful systems known as *expert finders or expert/expertise recommenders*. These systems aim at mitigating the shortcomings by trying to automatically discover up-to-date expertise information from implicit/secondary sources instead of relying on experts or other human sources only, although experts and their proxies can still complement/refine the automatically generated expertise information.

Attempts to develop systems that exploit implicit evidence of expertise to augment the process of finding the right expert date back at least to the visionary work of Maron, Curry, and Thompson (1986). Their experimental system, called HelpNet, accepts requests for information and responds with names of people ranked by the probability that the individual will provide a satisfactory answer. This probability is computed using probabilistic models of information retrieval that combine the estimation of people's expertise in answering a question on a topic with the probability that a given user would be satisfied with the response provided by the source. To do this, the system constructs a profile by asking people to indicate their expertise by selecting from a list of topics along with a probability estimate of their ability to provide a satisfactory answer to questions on that topic. Maron and his colleagues envisioned such systems enabling the emergence of "a large, active and fruitful future network of informationally rich people providing help to one another."

The next notable system was the Expert/Expert-Locator (EEL) (also called "Bellcore Advisor" or "Who Knows") (Streeter and Lochbaum 1988a; 1988b). This system takes natural-language requests for technical help or advice and, using Latent Semantic Indexing (LSI), returns pointers to "nearby" research groups. The system constructs an expertise index of research groups based on a representative collection of the technical documents they produce. In a test using EEL (Furnas et al. 1988), descriptions of individual experts' current projects are used as query to compare how well the system managed to predict which of the 480 Bellcore work groups an expert belonged to.

ContactFinder (Krulwich and Burkey 1995; 1996) is an intelligent agent that monitors discussion groups and extracts contacts in some specific areas, which it then uses to respond to postings that ask questions with referrals to relevant contacts. This system uses various heuristics to extract contacts from e-mail messages and to identify those postings that ask for technical help. Mattox, Maybury, and Morey (1999) developed an expert finder system that exploits MITRE Corporation's corporate intranet to enable the location of relevant experts by identifying relationships between experts and documents.

Kautz and his group approached the expert-finding problem from a different perspective (Kautz, Selman, and Milewski 1996; Kautz and Selman 1998; Kautz, Selman, and Shah 1997). Their work is based on the observation that expert finding is an inherently complex process. Hence, they postulate that the best way of finding an expert is through what is called "referral chaining," whereby a seeker finds the needed expert through referral by colleagues. Schwartz and Wood (1993) have also tried to enable locating people with related interests or expertise by analyzing the graph—which they called "specialization subgraph"—formed by e-mail communication patterns (rather than their contents).

They use a set of heuristic algorithms to uncover shared-interest relationships among people and derive a list of people who share a given interest.

Vivacqua (1999) describes an expert finder agent that is reminiscent of the earlier ideas in (Kautz, Selman, and Milewski 1996) in that it employs a personal agent that both profiles the expertise of a user and searches for other experts when help is needed. This agent was developed for the domain of Java programming. Yenta (Foner 1997) is also an agent-based system that creates personal profiles of people's interests and uses interagent communication to find people that have interests close to a query as well as to cluster people based on their shared interests. Expertise Recommender (McDonald and Ackerman 2000; Ackerman et al. 1999) is a system composed of components that implement the functionality and heuristics its creators identified from their field study in a software development company (McDonald and Ackerman 1998). Expertise Recommender provides four major components called profiling supervisor, identification supervisor, selection supervisor, and interaction management that maintain and manipulate expertise profiles.

There also exist some recent commercial knowledge management systems that provide features supporting expertise profiling and retrieval in organizations. Agentware Knowledge Server, from Autonomy, for example, includes a feature that identifies employees' areas of expertise based on the documents they access in and submit to the organizational intranet. Similarly, KnowledgeMail, from Tacit Knowledge Systems, supports finding experts by building profiles of people's skills from their e-mail messages as well as other documents they submit. AskMe Enterprise is another similar product.

Also noteworthy are organizational memory systems like Answer Garden (Ackerman and McDonald 1996), the Chicago Information Exchange (CIE) system (Kulyukin, Hammond, and Burke 1998), and Orbital Software's Organik, which include expert-finding components. These systems are basically question-answering and routing systems that respond to requests for technical help by retrieving stored question-and-answer pairs but also provide facilities to route unanswered questions to a defined group of experts. Similar to such systems are works that incorporate expert-finding capabilities as part of peer help systems in education and training environments. PHelpS (Greer et al. 1998a; 1998b) is one such system that enables finding peer helpers among course participants or task-specific groups of people.

There are also other systems that considered people's WWW browsing patterns as indicators of expertise. The MEMOIR system (Pikrakis et al. 1998) enables one to find experts in a certain domain based on a log database called "trailbase," which consists of URLs people visited as well as keywords for these pages. Similarly, the Expert Browser (Cohen, Maglio, and Barrett 1998) enables people in organizations to use logged and indexed browse paths of experts to find relevant documents. (However, the authors only describe those features that require the user to know the expert or her group a priori.) In general, as regards such systems, one may question their basic assumptions on the ground that browsing just shows someone's *interests* rather than expertise.

Apart from such implemented systems, there are also a few authors who tried to formulate techniques that enable finding experts by mining organizational and personal document repositories. Kimbrough and Oliver (1994) suggest a retrieval method called associative retrieval, which uses binary term-weight matrix-based procedures called DCB algorithms to identify resources (including people) in organizations that are closely linked to a given documented issue. Kanfer, Sweet, and Schosser (1996) present the idea of an agent called "know-who agent," which can use TF-IDF weighting to trace relevant experts based on e-mails they receive.

13.3   Positioning Automatic Expert Finders

Before going on to the domain analysis where we consider the functionality of expert finders, we survey the potential application contexts for these systems, with particular reference to other related organizational systems and services. This survey outlines the bounds of the expert finders' domain and crudely represents the context analysis phase required prior to domain analysis.

As part of organizational information systems, expert finders can either stand on their own or form part of other, broader systems in the organization. We believe that their great potential is unleashed only when used in integration with other organizational information systems, namely, knowledge management systems, recommender systems, CSCW systems, and electronic markets for human expertise.

As mentioned earlier, expert-finding capabilities form an important part of knowledge management systems, whose aim is to provide access to knowledge in all forms, including knowledge held by people. Davenport (1996) called this the "hybrid approach to knowledge management." Kautz, Selman, and Milewski (1996) also discuss the importance of integrating both the "ask a program/document" and "ask a person" paradigms into information seeking. These two approaches are mostly used in an interdependent manner, that is, one is used to find the other (Hertzum and Pejtersen 2000). Organizational memory systems like question answering and routing systems, for example, Answer Garden (Ackerman and McDonald 1996), can be cited as one realization of this paradigm, which necessarily calls for expert-finding capabilities.

Social recommender/collaborative filtering systems, too, can enhance their services by integrating expert-finding support. For example, as Höök, Rudström, and Waern (1997) note, a user of such a system might be much more interested in what particular experts regard as important information than in the recommendation of a large group of peers. One can reasonably conjecture that users may want to judge the relevance of a piece of information based on its *quality* (as reflected in the expertise of the recommender) in addition to *quantity* (the number of people recommending it). Obviously, expert finders can play important roles here. For example, their integration allows users to inquire the extent of expertise of recommenders or enables the recommender systems to factor expertise of the recommenders in their weighting schemes.

Those systems that fall under the rubric of CSCW systems, too, can integrate expert-finding components to permit the identification of individuals to collaborate with, in addition to supporting collaboration among those who have already identified each other (Hattori et al. 1999).

With expert-finding capabilities as a core, so-called electronic markets for expertise/human competencies, wherein expertise sellers and buyers transact, are suggested by Lang and Pigneur (1997). Moukas et al. (2000) propose a software-agent-based infrastructure that allows such transactions to take place. Recently booming services like XpertSite.com, exp.com, and ExpertCity.com, where users can post their questions and get quick expert answers for pay are other examples of such a market.

13.4   Domain Analysis

Domain analysis is a method for analyzing an application domain by studying and characterizing existing systems, emerging technologies, and development histories within a domain of interest (Lung and Urban 1993). In domain analysis, common characteristics from similar systems are generalized, objects and operations that are common to all systems within the same domain and that vary from system to system are identified, and a domain model is defined to describe their relationships (Prieto-Diaz 1987). For our purpose, we used the analysis method based on faceted classification suggested in Prieto-Diaz and later improved by Birk (1997).

Before proceeding, we would like to state that our aim here is far less ambitious than conducting a full-fledged domain analysis of expert-finding systems (for which we concur the expert-finding domain is not mature enough) as is done in software reuse efforts, where the approach is mainly employed. Our aims are (1) to come up with a systematic and structured way to characterize expert-finding systems, and (2) to investigate whether better systems that can be used in a wide variety of contexts can be designed. We analyze the literature of five expert finder systems (Krulwich and Burkey 1996; Mattox, Maybury, and Morey 1999; Kautz and Selman 1998; Vivacqua 1999; Streeter and Lochbaum 1988a; 1988b) to identify and define the feature space of the domain, and we map both implemented and potentially applicable technology to develop an intuitive domain model. Along the way, we also introduce terminology and structure that summarize the common as well as the distinct characteristics of these systems.

An Intuitive Domain Model
According to Birk (1997), an intuitive domain model is a faceted classification scheme that summarizes findings of a domain analysis and describes the domain using terms from the language of software pro-

fessionals. Each *facet* in the domain model is represented by a *domain factor* (attribute shared by systems). Each domain factor is defined through a set of discrete values (*"possible values"*). A facet of a concrete domain is characterized through one or more values (*"actual values"*) from the set of possible values. A domain factor together with its actual values is called *domain characteristic*. For the expert-finding systems domain, we identified seven facets/domain factors, as shown in table 13.1. Each column represents one facet/domain factor and its possible values, which are possible implementations of the respective domain factor. Hence, we can classify a given expert-finding system using its domain characteristics, which consist of the domain factors along with their values.

In the following discussion of the seven domain factors, we use the term *expertise indicator* to refer to the data gathered as evidence of expertise and input to a process of analysis to generate/infer the expertise of people. By *expertise indicator source*, we mean any source of expertise evidence that includes different types of documents, databases, individuals, and so on.

Basis for Expertise Recognition   Expert-finding systems use various pieces of evidence as indicators of expertise. In general, these can be grouped as explicit and implicit evidence. Although explicit evidence is very helpful when available, the focus of automatic expert finders is on employing implicit evidence because it is usually far more common and does not impose burdens on the experts. Some of the implicit pieces of evidence considered as indicators of expertise are document authorship (formal and informal, individually or in group), name occurrence in nonauthored documents, use of information sources or system functionality, queries sent to an information retrieval system, and the departments/projects experts work in.

In theory, all documents in an organization are potential sources of expertise evidence because they are created *by* or *about* somebody. However, for various reasons including computational difficulty, privacy, and coverage, not all sources can actually be used. Hence, expert-finding systems need to employ a procedure for recognizing and gathering potential sources of expertise indicators. We refer to this

Table 13.1
An Intuitive Domain Model of Expert-Finding Systems

Basis for Expertise Recognition	Expertise Indicator Extraction Operation	Expertise Modeling	Query Mechanisms
Explicit • Self-declaration by expert • Professional (organizational) position *Implicit* • Document authorship • Name-topic co-occurrence in documents • Projects worked on • Frequent usage of particular service/ information source/ software feature • Citations received	*Domain knowledge– driven* *Domain knowledge– independent* • Keywords from expert (or other people) • Name-concept co-occurrence (proximity) in documents • Frequently used software features	*Query time– generated* *Personal agent– based (distributed)* *Association to aggregated (centralized) expertise model* • Expert-to-canonical topics • Expert-to-publications • Expert-to-organizational structure • Expert-to-profile/expertise descriptor (database, Web page)	*Explicit query for expert* • Keyword queries • Natural language queries • Parameterized queries (e.g., keyword plus social radius of experts) *Induce information/expert need* • Observation by personal agent • Analysis of communication (e.g., newsgroup posting)

mechanism as *source recognition logic*. This can be static in that the system mines a predefined type or format of sources, or it may be designed to dynamically identify sources of expertise information from the large mass and variety of electronic as well as human resources.

Expertise Indicator Extraction   Once the sources are identified and gathered, expertise indicators are extracted from them. The expertise indicator extraction techniques that are applied on the aforementioned resources can be grouped as domain knowledge–independent or domain knowledge–driven. An example of the latter is described in Vivacqua (1999), where Java documentation is employed as a domain knowledge base to extract indicators of Java programming expertise.

Table 13.1
(continued)

Matching Operations	Output Presentation	Adaptation and Learning Operations
Exact/overlap matching *Statistical/similarity–based matching* (e.g., Latent Semantic Indexing) *Inference matching* • Inference on relation between concepts (ontology-based) • Inference on relations between experts • Inference on expertise level of people	*Ranked list of names* • Unidimensional ranking • Multidimensional ranking *Ranked list plus personal details* *Experts contextualized in their social network* *Documents/ organizational groups containing relevant experts*	*Adaptation using user's expertise models* *User modeling* *Gathering relevance feedback* *Community expertise evaluation/rating*

Expertise Models   We use the phrase *expertise model* to refer to a meta-description of an individual's expertise and skills, or a link to an expert from an independently maintained organized structure of such descriptions. Being an inferred *model*, it differs, for example, from a record in an expertise database in that it involves a degree of uncertainty about how well it matches the actual expertise of people. Similarly, we use the phrase *expertise modeling* to refer to the process of generating the expertise model through an analysis of the expertise indicators, including possible inferences on the basis of the findings. Hence, there is always a degree of uncertainty about how well the expertise model matches the actual expertise of people. An *expert model (profile)* refers to all information peculiar to an individual expert, including personal details, his expertise model (or links to one), his relationships with other experts, and so on.

Expertise models can be dynamically generated at query time from expertise indicator sources, or extracted and stored either by personal agents or as aggregated models to which experts are associated. In *query-time–generated models*, source databases are searched employing information retrieval systems, and the matching sources are mined for experts and expertise indicators (e.g., Mattox, Maybury, and Morey 1999). In *personal-agent–based systems*, expertise modeling is distributed to self-managing agents that belong to each individual expert and reside on his machine. As such, the whole system becomes a multi-agent system composed of personal agents, which carry out the dual tasks of modeling expertise (from authored documents and other sources) as well as assisting their owners in searching other experts. These agents can be endowed with mobility as well as autonomy to do all the processing and control of expertise modeling on their own. In the approach of associating experts to *aggregated expertise models*, experts are linked to a pre-constructed or dynamically generated central representation of expertise which can be a kind of knowledge model (ontology) or organizational structure.

Query Mechanisms   The system can either require the user to explicitly ask the system for experts, or it may infer expertise need from users' communications, activities, errors, and help-seeking actions.

Matching Operations   So as to identify experts, information or expertise needs are matched with expertise models or expert profiles using retrieval techniques including exact keyword matching or similarity matching, like vector-space-based methods. Furthermore, some inference mechanisms can be applied to either or both queries and expertise models. This will allow such inferences as "If x is expert on topic y, then she may also/not know topic z" or "If x knows topic y, then she may know someone who is expert on topic z."

Output Presentation   Expert-finding systems may present their outputs with a varying degree of details and functionality for further exploitation. As in information retrieval systems, some mechanism of ranking the identified experts (which we call expert differentiation) is applied. The ranking of experts may be *multidimensional* in that various criteria need to be taken into account. Apart from relevant details about each returned expert, the organizational and social context and network of the experts can be presented. Some systems also provide the sources in which experts are mentioned, leaving the task of identifying the experts in them to the user.

Adaptation and Learning Operations   These operations enable the customization of output by identifying users' preference and domain knowledge as well as gathering user feedback (both positive and negative) to the system's output. The system should not only be able to identify those people with required expertise but also be able to identify the most suitable ones meeting the needs and context of the user. For instance, the system can employ user models (including expertise models) to compare the experts' competence level with that of the user, make user-tailored rankings, and attempt to describe expertise at a level of granularity that matches queries (if an ontology is used). User feedback on the system's accuracy, ranking scheme, and so on, can be gathered and used to refine its expertise and expert models. Since expertise is in part a social construct, the system can also gather expertise evaluations and ratings from users and incorporate it into its expert differentiation scheme. Users can also be allowed to bring new experts into the system. This facet is implemented in only a few of the systems we studied. In Vivacqua (1999) an expert profile of users is employed to enable expertise-level matching. Mattox, Maybury, and Morey (1999) mention their plan to enable their system to learn over time based on results of each query to the system.

Discussion

In this section we relate the expert-finding problem as discussed earlier to the space of solutions that we reviewed and analyzed, and describe the gaps that came to light during this process.

As we saw in the problem analysis, a user turns to an expert as a source of information, as a candidate for a given organizational role, or as a mixture of both. Each of these purposes imposes its own requirements on system functionality. As noted, a user with an information need tends to seek experts before documents. The reasons for this include using them as filters (guides) to documents, avoiding searching for documents altogether, or the user's being interested in the situated interpretation and application of a piece of information rather than in the mere information itself. Such needs imply a role for expert finders of giving the user an expert-oriented access to the information space. Given a certain information space, an expert-finding system must then enable the user to find the right expert who can be used as a gateway to, or in lieu of, the information space. This justifies the approach of mining the information space as an implicit source of expertise indicators, as we saw in the domain analysis.

Even for those users who seek experts because they believe that the information is not documented, an expert finder that mines the information space can serve useful purposes. To begin with, it can complement information retrieval systems in ascertaining the belief that the information is actually not documented. Besides, it can be used to trace those who work in the problem domain at hand. But to help the user find an expert on something not documented, the expert finder must use other means for determining expertise beyond the organizational information resources.

The fact that users need experts as information sources also substantiates the claim that expert-finding systems need to be deployed in complement to, and as part of, knowledge management, information retrieval, CSCW, collaborative filtering, and related services. Furthermore, since expert seeking arises during day-to-day work, it is beneficial if expert-finding systems are embedded in the day-to-day problem solving and information search environments.

Users seeking experts who can perform some organizational function need more than just information. These users mainly focus on evaluating and comparing the expertise of people. Viewed in the light of McDonald and Ackerman's (1998) classification of expert finding into two phases as *expertise identification* and *expertise selection*, these users need more support for the later phase than those who are seeking experts as information sources. However, in the works we reviewed—with the exception of Expertise Recommender by McDonald and Ackerman (2000) —only expertise identification is targeted.

Specifically, while mapping the domain model to the expert-finding problem, we have identified four gaps, namely, source heterogeneity gap, technique optimality gap, analysis support gap, and reusability and interoperability gap. In the following, we describe each of these shortcomings and suggest some ways to tackle them. This discussion also forms the foundations for the approach we present in the next section of the chapter.

Source Heterogeneity Gap   In order to adequately exploit the information space as a source of expertise indicators, expert finders need to handle the heterogeneity and distributedness of the information space. This is also reflected by the wide variety of expertise indicator sources observed in the domain analysis. However, so far each of the current systems exploits a few types of mostly centralized sources only. Hence, architectures that are flexible enough to address this problem are needed.

A number of dimensions of heterogeneity and distributedness can be identified. One aspect of heterogeneity that needs to be addressed is the heterogeneity of sources in reflecting expertise. How well expertise indicators like terms and phrases reflect expertise is mainly a factor of how the *source* in which these indicators occur relates to the expert, irrespective of the indicators' direct statistical (or otherwise) correlation with the expert. For example, the occurrence of the term *software agents* in Dr. X's resume and its occurrence in one of her publications may not weigh the same. Moreover, the occurrence of this term in the title of a document shows different distance to her actual expertise, compared to its occurrence anywhere in the body. Therefore, expert finders need to determine how a document relates to an expert before going on to extract expertise indicators from it.

Another aspect of heterogeneity of sources that is important in expertise recognition arises from their differing provenance. The sources include a range of organizational resources, personal information resources of experts as well as the experts themselves. This calls for functionality that specializes in monitoring each of these sources as well as mechanisms to calibrate their differing ability of indicating expertise.

There also remains a lot to be done in addressing the common situation where expertise indicators are physically distributed across the organization and stored in various formats (databases, document repositories, Web sites, and the like). Furthermore, exploiting personal information resources brings in a range of privacy issues. Unlike the traditional expert database approach, where experts *actively* supply all information that will be accessible to the outside for evaluation, here *all* available information about the expert will be evaluated by default unless the expert is allowed to actively *block* certain pieces of information from being scanned and evaluated. This calls for the need to enable experts to guide and control the system in monitoring their personal sources.

The Expertise Recognition Methodology Gap   Being a relatively nascent research area, the work in the expert-finding domain until now focused more on ascertaining the feasibility of a solution to the problem than on seeking optimal approaches and techniques. Consequently, the techniques employed and their underlying assumptions also fall short of realizing systems that properly address the expert-finding problem.

Admittedly, expertise identification and representation pose immense challenges: the pool of expertise indicators is large and amorphous, the descriptors of expertise are difficult to extract, expert qualities are multidimensional and users' expertise needs are mostly fine-grained. The methods adopted by the existing systems to deal with these challenges are mainly based on generalizing expert finding with information retrieval assumptions and theories. Although this sort of reductionist approach helps to a certain extent, we believe there is a need to explore the unique features and requirements of expertise identification and modeling as well as expertise query formulation.

Expertise Analysis Support Gap   As already noted, current expert finders scarcely address expertise selection. Support for this can be based on the information space as well as on other sources. From the information space, an expert finder can provide access to the output of the expert as demonstrated by documents produced, and determine the expert's influence as demonstrated by citations received, co-authorship, and other relationships with other experts.

While setting out to support expertise selection, one should not forget that it is the user who does the selection and that the system can only support this process by providing appropriate analysis functionality. For example, the following system capabilities may considerably enhance the selection of the right expert:

• The ability to rank and contrast experts using different user-selected criteria (rather than the mere provision of a linear listing based on a predetermined criterion).

• Example-based search for experts using one expert's model as a query (or as a frame of reference).

• The presentation/explication of multiple relationships among experts. This can be used for visualizing (and catalyzing) collaboration, co-authorship, citation links, and project groups. (Note that two experts who are otherwise related may be far apart with respect to a query, and conversely two experts may be close with respect to a query but have little relationship to each other.)

• Using an ontology-based (knowledge-based) presentation/ranking of experts (subset-superset relationships, multidisciplinary and interdisciplinary expertise, and so on).

One way to help users in expertise selection is to increase the system's transparency. Viewed within the framework of our domain model, this can be done by providing interfaces to access the expertise indicator sources, the expertise model, and the expert model as well as the expertise recognition logic. This, in turn, permits the incorporation of functionality that can assist the user in evaluating and exploring (visualizing) the expertise information.

Reusability, Interoperability, and Extensibility Gap   Probably because of the embryonic stage of research on expert finders, current systems focus on solving a particular problem and coming up with a stand-alone solution (what Cohen and Northrop (1998) referred to as the "single-system mentality"). However, in order to live up to the wider variety of applications where expert finders are needed, these systems should be both readily transferable from application to application and interoperable with other systems. Moreover, since different applications and organizational constraints may require tailored implementations of the same facet, their components need to be substitutable and extensible as appropriate. Hence, as much as possible, expert finders should be designed in a generic architecture, keeping modularity and reusability in mind.

To this end, partitioning the whole system into loosely coupled modules that implement each facet appears to be promising. We believe the domain model presented in this chapter will be useful in this regard.

13.5 The DEMOIR Approach

Which Type of Expertise Model to Use?

In the previous section we argued that there is a need for an expert-finding system that can exploit heterogeneous sources of expertise indicators, use better techniques of expertise modeling and identification, be flexible enough to be integrated with other systems, and can support analysis as well as other exploitations of expertise information. A closer look at the seven facets shown in table 13.1 reveals that expertise models form the critical architectural foundation that determine performance and usability. We thus briefly examine the various alternatives for implementing this facet with regard to their ability to form a foundation for a solution that attacks the aforementioned gaps.

As we indicated before, we have three alternative expertise models: query-time–generated, personal-agent–based, and aggregated expertise models. While the query-time–generated approach uses dynamically generated expertise models, the other two are a priori constructed. The personal-agent–based models suggest a decentralized architecture, and the aggregated expertise models suggest a centralized approach.

Mattox, Maybury, and Morey (1999) argue that query-time–generated expertise models have the advantage of avoiding the maintenance of (possibly outdated) information internally and would permit operation in real time using the most recent information available to locate experts. However, not surprisingly, the authors reported that their system suffers from high latency in query processing. We also witnessed the same shortcoming in a comparable expert-finding system we developed for a research department. We feel that given the availability of search robots that can routinely gather sources of expertise indicators and can construct and update expert profiles, the advantage of query-time–generated models is not important any more. Besides, this approach allows for limited manipulations on the expertise information (like analysis, visualization, browsing, and comparison of expert profiles). The reason is that the approach lacks persistent expertise data and cannot exploit all types of documents (e.g., e-mails and other personal sources are difficult to include). It is also difficult to exploit diverse sources of expertise data other than documents (e.g., recommendations from people, social relations, feedback are difficult to incorporate).

The trade-offs between the other two approaches (aggregated expertise model and distributed personal-agent–based model) are more difficult to weigh. The advantages of using distributed personal agents include easy privacy maintenance through locality of expertise modeling, which in turn may give experts the feeling of being in control (although any access restrictions that may be imposed on an agent-based model can also be realized for aggregated models as well). However, this approach suffers from the limitations of relying on personal sources of information only. The fact that the expertise data are distributed results in limited accessibility and suboptimal utilization. The approach also suffers from problems of scalability when the number of experts grows large, since having individual expertise-modeling agents for numerous people overloads the network during querying because every query is matched to all distributed personal agents.

Maintaining an aggregated expertise model overcomes the aforementioned shortcomings of the other two approaches to a great extent while introducing its own shortcomings. This approach allows for an open and multipurpose exploitation of the expertise information, manipulation of the expertise information in the aggregate, and monitoring a wide range of organizational sources for up-to-date expertise data. It also facilitates using both knowledge-based and statistical expertise modeling (e.g., allows the analysis and grouping of experts based on their expertise profiles, facilitating inferences on the relationships among experts). However, it fails to afford localization, access to personal information sources of individual experts, and privacy of the expertise data. A more detailed discussion of this point can be found in Yimam-Seid and Kobsa (2000a; 2000b).

An optimal solution is one that can integrate the aggregated expertise models with personal-agent–based approach. The DEMOIR architecture (DEMOIR stands for Dynamic Expertise Modeling from Organizational Information Resources), which we briefly discuss in the following section, is motivated by the desire to implement such a hybrid and flexible solution. This approach is our attempt to lay the foundations for the development and testing of better algorithms and heuristics for expertise modeling and identification based on implicit sources of expertise evidence.

The DEMOIR Architecture

The DEMOIR architecture, shown in figure 13.1, is a modular architecture for expert-finding systems that is based on centralized expertise models while also incorporating decentralized expertise indicator source gathering, expertise indicator extraction, and distributed clients. It manages to do this by dissociating functions like source gathering, expertise indicator extraction and expertise modeling, and delegates them to specialized components which can be separately implemented and readily combined to suit an application environment. Specifically, this architecture has the following characteristics:

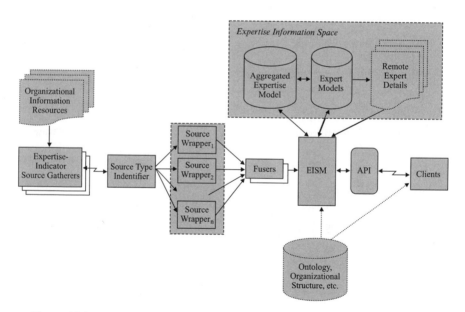

Figure 13.1
The DEMOIR architecture.

• Configurability and extensibility at all of its modules, thereby effectively addressing the reusability and interoperability gap.

• Expertise modeling that considers the heterogeneity of sources as valuable meta-information that must be exploited rather than a hodgepodge that must be made uniform. For instance, DEMOIR tries to explicitly capture how the sources relate to experts and where the expertise evidence stems from, and to factor this information into the expertise-modeling process.

• A combination of distributed and centralized monitoring of expertise data from both organizational and personal information sources. DEMOIR allows distributed and expert-controllable expertise indicator–gathering components (like robots), which can be tailored to the specific requirements of both organizational and personal sources. This enables us to tackle some aspects of the source heterogeneity gap and privacy problems.

• A centralized expertise information server that aggregates, stores, and supplies expertise information and provides application programming interfaces for client implementations and integration with other systems.

• A framework to integrate domain knowledge at all steps along with statistical and heuristics-based methods internal to components.

• Delegation to clients of application-specific exploitation of the expertise information (e.g., searching, browsing, analysis, visualization).

These characteristics are realized by the following DEMOIR components (also see figure 13.1):

Expertise Indicator Source Gatherers   These are agents that serve as informers to the centralized expertise-modeling server by routinely gathering expertise indicator sources from various parts of the organizational information resource like Web sites, databases, repositories, and personal sources. They are envisaged to be independent, adaptable to local constraints of the expertise indicator source they exploit, and not to be controlled by any central system. They are equipped with heuristics to recognize potential sources of expertise data (like memorizing names of experts and resolving name variations). They can also use techniques to trace name occurrences without a priori knowledge of expert names using, for example, proper noun identification methods employed in natural language processing (e.g., Wacholder, Ravin, and Choi 1997).

Source Type Identifier   This is a module that analyzes clues in the content and structure of sources to determine how they relate to the experts whose names are contained in or linked to these sources. The output of the source type identifier is used to invoke the appropriate source wrappers. Hence, the source type identifier, along with the source wrappers, implements differentiated extraction of expertise indicators based on types of source-to-expert relations.

Source Wrappers and Fusers   Wrappers are sets of modules that handle the extraction of expertise indicators from heterogeneous sources. Employing both statistical techniques and heuristics, each source wrapper extracts expertise indicators from a particular source type. The expertise indicators thus extracted are merged into aggregated expertise models by the fusers. The expertise models thus constructed, along with expert profiles and other related information (like the local archive of sources, expert networks) constitute what we call an *expertise information space* maintained and managed by the expertise information space manager.

Expertise Information Space Manager   This component manages the storage of, and retrieval from, the expertise information space. It specifically handles the low-level representation and maintenance of, as well as access to, the aggregate expertise model, the local expert models, and the remote expert details, which are the constituents of the expertise information space. It also executes the requests from the application programming interfaces. Moreover, the expertise information space manager enables a flexible integration of domain models (ontologies) or modules to generate them using methods such as concept clustering.

As we stated earlier, the aggregated expertise model represents the expertise space in a certain domain (like an organization) whereas expert models represent the individual experts, including a link to the aggregated expertise model and other peculiar information like personal attributes and links to other experts. In other words, the expertise model represents the conceptual relation and proximity among experts whereas the expert models represent other relations (like social ties, organizational relations, co-authorship relations). In terms of McDonald and Ackerman's (1998) dichotomy, we can also view expertise models as supporting expertise identification (Who are the experts on topic x?) while expert models/profiles support expertise selection (What does expert z know? How extensive is his knowledge? Which other experts relate to him?).

The Application Programming Interface   This facilitates the implementation of various clients to enable search, browsing, and analyses. The interface also supports the integration of the DEMOIR server in other applications.

13.6   Conclusion and Future Research

In this chapter we analyzed the expert-finding problem by classifying what motivates people to look for experts into two groups, namely, information needs and expertise needs. Then, we took a closer look at the expert-finding systems domain using the approach of domain analysis and presented our findings as a domain model. By overlaying the findings of these two analyses, we discussed the gaps that remain to be addressed and argued that it is more fruitful to approach them with a relatively generic architecture. In line with this, we described the DEMOIR approach, which we employ as a modular framework for expert finders, and demonstrated how it tackles the observed gaps to a considerable extent.

As we suggested throughout this chapter, a number of issues still remain open. Among the questions that need further investigation are How can expertise indicator sources in organizations be identified and exploited? How should expertise and expert models be structured and represented? How should one apply inference rules and algorithms on expert and expertise relationships? and How should users be supported in searching, visualizing, and analyzing the expertise information space?

An investigation of the contextual and integration issues is also important for the proper positioning and deployment of expert-finding systems within organizations. At the level of the individual user, adaptive features in the sense of identifying and fulfilling expertise needs from users' daily activities are necessary (see Kobsa, Koenemann, and Pohl 2001 for available methods). At the organizational level, the proper organizationwide applications, services, and systems into which expert finders can be incorporated also need to be identified. And finally, issues of privacy and security also must be taken into account. Kobsa (2002) discusses privacy concerns of Internet users and international privacy laws that directly affect expert finders. Schreck (forthcoming) presents a reference architecture for pseudonymous interaction in the area of user modeling that can also be adopted in the area of expert finding.

We aim to investigate some of these issues by pursuing the development and testing of the DEMOIR Server architecture employing various techniques. Specifically, we intend to continue working on (1) the development and testing of heuristics for source identifiers and wrappers, (2) methods of versatile representation of the expertise information space to support a range of purposes including exploitation (search and inference), visualization, and analysis, and (3) evaluation of our approaches and techniques through implementation and testing with users.

Acknowledgments

An earlier version of this paper appeared in the *Journal of Organizational Computing and Electronic Commerce*. Much of the research described here was carried out while the authors were affiliated with GMD—German National Research Center for Information Technology. A great many of the ideas presented in this chapter benefited from discussions with the information-brokering team members Jürgen Koenemann, Christoph Thomas, Roland Klemke, and Achim Nick as well as Mark Ackerman, Wolfgang Pohl, and Reinhard Oppermann.

References

Ackerman, M. S., and D. W. McDonald. 1996. Answer Garden 2: Merging Organizational Memory with Collaborative Help. In *Proceedings of the ACM Conference on Computer-Supported Cooperative Work (CSCW '96)*, 97–105.

Ackerman, M. S., D. McDonald, W. Lutters, and J. Muramatsu. 1999. Recommenders for Expertise Management. In *Proceedings of ACM SIGIR '99 Workshop on Recommender Systems: Algorithms and Evaluation*, Berkeley, California.

Birk, A. 1997. Modeling the Application Domains of Software Engineering Technologies. In *Proceedings of the Twelfth IEEE International Conference on Automated Software Engineering*, 291–292.

Cohen, A. L., P. P. Maglio, and R. Barrett. 1998. The Expertise Browser: How to Leverage Distributed Organizational Knowledge. In *Proceedings of the Workshop on Collaborative and Cooperative Information Seeking in Digital Information Environments, Conference on Computer-Supported Cooperative Work (CSCW '98)*.

Cohen, S., and L. M. Northrop. 1998. Object-Oriented Technology and Domain Analysis. In *Proceedings of the Fifth International Conference on Software Reuse*, Victoria, B. C., Canada, 86–93.

Davenport, T. H. 1996. Some Principles of Knowledge Management. Available at http://www.bus.utexas.edu/kman/kmprin.htm.

Davenport, T. H., and L. Prusak. 1998. *Working Knowledge: How Organizations Manage What They Know*. Boston: Harvard Business School Press.

Foner, L. N. 1997. Yenta: A Multi-Agent, Referral-Based Matchmaking System. In *Proceedings of International Conference on Autonomous Agents (Agents '97)*, 301–307.

Furnas, G. W., S. Deerwester, S. T. Dumais, T. K. Landauer, R. A. Harshman, L. A. Streeter, and K. E. Lochbaum. 1988. Information Retrieval Using a Singular Value Decomposition Model of Latent Semantic Structure. In *Proceedings of ACM SIGIR Conference*, Grenoble, France, 465–480.

Greer, J. E., G. McCalla, J. Collins, V. Kumar, P. Meagher, and J. Vassileva. 1998a. Supporting Peer Help and Collaboration in Distributed Workplace Environments. *International Journal of Artificial Intelligence in Education* 9: 159–177.

Greer, J. E., G. McCalla, J. Cooke, J. Collins, V. Kumar, A. Bishop, and J. Vassileva. 1998b. The Intelligent Helpdesk: Supporting Peer-Help in a University Course. In *International Intelligent Tutoring Systems Conference (ITS '98)*, 494–505.

Grief, I. 1998. Everyone Is Talking About Knowledge Management. In *Proceedings of ACM Conference on Computer-Supported Cooperative Work (CSCW '98)*, 405–406.

Hattori, F., T. Ohguro, M. Yokoo, S. Matsubara, and S. Yoshida. 1999. Socialware: Multiagent Systems for Supporting Network Communities. *Communications of the ACM* 42 (3): 55–61.

Hendriks, P. H., and D. J. Vriens. 1999. Knowledge-Based Systems and Knowledge Management: Friends or Foes? *Information and Management* 35 (2): 113–125.

Hertzum, M., and A. M. Pejtersen. 2000. The Information-Seeking Practices of Engineers: Searching for Documents as well as for People. *Information Processing and Management* 36 (5): 761–778.

Höök, K., A. Rudström, and A. Waern. 1997. Edited Adaptive Hypermedia: Combining Human and Machine Intelligence to Achieve Filtered Information. In *Proceedings of the Flexible Hypertext Workshop, Eighth ACM International Hypertext Conference (HYPERTEXT '97)*. Available at http://www.sics.se/~kia/papers/edinfo.html.

Kanfer, A., J. Sweet, and A. Schlosser. 1997. Humanizing the Net: Social Navigation with a "Know-Who" Email Agent. In *Proceedings of the Third Conference on Human Factors and the Web*. Available at http://www.optavia.com/hfweb/history.htm.

Kautz, H., and B. Selman. 1998. Creating Models of Real-World Communities with ReferralWeb. In *Working Notes of the Workshop on Recommender Systems, Fifteenth National Conference on Artificial Intelligence (AAAI '98)*, 58–59.

Kautz, H., B. Selman, and A. Milewski. 1996. Agent-Amplified Communication. In *Proceedings of the Thirteenth National Conference on Artificial Intelligence (AAAI '96)*, 3–9.

Kautz, H., B. Selman, and M. Shah. 1997. The Hidden Web. *AI Magazine* 18 (2): 27–36.

Kimbrough, S. O., and J. R. Oliver. 1994. On Relevance and Two Aspects of the Organizational Memory Problem. In *Proceedings of the Fourth Annual Workshop on Information Technology and Systems (WITS '94)*, 302–311.

Kobsa, A. 2002. Personal Hypermedia and International Privacy. *Communications of the ACM* (May 2002): 64–67.

Kobsa, A., J. Koenemann, and W. Pohl. 2001. Personalized Hypermedia Presentation Techniques for Improving Online Customer Relationships. *The Knowledge Engineering Review* 16 (2): 111–155.

Krulwich, B., and C. Burkey. 1995. ContactFinder: Extracting Indications of Expertise and Answering Questions with Referrals. In *Working Notes of the 1995 Fall Symposium on Intelligent Knowledge Navigation and Retrieval*, 85–91. Technical Report FS-95-03. Cambridge, Mass.: AAAI Press.

———. 1996. The ContactFinder Agent: Answering Bulletin Board Questions with Referrals. In *Proceedings of the Thirteenth National Conference on Artificial Intelligence (AAAI '96)*, 10–15.

Kuhlthau, C. C. 1993a. *Seeking Meaning: A Process Approach to Library and Information Services*. Norwood, N.J.: Ablex.

———. 1993b. A Principle of Uncertainty for Information Seeking. *Journal of Documentation* 49 (4): 339–355.

Kulyukin, V. A., K. J. Hammond, and R. D. Burke. 1998. Answering Questions for an Organization Online. In *Proceedings of the Fifteenth National Conference on Artificial Intelligence (AAAI '98)*, 532–538.

Lang, A., and Y. Pigneur. 1997. An Electronic Market of Individual Human Competencies for Team Building. *Virtual-organization.net Newsletter* 1 (3): 4–13. Available at http://www.virtual-organization-net/files/articles/nl1-3.pdf.

Lewis, T. 1999. Where the Smart Money Is. *IEEE Computer* 32 (11): 136.

Lung, C., and J. E. Urban. 1993. Integration of Domain Analysis and Analogical Approach for Software Reuse. In *Proceedings of the ACM/SIGAPP Symposium on Applied Computing*, 48–53.

Maron, M. E., S. Curry, and P. Thompson. 1986. An Inductive Search System: Theory, Design and Implementation. *IEEE Transaction on Systems, Man and Cybernetics* SMC-16 (1): 21–28.

Mattox, D. 1998. Expert Finder. *The Edge: The MITRE Advanced Technology Newsletter* 2 (1). Available at http://www.mitre.org/pubs/edge/June_98.

Mattox, D., M. Maybury, and D. Morey. 1999. Enterprise Expert and Knowledge Discovery. In *Proceedings of the Eighth International Conference on Human-Computer Interaction (HCI '99)*, 303–307.

McDonald, D. W., and M. S. Ackerman. 1998. Just Talk to Me: A Field Study of Expertise Location. In *Proceedings of the ACM Conference on Computer-Supported Cooperative Work (CSCW '98)*, 315–324.

———. 2000. Expertise Recommender: A Flexible Recommendation System Architecture. In *Proceedings of the ACM Conference on Computer-Supported Cooperative Work (CSCW 2000)*: 231–240.

Moukas, A., G. Zacharia, R. Guttman, and P. Maes. 2000. Agent-Mediated Electronic Commerce: An MIT Media Laboratory Perspective. *International Journal of Electronic Commerce* 4 (3): 5–22.

O'Leary, D. E. 1998. Knowledge-Management Systems: Converting and Connecting. *IEEE Intelligent Systems and Their Applications* 13 (3): 30–33.

Pikrakis, A., T. Bitsikas, S. Sfakianakis, M. Hatzopoulos, D. C. DeRoure, W. Hall, S. Reich, G. J. Hill, and M. Stairmand. 1998. MEMOIR: Software Agents for Finding Similar Users by Trails. In *Proceedings of the Third International Conference on the Practical Applications of Intelligent Agents and Multi-Agent Technology (PAAM '98)*, 453–466.

Prieto-Diaz, R. 1987. Domain Analysis for Reusability. In *Proceedings of the Eleventh Annual International Computer Software and Applications Conference (COMPSAC '87)*, 23–29.

Schreck, J. forthcoming. *Security and Privacy in User Modeling*. Dordrecht, the Netherlands: Kluwer.

Schwartz, M. F., and D. M. Wood. 1993. Discovering Shared Interests Using Graph Analysis. *Communications of the ACM* 36 (8): 78–89.

Stewart, T. 1997. Leading Lights: Author Tom Stewart on Intellectual Capital. *Knowledge Inc.* (May).

Streeter, L. A., and K. E. Lochbaum. 1988a. An Expert/Expert Locating System Based on Automatic Representation of Semantic Structure. In *Proceedings of the Fourth IEEE Conference on Artificial Intelligence Applications*, 345–349.

———. 1988b. Who Knows: A System Based on Automatic Representation of Semantic Structure. In *Proceedings of the Conference on Computer-Assisted Information Retrieval (RIAO '88)*, 380–388.

Vivacqua, A. S. 1999. Agents for Expertise Location. In *Proceedings of the AAAI Spring Symposium on Intelligent Agents in Cyberspace*, Stanford, California, 9–13.

Wacholder, N., Y. Ravin, and M. Choi. 1997. Disambiguation of Proper Names in Text. In *Proceedings of the Fifth Conference on Applied Natural Language Processing*, 202–208.

Wilson, T. 1995. Information-Seeking Behavior: Designing Information Systems to Meet Our Clients' Needs. In *Proceedings of ACURIL (Association of Caribbean University, Research and Institutional Libraries) Twenty-fifth Conference*, San Juan, Puerto Rico.

Yimam-Seid, D., and A. Kobsa. 2000a. Centralization vs. Decentralization Issues in Internet-Based Knowledge Management Systems: Experiences from Expert Recommender Systems. In *Workshop on Organizational and Technical Issues in the Tension Between Centralized and Decentralized Applications on the Internet (TWIST 2000)*. Available at http://www.ics.uci.edu/~kobsa/papers/2000-TWIST-kobsa.pdf.

———. 2000b. DEMOIR: A Hybrid Architecture for Expertise Modeling and Recommender Systems. In *Proceedings of the IEEE Ninth International Workshop on Enabling Technologies: Infrastructures for Collaborative Enterprises*, 67–74.

14

Automated Discovery and Mapping of Expertise

Mark Maybury, Ray D'Amore, and David House

The MITRE Corporation is a nonprofit corporation whose mission is to serve the public interest by creating solutions to pervasive, cross-organizational problems facing government in civil aviation, tax administration, and national security. MITRE's sponsors need it to help them be agile in response to world changes, be interoperable with national and international partners, and counter the loss of government experts. The corporation, employing approximately 4,500 people, is distributed globally (in the United States, Europe, and the Far East) and includes both technical and mission, or operational, experts. To support MITRE's sponsors, we are exploring knowledge partnerships with them and with site organizations to broaden MITRE expertise and enhance impact through partnership with other expert organizations.

As figure 14.1 illustrates, our efforts are aimed at providing full knowledge life cycle management, including Web-based expert-finding services, capture/reuse of knowledge and lessons learned, project and partnership creation (leader identification, team formulation, team facilitation/collaboration), and knowledge delivery. We are also exploring new virtual organizational models to enable efficient distributed teaming of expert talent.

To enable effective distributed knowledge management, MITRE employs global video teleconferencing, the MITRE Information Infrastructure (MII) intranet,[1] and public key infrastructure enabled extranet services. Knowledge resources such as "ask the expert," online knowledge repositories of risk management experience, and system engineering lessons learned are also available. Tools for staff and project discovery, information sharing (e.g., transfer folders), and virtual place-based col-

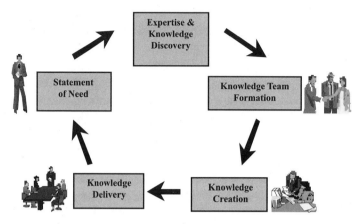

Figure 14.1
Knowledge management processes.

laboration such as the MITRE-created Collaborative Virtual Workspace (CVW)[2] are used to enable agile team formation and support. Corporate activities such as regular technical exchange meetings and upper management support for collaboration also foster a collaborative environment. Finally, external partnerships (e.g., with SEI, RAND, Aerospace, universities) ensure access to leading experts.

Effective expert and expert team discovery raises a series of complex issues: What is an expert? How do we characterize various levels of expertise or competence (e.g., student, master)? How do we authenticate or validate an expert? How do we characterize the evolution of what it means to be an expert or an individual's level of expertise over time? How can we systematically support this in a cost-effective manner?

This paper addresses related work in this area, describes and evaluates MITRE's Expert Finder and XperNet prototypes, and discusses plans for future research.

14.1   Previous Work

Several investigators have explored automating the process of expertise discovery and assessment. For example, in the Dataware II Knowledge Directory,[3] experts can self-nominate and subsequently be discovered through directory search; however, this manual process is expensive to maintain and becomes quickly out-of-date. In contrast, Autonomy Agentware Knowledge Server[4] analyzes users' search and publication histories to determine concepts that are indicative of their expertise. Yenta (Foner 1997) determines user expertise from e-mail message traffic, as does Tacit KnowledgeMail.[5] Other systems (Cohen, Maglio, and Barrett 1998) determine expertise from WWW-browsing patterns. MIT's Expert Finder (Vivacqua 1999) instruments software library usage to determine expertise level. Referral Web, from AT&T (Kautz, Selman, and Shah 1997), provides access to experts across an enterprise or community, aiming to make the basis for referral transparent to the user. It generates social networks based on bibliographic information and supporting context to deduce actual experts and associated referral paths. U.S. West's Expert-Expert Locator (Streeter and Lochbaum 1988) finds experts across an enterprise using Latent Semantic Indexing (LSI) techniques. A more detailed history of expert-finding systems and a domain model of such systems are presented in Yimam-Seid (1999).

Abuzz's Beehive[6] is one of many systems that provide an online community environment to support question-answer dialogues between users and registered experts. Users can learn from other users' question-answer dialogues posted under specific topics such as "cooking." Communities of experts are grouped in "web circles" that provide a domain-specific context for registering as an expert, for users to ask questions or initiate a group discussion. This is similar to the Answer Garden (Ackerman and Malone 1990), which categorizes questions into an ontology that could be browsed by users to find questions and answers similar to their own questions. If users do not find a related question, they are referred to an expert. The emerging online commercial systems attempt to also track each experts' performance; and the general trend is to use user ratings and experts' response times as a basis for measuring competence. Essentially, social filtering is used to qualify the level of expertise of registered experts. Such systems often suffer from the cold-start problem, where there is a mismatch between the number of experts and the number of users. In some cases, experts outnumber users, discouraging experts' participation or affecting revenue. In other cases, there is a dearth of experts (or qualified experts), and users become frustrated because of poor response times or low-quality answers. While these systems (e.g., XperSite.com[7]) present interesting expertise management paradigms, a number of core problems remain, including representing and measuring an expert's qualifications and matching questions to the appropriate experts.

14.2   Evolving Framework for Expertise Management

MITRE is a highly diversified organization focused on a wide range of problems and technologies. Much of the work is multidisciplinary, and project teams often need to be augmented with expertise not anticipated at project inception. This poses special problems in identifying and selecting individuals with the necessary expertise. Locating the right person to work a project or provide an answer to a question rests on a more fundamental issue: What is expertise? McDonald and Ackerman (1998) defined expertise as "the embodiment of knowledge and skills within individuals." At MITRE, expertise is operationalized as knowledge of MITRE's mission and sponsor program areas coupled with specific technical, management, and business skills needed to support clients and conduct research. However, measuring levels of expertise is a highly situated activity and, within an organization, often based on peer review and assessment. As such, the cost to build and maintain an aggregate view of an organization's knowledge and skills (to formally capture and manage expertise) is beyond what most organizations can support and would likely be inaccurate and an unreasonable goal for cultural reasons as well. An effective expertise management system needs to provide a reasonable balance between human and automatic expertise assessments.

Expertise location can be broken down into *identification* and *selection* phases (Ackerman et al. 1999). In the broader context of expertise management, we extend this to include expertise *measurement* and *representation* as fundamental to the overall problem of capturing and exploiting expertise. Decomposing expertise management into four segments has advantages in a addressing a number of system architecture issues. However, methods of assessing expertise depend on work context, organizational culture, and human judgment. As such, a system can

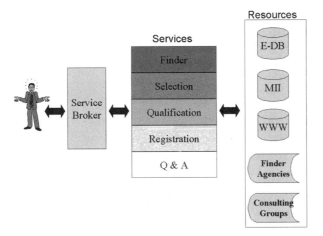

Figure 14.2
General architecture.

at best provide recommendations, with users ultimately determining who has the appropriate blend of knowledge and skills needed.

The MII is MITRE's corporate knowledge management system, accessible to all staff members across all locations. While the MII provides a wide range of services for exploiting MITRE work products (e.g., technical documents), it is largely document-centric and limits ways in which staff members can share knowledge and collaborate. The MII is evolving from a content management system into an expertise management system. In that regard, MITRE's expertise management system will be person-centric and focus on collaboration and expertise sharing. A general expertise management architecture is shown in figure 14.2. It is a component-based architecture that supports a wide range of services, largely built on top of the MII intranet and evolving extranet.

Early expertise management tools, evaluations, and workplace studies of how people identified and shared expertise provided the motivation for a number of the initial services described in this architecture. The major services include the following.

Service Broker

The Service Broker handles transactions between the user and enabling services. The broker includes a forms interface for expert registration and a multimodal interface supporting standard searches to the Expert Database (E-dB). It also utilizes other collections or access services such as the MII search engine, WWW search engines, and expert requisition forms for tasking commercial agencies to initiate searches. The Service Broker provides a number of lower-level services supporting query translation, question generation, and results presentation to the user. Questions can be directed to registered experts or broadcast to a wider corporate audience.

Registration Service
The Registration Service can be invoked to handle new-user registration or modifications to current user records. User-submitted registration information is extracted from forms and submitted to a database update process that adds or updates user registration records in the E-dB. The Registration Service also supports system-generated expert registration resulting from the automatic identification of users using the Finder Service. Experts located through automatic identification techniques (e.g., the MII Expert Finder or MII XperNet) are added to the E-dB with algorithm-generated ratings or with ratings assigned by actual users.

Finder Service
The Finder Service supports customized access to a range of collections or to external access services. User queries are translated by the Service Broker into a collection-specific syntax and used to search specific collections (e.g., the E-dB is searched for user- or system-registered experts). Various finder programs are used to address the cold-start problem, when the E-dB underrepresents the population of corporate experts. The MII Expert Finder algorithm is used to identify MITRE experts based on various levels of document processing and data in corporate databases. The MII XperNet algorithm is used to extract expertise networks or affinity groups across MITRE project areas.

Qualification Service
Users can rate experts in the context of a specific query and add comments. Ratings can also be based on the degree of match between candidate experts and a user query. This is computed automatically by the MII Expert Finder and MII XperNet algorithms.

Selection Service

The Selection Service is used to generate multidimensional views of an expert within the context of a query and other selection constraints. An expert's rank can be adjusted to be consistent with organizational or workflow parameters such as labor cost, availability, home organization, and access privileges. Users can adjust weights applied to specific selection criteria to tailor the selection list, or they can select experts based on a more holistic basis.

Question-and-Answer Service

Users can submit questions to a question-posting service. Questions can be posted within a prespecified topic category monitored by a team of experts or can be forwarded to a wider MITRE audience using discussion groups and e-mail. Question-answer dialogues captured from posted questions are retained in the E-dB and used to compute or update expert profiles and to track question topics over time.

Two finder services that exploit MITRE's intranet (the MII) are discussed next. The MII Expert Finder exploits the MII publishing space primarily to locate staff members who have specific expertise. The focus here is on the core algorithm and evaluation with real users. The MII XperNet tool complements the query-based finder tools and is used to automatically identify and track groups of individuals with related expertise. This tool extracts expertise networks using clustering and network analysis techniques. Users can navigate through expertise networks associated with a specific expertise area or can scan networks associated within organizational units such as a MITRE Technology Center. As a secondary option, user queries can be used to retrieve expertise networks, much like cluster searching is used as a recall-enhancing approach in traditional information retrieval applications.

14.3   MITRE's MII Expert Finder

Distribution of staff, decreasing project size, and cost/time pressures are driving a need to leverage enterprise expertise by quickly discovering who knows what and forming expert teams. Those in need typically have little or no means of finding experts other than by recommendation. Unfortunately, busy experts do not have time to maintain adequate

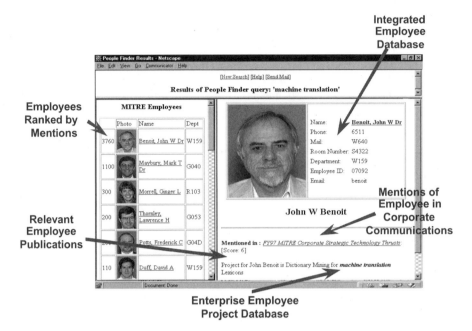

Figure 14.3
MII Expert Finder machine translation example.

descriptions of their continually changing specialized skills. Past experience with skills databases at MITRE indicates that they are difficult to maintain and quickly outdated.

MITRE's MII Expert Finder (Mattox, Smith, and Seligman 1998) fills this gap by mining information and activities on the MII related to experts and providing this in an intuitive fashion to end users. Figure 14.3 illustrates the system in action. In this example, a user is trying to find machine translation experts in the corporation. When the user searches using the term *machine translation*, the system ranks employees by the number of mentions of a term or phrase and its statistical association with the employee name either in corporate communications (e.g., newsletters) or based on what they have published in their resume or document folder (a shared, indexed information space). Integrated with MITRE's corporate employee database, employees are ranked by frequency of mentions, pointing to sources in which they appear.

The MII Expert Finder exploits the MII and thus avoids maintaining information internally. By doing so, Expert Finder operates in real time, using the most recent information available to locate experts. The MII contains many different sources of information that can be used to locate relevant expertise. Staff members can easily and quickly publish documents in individual staff document folders on the MII. These include technical papers, presentations, resumes, and home pages. Also, information is published about MITRE employees in project descriptions, announcements, and internal and external newsletters. At MITRE, all these documents are indexed by a common text search engine.

MII Expert Finder Process

The MII Expert Finder works by integrating expertise-related information found through queries to the MII's search engine. In and of itself, each source of employee information is generally not sufficient to determine if an employee is an expert in a particular topic. Expert Finder relies on the combination of evidence from many sources, and considers someone an expert in a particular topic if they are linked to a wide range of documents or a large number of documents about that topic.

Expert Finder has two main components: a set of scripts to call the MII's search engine and process the results, and a Web-based user interface. The steps that Expert Finder goes through when processing a query are shown in figure 14.4. The user is initially presented with a Web page that contains a search box for entering a Boolean query. A recognized problem with purely automatic approaches that process all data at query time (Yimam-Seid 1999) is critical speed inefficiency. Because some queries with many documents can take 30–45 seconds to process, the results of some commonly asked queries are cached by Expert Finder and the user is offered the option of viewing these cached results when available. If the resulting query has not been cached, the MII Expert Finder takes a keyword phrase (e.g., *chemical weapons*) or other Boolean search string and passes it to the underlying search engine, which then returns a set of documents (including resumes, home pages, presentations, newsletters) as a set of hyperlink pointers.

The documents used by the MII Expert Finder fall into two main categories: documents about a topic that are published by an employee

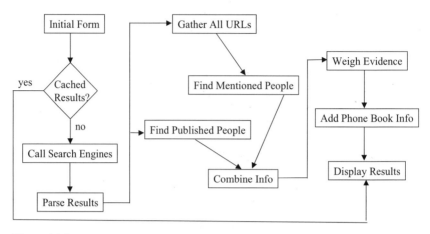

Figure 14.4
MII Expert Finder process.

and documents that mention employees in conjunction with a particular topic. For the self-published case, the MII Expert Finder relies on the number of documents published by an employee about a given topic to provide an "expert score" for that employee. The only exception is an employee's resume, which is given additional weight as a self-definition of an individual's expertise.

Managing the second class of documents, those that mention employees and topics, is more complicated. Whereas with the self-published documents there is an explicit linkage between the documents and employee (they are indexed by employee number), with documents that mention employees the linkage must be derived from the underlying text. The first step after the documents have been returned from the search engine is to locate the proper names within the text using a commercial product that tags names within a document.[8] Once all the person names in the document have been located, we use a database of MITRE employee names and a list of common nicknames (Thomas/Tom, David/Dave, Robert/Bob) to decide which people referenced in the document are MITRE employees. Note that this approach will run into problems for cases in which MITRE employees and nonemployees share the same name (e.g., a MITRE employee named John Smith might be confused with a nonemployee with that name).

The next step is to associate the MITRE employees mentioned in the document with the query topic. All the documents returned by the search engine contain the query string, but there are several distinct types of documents, and each type has a structure that must be exploited differently. For example, MITRE publishes an internal newsletter that contains short paragraphs describing accomplishments by MITRE staff (e.g., "Dr. John Smith presented a paper titled 'Intelligent Agents and Data Management' at the Tenth International Conference on Autonomous Agents"). In this case, the MII Expert Finder uses proximity as a metric for expertise (e.g., the name "John Smith" is five words away from the keyword phrase "Intelligent Agents"). In addition, the HTML tags of the document can be used to further refine the score. In this case, a paragraph marker ($\langle p \rangle$) breaks the linkage between a name and a topic because the announcements are always contained within a single paragraph. However, the heuristics used for the newsletter do not work well with other documents. For example, in technical reports the authors' names appear at the top of the document and may be several paragraphs away from the relevant keywords and therefore require different heuristics to determine the linkage between names and keywords.

Once each document has been examined, the evidence gathered about each person found is combined into a single score for that person. The increased likelihood of false positives among the "mentioned employees" results in less weight being given to names found via that approach compared with the weights given to "publishing employees." The person names are then matched against a database of MITRE employees, ordered by their final score, and displayed in a two-framed Web browser window. This means that the people who are most likely to be experts are displayed at the top of the list (see figure 14.3). In the left frame of the results window is a photo of the employee, the employee's name, and the employee's department (all taken from the MII phonebook). If the user clicks on an employee's photo or an employee's name, the right frame displays detailed employee contact information (including name, telephone number, e-mail address, department, room number) taken from the MII phonebook, followed by an ordered listing of hyperlinks to the relevant documents that are associated with an employee's expertise.

Table 14.1
Human and Expert Finder Performance

Expert Specialty Area	Human Agreement (1st, 2d, 3d) (%)	Expert Finder Precision (%)	Expert Finder Recall (%)
Data mining	70, 49, 24.5	60	40
Chemical	40, 8, 0.8	60	40
HCI	90, 36, 11	60	40
Network security	50, 10, 0.4	20	20
Collaboration	70, 35, 17.5	5	5
Average	63, 28, 11	41	29

MII Expert Finder Performance

Overall, the results obtained by the MII Expert Finder system are quite good. The original goal was to place a user within one phone call of an expert. That is, even if the people listed as the result of an MII Expert Finder query were not the experts, they would be able to provide the name of someone who was. However, in the majority of the cases tested, reasonable candidates for the title "expert" are listed as the top three or four candidates, where the likelihood of randomly selecting a correct expert is the total number of experts divided by 4,500 total staff, often significantly less than a 1 percent chance of getting any right. Table 14.1 illustrates preliminary results, contrasting the performance of ten technical human resource managers, professionals at finding experts, with the MII Expert Finder for the task of identifying the top five corporate experts in specialty areas listed in the table. The "Human Agreement" column in table 14.1 shows the degree of intersubject variability in reporting experts (measuring percentage of agreement on first, second, and third of five experts). The next two columns show results for "precision," the degree to which a staff member found by the MII Expert Finder is considered expert by human beings, and "recall," the degree to which a priori human-designated experts are found by the MII Expert Finder. In table 14.1, we use harsh measures, where "precision" measures how many of the top five MII Expert Finder results were also identified as experts by people. In contrast, "recall" measures how many of the top five experts that people identified were included in the top five MII Expert Finder results. In spite of human variability (e.g., note the difficulty that people had in identifying chemical and network security experts), the MII Expert Finder works remarkably well except in network security and collaboration (ironically, a result of few expert collaboration staff members' publishing on the MII, perhaps because they use specialized collaboration environments that were not instrumented).

Users of the MII Expert Finder have had generally positive comments about the system, in particular because the system tends to find an expert, a list of experts, or someone who is one phone call away from an expert, for a large variety of queries. Cases in which expert names appear as a surprise to people testing the system tend to lead either to refining the query or learning about a new expert (or at least someone working in a related field) within the company. Some of the user complaints about this approach result from not enough employees regularly publishing information and also from old information currently receiving the same importance as new information.

14.4   MII XperNet

At MITRE, Technology Centers support application development and applied research in a number of technology areas related to the sponsor's mission. As such, center staff often partner directly with project departments, forming teams with diverse but complementary skills and problem knowledge. Organizationally, staff working on related technologies and problems can be modeled as social networks that form the basis for abstracting expertise. According to Ackerman et al. (1999), expertise networks can be defined as "specializations of an organization's social network. They consider not only how people are socially arranged but what expertise they have and trade." However, in large, dynamic organizations expertise networks are often difficult to discern from the formal organizational structure as represented by the typical organization chart. As such, formal views of organizations may not always reflect actual interest areas, roles, and relationships of people within. XperNet is designed to detect actual work relationships across the enterprise as a basis for assessing workflow and areas of expertise and collaboration. Because work groups can form and disperse quickly to meet project demands, we have what can be characterized as emergent networks to complement what may be in formal organizations. XperNet is designed to extract expertise networks and integrate them into the overall expertise management system.

XperNet Model

The core model associates activities with workplace semantics and social context. In the baseline design, activities are represented by an activity identifier and associated with a membership list (individuals involved in the activity) and a semantic context (a set of terms or other descriptors that describe key themes or topics associated with the activity). For example, a technical exchange meeting (TEM) addressing "mobile computing" consists of the TEM identifier (title, corporate activity number, date, and location), a list of participants or contributors, an "owning" organization, and an activity description. Similarly, corporate share folders assigned to each staff member can be represented as a dissemination activity, with membership (the share folder's owner) and semantics extracted from the associated items (e.g., briefing paper). Note that each staff member has specific attributes such as job title or position, organizational home, and technical level (seven technical levels cover the technical staff). These attributes provide another basis for identifying relationships between staff members.

Computationally, XperNet maps an *n*-partite graph into a unipartite graph (an expert network). We start with a bipartite graph, such as a mapping of people to their associated projects. This graph consists of nodes and links such that all the nodes of one subset are linked to the nodes of the second with no edges between nodes in the same subset. This concept can be extended to *n*-partite graphs. For example, in a tripartite graph the nodes are partitioned into three subsets so that no two vertices contained in any one partition are adjacent. In this initial version, XperNet generates a corporate tripartite graph consisting of the following modes (node types): people, activities, and organizations (figure 14.5).

This tripartite (or more generally *n*-partite) graph is reduced using a composite similarity computation. Each instance of a person involved in an activity is represented by a vector, V. This instance vector consists

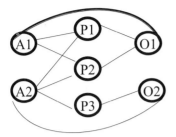

Figure 14.5
A sample tripartite graph consisting of activity (A), people (P), and organization (O) modes.

of the Person identifier (name, position, title, and employee number), a set of Activity attributes (activity type, time, location), Organizational descriptors (person's home organization, location), and a Thematic description (simple keywords, phrases, or terms from a classification taxonomy or some domain-specific estimate of expertise). It is noted that there may be several vectors for a person, and similarly a person may have several vectors for an activity. For example, if a person wrote several papers for a workshop, there may be an instance vector for each paper.

A relationship measure, R, is computed between all vector pairs. The general form of R computed between vectors i and j is

$$R_{i,j} = \sum V_i * V_j \quad \text{for all vectors } i \neq j, \tag{1}$$

where

$$V_i * V_j = a * O_{ij} + b * A_{ij} * (S_a) + c * S_{ij}, \tag{2}$$

where

O_{ij} = organizational similarity between persons i and j; O_{ij} is $[0,1]$;

A_{ij} = activity co-membership for persons i and j; A_{ij} is $[0,1]$;

S_a = measures the extent that activity A, and persons i and j have a common theme;

S_{ij} = thematic similarity between persons i and j.

Finally,

$$a + b + c = 1, \tag{3}$$

a setting of weighting parameters.

Note that (2) has three measures of association on which link strength is based. The O_{ij} term computes the level of association attributed to co-membership in a formal organization (such as a department). The A_{ij} term adds the dynamic ties associated with being involved in the same activity (e.g., project). A_{ij} is adjusted by the term (S_a) so that if the activity is thematically consistent with the content signature (terms) for person i and person j, $S_a > 0$, and the activity contribution to R increases. Finally, the S_{ij} term provides a measure of the related interests between the two persons. Based on the application, this can be based on a document similarity computation (cosine measure) often used in information retrieval or be based on some more sophisticated measure of skills and expertise. Again, from (2), we expect that R is maximized when staff members have similar interests and skills, and work across a common set of activities within the same organizational unit. In practice, however, we often find links between people with similar skills who are not in the same organization, nor do they work on the same tasks. These links or subnetworks are especially interesting in the context of finding highly diffused or even hidden areas of expertise.

The association measure, R, provides a measure of organizational, activity, and skill/interest area similarity between staff members. R is used as basis for clustering people, which essentially reduces the n-partite representation into a unipartite graph. While the performance of the clustering method is of interest, it is beyond the scope of this brief overview. The main point here is that the statistical clustering method provides a basis for grouping people based on organizational structure, workflow, and semantic similarity. The clusters produced are viewed as expertise networks. Note that each network member (node) has linkages to other members and nodal attributes that can be used to further determine what functional role a person may play within the network. For example, a network member who is an administrator would be easily distinguished from those who were research scientists or engineers.

XperNet Use

On a daily basis, XperNet collection agents mine various MITRE work spaces to identify activities such as projects, technical exchange meetings, and public share folders that may be new or may have changed since the last update. The system automatically generates new activity vectors or updates current vectors associated with an existing activity. If new vectors are created, they are first matched to existing expertise networks (a classification step); if they don't match, the vector is added to a singleton list and processed by the clustering algorithm. This second-stage clustering provides a basis for identifying emerging groups.

XperNet works without user queries to identify expertise areas; a distinction between it and other expertise locator tools. While the system supports queries, its main distinction is the automatic generation of expertise networks in skill or technology areas not necessarily known in advance. A first-generation browse interface is shown in figure 14.6. Typically, users can browse through a fairly large number of expertise networks (clusters) that can be ordered according to network size or diversity (a measure of the range of organizations represented by network members).

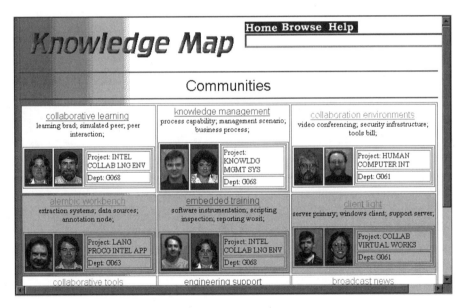

Figure 14.6
XperNet user's browse interface.

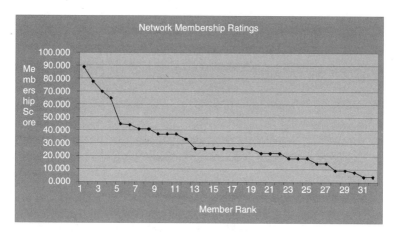

Figure 14.7
Expertise ratings.

Note that each network listed is represented in thumbnail or folder form. In particular, the network summary consists of the top two most central people in the network, the activities (e.g., project) that contributed most to network formation, and a short text summary describing the network theme. Opening the folder, the user is provided a list of network members, their rank, and their home organization; contributing activities; and documents within the MII that contributed to generating the network theme. User queries produce a list of matching expertise networks. In both the browse and query interfaces, the expert rating of each network member is provided, as illustrated in figure 14.7. Ratings are used to rank experts for selection or to highlight experts within a network visualization. A planned extension is to allow network members to modify the social network (e.g., add new members); modify the description, such as changing the expert area descriptors; and use the network for communicating with members and outside communities.

XperNet Evaluation
The current XperNet algorithm is under evaluation at MITRE's Information Technology Center. In earlier experiments, expertise networks, generated from user surveys, were compared to automatically generated expertise networks. The survey was sent to the center's technical staff.

Table 14.2
Scoring XperNet Using Survey Results

Cutoff	Average Precision (%)	Average Recall (%)
10	70	42
20	63	73
30	46	77

Each survey respondent nominated MITRE staff that had expertise in the specified technology area. Respondents nominated those they worked with as well as other known corporate experts, typically outside their home organization. In results from one center, four core expertise areas were noted (with a number of subspecialties): collaboration, knowledge management, advanced instructional training, and language processing. These areas match up fairly well with four separate departments within the center; however, many of the identified experts come from other organizations outside the center.

The XperNet algorithm was run, and the standard precision and recall measures, traditionally used in information retrieval experiments, were used to assess the overlap between the manual (human) and XperNet-generated networks. The surveys did not provide a ranking of experts, so precision at a particular cutoff was defined as the percentage of manually identified experts who were in the automatically generated list. Similarly, recall at a specified cutoff is the percentage of automatically ranked members who were in the total manually generated expert list. As shown in table 14.2 and in figure 14.8, approximately 70 percent of the top ten automatically identified experts were in the manually identified list. Precision dropped about 10 percent when computed over the top 20. Recall at the top 10 cutoff was also fairly high, but this is partly a function of the relatively small number of experts identified manually. Looking at the top 30, approximately 75 percent of the experts were identified automatically with approximately 50 percent accuracy.

The current results suggest the feasibility of automatically extracting expertise networks. However, there are a number of research issues to be addressed in the next generation of XperNet.

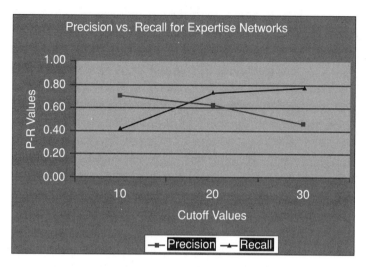

Figure 14.8
Average precision vs. recall for expertise networks.

14.5   Lessons Learned/Future Work

The MITRE expert- and community-finding tools represent a valuable first step toward achieving the objective of automated discovery and mapping of expertise. However, there are several system and user issues that require further investigation, including sources, processing, and usage.

First, these systems depend upon multiple sources of knowledge and accordingly require some mechanism for assessing source reliability and combining evidence from a range of sources of varying uncertainty. For example, in Expert Finder, one major activity is the addition of a Bayesian network to manage the evidence combination from the various sources. The current method of evidence combination is fairly arbitrary. The addition of a Bayesian net would allow the system to learn over time by using the results of each query to adjust the weights of each term. For example, we assume that someone can only really be an expert in one or two subjects. So the probability that someone is an expert is inversely proportional to the number of times they show up for distinct queries. So as Expert Finder operates over time it would adjust the prior probabilities in the network based on empirical evidence.

Analogously, in the current XperNet system, expertise indicators are extracted from a sample of documents and activities taken from the corporate information space. We are currently investigating the effect of sample size and sample selection on network accuracy and coverage. Hybrid sampling schemes that weight samples based on spatial location and currency can be used to bias the system or to provide a basis for selectively weighting indicators. For example, an indicator extracted from a recent project activity within a research program area may carry more weight in determining a network's shift in focus.

A second issue is one of timeliness and performance. For example, expensive tagging and analysis of source documents requires time. In Expert Finder, the average response time for five queries described in the evaluation was approximately 30 seconds. The majority of the time is spent in the name-tagging process. More significantly, the use of the preexisting MII is a double-edged sword. It makes it easy to maintain because Expert Finder does not actually maintain any indexed information. However, it also means that Expert Finder and XperNet are totally dependent on outside entities to maintain the necessary information. In the case of the MII, it is the employees themselves who maintain most of the information through self-publication. Of course, when some person does not publish, they do not show up as an expert or in an expert community. Another problem occurs when people publish documents that they did not create. For example, the secretary for the MITRE vice president in charge of the research program regularly publishes the research overview presentations given by the vice president. Because these presentations contain a wide variety of technical information, the secretary is routinely listed as an expert in a great number of areas. This problem generalizes to one of "buzzword pollution." People who make liberal use of technical jargon can show up as experts even when they are not.

We are continuing to improve these systems to address these problems. In Expert Finder, we are caching some results to have very fast response times for common queries. We are planning to expand the use of results caching to include a much greater number of queries, and to use these cached queries to create a navigable Yahoo-style hierarchy of expertise areas for easier browsing. Using these expertise areas, we also plan to allow users to search by name and by department, so that users can learn about the known skills of themselves and their co-workers, and encourage the increased publication of documents to increase the likelihood of an expert's name appearing in a subject area. Also, the MII contains information about an employee's job title, which could be used to filter the set of potential experts that could be suggested by the system.

Other improvements include decreasing the importance of older documents found by the system, adding additional sources of information, incorporating more standard information retrieval techniques such as query expansion and Boolean operations, and adding the capability to define standing queries so that a user can be notified when new experts appear.

Within XperNet, expertise networks provide a rich context to navigate within. In the next version of the system we are exploring user interaction with the network as a basis for selectively pruning nodes or links to construct special graphs for building project teams or distributing information. Finally, we continue to explore new methods for qualifying levels of expertise. This remains a tough problem, especially where it is problematic to develop domain models or where expertise changes rapidly. The general approach taken here is to support a user feedback loop used to train the system, that is, to provide examples of the classes of information useful in assessing expertise as a basis for adapting indicator extraction and weighting schemes.

Acknowledgments

We are indebted to David Mattox for his assistance with the creation of MITRE's Expert Finder. We would also like to thank Inderjeet Mani, whose research efforts supported the development of this application, and Chris Elsaesser for the original idea for an expert finder. We thank Manu Konchandy for his contribution to the development of XperNet tools.

Notes

1. The MII was awarded the *CIO Magazine* 1999 Enterprise Value Award (EVA).

2. The open source is available at http://cvw.sourceforge.net/.

3. Dataware Knowledge Management Systems white paper, http://www1.dataware.com/forum/kms/kmsfull.htm.

4. Autonomy Technology white paper, http://www.autonomy.com/tech/wp.html.

5. Tacit KnowledgeMail, http://www.tacit.com/products/knowledgemail.html.

6. Abuzz, "Ask Anything," http://www.abuzz.com/.

7. XperSite.com, http://www.xpersite.com/.

8. NameTag, from IsoQuest Corporation.

References

Ackerman, M. S., and T. W. Malone. 1990. Answer Garden: A Tool for Growing Organizational Memory. In *Proceedings of the ACM Conference on Office Information Systems*, 31–39.

Ackerman, M. S., D. McDonald, W. Lutters, and J. Muramatsu. 1999. Recommenders for Expertise Management. In *Proceedings of ACM SIGIR '99 Workshop on Recommender Systems: Algorithms and Evaluation*, Berkeley, California.

Cohen, A. L., P. P. Maglio, and R. Barrett. 1998. The Expertise Browser: How to Leverage Distributed Organizational Knowledge. Paper presented at the Workshop on Collaborative Information Seeking, Conference on Computer-Supported Cooperative Work (CSCW '98).

Fenn, J. 1999. *Skill Mining: An Emerging KM Technology*. Gartner Group Report. Available at http://www4.gartner.com/Init.

Foner, L. N. 1997. Yenta: A Multi-Agent, Referral-Based Matchmaking System. In *Proceedings of International Conference on Autonomous Agents (Agents '97)*, 301–307.

Kautz, B., B. Selman, and M. Shah. 1997. The Hidden Web, *AI Magazine* 18 (2): 27–36.

Maybury, M., and W. Wahlster, eds. 1998. *Readings in Intelligent User Interfaces*. Menlo Park, Calif.: Morgan Kaufmann.

Mattox, D., M. Maybury, and D. Morey. 1999. Enterprise Expert and Knowledge Discovery. In *Proceedings of the Eighth International Conference on Human-Computer Interaction (HCI '99)*, 303–307.

Mattox, D., K. Smith, and L. Seligman. 1998. Software Agents for Data Management. In *Handbook of Data Management*, ed. B. Thuraisingham, 703–722. New York: CRC Press.

McDonald, D. W., and M. S. Ackerman. 1998. Just Talk to Me: A Field Study of Expertise Location. In *Proceedings of the ACM Conference on Computer-Supported Cooperative Work (CSCW '98)*, 315–324.

Streeter, L. A., and K. E. Lochbaum. 1988. An Expert/Expert-Locating System Based on Automatic Representations of Semantic Structure. In *Proceedings of the Fourth IEEE Conference on Artificial Intelligence Applications*, 345–349.

Vivacqua, A. S. 1999. Agents for Expertise Location. In *Proceedings of the AAAI Spring Symposium on Intelligent Agents in Cyberspace*, Stanford, California, 9–13.

Yimam-Seid, D. 1999. Expert Finding Systems for Organizations: Domain Analysis and the DEMOIR Approach. In *Proceedings of the European Conference on Computer-Supported Cooperative Work (ECSCW '99)*.

15

OWL: A System for the Automated Sharing of Expertise

Frank Linton

People possess many kinds of expertise and have many methods for sharing it. This chapter focuses on one kind of expertise, the use of desktop application software, and presents an automated method for sharing that expertise.

New workplace technologies enable new methods for sharing expertise. In the last decade, an enormous change has taken place in the workplace: there is a PC on every desk, and much professional office work is performed in the medium of software. Mastering one's software—at least the portion of it that is relevant to one's job tasks—has become a key enabling skill for performing well on the job. It also happens that work performed in software is easily observable by automated processes. This observability provides new opportunities for the automated sharing of expertise, provided the software is *instrumented*.

Software is instrumented by adding a small amount of code to the software or to the computing environment that observes and reports actions users take on the software's interface. Thus, the user's every menu selection, button-click, and keyboard command can be observed and reported. MITRE has developed software tools to instrument user actions in UNIX applications (Cheikes et al. 1998), Java applications, and the Microsoft Office suite.

Instrumentation can capture users' actions on the job. Logging these actions automatically captures data about how work is done, in great detail and from a large number of users. In OWL (Organization-Wide Learning), the software reported on here, expertise is captured from anyone who displays it and delivered to everyone who needs it. The distinction between expert and novice blurs, as individuals prove to be experts in some areas and novices in others.

The phrase *sharing expertise* implies a transaction involving the transfer of expertise from a giver to a receiver. OWL reduces the effort on the part of the giver to nearly nil, and ensures that the receiver gets expertise of proven value. However, OWL cannot implant expertise directly into the receiver's brain; the receiver has to make some effort to internalize it. We characterize this effort as *learning*. OWL helps users learn by providing them with rudimentary instruction; it directs them to an appropriate spot in the application's help system.

15.1   Recommender Systems

OWL is a kind of recommender system (Resnick and Varian 1997). Recommender systems are frequently used in electronic commerce to recommend purchases to consumers. In contrast, a recommender system is used here to transfer expertise among application users. OWL's recommender system is similar to those of e-commerce Web sites, such as Reel.com, that are based on individuals' patterns of purchases (or in OWL's case, the software users' knowledgeable selections of functionality). For example, consider a group of people who like the movies you like and dislike the movies you dislike. Some members of this group will undoubtedly have seen and liked movies that you have not yet seen. The Reel.com recommender system would suggest those movies to you. Similarly, OWL compares each software user to others to find those who share patterns of command usage, then recommends new commands for each user to learn based on the pooled knowledge of similar users.

The functionality of a modern application, such as Microsoft Word, may consist of more than 1,000 distinct commands. Most of those commands are irrelevant to the job tasks of any one user, so any attempt to master the full functionality of an application is counterproductive. On the other hand, most users learn only a small part of the relevant functionality of an application in formal training. Knowledge of the remaining relevant functionality is acquired, if it is acquired at all, slowly and sometimes painfully over the years by the informal sharing of expertise. Meanwhile, the lack of knowledge results in reduced efficiency. An automated system for sharing expertise helps users acquire the relevant functionality of their applications quickly by suggesting to each user functionality that their peers have already found useful. "In many workplaces ... mastery is in short supply, and what is required is a kind of collaborative bootstrapping of expertise" (Eales and Welch 1995, 100).

OWL has been gathering data from users for several years, and my colleagues and I have recently implemented the software that makes recommendations to OWL users. With the empirical evidence now available, we cannot claim that the OWL recommender system successfully promotes expertise sharing, but there are several reasons to expect it will. First, recommender systems for e-commerce are known to work. Recommender systems are acknowledged to account for a large part of Amazon.com's success. Second, the recommendations are timely. New knowledge is presented to a user at the time most appropriate for her to learn it, that is, when it fills a gap in her knowledge or extends the boundaries of her knowledge. Third, the functionality OWL is recommending is known to be relevant because the user's peers in the same work context are already using it. OWL does not recommend commands the user already knows nor commands that none of her peers have found useful.

Fourth, the recommendations are expected to be time-saving. To learn more about an application, an individual can turn to expertise in many formats: advanced courses, self-study and reference materials, help, the World Wide Web, and so on. Nevertheless, the user faces a difficult task. He must not only perceive a need but also perceive the application as having the possibility of fulfilling it. He must then explore the source or sources of expertise to find the function or set of functions that enables him to do the task with the software. Because the user and the other experts often define the same task in different terms, such explorations are often fruitless and are correctly seen as high-risk, low-return ventures. It should come as no surprise, then, that any new learning resulting from these perceptions and explorations is rare, and that as a result much of the productivity gain made possible by desktop software is never realized (Landauer 1996).

OWL provides a potential solution to the high-risk, low-return exploratory learning situation. OWL pools the expertise of all users in an organization by recording each use of each function. Each use of a function is interpreted as a vote for its utility. OWL then compares the functions used by each individual to the functions used by the pooled group of users. It finds the gaps in, and the boundaries of, each individual's knowledge and makes recommendations to each individual that fill in the gaps and extend the boundaries. OWL provides a current, peer-based answer to the question Given all the functionality of this application, which is the next-most useful function for me to learn? OWL provides users with a means of learning that is better than exploring, yet OWL does not discourage or inhibit exploration, and when a user discovers something and begins to use it, it is added to OWL's database and will, at the appropriate time, be recommended to each of the other users.

A later section describes how OWL computes recommendations for each user. The characteristics of expertise are defined as the number and relative frequency of commands used. While this is a relatively shallow definition of expertise compared to a task-based definition, it has one great advantage: there is no need to capture expertise before installing the system. Whenever someone begins to use a new command, the event is captured, and eventually the command is recommended to others. Because individuals' use of commands will vary, data are observed and pooled from multiple individuals for the recommendations. The automatic capture of command usage means that no effort is required of experts for them to share their expertise (see chapter 1). They may, however, hide their expertise by turning off the OWL logger.

The system is intended to continually improve the performance of application users by providing individualized recommendations in the form of OWL Tips. The OWL system compares the individual users' data to the pooled data of their peers to make recommendations. The system attempts to time the recommendation such that the user already will have felt a need for the knowledge the system is offering to transfer ("There must be a better way to do this, but I don't have time to look for it now").

Applications are frequently upgraded, work processes are refined, and clever users discover better ways of doing things; thus expertise is not static, but rather it evolves. To capture evolving expertise, the system must update its recommendations frequently. The updating process begins by analyzing user data. Some users are generally innovative practitioners, yet any user may be the first to apply a command. As users discover and apply new commands, these will appear in their logged data. Other users' data will reflect their ignorance of these new commands; at the appropriate time, the recommender mechanism will recommend them, users will adopt them, and the knowledge will spread.

15.2   User Observation

This section describes how OWL observes and logs users' software-based activities, and the demographic characteristics of the users whom OWL has been observing at the MITRE Corporation. It presents a summary view of their usage of Microsoft Word, the desktop application used for this research.

The OWL Logger

To share expertise automatically, it must first be observed and captured. This task falls to the OWL logger. Each time a user issues a Word command, such as Cut or Paste, the command is written to the log, together with a time stamp, and then executed. Logging is initiated when the user opens Word; a separate log is created for each file the user edits, and when the user quits Word, the logs are sent to a server, where they are periodically loaded into a database for analysis. A toolbar button (figure 15.1) labeled "OWL is ON" (or OFF) informs users of OWL's state and allows users to choose not to be logged.

The first few lines of each log record general information: the logger version, the date and time stamp, and the user's name, followed by the platform, processor, and version of Word. Then detailed logging begins. Each time the user enters a Word command, the logger adds a line to the

Figure 15.1
The OWL toolbar.

log file. Each line contains a time stamp, the command name, and possibly one or more arguments. For example, one log entry recorded these facts: at 5:11:34 p.m. the writer used the File Open command to open a file titled "Notes for ITS 2000." Other entries record editing commands (Copy, Paste) and Save and Print commands. The logging process does not record the text a user enters; this omits some potentially useful information but preserves users' privacy.

Logging captures a detailed record of a user's activities, but the record may be sketchy for several reasons. First, an individual may also perform work on other systems without loggers, so some of his activity may not be captured. Second, in addition to omitting text, the logger does not capture certain other keyboard actions such as Tab and Return, nor does it capture certain mouse actions such as scrolling. The logger does not distinguish whether a command is entered by a menu selection, a mouse-click on an icon, or a shortcut key. Finally, permitting user control over logging means that logging can be turned on and off at will, although the default is that OWL is on. To summarize, the logged data are not a census of the user's actions nor a random sample but rather a semi-arbitrary selection of them.

OWL Users

The Word usage data reported here were obtained from thirty-seven users; the period of logging ranged from one to nine months per person. (Data have been collected continuously from early 1997, beginning with Word 6 users on Macintosh computers.) The data were obtained for the Windows version of Microsoft Word 97. The majority of the users are members of the MITRE Corporation's Center for Integrated Intelligence Systems. MITRE is a federally funded not-for-profit corporation performing research in the public interest. The users include four department heads, thirteen systems engineers at six levels of responsibility, eight support staff, and a variety of other technical and professional staff. There are fourteen males and twenty-three females. The users have been employed at MITRE from one to thirty-nine years with a median of twelve years. During the time they were logged, the Word users as a group used 163 distinct commands a total of 130,274 times. The average person used 58 ($SD = 19$) distinct commands during the logging period.

Table 15.1
Command Sequences and Percentages of Use

Sequence	Command	Percent of Use	Cumulative Percent of Use
1	Edit Delete[a]	34.2	34.2
2	File Save	10.5	44.8
3	File Open	8.7	53.5
4	Edit Paste	7.9	61.4
5	File DocClose	5.1	66.5
6	Edit Copy	4.2	70.7
7	Format Bold	3.7	74.4
8	File Print	2.8	77.2
9	Edit Cut	2.4	79.7
10	File SaveAs	1.7	81.3
11	Edit Undo	1.5	82.8
12	File PrintPreview	1.3	84.1
13	File PrintDefault	1.2	85.3
14	File ClosePreview	1.1	86.4
15	Format Italic	0.9	87.3
16	Format Underline	0.8	88.0
17	Window DocMinimize	0.7	88.7
18	Format CenterPara	0.6	89.4
19	Edit Find	0.5	89.9
20	Insert Break	0.5	90.3

a. "Edit Delete" is the command that deletes the character to the left of the cursor.

Pooled Knowledge

Table 15.1 lists the 20 most frequently occurring Word commands sequenced by their frequency of occurrence in the data, the percentage occurrence of each, and the cumulative percent of usage for all commands up to that point in the sequence. Command names are preceded by their main menu type, for instance, File Open is the Open command in the File menu. The first two commands account for 45 percent of all command use, the first 10 commands account for 80 percent, and the first 20 commands account for 90 percent.

The unequal values of nominally paired commands (for example, the log shows more File Open commands than File DocClose commands) may be understood by recalling that there are multiple ways of accomplishing the same effect, that is, a file may be closed by File Close, File Exit, File SaveAs, crashing the system, and so on.

If we take each use of a command as a vote for its utility, then the data in table 15.1 provide us with a rough measure of the value of each command as used by this group of individuals at this point in time. Thomas (1998) reports similar results for another editing application.

One may obtain a sense of how much expertise there is in an organization for an application by looking at how many of its users know its most frequently used command, its second most frequently used command, and so on. One might expect that, in the case of Word, where our average user knows 58 commands, all users would know perhaps the 30 most frequently used commands, but that expectation would be incorrect. Most users do know all of the top 10 commands, but then the number of users who know any particular command gradually decreases.

Figure 15.2 displays data for the twenty-one users who have logged at least 1,000 data points. The top 50 commands are sequenced along the horizontal axis according to their frequency of occurrence, which is

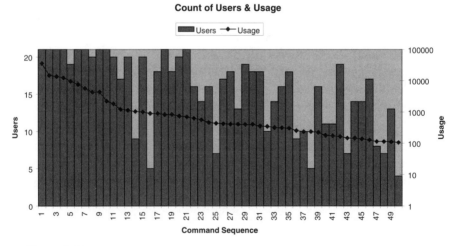

Figure 15.2
Counts of users and usage of each command.

plotted as a line whose values can be read on the logarithmic scale on the right axis. The number of individuals who have used the command at least once is plotted as a vertical bar whose values can be read on the left axis. The number of users of a command decreases in rough correspondence to the command's frequency of occurrence.

One can interpret the vertical bars as a measure of organizational knowledge and the space above the vertical bars as a measure of organizational ignorance. In general, the number of users decreases as command usage decreases. At about the sixty-fifth command, there is more ignorance than knowledge. That is, on average, any given command beyond the sixty-fifth is unknown to more than half the users. The expertise-sharing mechanism in OWL focuses on overcoming ignorance individual by individual, beginning with the gaps in each individual's knowledge and then extending the boundaries of her knowledge.

The usage characteristics of desktop applications described in this section may be of value to software designers, user interface designers, instructional designers, and others. This information was acquired in the process of developing automated knowledge-sharing mechanisms using a recommender system approach. A more detailed analysis of these data may be found in Linton, Joy, and Schaefer (1999), and in Linton and Schaefer (2000).

15.3   Individualized Recommendations

The hypothetical OWL user is hardly aware that she is using OWL as she proceeds about her normal job tasks. In the background, OWL records and logs the commands of the application she is using; the user can turn OWL off with a mouse-click if the need should arise (figure 15.1). Whenever she exits the application, OWL sends her logs to a server, where they are loaded into a database. From the data OWL computes tips for each individual. The tips are stored in tip files on the server. Whenever the user decides to learn something more about the application and clicks on the OWL Tips button (figure 15.1), the user's current tip file is retrieved from the server and presented to her (figure 15.3). She reviews the tips and clicks on one she wants to investigate further, then reviews the Word Help for the command (OWL logs this

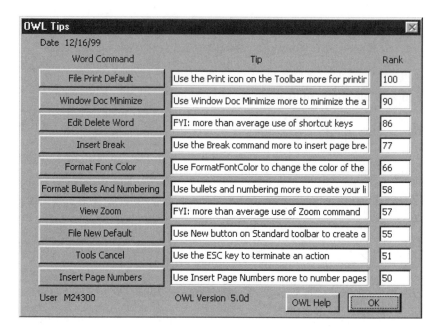

Word Command	Tip	Rank
File Print Default	Use the Print icon on the Toolbar more for printir	100
Window Doc Minimize	Use Window Doc Minimize more to minimize the a	90
Edit Delete Word	FYI: more than average use of shortcut keys	86
Insert Break	Use the Break command more to insert page bre.	77
Format Font Color	Use FormatFontColor to change the color of the	66
Format Bullets And Numbering	Use bullets and numbering more to create your li	58
View Zoom	FYI: more than average use of Zoom command	57
File New Default	Use New button on Standard toolbar to create a	55
Tools Cancel	Use the ESC key to terminate an action	51
Insert Page Numbers	Use Insert Page Numbers more to number pages	50

Figure 15.3
The OWL Tip Viewer.

information as well). The command provides functionality that the user may have felt "had to be there" but had been unable to find. She tries out the command a few times and later begins to employ it. Since she installed OWL, she has slowly but consistently increased her knowledge of, and satisfaction with, the application. This section describes how OWL computes these individualized recommendations.

OWL shares expertise by judiciously transferring it from those who have it to those who do not. It compares each user's expertise to the pooled expertise of similar users in order to fill in the gaps and extend the boundaries of each individual's expertise, thereby raising the level of expertise of all and increasing the effectiveness of the organization.

As soon as OWL has observed and logged an adequate sample of a user's behavior, the analysis process can begin. When an individual is seen not to use a command that his peers have found useful, OWL assumes he might find the command useful if he were told about it. Similarly, underuse of a command may indicate ignorance of further appli-

Table 15.2
Individualized Recommendations for User 274

Command	Expected Usage	Observed Usage	Recommendation
Edit Paste	170	274	OK
Edit Delete	129	0	New
Edit Copy	107	97	OK
Edit Cut	48	100	OK
Edit Undo	16	14	OK
Edit Find	12	1	More
Edit SelectAll	9	12	OK
Edit DeleteWord	4	0	New
Edit Replace	3	0	New
Edit PasteSpecial	2	0	New

Note: Data for this table slightly predate the data presented in table 15.1.
OK = the person is using this command as expected.
New = the person is not using this command; OWL recommends he learn how to use it.
More = the person rarely uses this command; OWL recommends she learn more ways to use it.

cations of the command. Overuse of a command may indicate reliance on a weak general-purpose command, such as Delete, when a more powerful but more specific command, such as DeleteWord, might be more appropriate.

A given volume of logged data will provide more reliable estimates of the user's knowledge of the more frequently used commands than of the less frequently used ones. OWL must be careful not to equate its non-observation of a command with a lack of knowledge of that command on the user's part. It may simply be that OWL has not yet acquired enough data to observe it. Rarely used commands indicate the boundary of a user's knowledge.

These learning opportunities (nonuse, underuse, overuse, and on-the-verge-of-use) can be prioritized and presented to the user in terms of learning recommendations. Table 15.2 shows a portion of one user's information.

The first column of table 15.2 lists the 10 most frequently used Edit commands (commands nominally under Word's Edit menu), sequenced by their overall frequency of use. Not shown are the vast majority of text-editing commands.

The second column of table 15.2 lists the expected value for each of these 10 commands. The expected value is the usage the command would have had if the individual had used it with the frequency that his pool of peers does.

The third column of the table lists the actual usage of these commands by this individual during the time he was logged.

The expected values are unique to each individual and each moment in time. The reason for differences between observed and expected values might have several explanations, such as the individual's tasks, preferences, experiences, or hardware, but we are most interested when the difference indicates the lack of knowledge or skill.

The fourth column of table 15.2 contains various symbols that result in recommendations for learning. The five symbols (not all are shown) are OK, (blank), New, More, and Alt.

A command whose expected value is zero need not be learned and can be ignored; its indicator is a blank. A command that has a nonzero expected value but is one the individual has never used is a command the individual probably would find useful if he were to learn it; its indicator is New. A command whose usage is reasonably close to the expected value can also be ignored. The current value of "reasonably close" was set arbitrarily. Eventually the value can be determined empirically. The indicator for a command reasonably close to the expected value is OK. A command that is used less than expected may be a component of text-editing tasks that are unknown to the user but potentially valuable; its indicator is More. A command that is used more than expected may indicate ignorance of more powerful ways of accomplishing some text-editing tasks; its indicator is Alt.

As mentioned, new sets of recommendations, known as tips, are computed monthly. (A month is about the minimum time required to see a significant change in users' behavior.) When the new tips are computed, each individual is sent an e-mail message telling her that she has a new set of tips. The tip file resides on the server. Whenever the person decides she wants to learn something more about the application, she clicks on the Tips button on the OWL toolbar (figure 15.1). The Tip Viewer (figure 15.3) then retrieves the individual's tip file and displays it to her. The Tip Viewer presents the tip name, a brief description, and a relative ranking of the top 10 tips. Users can then review their tips and click on any tip to learn more about the command. Today, the instruction is elementary; clicking on a tip simply brings up the appropriate Word Help page. The OWL Tips mechanism has been field-tested with about twenty users for several months and is now being scaled up, with the goal of having about one hundred users for the remainder of the research project.

15.4   Discussion

This section discusses OWL versus performance support systems, the rationale for believing that more expertise is better, and some limitations on learning by the expertise-sharing process.

OWL versus Performance Support

Performance support systems are another means of sharing expertise. Performance support systems require extensive up-front knowledge acquisition from experts. That knowledge, once acquired, is static. In contrast, OWL requires little up-front task analysis and its knowledge is dynamic. It is only necessary to ensure that there are pointers into the appropriate places in the application's Help system for each command that OWL recommends. These can be added incrementally as needed. Conventional performance support requires that the knowledge transmitted to the learner already exist. OWL transmits knowledge from user to user as that knowledge—of which commands are the most useful—is acquired by the organization. As soon as anyone finds some function of the software useful, OWL captures that knowledge and dispenses it as appropriate. Finally, performance support systems become obsolete when there are changes in the organizational context and individuals begin to perform new tasks and apply new skills. In contrast, OWL automatically adapts to changes in the organizational context, that is, when its users begin to use the software in different ways, OWL's recommendations will also change.

Possible Influences on Command Use Frequency

As mentioned earlier, there may be valid reasons why some people use commands that others do not. One's editing tasks may seem to require commands such as MailMerge and InsertTable. Another reason is users' experience with other software with different interaction models. A third reason is stylistic differences or individual preferences. Nevertheless, it is my observation that all users are focused on getting their jobs done. If they have only one method of accomplishing a task, they will use it. If they have two or more methods, they will usually choose the more appropriate one, where "more appropriate" depends on the immediate circumstances. For example, a person familiar only with tabs will create a table using tabs, but a person who knows both tab and table commands will create a table by choosing the more effective method, depending on the circumstances.

Limitations on Sharing Expertise

Much expertise can be transmitted by sharing. However, sharing implies reciprocity. The good you share with me one day, I may share with you the next. For software expertise in a professional setting, this reciprocity, as we have seen, largely holds true; most users have something to exchange, they use some commands that many others do not; and even the office guru who knows more than most may gain increased prestige as part of the exchange.

However, there are two cases of knowledge transfer where expertise sharing does not appear to be the mechanism at work. First, when experts are not conscious of their knowledge, they cannot consciously share it; nevertheless, the transfer of such tacit knowledge may be critical to an organization's success. Nonaka and Takeuchi (1995) indicate that this type of knowledge is transferred by socialization. Second, sharing implies reciprocity, and reciprocity implies exchanges among near-equals; thus knowledge sharing should not be considered a mechanism to replace conventional training or instruction, in which the knowledge of the participants is typically far from equal. Furthermore, formal training and instruction typically require social processes far more structured than informal exchanges do (Gagne 1985).

15.5   Further Work

This section discusses methods for refining OWL's recommendations, how OWL's effectiveness was evaluated, and the application of the OWL approach to information sources.

Refining the Recommendations

The current design of OWL produces good recommendations. However, these recommendations could be improved by three processes: age-weighting user data, clustering users, and finding meaningful sequences of commands.

As we saw, OWL currently computes its recommendations based on all the commands in its database. This is not a problem if the contributions from all users are roughly equal, but they are not: some users may have been logged for a longer period than others, and some are heavier users than others. Those users who have accumulated more data have a larger influence on the recommendations. In response to these issues of long-term versus new users and light versus heavy users my colleagues and I are considering age-weighting the data to reduce the influence of the length of observation while maintaining the influence of the relatively heavy users on OWL's recommendations. Commands would contribute less to the recommendation calculation as they aged, and all commands more than one year old would be ignored. This age-weighting would have the added advantage of producing recommendations that more strongly reflect users' evolving knowledge because the latest usage patterns will have the most weight.

Another method of improving OWL's recommendations may be cluster analysis. In general, cluster analysis is the process of placing individual items into groups based on the similarity of their attributes. For OWL, users were clustered based on similarities in their use (in percent) of Word commands. The assumption was that the groups would represent sets of individuals who used Word in similar ways, and that recommendations based on comparison with others in one's own cluster would be more valuable than recommendations based on all users. A cluster analysis using the Nearest Neighbor algorithm (Fukunaga 1990) was performed for the twenty-one individuals for whom there were more than 1,000 data points. The results were unexpected: five distinct clusters were found. The clusters did not correlate with any of the work-related demographic features mentioned earlier in the description of OWL users. Apparently the links from job title to job task to writing task to text-editing task are too tenuous to establish a correlation. Instead, one cluster of twelve users was quite similar to the whole group. The other four clusters were marked by excessive use—approximately 50 percent—of a single command (a different one in each case). Nevertheless, clustering is still expected to be a useful technique with large numbers of users.

Finally, OWL's recommendations might be improved by considering sequences of commands, or editing tasks. Up to this point, expertise has been considered to consist of using individual commands. However, some tasks, such as moving text, are achieved by issuing a sequence of commands, for instance, Edit Cut followed by Edit Paste. Thus, an automated means of detecting meaningful sequences of commands would be useful. The initial analysis of sequences of pairs and triplets of commands that occur more frequently than one would expect by chance alone has revealed such humdrum sequences as Save, Print, and Exit, but no clever tricks and no real surprises.

Evaluating the OWL Project

My colleagues and I have recently begun to compute tips and make them available to users; thus we can observe and quantify knowledge gained, and we are collecting the information that we require to make these calculations. To measure the effectiveness of OWL Tips, the use of the Tips window and the selection of individual tips are logged, revealing whether the user has looked at the Tips window and which of the individual tips she has chosen to investigate further. The command-logging process reveals whether the user tries out a command after seeing a tip recommending it. The continued use of a command that was introduced by a tip is used to measure learning. Knowledge gained by the organization (versus that gained by the individual) may be one of the more important outcomes of using OWL—or any expertise-sharing system—from a cost-benefit perspective. To date, a few users appear to have learned from a few tips, but based on a casual review, the rate of appearance of newly learned commands in the logs remains unchanged.

A command is determined to be "newly learned" as follows. Given the frequency of occurrence of a command once it appears in a users' log, how certain is it that its first appearance in the log is its first use? For example, if a command is now used 10 percent of the time, and it appeared among the first 100 commands in the log, it was probably known to the user before logging started. If it first appeared after 1,000 commands had been logged, it was probably unknown to the user until that moment. This measure is computed formally using the binomial distribution probability (Howell 1982).

What might account for this lack of learning? There are several possibilities to be explored. The first is bad recommendations. This is unlikely because of the fact that the user's peers have found the commands useful, and more expert users use more commands, not different commands. Also, many users are grossly inefficient, for example, they may delete hundreds of characters one at a time rather than doing a Select and Delete. The second possibility is low-quality instruction. For instruction, OWL points users into the Help system, and help is not training. Worse, not all help is directly accessible; sometimes users must pick their way through one or two mysterious Help system menus to reach help for the recommended command. Third, OWL does not emphasize the social aspect of learning (see chapter 12). While the recommendations are based on the usage of one's peers, to the user it may appear that OWL is making the recommendations. Users' photos are available on the corporate intranet, so perhaps each tip should be accompanied by the name and photo of someone who both uses the command and is likely to be known to the user. This approach might also help build communities of practice and generate increased informal communication regarding the application (see chapter 8). Also, perhaps a recorded demo of a command's use by a trustworthy source within the organization would be more motivating than impersonal Help text. Finally, while the goals of the OWL research correspond to those of Eales (see chapter 11), the methods described here are rather different. OWL tries to make expert input effortless and to provide users with low-cost, high-benefit learning on demand. Eales assumes a large amount of organizational support, and he attempts to increase communication among individuals. Perhaps judiciously combining elements of his approach with the OWL approach would increase learning without an undue increase in effort.

Recommender Systems for Learning about Data

The approach taken in OWL is applicable to sharing other kinds of expertise besides the application functionality that OWL recommends. For example, the same technique could be used to share data sources, such as URLs. In a pre-pilot test, my colleagues and I applied OWL methodology to recommend URLs from the MITRE corporate intranet to a group of users. For analysis, we selected a group of managers from one division and the URLs they had visited in the previous six-month span. We computed the potential recommendations for each manager by comparing the observed values and the expected values. If we expected the manager to visit the URL once or more, and he had not visited the URL (in the last six months), we included the URL; otherwise not. Finally, we determined the individualized set of recommendations for each manager by taking the "top 10," the ten unvisited URLs most visited by other managers. Research on this URL recommender is continuing.

15.6 Summary

Changes in workplace technologies now permit systems such as OWL to automate the sharing of expertise pertaining to desktop applications. OWL is a kind of recommender system, software that recommends objects or activities to individuals based on their membership in clusters of individuals with similar preferences. The OWL project has been gathering data about how individuals use one software application for several years. The data reveal that individuals—and organizations—use only a small portion of an application's functionality, that a few commands account for most of the usage, and that very few of even the frequently used commands are used by all individuals.

When users want to learn more about an application, they can learn about new functionality that their peers have already found useful by clicking on the Tip Viewer, the tool in which OWL makes available its frequently recomputed recommendations for each individual. In contrast to performance support systems, OWL's tips adapt as users learn and organizations evolve; OWL complements formal instruction. While OWL has been in use only briefly, it is already clear that its recommendations can be refined and its instruction improved. The recommender approach taken in OWL might be productively applied to areas other than applications; one such area is recommending data sources such as URLs, and a URL recommender is being implemented.

References

Cheikes, B., M. Geier, R. Hyland, F. Linton, L. Rodi, and H. Schaefer. 1998. Embedded Training for Complex Information Systems. In *Proceedings of the Intelligent Tutoring Systems Fourth International Conference (ITS '98)*, 36–45.

Eales, R. T., and J. Welsh. 1995. Design for Collaborative Learnability. In *Proceedings of the First International Conference on Computer-Supported Collaborative Learning (CSCL '95)*, 99–106.

Fukunaga, K. 1990. *Introduction to Statistical Pattern Recognition*. San Diego: Academic Press.

Gagne, R. 1985. *The Conditions of Learning*. New York: Holt, Rinehart and Winston.

Howell, D. 1982. *Statistical Methods for Psychology*. Boston: Duxbury Press.

Landauer, T. 1996. *The Trouble with Computers: Usefulness, Usability, and Productivity*. Cambridge Mass.: MIT Press.

Linton, F., and H. P. Schaefer. 2000. Recommender Systems for Learning: Building User and Expert Models Through Long-Term Observation of Application Use. *User Modeling and User-Adapted Interaction* 10: 181–207.

Linton, F., D. Joy, and H. Schaefer. 1999. Building User and Expert Models by Long-Term Observation of Application Usage. In *Proceedings of the Seventh International Conference on User Modeling (UM '99)*, 129–138.

Nonaka, I., and H. Takeuchi. 1995. *The Knowledge-Creating Company*. New York: Oxford University Press.

Resnick, P., and H. Varian. 1997. Introduction to Special Section on Recommender Systems. *Communications of the ACM* 40 (3): 56–58.

Thomas, R. 1998. *Long-Term Human-Computer Interaction: An Exploratory Perspective*. New York: Springer-Verlag.

Contributors

Mark Ackerman is an associate professor in the School of Information and the Department of Electrical Engineering and Computer Science at the University of Michigan. Previously, he was an associate professor at the University of California, Irvine, and a research scientist at MIT's Laboratory for Computer Science. Since 1990 he has examined organizational memory and its computer support, including expertise management. He has also published on topics such as computer-supported cooperative work, privacy, virtual communities, cooperative information access, multimedia, and human-computer interaction. E-mail: ackerm@umich.edu.

Wilfried Aulbur is head of business development and strategy for Daimler-Chrysler Research and Technology, India, Bangalore. E-mail: wilfried.aulbur@daimlerchrysler.com.

James Boster is a professor of anthropology at the University of Connecticut. E-mail: james.boster@uconn.edu.

Andrew Cohen is a senior director at Kanisa. E-mail: andrew.cohen@kanisa.com.

Raymond D'Amore is a senior principal scientist at the MITRE Corporation. E-mail: rdamore@mitre.org.

Jim Eales is a member of the Interaction Design Centre and a lecturer in the Department of Computer Science and Information Systems at the University of Limerick, Ireland. E-mail: jim.eales@ul.ie.

Kate Ehrlich is a senior research scientist in Viant Corporation's innovation center. E-mail: kehrlich@viant.com.

Thomas Erickson is a research staff member at the IBM T. J. Watson Research Center. E-mail: snowfall@acm.org.

Henrik Fagrell is a research manager at the R&D Company Newmad Technologies. E-mail: henrik.fagrell@newmad.se.

Geraldine Fitzpatrick is a senior experience modeller in the User Experience Domain, Sapient Ltd, London. E-mail: Gfitzpatrick@sapient.com.

Saul Greenberg is a professor in the Department of Computer Science at the University of Calgary, Alberta, Canada. E-mail: saul@cpsc.ucalgary.ca.

Roland Haas is managing director of DaimlerChrysler Research and Technology India, Bangalore. E-mail: roland.haas@rti.daimlerchrysler.com.

Pamela Hinds is an assistant professor in the Department of Management Science and Engineering at the Engineering School, Stanford University. E-mail: phinds@stanford.edu.

Joachim Hinrichs is a senior researcher in the department of computer science at the University of Bremen. E-mail: j.hinrichs@informatik.uni-bremen.de.

David House is a senior engineer at the MITRE Corporation. E-mail: dhouse@mitre.org.

Marleen Huysman is an associate professor of knowledge management in the Department of Economics and Business Administration at Vrije Universiteit Amsterdam. E-mail: m.h.huysman@tbm.tudelft.nl.

Wendy A. Kellogg is manager of the social computing group at the IBM T. J. Watson Research Center. E-mail: wkellogg@us.ibm.com.

Alfred Kobsa is an associate professor in the Department of Information and Computer Science at the University of California, Irvine, and a professor of computer science at the University of Essen, Germany. E-mail: kobsa@ics.uci.edu.

Frank Linton is a lead scientist at the MITRE Corporation. E-mail: linton@mitre.org.

Wayne Lutters is an assistant professor in the department of information systems at the University of Maryland, Baltimore County (UMBC). E-mail: lutters@umbc.edu.

Mark Maybury is executive director of the Information Technology Division at the MITRE Corporation. E-mail: maybury@mitre.org.

David W. McDonald is an assistant professor in the Information School, University of Washington, Seattle. E-mail: dwmc@u.washington.edu.

Bill Penuel is a senior education researcher at the Center for Technology in Learning, SRI International. E-mail: william.penuel@sri.com.

Jeffrey Pfeffer is the Thomas D. Dee II Professor of Organizational Behavior at the Graduate School of Business, Stanford University. E-mail: Pfeffer_Jeffrey@gsb.stanford.edu.

Volkmar Pipek is a research associate in the HCI and CSCW Research Group (ProSEC), Institute for Computer Science, University of Bonn. He studied computer science and economics at the University of Kaiserslautern, Germany, was a researcher in the POLITeam-Project, and now heads a project on organizational learning in virtual organizations. E-mail: pipek@cs.uni-bonn.de.

Mark Roseman is the founder and chief technology officer of Team Wave Software Ltd. E-mail: mark@markroseman.com.

Sunil Thakar is a scientist with DaimlerChrysler Research and Technology, Germany, Berlin.

Dawit Yimam-Seid is a doctoral student in the Department of Information and Computer science at the University of California, Irvine. E-mail: dseid@ics.uci.edu.

Volker Wulf is a senior researcher at the Fraunhofer Institute for Applied Information Technology and an associate professor at the University of Siegen. Recently he was a research scholar at the Massachusetts Institute of Technology. He previously headed the HCI and CSCW Research Group (ProSEC), Institute for Computer Science, University of Bonn. His research interests lie primarily in the areas of computer-supported cooperative work and learning, knowledge management, human-computer interaction, and participatory design. E-mail: wulf@fit.fraunhofer.de.

Index